INTERNATIONAL ASPECTS OF OVERPOPULATION

Proceedings of a Conference held by
the South African Institute of International Affairs
at Johannesburg

Edited by

JOHN BARRATT and MICHAEL LOUW

MACMILLAN

ST. MARTIN'S PRESS

First published 1972 by
THE MACMILLAN PRESS LTD
London and Basingstoke
Associated companies in New York Toronto
Dublin Melbourne Johannesburg and Madras

Library of Congress catalog card no. 71–179498

SBN 333 13121 5

Printed in Great Britain by
RICHARD CLAY (THE CHAUCER PRESS) LTD
Bungay, Suffolk

Contents

Foreword

Many aspects of the world's 'population explosion' have been considered at conferences and in published studies, but its impact on the relations between states is one aspect which has not received much serious attention. The South African Institute of International Affairs felt, therefore, that this would be a fruitful theme for a conference of international experts, and that from their deliberations might come a constructive contribution to world thinking and action on this urgent problem affecting all mankind. It is hoped that this report, which contains the main papers and summaries of the discussions, as well as the conclusions reached after nearly a week of deliberations, will make such a contribution.

It was appropriate that this Conference was held in 1970, the centenary of the birth of Jan Christiaan Smuts, because, as the Conference President, Dr. Anton Rupert, said in his opening address, Smuts was 'a man who gave such deep thought to global problems'. The venue of the Conference was Jan Smuts House in Johannesburg, which was established in 1960 as a living memorial to Smuts, and which is the home of the Institute.

The success of the Conference, which is reflected in this report, was due to the efforts and generosity of many people, only some of whom can be mentioned here. The outstanding contributions of the main speakers, rapporteurs and other participants can be judged in the pages which follow. In an annexure appear the names of Corporate Members of the Institute and other South African companies, as well as individuals, without whose support the Conference would not have been possible. A special word of thanks is also due to the Conference President, Dr. Anton Rupert, and to the other officers who assisted in presiding at the working sessions. The advice of Dr. Ben Cockram, who originally conceived the idea of this Conference, of his successor as Smuts Professor of International Relations, Dr. Michael H. H. Louw, and of Professor Jan L. Sadie, was invaluable in the planning of this project.

The Institute and all those who participated in the Conference are greatly indebted to the Director, Mr. John Barratt, and his staff, on whose shoulders fell the burden of the preparatory work, which began two years beforehand, and of the organisation of the Conference itself. Their untiring efforts were reflected in the smooth functioning and undoubted success of the Conference.

Mr. Barratt and Professor Louw were responsible as editors for the preparation of these proceedings for publication. In this task they received valuable assistance from Miss Joan Knox and Dr. Denis Worrall.

Finally, mention must be made of the willing co-operation of the University of the Witwatersrand, on whose campus Jan Smuts House is situated.

LEIF EGELAND
National Chairman

South African Institute of
International Affairs

Preface

The papers reproduced in this volume are those which were presented at a Conference held at Jan Smuts House in Johannesburg during the week 23 June to 1 July 1970. The theme of the Conference was 'The Impact on International Relations of the Population Explosion', and it was organised by the South African Institute of International Affairs.

The Conference programme was structured so as to allow for consideration firstly of various aspects of rapid population growth, mainly on a national level, leading to a consideration of the international implications, including population factors on a regional level. The order of the programme has been maintained in this volume.

After the presentation of each paper, the topic was discussed by a panel of experts, including the author, and then opened for general discussion. Brief summaries of the main points raised during these discussions are given after each paper. The summaries are based on reports prepared by the Rapporteurs, which were circulated at the Conference. (The names of the Rapporteurs are listed in Annexure 6.)

Information concerning the authors of the papers, including the Background Paper (reproduced in Annexure 1), is given in Annexure 4. The names of panel members and other participants appearing in the discussion summaries are listed alphabetically in Annexure 5.

The Conference Conclusions which appear in Chapter 16 were drafted by a representative committee of the Conference, and were then discussed and approved at the closing session, as representing a general consensus among all participants.

The President of the Conference was Dr. Anton Rupert, and the Chairman of the working sessions was Dr. Leif Egeland, National Chairman of the Institute. He was assisted by two Vice-Chairmen: Mr. W. T. Ferguson and Mr. A. J. Karstaedt, who are the Chairmen, respectively, of the Cape Town and Eastern Province Branches of the Institute.

John Barratt
Director, S.A.I.I.A.
Conference Secretary

Introduction

MICHAEL H. H. LOUW

From the perspective of the seventies, a significant evolution of international relations as an academic discipline may be observed. In the twenties its central concern was world peace, and how this could be ensured through conscious, planned organisational structures and procedures, based on the assumption that peace is indivisible and that the key to its attainment was collective security. Although some of these assumptions proved to have been built on somewhat shaky ground, especially, for example, the idea of collective security, many of them were for want of appropriate substitutes continued in post-war peace machinery. This period, however, is marked by some significant new approaches to world peace, the most important of which were based on the assumption that social and economic factors played an important role in the kind of world situation in which peace could survive and grow. Interest in the consciously planned organisation of world peace and collective security probably did not diminish, but somehow a lessening of confidence in the effectiveness of the United Nations machinery to resolve a number of continuing violent conflicts did become noticeable, and this led to an emerging contemporary belief that world peace is perhaps dependent more upon a fortuitous balance and convergence of the interests and actions of the great powers, than upon deliberate organisational procedures based on the mechanics of voting by unequal states, through which artificial majorities legitimate collective action. This belief that one cannot always 'organise peace' has led, among international organisations, to some subtle but important shifts in their perceptions of contemporary world problems.

Among these the most important development was the emergence, first, of international awareness and concern (an 'international conscience') with broad and long-range, but decisive, conditions and problems in the underlying socio-economic patterns of the world. This conscience, for example, saw the condition of poverty and misery and the widening gap in living standards between the rich and poor countries as an unnecessary and intolerable situation in a world where enough natural resources and material wealth were available to eliminate them. Hence the strong belief in 'development' as a solution of some of the ills which could disturb world peace. A comparable belief is expressed in the constructive role which science and technology could play in improving the levels of living in less developed countries, exemplified in the United Nations conference on science and technology in Geneva in 1963 and the subsequent arrangements to continue its work. The obverse side of the technology coin, viz. the tremendous advance of military (especially nuclear) technology, and its obvious attendant dangers of total annihilation, did not go unnoticed either, and the international conscience and problem perception came into operation to bring about, for example, the Test Ban Treaty, the Non-Proliferation Treaty and the Strategic Arms Limitation Talks.

Second, this awareness was accompanied by a perception of the role which international action could and should play in the solution of these problems. This led to the establishment of many institutions and programmes, international, national, official and private, to achieve real and concrete results. The outstanding example here is the United Nations Development Programme, with its intricate web of interrelated organisations, programmes and operations.

Third, this awareness and its attendant role perceptions have tended to become global in scope, not of one or a few countries, or even a region, but of the totality of man's physical environment, i.e. the whole earth, including its associated space. This global and spatial perspective is exemplified in the Test Ban Treaty and the planned United Nations conference on environment in 1972.

It is within this context of an international concern with socio-economic problem areas, a perception that international action is appropriate and legitimate and of a global total perspective, that the problem of overpopulation should be seen. It was essentially during the period after the Second World War that an awareness developed of the dramatic pace of the rate of world population growth and of depressing implications for levels of living and resources. Normal population growth could still be seen as an element in the socio-economic equation, but population as an 'explosion' of sheer numbers was seen as a problem with serious implications, not only for national levels of living, but also possibly for social and for international peace.

In the process of perception of the problem and of appropriate international action, it soon became clear that the problem of overpopulation was not one involving political issues and differences between nations and that there was no real conflict between states or bloc formation caused by the population problem. In fact, some of the strongest proponents of birth control, for example India, were countries with serious overpopulation problems, while some of their opponents had no such problems but opposed some forms of birth control on moral or religious grounds. It was also realised that population growth in the mass was based on the cumulative effects of the single case and the individual act of procreation, and was thus first and foremost a personal and private affair, not subject or amenable to national or international sanctions. As a personal decision, this act was linked to complex psychological, cultural and economic motivations. If it was agreed that one of the most urgent and effective solutions was the reduction of population through birth control (or, to use the more scientific term, 'family planning'), then international and national policies would have to be designed so as to influence and persuade participating individuals to practise birth control. Such persuasion, through family planning campaigns and appeals, would be all the more effective if linked to basic cultural and other motivations and if supported by objective, scientific evidence on the social implications and effects of over-population and on the helpful role of contraceptive technology. For this purpose, continuing studies and research on these matters are not only relevant but essential. However, equally important as a parallel activity is the study of the contemporary population problem in its international implications, i.e. its impact on international relations in general, at the present time and in the future, and of the ways in which international action is appropriate or can be made more effective. It was in this context then that the Conference saw its task and the dimensions of this task.

A closer look at this broad theme of overpopulation shows how complex it is and that for understanding it in an international setting, an analysis would be necessary, not only of the factors which bear on overpopulation, but also of the way in which they are interrelated, in terms of cause and effect. Such an analysis would also indicate, from the operational point of view, how the general problem of overpopulation can be subdivided into its constituent problems and how they can be viewed in a national, a regional and an international perspective, and how their solutions would involve differentiated but complementary institutions, procedures and approaches. Many of these problems and their solutions are still changing and developing (for example, contraceptive technology) and the complete perception and identification of problems and the formulation of agreed solutions have not yet reached finality. The problem of overpopulation is therefore both complex and changing.

It would be useful here to indicate briefly some of the major international issues involved in the population problem. Perhaps we should start first with the value dimension, because this constitutes the basic set of premises or the point of departure in individual, national and international decisions on population. Although personal decisions on family size are influenced by cultural factors, there is also the moral issue of the rights of both parents and children.

The right of the parents as individuals and as citizens to procreate, and thus to perpetuate a name, must be considered a fundamental human right. Similarly, the right of an infant to proper care and a decent life must also be considered inviolate. But if the parents have more children than the resources (both personal and national) to ensure their proper care and decent life would permit, thus leading to misery, the two rights come into conflict. This is a moral dilemma, and the only solution seems to lie in the voluntary decision of the parents to plan their families in accordance with reasonable expectations of an adequate standard of living for all. But how, from the international and national points of view, can individuals be persuaded to take decisions appropriate to resolving the larger overall problem of excess population? What moral formula can be helpful here?

A second important issue is how a reasonable quality of life for growing children and adults (which may also be considered one of the 'human rights' of the individual) can be ensured in concrete, tangible terms. These conditions are dependent on the resources of a country to provide them, and these again are dependent on a complex pattern of interacting factors which provide for the production and distribution of material means and the social services which would ensure a reasonable level of living for a tolerable population level, as well as a minimum level for survival for an excessive population. As these conditions of living are normally provided within a national context, they are related to the national resources of a country, the country's capacity to exploit and develop these (a capacity which in turn is related to financial and manpower resources), its economic system and the quality and stability of its government.

A third major issue is finding appropriate formulas for *accelerating* the development of the poorer countries which are generally also 'overpopulated' in terms of their resources. Their problem is how to raise and to ensure a continuing rise in their standards of living. The wealthier countries are succeeding in this through the development of their technologies and their financial systems, and, in addition, are producing exportable surpluses of food, know-how and capital which could alleviate the misery of the poorer and overpopulated nations. But the transfer of food, knowledge and capital involves complex problems of trade, intercultural relations and the control and channelling of financial arrangements. There is also the problem of finding appropriate moral formulas, for example, to guide the volume of aid which the wealthier countries should give, the subtle but sensitive difference between development, aid and welfare, and the moral or other obligations of the recipient countries.

Turning now to the operational side, it is clear that for a proper understanding of world population problems a distinction should be made between population as a normal phenomenon and component of a politico-economic society, and population as a problem situation. A certain tolerable or optimal population level (i.e. one based on the ratio between population and resources) in a country is functional, because it provides the basis for manpower for production and for military capability, a market in the economic system and the essential human resources for socio-economic development and for the survival of the national or human species. But when a certain population is either too small to fulfil these functions, or too large for available resources, then it does become a problem. The purpose of this Conference was to focus attention on the problem not of inadequate or tolerable national population, but of excess population on a world scale, and this in terms of its international ramifications. If it is recognised and perceived as a world problem, then its solution requires the development of appropriate policies and programmes, by authorities or organisations on both national and international levels and in both the governmental and private spheres.

Furthermore, such policies and programmes in all four of these contexts would obviously only be effective if they were complementary rather than competitive. This means that the overall problem of the 'population explosion' (to use the more dramatic but currently accepted term) has to be split into sub-problems appropriate for perception and action in the four contexts, i.e. the national, international, governmental and private contexts. It should also be seen in terms of various fields of specialised knowledge applicable to its solution, for example, contraception, food distribution, demography, development, etc., which have to be integrated and thus require an interdisciplinary focus and integrative thinking.

In order to come to grips with the problem of overpopulation, a first requirement would be to get some idea of its dimensions. This would include statistics on world population and its distribution over the globe, the varying structures (age, sex, etc.) in different countries (for example, relative high percentages of old people in some developed countries and high percentages of children and young people in most less developed countries), trends, growth patterns, fluctuations and projections for the future, etc. Information is also needed on causes and motivational factors (incentives and disincentives) of population changes, the psychological and cultural aspects of reproduction ('reproduction *mores*'), population movements (migrations, such as rural-urban or international migrations), food and other resources in relation to population, dietetic patterns, standards of living, etc.

The second step would be to understand the implications and effects of overpopulation. This would include the pressures of population on resources and the resultant lowering of the levels of living (food, diet and social services), the possibilities of social unrest resulting from frustrations and hunger among large masses of population, the over-exploitation of natural resources resulting in their destruction or pollution and the social evils of uncontrolled mass urbanisation. In developing solutions for these problems attention would be drawn to the urgent need for improved industrial and agricultural systems and technology, for the rational exploitation of natural resources and greater social justice in their allocation. Other aspects requiring study are the extent to which food, funds and technological and organisational skills can be transferred from the developed to the less developed countries, and the moral issues of individual, family and national rights and duties regarding procreation.

Third, an accurate and complete perception of overpopulation as a problem would have to be made. This would include formulations, evaluations and decisions regarding its solutions. What would be the specific, realistic and workable solutions for the many subproblems of world overpopulation perceived by the many organisations as their appropriate roles? Who should do what in a total yet complementary pattern of specific action programmes?

In considering these solutions a distinction has to be made between those with short- and those with long-term effects. On the one hand, there are at this moment many areas of overpopulation with malnutrition and poverty, and these require immediate and urgent solutions such as food programmes, employment opportunities and direct social services, such as health and welfare services. But it is essential that such short-term programmes be complemented by long-range programmes, for example, family planning campaigns, mass contraceptive services and a general improvement of the levels of living through economic development and education. These two types of programmes should be carried out not as abstract exercises but within the broad context of an optimum population policy and a national development policy, specifically designed and implemented by its government for the unique population situation of each country. International programmes fulfil a different function; they are focused more on the collection and dissemination of information gained through research and through comparative studies in many countries and of the various regions of the world, which is relevant to the formulation of the national population policies of individual countries. International organisations also help to establish, through international discussion, the broad criteria and guide-lines for such policies and programmes.

Because of the nature of its task, the Conference therefore had to concern itself primarily with the wider international dimensions of the problem of world population. It had to examine this problem as it exists today, its implications for the present and the future, and appropriate solutions and their implementation. This exercise thus came to have both an inter-disciplinary and a global focus, and led to an examination of world population in relation to the global environment, a new and possibly more inclusive approach to a complex problem; an approach on which an important contribution has already been made by Harold and Margaret Sprout with their 'ecological triad' (environment, environed organism(s) and inter-relationships), which provided the basis for their statement that 'interrelatedness within and between national communities, and the increasing irrelevance of the time-honored distinction between domestic and international questions, constitute major datum points in the ecological perspective on international politics.'* It may be expected that, if further studies of this important problem of our times are to be fruitful, they should be carried out within the context and framework of a world ecology; the parameters of this problem having now shifted to the limits of the globe and of world humanity, thus establishing a truly appropriate challenge to the study of international relations.

* Harold and Margaret Sprout, *An Ecological Paradigm for the Study of International Politics* (Center of International Studies, Princeton University, 1968) p. 56.

1 Contemporary world demographic trends

J. L. SADIE

By way of introduction the reader is to be warned that, as yet, we do not have complete statistical coverage of the earth's population through comprehensive and reliable censuses and current registration of births, deaths and migration. Fortunately for the world as a whole, net migration is nil, and this fact reduces the sources of error, the presence of which should always be allowed for in interpreting the statistical estimates presented in this paper. The further in time we move away from the present moment in either forward or backward direction, the greater the probable degree of error. Once, however, we dispose of reliable demographic data on mainland China, the most populous country in the world, the statistically most significant element of uncertainty will have been removed.

1. HISTORIC GROWTH

Contemporary demographic trends can be most readily appreciated by viewing them against the background of the course of events in the past as revealed by estimates of population size.[1] This is most vividly portrayed in graph 1.1 which is based on Table 1.1, and which

TABLE 1.1

World Population '000,000

Year	Population
A.D. 1	300
1750	791
1800	978
1850	1262
1900	1650
1950	2515
1970	3632

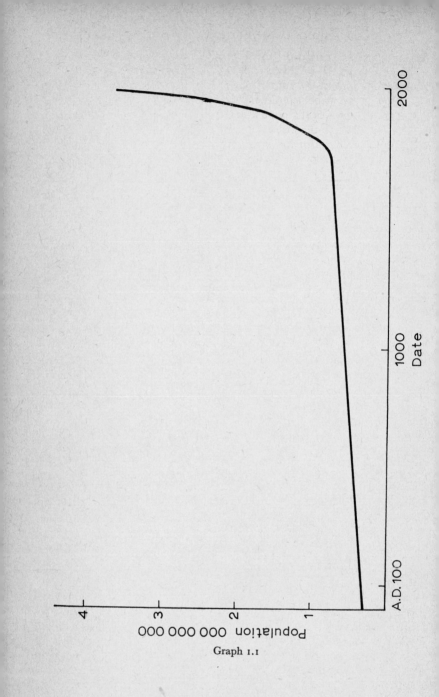

Graph 1.1

demonstrates the origin of 'the population explosion' as the most widely used phrase in the world today. While there might have been fluctuations in the rate of growth before 1750, whose upward phases could have been considered explosive, the tempo of sustained expansion of the world's population during the past two centuries is unprecedented in the history of mankind. Having been of minuscule proportions for many hundreds of years since the birth of Christ, the growth-rate started to increase around the sixteenth century and remained ostensibly on a fairly even keel of one-half of 1 per cent, on average, until the beginning of this century. The figure rose to 0·6 per cent during 1900–20, which period included the First World War, to 1·0 per cent during 1920–50 despite the ravages of the Second World War, and to 1·85 per cent, on average, in the two post-war decades. This acceleration in the rate of increase has been responsible for a net addition of 1390 million to the inhabitants of the earth since the year 1900. In other words, without it they would have numbered some 2240 million in 1970 instead of the actual 3632 million.

At the moment they are increasing at a rate of 2·0 per cent per annum which implies a doubling of their number within 35 years. When the latter is compared with a doubling time of 65 years in the immediately preceding period 1900–65, of 150 years between 1750 and 1900 and of some 1700 years before that, contemporary performance on the demographic front strikes one as being on a par with technological or scientific progress as the most remarkable feature of our age.

The accelerating rate of growth superimposed on an ever-expanding base is making continuously rising absolute contributions to the number of earthly dwellers. While the first aggregate of 1000 million was attained around the year 1800; the second by 1930, or 130 years later, the third by 1960, or within 30 years, the fourth is due to be recorded in 1975, only 15 years after 1960. In the absence of unforeseen changes the 10 years 1975–85 might produce the fifth one-thousand million. During the next 12 months some 124 million babies will be born and around 51 million persons will die, to leave the earth with a net new crop of 73 million people, enough to replace the population of France, Switzerland and the Netherlands. The United Nations projections[2] have revealed that if the conditions of stable fertility and declining mortality prevailing during the fifties were to be maintained, the earth's inhabitants would add up to more than 7500 million persons at the end of this century. To reinforce this alarmist note one may mention that at this rate of growth the number would be 40,000 million a hundred years hence. To forestall the indictment of statistical juggling we hasten to add that these figures do not constitute predictions, but serve as a warning that unless the rate of population growth were decelerated voluntarily or some revolutionary discoveries and inventions bring about radical changes in the ability of man to sustain human life at a reasonable level, calamities appear to be inevitable. In this regard, however, the simple global aggregate figures and tendencies are not adequate for analytical purposes.[3] The cause of concern is, namely, first and foremost the inverse relationship existing between the rates at which various communities are growing in size and their ability to accommodate the increasing numbers.

2. THE RICH AND THE POOR

In Table 1.2 are summarised the salient demographic features of three main categories of countries, classified according to level of gross national product (G.N.P. converted into U.S. dollars) per capita.[4]

TABLE 1.2   1970 Demographic magnitures and level of G.N.P.

Population in millions	Rate per thousand of population				Age structure		
	Births	Deaths	Natural increase	Total	0–14	15–64	65+
I. *Countries with G.N.P. per capita of $750 and over (Average $1700)*							
954	18	9	9	100	28	62	10
II. *Countries with G.N.P. per capita of $250–750 (Average $570)*							
A. 137	20	9	12	100	28	62	10
B. 23	33	8	25	100	42	55	3
C. 138	42	9	32	100	45	52	3
Aggre-gate 298							
III. *Countries with G.N.P. per capita below $250 (Average $135)*							
2380	41	17	24	100	41	55	4
World total 3632	34	14	20				

The countries in the high-income category, which contain 26 per cent of the world's population, have[5] already reached the last phase in the demographic cycle with a birth-rate which averages 18 per 1000 and a crude death-rate which is slowly rising because of the influence of the ageing process even while mortality, already low, is tending downward still further. That the growth-rate of less than

1 per cent per annum presents no problems of Malthusian proportions does not mean that the inhabitants are necessarily happy about the absolute size of population additions involved. Remarked one writer, referring to the situation in the United States, 'when a city dweller observes the overloading of all public facilities – for education, culture, recreation, transportation, power and communications; when he feels oppressed by crowded streets and jarred by high-decibel cacophony; when he observes the increasing irritation and incivility with which otherwise normal citizens treat one another . . . he may conclude that adding another 100 people to this country's problems is not such a good idea.'[6] When sheer numbers have reduced the space available per capita – a very important ingredient of high standards of living – to the proverbial (actual or imagined) 'standing room only', the zero population growth-movement may gain a great deal of support, and depress the relatively low level of fertility still further.

The populations in this category are those of western and northern Europe, three of the six eastern European countries (Czechoslovakia, East Germany and Hungary), Italy in southern Europe, the Soviet Union, the United States, Canada, Japan, Australia, New Zealand, Argentina, Venezuela, Puerto Rico, Israel and South Africa (the white community only).

In the second or middle-income category three sub-groups can be distinguished:

II A: Southern Europe, Italy excepted, and three eastern European countries. They are in the same phase of the demographic cycle as Category I, their average growth-rate being only slightly higher. Some of them have lower birth-rates than those in the first category.

II B: A few countries in Asia and Africa whose total population adds up to only 23 million. They have advanced some distance in the transition from high to low fertility.

II C: This group encompasses the sixteen Latin American countries which remain after two of the sub-continent's republics have been classified in Category I, and seven in Category III. A few of these have been experiencing for some time fertility rates below the traditional maximum, but as yet there is no clear evidence that the group as a whole is embarking on the transition from high to low fertility. At 42 per 1000 their average birth-rate could be somewhat higher even than that of the third category which had been estimated at 41. The continued decline in mortality, on the other hand, is an indisputable fact which has been responsible for a progressive rise in the rate of natural increase from around 1·8 per cent per annum in the twenties to 3·2 per cent at the moment.[7] This sub-category is the furthest advanced of all in the explosive phase of the demographic cycle. The only comfort to be derived from the statistics is that a further decline in mortality cannot add more than 0·3 percentage points to the growth rate. This group II C provides an example of what might conceivably (or theoretically) happen to the populations classified in III.

In the third or low-income category we find nearly 66 per cent of the world's population, most of whom are eking out an existence on an average per capita G.N.P. of $135, and producing 15 per cent of the gross world product, compared to the 77 per cent of G.W.P. earned by the Category I population representing 26 per cent of the earth's inhabitants. Their rate of natural increase of about 2·4 per cent per annum is the outcome of a crude birth-rate of 41 and death-rate of 17 per 1000, and is responsible for 77 per cent of the annual increment in the world's population. In their relatively high crude death-rate lurks considerable scope for a further rise in the growth-rate. A decline of the former to the level of Category II C would raise the latter by nearly 1 percentage point, or from 2·4 to 3·2 per cent per annum.

The response to the presentation of this sort of sombre picture is to refer to the phenomenon of the demographic transition and to hold up the experience of the Category I countries as an example of why the demographic gap – or the growing disparity between birth- and death-rates – need not worry us unduly. The rebuttal would be briefly in the following terms. Firstly, the basic cause of the gap continues to operate: unlike fertility, barring the possibility of a successful intervention of family planning campaigns, the level of mortality in the poorer countries can be, and has been, divorced from economic, social and scientific developments as an endogenous process. Its reduction can be exogenously induced. It was, and is, not necessary for the low-income countries to generate for themselves new knowledge and means to combat and control disease. Public health techniques, chemotherapy, pesticides, disinfectants and the like can be imported from the high-income countries who are eager to provide them at little and often no cost to the former. A willingness to limit births cannot be imported thus. Even where mortality control is an endogenous process, as is the case where the observation of a few simple rules of hygiene can save the lives of large percentages of new-born babies – a most important element in declining mortality – the change in the way of life required is much less radical than would be necessary for family control. Secondly, a growth rate of 2·4 per cent per annum is already too high and is inhibiting of the attainment of those 'threshholds' of economic and social conditions which are required to produce changes in reproductive *mores*. Thirdly, a very considerable decline in the birth-rate from the present 41 to 33 per 1000 will not make any difference to the rate of growth in the poorer countries if their death-rate were reduced from 17 to 9 per 1000; a figure not very difficult to achieve. Fourthly, whatever may reasonably be expected to happen to fertility, the absolute numbers of births to mothers in low-income countries are almost bound to increase since the potential number of mothers at the most fertile period of their lives, i.e. between 20 and 30 years of age, will double between now and 1985. Thus rapidly growing populations have their own built-in momentum.

A rise in the share of the third as well as the IIC category of countries in the world's population seems to be inevitable. Reductions in the birth-rates have indeed been noted in a few countries, but there is no indication that an appreciable change in reproductive performance is imminent to release the fertility drag on the transition to lower rates of growth.

In the demographic literature usually only two categories of countries or areas are distinguished, viz. the developed and the less developed (or developing) countries. To facilitate the use of available international statistics we shall have recourse to this classification in our further discussions. To this end, just over one half of population classified in our Category II has to be transferred to Category III to make up a total of 2541 million persons (70 per cent) residing in less developed areas, and the remaining number – those of southern and eastern Europe and temperate Latin America – to Category I to yield a total of 1090 million (or 30 per cent) found in developed countries.

3. POPULATION PROSPECTS

The United Nations Secretariat has computed projections of world population by country, in which three variants, a 'high', 'low' and 'medium', were distinguished, the variations being a function of the alternate rates of decline in fertility assumed. The 'medium' variant, because it falls between the high and the low, appears more or less reasonable even if only by definition, and is most often quoted.[8] We, too, shall make use of them. The underlying assumptions defy simple description in a few sentences, since they differ from one region and country to another depending on the specific conditions obtaining in each during recent times. Translated into aggregated crude rates per 1000 of the population the implications of the assumptions regarding fertility and mortality – measured in magnitudes standardised for sex and age for the employment in projections – are as follows:[9]

More developed regions	1965–70	1970–75	1975–80	1980–85	1985–90	1990–95	1995–2000
Birth-rate	18·5	18·7	19·4	19·3	19·0	18·5	18·3
Death-rate	8·5	8·6	9·0	9·1	9·2	9·4	9·6
Natural increase	10·0	10·1	10·4	10·2	9·7	9·1	8·8
Less developed regions							
Birth-rate	39·4	38·2	36·5	33·9	31·8	29·7	28·0
Death-rate	17·3	15·7	14·4	12·5	11·2	10·0	9·2
Natural increase	22·1	22·5	22·1	21·4	20·6	19·7	18·8

It will be seen that the population of the more developed regions is projected to grow at a declining rate after 1975–80 arising from an increasing crude death-rate – the result of the larger percentages of old people – and a birth-rate which remains approximately constant. The projections for the less developed areas provide for a birth-rate which diminishes somewhat more rapidly than the death-rate so that the rate of natural increase decelerates at a fractionally faster pace than in developed regions. The 1963 assessment of world population based on these assumptions produced a 1970 estimate which a subsequent revision[10] intimated to be too low by 40 million or by 0·7 and 1·23 per cent respectively for developed and developing areas,[11] and a 1985 estimate which could be out by 1·5 and 4·8 per cent respectively. The author has used the latter percentages, and correspondingly derived ones for sub-regions, to blow up the figures for the year 1985 and 2000 as assessed in 1963, to obtain a rough 'minimum medium' estimate. The results are summarised in Table 1.3.

TABLE 1.3   Projected populations of the world in millions

	1970	1985	2000
Developed regions	1090	1275	1460
Less developed regions	2541	3658	4926
Total	3632	4933	6386

Sources: Adapted from U.N. *World Population Prospects as assessed in 1963*; U.N. *Population Newsletter* (December 1969).

If these projections were to be realised in fact the earth's inhabitants will increase by 2754 million during the next 30 years, or by 76 per cent. The contribution of the poorer nations to the increment would be 2384 million (or 87 per cent) as against a meagre 370 million (13 per cent) by the richer nations. Barring a fertility *risorgimento* among developed nations – an improbable event – their future populations are not likely to be underestimated to any greater extent than those of the less developed countries. Nothing that is foreseen can bring about a drastic change in the 87:13 incremental ratio mentioned above.

4. THE TOP TEN COUNTRIES OF THE WORLD

The ten countries with the largest populations in the world are as follows, in descending order: China (mainland) 760 million, India 555 million, Soviet Union 243 million, United States 205 million, Pakistan 137 million, Indonesia 121 million, Japan 104 million, Brazil 93 million, West Germany 59 million, United Kingdom 56 million. Together these top ten contain 2333 million, or 64 per cent, of the world's inhabitants. The remaining 36 per cent are spread over some 140 political units. Emphasising the unequal distribution even more starkly is the fact that the numbers in Communist China and India alone add up to more than one-third of the world total, and in 10 years' time their present 1315 million may have grown into 1600 million. The five developed nations among the top ten stand to lose some of their relative numerical strength in the years to come. Brazil will move up from eighth to seventh in the ranks.

These top ten countries contain 64 per cent of the world's population. The remaining 140 or so political units contain the other 36 per cent. It is quite probable that the former are not going to maintain their relative share over the next 30 years.

5. CONTINENTS AND SUB-CONTINENTS

East Asia has lost its position at the top of the regional log to south Asia whose demographic ascendancy is growing over time, to attain a 36 per cent share by the end of the century compared to 25 per cent in 1920. The former has China (mainland) and Japan as its most important components, while the latter contains, among others, India, Pakistan and Indonesia. The whole of Asia – the Asian portion of the Soviet Union excluded – accommodated 55 per cent of the earth's inhabitants in 1920, 56·6 per cent of them in 1970 and a probable 57·6 in 30 years' time. Europe's population has experienced the largest decline of all regions, from 17·5 per cent in 1920 to 12·7 per cent at the moment, to reach a probable 8·6 per cent at the end of the century. This contrasts sharply with the situation during the nineteenth century when Europe led the rest of the world, as emerges when northern America and Oceania, the areas of European settlement, are included. The relative numbers

TABLE 1.4   Population growth in larger regions in millions

	Growth % 1970–75	1920	1950	1970	1985	2000	Ratio 2000 1970
East Asia	1·68	553	684	930	1182	1377	1·48
South Asia	2·85	470	697	1126	1693	2302	2·04
Europe	0·73	325	392	462	515	551	1·19
Soviet Union	1·05	155	180	243	287	341	1·40
Africa	2·80	143	222	344	530	793	2·31
Northern America	1·28	116	166	228	280	350	1·45
Latin America	2·93	90	162	283	435	638	2·25
Oceania	2·98	9	13	19	27	34	1·79
Total	2·06	1860	2515	3632	4933	6386	1·76

Sources: As in tables 1.2 and 1.3.

residing in the Soviet Union and northern America are expected to decline between now and the end of the century, after the latter has maintained its position during 1920–70. Latin America has been registering the highest relative increase, viz. from 4·8 per cent in 1920 to 7·8 per cent of world population at present. From now on there is evidently going to be a race between this sub-continent and Africa for growth leadership as indicated by the 2000/1970 ratios in Table 1.4, with Africa in the lead by a short head and accommodating 12·4 per cent of the world's population in A.D. 2000 compared to Latin America's 10 per cent. In the latter Brazil, with 93 million inhabitants, representing one-third of the region's total, is the giant. The next in line is Mexico with 51 million, followed by Argentina (24 million) and Colombia (22 million). These four republics contain two-thirds of Latin America's population.

In Africa Nigeria, with 55 million inhabitants, is the most populous country. Its relative share in the continent's population is, however, only 16 per cent and that of the top four (the other three being the United Arab Republic, Ethiopia and South Africa) no more than 38 per cent. The population scatter is greatest in this continent.

6. AGE STRUCTURE

Differing age structures are the most distinctive characteristic of populations at various stages of the demographic cycle. The higher the level of fertility the more youthful the structure. A drop from a high to a lower level of mortality, which usually has the greatest impact among infants and children, tends to have a similar effect. Reference to Table 1.2 will indicate that the countries furthest advanced in the explosive phase have the most youthful populations, while those which have been coursing along the last phase in the demographic cycle have the oldest populations. The following schematic presentation of the ageing process may facilitate understanding:

(1) Populations experiencing unrestricted fertility and mortality levels have high percentages in the 0–14 age group (40–43 per cent), small proportions in the 65+ age group (2–3 per cent) and relatively small numbers in the 'productive' age groups 15–64. Some of the Category III countries are in transition between this and the next phase.

(2) If mortality declines while fertility remains unchanged at traditional or near maximum levels, juvenescence takes place. The percentage of youths increases and the productive age group shrinks somewhat in relative size. Most Category III or low-income countries have embarked on this phase, while Category II C (as in Table 1.2) are approaching the end of it.

(3) When fertility declines, and especially if it does so at a more rapid rate than mortality, the proportions under 15 years diminish and the productive group is strengthened. A few individual countries in Category II B, II C and I are experiencing these conditions.

(4) When both fertility and mortality have reached and maintained low levels over a long period, the decline in the youthful population is now being more than offset by the relative increase in old people, and the proportions in the 'productive' ages are now diminishing. Some of the Category I – the most highly developed – nations are at this stage.

If the assumptions underlying the projections in section 3 were to be realised the percentage of the population in the productive ages will deviate very little from 63 per cent during the next 30 years in the more developed regions, and will rise from 56 to nearly 61 in the less developed regions. If the assumed reduction in fertility is not going to take place, the expected rise in the proportion will not eventuate either.

As it is, the supremacy of less developed regions is reduced somewhat when not total populations but only the manpower age groups are compared. Moreover, because of its economic effects, the age composition of the lesser developed countries is a source of weakness, that of the developed countries a source of strength, in that in the latter smaller 'demographic investments', and less of a 'widening of capital', are required to accommodate non-productive elements of the population and new additions to the labour force, and more resources can be devoted to improving the efficiency of each member of the community. The school age population is projected to increase by 1·5 per cent, the manpower group by 10·9 and the old-age population by 23·7 per cent during the next decade in the more developed areas. The comparable rates for the less developed areas are 28·5, 28·7 and 38·2 per cent respectively.[12] Even if the marginal product per worker were the same in the two categories of countries, it must be abundantly clear that the latter category would be much harder put to it to generate productive employment for the labour force emanating from the manpower age group, and to supply their children of school-going age with schools, teachers and books.

At the same time it needs to be pointed out that the developed nations have the problem of the aged to contend with inasmuch as they have more than half the world's old people and only 25 per cent of the world's people younger than 65 years.

7. URBAN–RURAL DISTRIBUTION

Table 1.5 indicates that the populations of the developed regions are urbanised to a much greater extent than those of the less developed areas: according to 1960 figures 60 per cent as against 20 per cent. With regard to continents, northern America is found to be in the lead (70 per cent) with Africa exhibiting the lowest percentage (18 per cent). Among the lesser developed areas Latin America's degree of urbanisation is outstanding and equals that of the Soviet Union.

The growth of towns and cities has been of much more explosive dimensions than that of total populations, leading to huge metropolises, megalopolises and conurbations in some countries. Between 1920 and 1960 the world aggregate increased by 61 per cent; the urban dwellers (as nationally defined) grew by 175 per cent, the pace having been considerably faster in the less developed than in the more developed areas. These tendencies are projected to continue, but even the doubling of the urban component in the former cannot prevent the population from remaining predominantly rural.

During the 40 years 1960–2000 some 1610 million persons in the poorer countries may be added to the population of their towns and cities, many of them without any hope of finding employment because of an absence of opportunities or because they lack the literacy

TABLE 1.5   Percentage of population in urban areas

	1920	1960	1980	2000
World total	*19*	*33*	*46*	*51*
More developed areas	*39*	*60*	*71*	*81*
Europe	46	58	65	71
Northern America	52	70	81	87
Soviet Union	15	49	68	85
Oceania	47	64	75	80
Less developed areas	*8*	*20*	*30*	*41*
East Asia	9	23	31	40
South Asia	9	18	25	35
Latin America	22	49	60	80
Africa	7	18	28	39

Source: U.N. *Growth of the World's Urban and Rural Population 1920–2000* (ST/SOA/Ser.A/44, New York, 1969).

and skills needed in modern industry. They constitute fertile breeding ground for social unrest. Even so an increment (under the medium variant projection) of 1300 million persons will have to be accommodated in the rural areas which are already rife with underemployment, and for which estimates of the proportions of 'superfluous' agricultural population range from 10 to 40 per cent.[13]

And so it would appear that a major aspect of proliferating mankind on the rampage is the ability or inability to provide them with economic opportunities, or simply employment at reasonable rates of remuneration. The poorer countries have learned to live with underemployment. Could these communities adapt themselves equally well to unemployment, the product of urbanisation and modernisation?

Notes

1. Adapted from John D. Durand, 'The Modern Expansion of World Population', *Proceedings of the American Philosophical Society*, III 3 (June 1967) 136–59; United Nations, *World Population Prospects as assessed in 1963*, ST/SOA/Ser.A/41 (New York, 1966); Population Reference Bureau, *1970 World Population Data Sheet*; United Nations, Population Division, *Population Newsletter*, December 1969, reporting on *World Population Situation* (Document E/CN.9/231).
2. U.N. *World Population Prospects as assessed in 1963*, pp. 125–7.

3. Cf. e.g. A. Sauvy, *La Situation Demographique du Monde d'Aujourd'hui* (International Population Conference, London, 1969).
4. Refers to G.N.P. around 1966–7. The usual qualifications concerning international comparability apply. Cf. United Nations, *Yearbook of National Accounts Statistics 1968*.
5. With one exception.
6. Rufus E. Miles, 'Whose baby is the population problem?', *P.R.B. Population Bulletin*, February 1970.
7. Cf. Carmen A. Miro, *Los cambios demograficos en America Latina y su influencia* (C.E.L.A.D.E., April 1967).
8. U.N. *World Population Prospects*, p. 6, maintains: 'The "medium" estimates are intended to represent the future population trend that now appears most plausible in view of what is known of past experience and present circumstances in each region.'
9. Ibid., pp. 34–6.
10. U.N. *Population Newsletter* (December 1969).
11. It will be seen that the growth-rate in less developed areas postulated for 1965–70 was lower than the rates mentioned in table 1.3.
12. Cf. U.N. *Population Newsletter* (December 1969) p. 1.
13. Cf. J. L. Sadie, *Demographic Aspects of Labour Supply and Employment*, Background Paper A.5/19/E/484, World Population Conference 1965.

DISCUSSION

Panel Members: Mr. Jean Bourgeois-Pichat, Professor H. V. Muhsam, Dr. B. J. Piek

Mr. Bourgeois-Pichat thought that Professor Sadie had been unduly pessimistic in his view of the problem. Firstly, he argued that the implications for international relations might not be as serious as a consideration of the population of the world as a whole suggested. Unless a country was of at least a certain minimum size, it found it difficult to make its views heard effectively in international affairs. The effect of the population explosion would be to increase the proportion of the population in various regions living in countries with populations of 10 million or more people. The increase in the number of countries in the ' 10 million club', he argued, would alter the distribution of political influence in a way conducive to more harmonious international relations.

Secondly, he felt that Professor Sadie might have underestimated the rate of decline of fertility. Once the decline in fertility began, it tended to proceed quite rapidly. As examples he mentioned the case of Singapore (where the crude birth-rate had fallen from 45·8 in 1953 to 24·7 in 1968) and the Caribbean area. He pointed out that measures aimed at reducing the level of infant mortality tended also to reduce the desire for large families.

Thirdly, on the question of urbanisation, he said that some of the best features of our civilisation were the products of this phenomenon. While the rates of departure from rural areas were much the same for both developed and underdeveloped areas, the rate of arrival in urban areas relative to the existing urban population was much greater in underdeveloped than in developed countries. He suggested that the problems associated with urbanisation tended to be exaggerated, and that in the future as in the past the growth of cities might be facilitated by improved means of transportation. The motor car had increased the amount of space required per person, but new means of rapid mass transportation were already being developed, and these and subsequent developments would make it possible for people to live at increasingly greater distances from their places of work in cities.

Professor Muhsam questioned Professor Sadie's use of the phrase 'the last phase in demographic development', as other phases might possibly arise in the future. In socialist countries, for instance, abortion was playing a larger part in population control, and he wondered whether one could expect future population growth to be determined to a greater degree by planned government action.

B

Although the latter might be effective, there was the danger of government controls involving modern scientific methods being allowed to go too far, and generally he questioned the advisability of extensive government controls. He suggested that the present population explosion was not unprecedented in the history of mankind, and that the emergence of man from earlier forms of life, for instance, must also have involved a population explosion.

Dr. Piek said that world population might be lower at the end of the century than the medium projection mentioned by Professor Sadie suggested. The United Nations paper upon which this estimate was based assumed a 50 per cent decline in fertility over 30 years, but did not make allowance for the impact of government programmes. In addition, certain inner controls related to changing social and economic conditions might come into operation. These inner controls might eventually become institutionalised in the developing countries, and could result in the low projection being realised and the world's population at the end of the century being between 5·5 and 6 billion, with the prospect of a declining rate of growth.

Professor Muhsam commented, in reply to a question, that all species had the capacity to reproduce at a rate greater than their environment allowed, but that the human race was the most adaptable of all species. He stressed the danger that, just as insects were controlled by spraying, governments might attempt to check population growth by introducing chemical substances into the supply of drinking water. Such measures might be reversible, but governments might easily move on to irreversible measures.

Professor D. G. Haylett pointed out that bacteria grew rapidly at first, but that their numbers levelled off and then declined, and he asked whether there might not be similar built-in controls operating in the case of humans. *Dr. Piek* replied that the controls operating in the case of man were likely to be social ones, while *Professor Sadie* said that an increasing death-rate might be such a built-in control, but that this was not an acceptable means of checking population growth.

In reply to a statement that population studies in the Caribbean had revealed a relationship between fertility and malnutrition, in that malnutrition tended to increase the sexual urge and hence population growth *Mr. Bourgeois-Pichat* commented that malnutrition and venereal disease checked the rates of population growth, but that medical treatment had reduced the latter and thus increased fertility. Thus while the birth-rate appeared to be constant, behind this constancy there lay perhaps the beginning of control hidden by the tendency of medical advances to raise fertility.

Professor H. L. Watts said demographers fell into two categories, optimists and pessimists, depending on the assumptions underlying their projections. All papers, however, showed the danger that population would outstrip food supplies. Family planning depended on the longer-term goals of the society and the individual, such as the raising of the standard of living. Whereas mortality could be reduced without changing the whole culture, family planning could not. Perhaps, therefore, the medium population estimates were too optimistic.

Professor Sadie, commenting on points raised in the discussion, said that, while there probably had been earlier population explosions, these were, unlike the present one, not sustained over long periods. In dealing with urbanisation in his paper, he had been thinking particularly of developing countries where population moved to urban areas in advance of jobs being available, and where also they did not have the resources to counter congestion by providing rapid mass transport systems. He agreed with Professor Muhsam that other phases in the demographic cycle might yet emerge in which other than the familiar social and economic forces might be dominant.

Professor E. S. Munger pointed out that power was not simply a function of population size, but also of certain qualitative factors. Another participant commented that while the size of countries would increase this would not necessarily change the relative distribution of countries by size, and that this was the more relevant condition in international relations.

Professor Louw asked what, in regard to government interference, demographers thought was desirable; what would they advise governments to do? *Dr. Piek* replied that there was no golden rule. Social and economic conditions played an important role, so that demographers could not make assumptions independent of those conditions. *Professor Muhsam* said the demographers' role was to study what factors influenced population growth. The setting of goals, which required the introduction of valued judgements, was the responsibility of others, not demographers.

2 World resources, their use and distribution

WILLEM BRAND

Resources may be defined as means employed by man for his welfare or well-being. Most resources are not free and can only be acquired through the application of man's brain and brawn. As a first approximation of the distribution of world resources, the division of the world national product between the various continents comes to mind. The national product is hereby seen as a comprehensive index for measuring the level of development, which reflects at the time man's mastery over nature and the manner in which resources are allocated. Following this idea, Table 2.1 below shows the distribution of world population and world national product between the various continents (divided into rich and poor) and national proproduct per head in 1960 and 1970.

TABLE 2.1   Population: national product and national product per head. 1960 and 1970

	Population (in millions)				National Product (in billions of $)				Nat. Product per head in $	
	1960	In %	1970	In %	1960	In %	1970	In %	1960	1970
World	*3000*	*100*	*3600*	*100*	*1350*	*100*	*2640*	*100*	*450*	*730*
Poor areas	*2050*	*68*	*2550*	*71*	*220*	*16*	*400*	*15*	*100*	*157*
Asia	1570	52	1920	53	130	10	240	9	95	125
Africa	270	9	350	10	30	2	50	2	120	143
Latin America	210	7	280	8	60	4	110	5	320	393
Rich areas	*950*	*32*	*1050*	*29*	*1130*	*84*	*2240*	*85*	*1190*	*2130*
Europe incl. Soviet Union	640	21	700	19	530	40	1070	40	820	1530
North America	200	7	230	7	540	40	990	38	2700	4300
Oceania and Japan	110	4	120	3	60	4	180	7	550	1500

The population date can be found in a United Nations publication.[1] The national product figures have been derived from United Nations sources and extrapolated with some guesswork until 1970.

As can be seen at a glance, the world national product has almost doubled in the period 1960–70 and the growth-rate in the poor and rich areas has been about the same. On the other hand, because of the higher rate of population growth in the poor continents (from 2·0 per cent in 1960 to 2·5 per cent in 1970) as compared with the rich ones (from 1·2 per cent in 1960 to 0·8 per cent in 1970), it appears that national product per head has advanced less rapidly in the poor than in the rich nations. Thus the gap in the levels of living between developing and developed countries has further been widened.

The most striking result from our calculations is that the inhabitants of the poor continents, though forming 70 per cent of the world population, produced only 15–16 per cent of the world's goods and services embodied in the national product in the period 1960–70. Though no accuracy is claimed for this outcome, the data as found in the United Nations *Statistical Yearbooks* confirm that in the period 1938–61 the share of the less industrialised countries in the world domestic product (excluding the communist bloc) remained more or less steady at 17·5 per cent, while its proportion in the world population increased from 67 to 70 per cent.

The resource distribution pattern may be further approached in more conventional terms. The earth's surface consists roughly of 30 per cent land (135 million km^2) and 70 per cent water (seas and oceans: 375 million km^2). A few years ago, it was reckoned[2] that about half of the world population was concentrated on 5 per cent of the earth's surface, while 57 per cent of the land supported only 5 per cent of the people. This pattern is probably still true today. Due to topography, climate and soil, population is bound to be unevenly distributed over our planet. Because of severe cold, insufficient rainfall and infertile soils only an estimated 20 per cent of the earth is considered habitable. The following table gives an indication of the skewed distribution of land resources between the various continents according to recent data supplied by the Food and Agriculture Organisation (F.A.O.).

From this table it can be calculated that the poor regions, having as said 70 per cent of the world population, possess 58 per cent of the land, 54 per cent of the arable land, 58 per cent of the meadows and pastures and 53 per cent of the forested area. This implies that they have more 'other', probably unusable land. It can also be seen that the Far East, Europe and Japan have little arable land per capita, which points to intensive cultivation, while the more favourable man/land ratio for the Soviet Union, North America and Oceania indicates the possibility of extensive cultivation. One should however not read too much into these figures. They do not show

TABLE 2.2   Total and per capita land utilisation in the world and by regions

	Land area (millions of ha.)	per capita ha.	Arable land (millions of ha.)	per capita ha.	Meadows and pastures (millions of ha.)	per capita ha.
World	*13,422*	*3·99*	*1440*	*0·42*	*2880*	*0·86*
Poor regions	*7810*	*3·32*	*780*	*0·33*	*1671*	*0·71*
Far East	2036	1·20	377	0·22	287	0·17
Near East	1218	8·11	77	0·51	194	1·30
Africa	2497	9·32	217	0·81	682	2·55
Latin America	2059	8·37	109	0·44	506	2·06
Rich regions	*5592*	*5·56*	*660*	*0·66*	*1209*	*1·20*
Europe	493	1·11	151	0·34	91	0·20
Soviet Union	2240	9·70	241	1·04	373	1·61
North America	1971	9·20	223	1·04	281	1·31
Oceania	851	48·63	39	2·23	483	27·24
Japan	37	0·38	6	0·06	1	0·01

	Forests (millions of ha.)	per capita ha.	Other land (millions of ha.)	per capita ha.
World	*3999*	*1·19*	*5083*	*1·51*
Poor regions	*2104*	*0·89*	*3255*	*1·39*
Far East	490	0·28	900	0·53
Near East	123	0·83	824	5·53
Africa	496	1·86	1102	4·13
Latin America	1015	4·13	429	1·74
Rich Regions	*1895*	*1·89*	*1828*	*1·82*
Europe	139	0·31	112	0·25
Soviet Union	910	3·94	716	3·10
North America	739	3·45	728	3·40
Oceania	82	4·82	267	15·71
Japan	25	0·26	5	0·05

that in most of the developing world forests consist of heterogeneous stands which are inaccessible while in Europe with the least forest per capita about all available timber is being exploited. The main weakness of the above data is that they convey no information on the productivity of the land or of farm animals. It may be interesting to know that the developing regions possess 66 per cent of the world's number of livestock. However, it should then also be pointed out that most of the cattle in the poor regions serve as draught-animals, while in the rich countries this function has been more and more taken over by tractors.

Thus also with the aid of F.A.O. data the following table has been constructed showing the regional shares in the world production of the most important cereals (barley, maize, rice and wheat) and of milk for the year 1967.

The table shows that the poor regions, having 70 per cent of the world population, are only responsible for 48 per cent of cereal production, which reflects the inadequate amount of calories consumed there by the average inhabitant. That the share of the richer regions is not larger than 52 per cent can partly be explained by the inelastic demand for food products at a high-income level so that in certain countries cereal output is curtailed to avoid unmarketable

TABLE 2.3   Regional shares of cereals and milk production plus population 1967

	Cereal production (million tons)	In %	Milk production (million tons)	In %	Population (millions)	In %
World	957	100	385	100	3420	100
Poor regions	453	47·5	71	18	2394	70
Africa	37	4	12	3	328	10
Asia	371	38·5	42	11	1807	53
South America	45	5	17	4	259	7
Rich regions	505	52·5	315	82	1026	30
Europe	151	16	149	39	452	13
North America	212	22	68	18	220	6·5
Oceania and Japan	30	3	18	5	118	3·5
Soviet Union	112	11·5	80	20	236	7

surpluses. Such surpluses have in the meantime served to fill the mounting gains deficit (from 1·2 million tons as an average in the period 1955–7 to 14 million tons in 1967) in some parts of the poor regions. It may also be pointed out that in the period 1957–9 to 1964–6 in the developed continents agricultural production (for 12 major crops) increased by 16 per cent, while the cultivated area declined by 1 per cent. In the same period in the developing regions agricultural production rose by 22 per cent, accompanied by an increase of 11 per cent in cultivated areas so that only 50 per cent of the increase in output was attributable to an improvement in yield per hectare. Considering that the increase in yield per hectare is partly caused by the application of fertilizer, it is understandable that in 1966–7 of total commercial fertilizer (N, P_2O_5 and K_2O) 95 per cent was produced and 90 per cent consumed in the developed regions.

The small proportion of the developing countries in the world's milk production forms an indication of the deficiency in fats and proteins consumed, which defect has been amply underlined by other F.A.O. information. This fact together with other data on nutrition forms a sign of the physical and mental inadequacy of human resources in the poor regions.[3]

It needs further to be emphasised that in the poor regions 60–80 per cent of the economically active population is engaged in primary production, while in the rich countries only 5–20 per cent is thus employed. Cereal production per male employed in agriculture for this reason is a better indicator than output per hectare to demonstrate the level of agricultural development.[4]

The backwardness of the agricultural sector in the developing countries has been ascribed to technological and institutional factors, but also the innate quality of the soil in the tropical regions has often been advanced as a reason. Thus P. Gourou[5] has pointed out that such soils are poorer and more fragile than those of temperate regions. As a result great care is needed in using them to avoid their impoverishment and destruction. Expanding deserts or erosion of the land due to indiscriminate felling of trees in Africa, Asia and Latin America bear witness that these aspects have not been heeded. It has also been observed that plants and cattle in the tropics are more susceptible to pests and diseases than elsewhere. Some authors, among them W. W. McPherson and B. F. Johnston,[6] seem to take the view that such handicaps can be overcome by appropriate knowledge and that the possibility of double or multiple cropping in irrigated tropical areas could more than offset any soil deficiencies. Without entering into the merits of this controversy, there seems no doubt that the green revolution which implies the utilisation of high-yielding seed varieties combined with adequate water, fertilizer, crop protection and other inputs (research, extension services, marketing and credit policies), which appears imminent in several developing countries, will upset any previous calculations about the food-producing capacity of our planet. Such projections, as made for example by W. W. Cochrane,[7] showing on the basis of data on population growth, likely increase in food production, income and elasticity of demand for food, that by the year 2000, $30 billion of food imports (as compared with $1 billion in 1960) would be required by the developing world, seem fortunately to have been overhauled by events.

It may be presumed that C. Clark,[8] who in the late fifties made the prognosis that the earth could accommodate 28 billion people had the implications of the green revolution in mind when in a more recent publication[9] he increased his estimate to 47 billion based on an American level of food consumption or 157 billion on an Asian diet.

It may hereby be noted that if the 3·0 billion people in the world in 1960 continued to grow at the rate of 2 per cent as in the sixties (which implies a doubling every 35 years), a figure of 48 billion would be reached in 130 years. In calculations such as those performed by Clark the technical and cultural difficulties of the transition from traditional food production to an industrial modern type of farming are more or less ignored.

We may further add that though the prospects of the sea, which now only provides 1 per cent of man's food supply, are considered promising, they will not substantially change the food situation. Neither is it expected that synthetic food production ('man-made' proteins and amino acids) will greatly alter the picture in the foreseeable future.[10] Thus our conclusion is that the limited amount of arable land on our earth puts a limit to the number of people which can be sustained. It may be pointed out that water is also a scarce commodity. Annual rainfall does not vary greatly, the tapping of underground reserves cannot continue for long and though no quantitative data on this topic seem to have been assembled, it would thus appear that the amount of available water also places a restraint on the number of humans which our planet can adequately feed. It needs to be stressed that even in the United States 80 per cent of the water is still consumed by agriculture.

Another way of looking at the distribution of world resources is to focus attention on industrial production. The following table shows the unequal distribution of manufacturing activity in the world, which implies the uneven consumption of industrial raw materials.

From the table can be seen that in the mining sector (especially

TABLE 2.4   Percentage distribution of total value added in U.S. $ by industry and regions (1963)

	Total manuf. mining and electr.	Total mining	Total petrol	Total manuf.	Total electr.
World	*100*	*100*	*100*	*100*	*100*
Industrial regions	*88*	*75*	*65*	*88*	*88*
North America	34	28	42	34	34
Europe	24	15	2	24	33
Soviet Union and eastern Europe	29	31	21	29	20
Oceania	1	1	—	1	1
Unindustrialised regions	*12*	*25*	*35*	*12*	*12*
Africa	1	5	3	1	2
East and south-east Asia	6	5	5	6	7
Middle East	—	7	15	—	—
Latin America	4	8	11	4	4

Source: United Nations, *The Growth of World Industry, 1967*, vol. 1 (New York, 1969) pp. 286–9.

petroleum) the share of the poor areas is higher (respectively 25 and 35 per cent) than for manufacturing and electricity (12 per cent). Some of this primary production is via trade consumed by the industrial countries and this trend is demonstrated for the energy sector (coal, petroleum, natural gas, hydro plus nuclear energy) in the table underneath, based on data found in the United Nations *Statistical Yearbook*.

TABLE 2.5   Energy distribution of the world, expressed in billions of metric tons of coal equivalent, 1959–67

	Production				Consumption				per capita cons. in kg.	
	1959	In %	1967	In %	1959	In %	1967	In %	1959	1967
World	4·1	100	5·8	100	3·9	100	5·6	100	1300	1650
Industrial regions	3·3	81	4·3	74	3·5	90	4·9	87·5	3500	4900
North America	1·4	34	2·0	34	1·5	38	2·1	37·5	7600	9700
Europe	0·6	15	0·5	9	0·8	20	1·1	20	2400	3150
Oceania	0·03	0·7	0·05	1	0·04	1	0·06	1	2800	3600
Soviet Union and eastern Europe	1·3	32	1·7	30	1·2	31	1·6	30	1220	1450
Unindustrialised regions	0·8	19	1·5	26	0·4	10	0·7	12·5	215	325
Africa	0·05	1	0·2	3	0·06	1	0·09	1·6	243	285
Asia	0·5	12	0·9	15	0·2	5	0·45	8	210	250
Latin America	0·3	7	0·4	7	0·1	3	0·2	3	600	780

Thus between 1959 and 1967 in the industrial regions as a whole energy production only increased by 30 per cent. In Europe even a decline of about 10 per cent can be observed. On the other hand, production of energy in the developing countries almost doubled, a sizeable part of which was exported mainly to Europe to make the increase in energy consumption of 40 per cent in the rich nations possible. This applies particularly to petroleum. Total petroleum production was 1·8 billion tons in 1967 of which almost 50 per cent originated in the developing regions. However, of gasoline production (373 million tons in 1967) less than 15 per cent was produced in the poor countries. For iron ore[11] a similar tendency can be observed. In 1937 the share of the developing countries in world exports of iron ore (25 million tons) was about 24 per cent, but for 1985 it has been estimated that their portion (in a total of 215 million tons) may rise to almost 68 per cent. For 1985 their share in the world's consumption of iron ore is expected to increase to 20 per cent, compared with 10 per cent in 1937.

If the 1963 data on the distribution of industrial production are compared with historical information,[12] it would appear that since 1938 the relative position of the developing world in manufacturing has hardly changed. Going back till 1870, the increasing importance of the United States, the Soviet Union and eastern Europe at the expense of western Europe in the index of world industrial production can be noticed. The seemingly slight rise in the share of Africa, Asia and Latin America in total manufacturing can probably be ascribed to the scarcity of data prior to 1938.

Another aspect of the uneven distribution of world industrial production may be touched upon. In view of the low income per head and thus a less varied structure of consumption, it seems clear that most industry in the developing countries is of the simpler kind. From United Nations information[13] based on data referring to value added for 1964, it can be observed that light manufacturing (food, beverages, textiles) was responsible for 36 per cent of industrial production in the rich nations and 56 per cent in the poor nations. The share of the latter nations in total manufacturing output of the developed countries was only 6 per cent. For textiles their portion was about 14 per cent, but for heavy manufacturing (chemicals, base metals, metal products) only 4·5 per cent. It appears likely that even if in the future the economic growth-rate in the developing regions is somewhat higher than in the rich countries, the composition of their industrial output will remain for a long time relatively slanted towards light industry, because of their 2·5 times higher rate of population increase and thus a relatively small rise in income per head.

The period for which data are available is still too short to determine whether this viewpoint can be supported. If, however, our conclusion is valid, it would imply that a relatively large share of the work force, because of higher population growth in the developing countries, would remain employed in those industries in which less skill and technology is applied.

Several studies[14] have been attempted of the requirements of industrial raw materials by the world at large should the poor regions attain the rich nations' level of consumption. A tripling of food output would be required to provide an adequate amount of calories, a five-fold increase in energy production, a similar rise in output of iron ore and ferro-alloys, somewhat less of copper, much more of aluminium and a quadrupling of lumber output. When such information together with foreseeable population growth is projected against available and potential reserves of some of the non-renewable resources, it appears likely that there is a limit as for cultivable land with regard to the amount of people our planet could support.

The unknown variable in such extrapolations is the future development of technology or the application of human intelligence to the harnessing of traditional or new resources. The problem posed appears to be a perennial one for the economist. The classical school (D. Ricardo, Th. R. Malthus) believed that unbridled population growth, given the scarcity of natural resources or the 'niggardliness' of nature, would limit the possibility of rising living standards. Moreover, due to the increase of population more and more marginal land and other resources of an inferior nature would have to be exploited, thereby raising the cost of food and other means of subsistence and thus curtailing the margin for elevating levels of living. The law of diminishing returns underlying these propositions, which implies that an additional resource unit could only be obtained at greater effort or cost, has so far not proved to be correct as far as the industrial countries are concerned. Historical data for the United States[15] show that since around 1870 until the late fifties agricultural (except for lumber) and mineral resources have been produced with less labour and at decreasing cost so that their prices have not risen in relation to the general price level. Though for Europe no similar study has been undertaken, there is no reason to doubt that a similar conclusion can be drawn. Due to (a) improved technology, which reduced the cost of extraction or led to the discovery of new resources, which were not necessarily dearer, (b) a substitution from resources becoming scarce for those being more plentiful, (c) a more economic use of resources, (d) the retrieval of original raw materials from scrap, (e) the shift in the economic structure towards more processing and services, the law of diminishing returns has not yet become manifest in the western world.

The classicists recognised that approaching deficits of resources could be postponed through the medium of international trade. Scarcities of natural resources in a particular country or region could be alleviated by importing the relevant raw materials from other countries possessing these resources in excess in exchange for manufactures. J. Stuart Mill[16] summed up this possibility succinctly for the United Kingdom: 'It is to the emigration of English capital, that we have chiefly to look for keeping up a supply of cheap food and cheap materials of clothing, proportional to the increase of our population; thus enabling an increasing capital to find employment in the country, without reduction of profit, in producing manufactured articles with which to pay for this supply of raw produce.'

The pattern of world trade proves to some extent the accuracy of this statement. Foreign supplies of certain raw materials have pre-

vented the prices of some resources from rising, but a rash conclusion
is not warranted. Comparative advantages of manufacture versus
material extraction within one country come also into play, while
trade restrictions and subsidies have further coloured the picture.
The world prices of wheat, sugar and cotton, for example, have no
relation to production cost. Internal prices are artificially kept high
in rich countries to assure a reasonable income to domestic producers. The relatively high domestic price often encourages an un-
intended expansion of output and the world price which applies
only to the relatively small amount traded, tends to be depressed
because world supply outruns world demand. Also for certain
minerals the policy of the United States has tended to discourage
imports. Still A. K. Cairncross[17] has shown that between 1913 and
1953 the share of the developing nations in world exports of raw
materials grew from 36·3 to 49·5 per cent. For the later years the
following table based on United Nations data has been drawn up.

TABLE 2.6   Share of developing areas in world exports in billions of $ and
percentage (1953–68)

	1953	In % of world exports	1968	In % of world exports
Total	20	28	41	20
Food products	8	50	10	35
Raw materials	6	46	7·6	34
Fuels	4	57	14	74
Chemicals	—	—	0·6	4
Machinery	—	—	0·7	1
Other manuf.	2	12	7·6	13

In the period 1953–68 the portion of the developing nations in
world trade has diminished from 28 to 20 per cent largely due to
the dynamic interchange of manufactures between the industrial
nations. In the total of exports of primary commodities their share
was only 45 per cent in 1968. Their part in food exports has decreased, due to their poor performance in grain production in the
light of their accelerated population growth. For coffee, tea, cocoa,
bananas, etc. the poor countries have a near monopoly, but the
inelastic demand for these products has meant that sales have not
risen in proportion to the increase in income in the rich world.
In the group of other raw materials (industrial raw materials, such
as cotton, rubber, natural fibres plus metals) their proportion in
world trade has declined, due to the emergence of substitutes.
However, we have already pointed out that for iron ore, and we can
add bauxite, copper, lead, tin and zinc, their share has continuously

been going up. In the fuel field, especially petroleum, their position has greatly improved and this sector presents an almost perfect illustration of the situation which the classical economists had in mind. It can further be computed that in the total exports of manufactures their part has been slightly going up from 6 to 7 per cent.

In addition it needs to be stressed that in the period 1953–68 the share of the western countries in the developing countries' exports has been slowly rising from 71 to 73 per cent. The communist world appears to be a stagnant trade partner, hovering around 5 to 6 per cent, while the reciprocal trade between the poor nations has declined from 25 to 22 per cent. It is important hereby to remember that a free flow of trade and of capital is a condition for an exchange of such resources, as by a fluke of nature or otherwise certain regions possess in abundance and others show a growing deficit.[18] Nationalistic policies or confiscatory measures towards foreign capital in the developing world may form an occasional hindrance, but not for long if it is realised that the western industrial nations are the largest and likely to remain the most reliable buyers of raw materials in the foreseeable future.

A few other resource aspects have still to be mentioned. Space is increasingly recognised as a necessity for human survival, though it is hard to state for the human animal in contrast with rodents or insects when the moment of social stress as a result of 'pathological togetherness' will arrive. It may be pointed out that if there were 48 billion people by the year 2100, the density would be 355 persons per km^2 on the land area (135 million km^2), almost equal to the situation now prevailing in the Netherlands. This prospect does not seem inviting, but becomes clearly appalling if world population should continue to increase by 2 per cent and in over a little more than 500 years the density on the land surface would reach 1 million persons per km^2. From the space angle, it thus also seems likely that in a relatively short period in the history of mankind population growth has to come to an end.

Partly correlated with the space problem, there is a growing uneasiness especially in the already affluent world about the 'diseconomics' of an ever-rising standard of living. The spoilage of nature due to sprawling cities, the pollution of water, air and soil as a result of industrial inputs and waste products will, as the ecologists warn, require drastic measures to preserve or restore a healthy environment. The dangers seem real. Water is polluted as sewage plants dispose of their waste in rivers and lakes. Pesticides are leaked out and carried into rivers, reducing the amount of diatones which are responsible for the replenishment of the oxygen supply. Use of chemical fertilizer flowing from farmland into canals and rivers and heated cooling water from electric plants affect the biological equilibrium in water life. The air is poisoned by carbon monoxide and tetraethyl lead from gasoline-driven vehicles. The burning of fossil fuels which raise the carbon dioxide content of the atmosphere may lead to a rise in the earth's temperature. The health of man is apparently threatened by the spewing of obnoxious gases and waste in the air we breathe. Though in the exhortations of the scientists concerned a certain emotional overtone is displayed, it seems likely that protective measures will be evolved to curtail the use of pollutants. Such a development may make the use of existing resources more expensive or perhaps cause a shift towards less dear resources. The effect of such a better control of our environment on future resource distribution cannot yet be predicted, but the problem does seem surmountable in the light of the technology and knowledge available in the western world. Similar problems as above described await the developing nations to some extent, as a result of the implications of the green revolution and their need to augment cereal supplies until the year 2000 with, say, 170 per cent and animal products with 210 per cent in order to meet the expected population growth and increase the available food and animal products per capita with respectively 25 per cent and 40 per cent as the F.A.O. has calculated.

Technically such an expansion appears feasible but it is mainly dependent upon the mobilisation of qualified manpower and the creation of the material and institutional infrastructure required for the task.

This brings us once more to the unbalanced quality and distribution of human resources in the world, which appear to be the most decisive factor in explaining the efficiency in the use of all other resources. According to UNESCO data 90 per cent of those with a tertiary education dwell in the rich countries. Largely due to the accelerated population growth in the developing nations and despite the sizeable budgets devoted to education, it has been estimated that the number of illiterates has risen from 700 to 800 million in the period 1960–70. Increased enrolments in primary, secondary and tertiary education are impressive, but disguise the fact that the wastage in all forms and levels of education averages over 50 per cent. Neither do these data take into account the brain flow from the poor to the rich nations caused by the structural defects in society. The relevance of the content of education to the specific problems faced by the unindustrialised world propounds another problem which appears to defy a solution. It may in this respect be observed that education as such is no substitute for the practical knowledge needed and the willingness to apply it to the job at hand. Available data[19] for the sixties indicate that in the developing countries the expansion of employment has been less than the natural growth of the labour force. Because of a rather capital-intensive industrialisation and other factors unemployment has risen and the flow towards marginal occupations in the manufacturing and services sector has increased due to the labour surplus existing already in the primary sector. For the period 1970–80 it is expected that in the poor world alone some 230 million new jobs, compared with 160 million in the sixties, will have to be found for the more than 300 million who are expected to offer themselves on the labour market. The International Labour Office (I.L.O.) together with interested governments is engaged within the framework of the second development decade in preparing projections about the absorption of this magnitude into productive employment. The preliminary results[20] of this exercise appear highly optimistic even given a growth-rate of the national product of 6 or 7 per cent in the light of past experience. This subject requires a separate paper to do it justice, but it may be ventured that the organisation of human resources in the poor part of our world in particular is likely to present a challenge as great as the husbandry of material resources in the future.

Notes

1. *World Population Prospects as assessed in 1963* (New York, 1966).
2. See C. Langdon White, 'Geography and the World's Population', *The Population Crisis and the Use of World Resources*, ed. Stuart Mudd (The Hague, 1964) pp. 15–25.
3. See Chapter IV, 'Food and Nutrition' (pp. 80–107) in United Nations, *Report on the World Social Situation*, New York, November 1967.
4. See Figure III-3 on p. 78, *The State of Food and Agriculture 1968*, Food and Agriculture Organisation of the United Nations, Rome, 1968.
5. *Les Pays Tropicaux*, Paris, 1953, p. 15.
6. 'Distinctive Features of Agricultural Development in the Tropics' (pp. 184–233) in H. M. Southworth and B. F. Johnston (eds.), *Agricultural Development and Economic Growth*, Ithaca, N.Y., 1967.
7. 'The World Food Budget: A Forward Look to 2000 and Beyond' (pp. 86–95) in *World Food Forum Proceedings*, U.S. Department of Agriculture, Washington D.C., January 1963.
8. 'World Population', *Nature*, vol. 181, May 1958, and 'The Earth can feed its people', *World Justice*, vol. I (September, 1959) pp. 35–55.
9. *Population Growth and Land Use* (London, 1967) p. 153.
10. See data given by P. V. Sukhatme, D. Basu and W. Schulte, 'The Problem of Population and Resources with special reference to Land Use and Food Supply', paper submitted to the conference of the International Union for the Scientific Study of Population, held in London, 3–11 September 1969.
11. See United Nations, *The World Market for Iron Ore* (New York, 1968).
12. F. Hilgerdt, *Industrialisation and Foreign Trade*, League of Nations, 1945.

13. United Nations, *World Economic Trends: Economic progress during initial years of development decade: Major economic indicators for developing countries*, Document E/4059, 29 June 1965.

14. See e.g. L. Fisher and N. Potter, *World Prospects for Natural Resources*, Baltimore, 1964 and references given by E. A. Ackerman, moderator of meeting B. 10, 'Population and natural resources' (pp. 259–68) in United Nations, *World Population Conference, 1965*, vol. I; Summary Report, New York, 1966.

15. See H. J. Barnett and C. Morse, *Scarcity and Growth: the Economics of Natural Resources Availability*, Baltimore, 1963.

16. *Principles of Political Economy*, 4th ed., 1857, II 311.

17. *Factors in Economic Development*, London, 1962, pp. 190–208.

18. See on this point e.g. Ch. F. Park Jr., *Affluence in Jeopardy: Minerals and the Political Economy* (San Francisco, 1968).

19. Reliable information on this subject is scarce, but our deduction is based on Chapter VII, 'Employment, Manpower and Income, 1967', *Report on the World Social Situation*, United Nations, New York, November 1967 and Table 39 (p. 75), *World Economic Survey 1967 – Part One*, United Nations, New York, 1968.

20. United Nations, *Developing Countries in the Nineteen Seventies; Preliminary estimates for some key elements of a framework for International development strategy*, Document E/AC,54/L. 29/Rev.1, 14 June 1968.
The I.L.O. plan is contained in I.L.O., *The World Employment Programme* (Geneva, 1969).

COMMENTS*

John Phillips

Bearing in mind the vast range of the subject and the space available, Professor Brand has presented a valuable background contribution. In the nature of the subject and the patchiness of our information it is inevitable that there would be divergence of view on a number of points. It is not proposed to raise these in this short note, but rather to concentrate upon several features of particular significance. (These comments are presented in summarised form.)

(1) So far as Africa is concerned – and particularly Africa south of the Sahara – from my knowledge and interpretation of the potential bioclimatic regions and units thereof,[1] I believe that very large amounts of food and other materials could be produced in the course of the next two decades, in the humid to the sub-desert regions and in sectors of the deserts, provided scientific knowledge, political co-operation, administrative wisdom and the mind, heart and body of the peoples themselves could be focused upon the mighty task. Professor Brand is wholly correct in considering whether the bending of the mind and body of man is not perhaps the greatest of the challenges for today and the future. Knowledge there is and will be in every increasing amount and quality; ways and means of translating this into practice will be learned. But from my long experience in Trans-saharan Africa and my various studies in a number of developing countries in south-east Asia and Latin America, I realise how recondite is the task of getting man to think for himself, to work for himself, to peer into the face of the future in terms of such simple (or seemingly simple to the western mind) matters as setting aside for the 'hungry' months a proportion of the results of good to fair harvests in any given season.

Community development – The development and encouraging of the 'felt need' is a splendid philosophy: but I have not found its application encouraging, except, very locally, in Africa. Some of the earlier rosy tales about its great success in Asia seem to be less bright today, after some years of further experience. I note this because it will be said that I am unduly pessimistic about the response of man in Trans-saharan Africa, that community development will change all that. I would be happy to be shown that I am wrong.

(2) Water need not be the scarce commodity it is at present described as being. I have shown in several communications that the

---

* Professor Phillips, who was to have led the discussion of this paper, was unable to be present. He submitted these written comments for circulation at the Conference.

water resources of Africa could be greatly developed; that much present waste swamp country could be managed so as to use the water gainfully and without despoliation thereof and of the land; that there are vast numbers of splendid catchment areas and dam sites awaiting development. Desalination of ocean water and brack water, occurring inland in some of the sub-desert/desert sub-regions, could be treated by modern techniques so as to provide water for primary and other purposes: this could be pumped great distances inland. (The pioneer studies in Israel, the United States, South Africa and elsewhere all bear on the fundamental features of these techniques and practices. Some of the work at the University of Arizona, based on the Gulf of California, bears on this, in relation to food/plant production in the Gulf of Arabia.)

(3) We have scarcely begun a 'management of the ocean': this could in time make a very much greater contribution to food supply and various other materials required for a range of industrial needs.

(4) I am not pessimistic about the probability of appreciable amounts of synthetic food and other materials being produced by chemical means. The extraction of leaf protein, alone, as pioneered by Pirie at Rothamstead, holds vast promise.

(5) Great areas in the sub-humid, mild sub-arid, sub-arid, arid, sub-desert and desert bioclimatic subregions in Trans-saharan Africa (i.e. south of the Sahara) could be developed for irrigation, particularly with the aid of nuclear energy. This will be costly; but if man works hard enough and if administrations think hard enough and set a courageous lead, money will be found.

(6) The dramatic production of very high yielding strains of rice, as the outcome of the co-operation of the Rockefeller Foundation and other interests, and the great success of the International Institute for the Improvement of Maize and Wheat in Mexico (C.I.M.M.Y.T.) are examples of what modern science, duly directed and concentrated, is able to do. A widening, deepening and great expansion of such researches and related trials will doubtless produce many other amazing developments during the next quarter of a century.

(7) While it is said by some that wood will be less wanted in the future than today, that a range of synthetic materials will take its place, it remains true that wood and compounded materials in which wood plays a significant part will be required for special requirements down the years. Here the still extensive evergreen and semi-deciduous humid forests and the vast wooded savannah of better quality (in the sub-humid regions) of Africa will play a great role. In comparison with the Amazon, of course, these are far less important: the Amazon – as I myself have had the privilege

of seeing – is still a vast relatively untapped source of timber, timber products and the like.

(8) Livestock production could be steadily improved . . . using indigenous cattle, sheep, goats in the first instance and for a long time. Later, when more is known and better facilities exist, suitable crossing programmes could be attempted, in an effort to provide types more suitable for particular purposes . . . all the time ensuring that the inherent resistance to climatic disease, pest and other hazards is not lost and the foraging habit is preserved. Tsetse fly (which still 'protects' about three-fifths of Tropical/Equatorial Africa from feckless livestock production and land deterioration) will in time be controlled and this would provide much more space for livestock production. Premature reclamation of tsetse areas – followed by uncontrolled mismanagement of the natural pasturage and soil thus freed of 'fly' – would be an appalling practice, which no administration should permit to happen. Suitably correlated reclamation and introduction of sound management, appropriate distribution of stock watering points and the provision of animal husbandry and veterinary services could make a great contribution in the course of the years.

(9) Africa's wild animals must play a greater role than ever before, not only for attracting foreign exchange through tourism, but in the form of food for the indigenous people. Although some attempts are being made by the International Union for the Conservation of Nature, the philosophy, art and practical science of encouraging the native peoples, country by country, to co-operate are still not applied more than very locally. Until this is done and proved a success, practical progress in conservation and management is certain to be disappointing.

(10) Professor Brand is correct in noting (p. 23) that the transition from traditional food production to an industrial modern type of farming are not always borne in mind. This is certainly one of the challenges in community development and agricultural extension and to technical experience and knowledge: I have seen this in various parts of Africa and elsewhere . . . and it is most conspicuous where the policy of 'cash farming' is introduced too enthusiastically and light-heartedly, often as the outcome of well-intended but not always wise recommendations by those experienced only in modern western agricultural production.

Time, experience, acceptance by the native peoples, and sustaining direction and credit are imperative to success in this transition. *Festina lente* must be the motto: not 'press on regardless'!

(11) Pollution of water, soil and the air, with special reference to agricultural and related production, is perhaps over-stressed by

the emotionally-minded educationists, the administrators, the 'kindly old gentlemen of the clubs'. So far Africa has escaped very lightly . . . even in her more developed parts. But all concerned must be awake to the threat. Attention has recently been drawn to this threat in the developing countries at a symposium organised by the Conservation Foundation, Washington, D.C., the proceedings of which are to appear as a book entitled *The Careless Technology* (edited by Milton and Farvar), Natural History Press, New York. I myself took the line* that too much has been claimed about the harmful effects of fertilizers in Africa: fertilizers are a valuable means of stimulating production of food and some other materials, provided they are applied with ecological knowledge and an economic sense. So it is with chemicals for the control of pests and disease: feckless application is of course *mad*, but application must be informed, careful and with all the necessary scientific and other checks. Scientific knowledge now and in the future certainly could ensure that common sense prevails . . . provided of course that politicians and administrators do their respective duties!

(12) The geological and related mining prospecting surveys of Africa have still far to go. With new techniques capable of penetrating below the upper burden of vegetation, soil and superficial rock, it should be possible to survey and develop with greater accuracy what may be available. This will be costly: but again, when the world demands materials, the world will find it possible to pay.

There is so much more to be said, but I close on the theme which I have attempted to make known down the years on all my travels and studies in the developing countries:

Scientists, technologists, educationists, economists – all must learn to think *ecologically* about production and development in the developing countries, more particularly. This should engender action based upon a sounder study of cause and effect, a better understanding of the prime facets in biological and economic problems.

Couple this and apply it to ways and means for the better educating of native peoples to control human reproduction and improve the conservation and productivity of the environment – then great progress could be made . . . assuming that every one from above to below works much harder and with ability.

* See my books: *Agriculture and Ecology in Africa* (Faber, London, 1959); *The Development of Agriculture and Forestry in the Tropics: Patterns and Problems and Promise (Africa, SE. Asia, Latin America)* (London, 1961–6); and various contributions to journals, etc.

DISCUSSION

Panel Members: Professor P. D. Tyson, Professor E. S. W. Simpson

Professor Tyson emphasised the time factor, as did *Professor Simpson*. The latter considered that the economic approach was not wholly viable. Due to the uneven distribution of natural resources, a gross measure of arable land was a poor yardstick. The biologist could probably give a better formulation of the environment.

The reason why countries were underdeveloped should be found in the inherent capacity of the ecosystems of which they are comprised. The potential had changed in the past and there was no reason to doubt that it would change again in the future.

Professor Brand said he saw no reason to be unduly pessimistic. Some situations had tended to be exaggerated by the more emotionally-minded, but he considered that man's ingenuity would undoubtedly provide adequate substitutes for the dearth of raw materials, even in those countries where development prospects were bleak. This view he also applied to the attendant evils of industrialisation – pollution, effluent and the like – which *Professor Tyson* considered could not be divorced from population and industrial growth. *Professor Tyson* argued that man could lessen the inhabitable area of the earth through creating irreversible changes in the environment. *Professor Brand* thought this could, and would, be contained. He concluded that man and his productivity were the keys (the ecologist would put biological fundamentals first). Education of the right sort must, however, be introduced to underdeveloped countries; otherwise natural resources would only be minimally exploited, resulting in an ever-shrinking, low quality environment. Education must have relevance to the society in which it occurred, and the manpower made available must be absorbed into the economic life and not frittered away in unproductive idleness, as was all too frequently the case.

Mr. M. W. Richards asked whether in table 2.1 the increase in national product per head (stated in terms of dollars) took account of inflation. In reply, *Professor Brand* said that the amounts were in 'constant dollars'. He added that, although comparative statistics for developing and developed countries might cause an exaggerated impression of the differences between them, the fact was that those differences were very real indeed.

Professor Marcus Arkin questioned Professor Brand's interpretation of 'the law of diminishing returns' associated with the classical economists, Ricardo and Malthus. In his paper Professor Brand stated that 'the law of diminishing returns . . . has so far not proved to be correct as far as the industrial countries are concerned'. *Professor Arkin* thought that it would be more correct to say that the operation of Malthus's law had been allayed by various factors. But it would be wrong to say that it had been disproved.

Mr. M. J. Fransman said that however one interpreted Malthus, or whether one was an optimist or pessimist, the fact was that the world population was increasing and hence required an increase in output. This in turn required capital in all its forms. But there appeared to be a fall-off in international aid in recent times.

Referring to Professor Brand's remarks on the role of education in development, *Professor S. P. Cilliers* raised the question of the extent to which the problems of the developing areas could be met with 'brain power' from the developed countries. He suggested that economists might be able to work out a formula in terms of which 'brain power' might figure in balance of payment calculations.

In response to a question regarding mineral resources, *Professor Simpson* said that scientists were discovering more and more mineral resources in the sea. In fact all 92 elements were to be found in the sea, and, provided countries were prepared to pay the cost, even gold could be obtained from the sea.

Mr. G. E. Lavin expressed the view that not sufficient attention had been given to the place of water as a natural resource. This was a problem in particular in Africa. Sea-water might be distilled for human use; but for agricultural purposes the cost would be prohibitive.

Professor H. L. Watts felt that not sufficient attention had been given to power as a resource, as also the possibility of other forms of productivity outstripping agricultural production, and so creating a problem of hunger. *Professor Watts* illustrated his point in relation to South Africa: peasants acquiring industrial skills were absorbed far more easily into the lower rungs of an industrial economy than they learnt modernised agricultural methods.

Mr. T. C. Robertson drew attention to the fact that in many developing countries the 'renewable' resources were being destroyed. He cited as an example the indiscriminate felling of trees. He expressed concern that if this process continued these countries would not have 'renewable' resources when they entered the industrial era.

Professor R. J. Davies said the difference in human resources was an important factor in the general disparity between developed and developing areas, and one which should be considered in the formulation of aid schemes. It was a mistake, for example, simply to transplant technology to developing areas without having regard to the special requirements of tropical and sub-tropical climates. He pleaded for more research on this problem.

In his concluding comments *Professor Brand* accepted Professor Arkin's criticism of his interpretation of Malthus. Regarding the question of power, while some power resources would be exhausted, he felt that most scientists were agreed that substitutes would be found. He concurred with a view expressed by *Professor Simpson* regarding the sea as a source of food, namely that its promise had been exaggerated.

Finally, *Professor Brand* declared himself an optimist on the question of overpopulation. For two million years man had overcome his problems and met his challenges; this problem, said Professor Brand, man would also overcome.

3 World food supplies

G. UGO PAPI

The ratio population/food is long established. The relationship between these two magnitudes has always been fundamental as an indication of the prosperity of a country. In the background there remains the intuition of Malthus. His reasoning may seem to have been defective, and his ideas have had to be modified in the light of the experience of more than one and a half centuries. Nevertheless, his intuition is still full of significance for us. Here we shall mention only some lines of thought which remain essential for our study.

The classification of populations into those 'with incipient decline', those 'with transitory increase' and those 'with a high development potential' is well known.[1]

1. INCIPIENT DECLINE

Falling within the first category are the populations of the north, west and centre of Europe, the United States of America, Australia and New Zealand. With a certain approximation Canada also falls within this category, as does, possibly with some doubt, southern Europe. The increase in the populations of these countries is slow as they have already reached low death-rates and the families are of modest size. One can expect that the populations here will grow for some time, because the age distribution tends to increase the birth-rate and decrease the death-rate, although the death-rate has already declined considerably. It is characteristic that the birth-rate in these countries is 'controlled'. Reproduction is sensitive to incentives for larger or smaller families. When the direct causes of variations disappear, the birth-rate will be sufficient to maintain a 'stationary' society; that is to say births will balance deaths.

2. TRANSITORY INCREASE

In the second category – 'populations with transitory increase' – fall the populations for whom the process of modernisation of the institutions has already begun to reduce the birth-rate as well as the death-rate. The birthrate, however, responds more slowly to change in the social environment than does the death-rate and, consequently, the population will increase for some time. In this category fall the populations of eastern Europe, the Soviet Union, Japan and some Latin American countries.

Despite increasing urbanisation and industrialisation, these countries will still depend primarily upon agriculture. The periods during which the populations increase can be shortened by political measures or may be lengthened due to unsuitable political measures. However, all things considered, this category represents a section of the human race which will in due course pass to the stage in which low death-rates and low birth-rates are recorded.

3. HIGH INCREASE POTENTIAL

In the third category – 'populations with a high increase potential' – one can place *more than half* of the world's population: practically the whole of the Far East (with the exception of Japan), a large part of Latin America, a large part of Africa and the greater part of the Middle East. Here things become complicated. Not only does the birth-rate show no sign of reduction, but it does not respond to changes in the environment.

Within this category one can try to make a further distinction. Some of the populations are spread over extensive territories: they are those of a large part of South America, Borneo, Sumatra, New Guinea, Africa and the Middle East. In those regions there are abundant possibilities of producing goods, but these possibilities are not used. Sometimes, as in the case of the Middle East, the presence of mineral products – for example oil – provides the funds necessary for economic development. Thus one is led to think of large flows of capital which can promote vigorous economic development which will allow for better health services and for measures to be taken by conscientious governments to solve the economic problems. No doubt, however, the result of every measure taken on both the national and international level will be an increase in the size of the population. At the end of colossal efforts it will be possible for a larger number of human beings to live in these territories, but there will be no improvement whatsoever in the standard of living.

Nevertheless, to the extent to which incomes increase at a faster rate than does the population – not only due to the possibilities for producing goods and services, but also due to a greater sense of responsibility and a greater liking for a higher standard of living –

the increase in the population will not constitute an insurmountable obstacle to the liberation from a stagnant situation of want and a high death-rate.

4. A STICKIER PROBLEM

The stickier problem appears in countries with a high population density, even though they may have a large development potential. Egypt, China, India, Korea, Formosa, Java and the greater part of the Caribbeans represent overpopulated areas with very low living standards of populations on poor land or land not yet developed. Here the increase in population negates any possibility of an improvement in nutrition and health. The size of these populations will increase if the death-rate does not rise. If the death-rate declines the rate of population increase will be higher. The problem confronting students and the authorities is to see whether the process of social, economic and political evolution can *arrest* the accelerated rate of increase of the population (as was the case for the low-density populations). Such an arrest is conceivable only through reducing the number of births – one cannot deliberately try to achieve this through a decisive increase in deaths.

It is not an easy task to promote reductions in the birth-rate among enormous masses of agricultural populations for whom the 'small family' cannot represent an ideal considering the kind of life they lead. It is however certain that unless the birth-rate is reduced any development effort will result in a larger number of people rather than in a higher standard of living.

5. BALANCE BETWEEN POPULATION AND SUBSISTENCE BY BIRTH CONTROL

These very brief remarks make it clear that it is impossible to speak indiscriminately of a 'world population' which is made up of very different aggregates which differ widely in respect of standards of living, level of economic development, political stability and other aspects of community life. It is not the size of the population itself but the low standard of living which gives rise to apprehension.

Barely a third of the world population is acquainted with an *elastic* rate of reproduction, regulated on the basis of preventive checks. The other two-thirds show a tendency to increase as the economy progresses. The balance between population and subsistence could be maintained if the progress was *faster* than the increase in population. Past experience, however, does not indicate that this is the case. Rather the lack of limitation on the birthrate reduced the most generous productive efforts to merely perpetuating a situation of great misery for ever-increasing numbers. It is not right to maintain silence on these problems, or to maintain a dogmatic insensitivity to the urgency of them.

The fostering of a greater sense of responsibility towards the lives of our sons in every human being represents a *first* step towards a more favourable relationship between population and subsistence.

6. THE FOOD 'DEFICIT': 'POPULATION EFFECT' AND 'INCOME EFFECT'

There is indeed an alarming prospect of a continually widening gap between population and food. It is a problem which leaves no room for complacency, despite encouraging progress in certain major food 'deficit' areas in these last years.

For the purpose of the F.A.O. Regional Studies the following classification was used: Zone A: Developed Market Economies; Zone B: Centrally Planned Economies; Zone C: Developing Countries. Within Zone C sixty-four countries were included in the 'regional studies'. This classification is not in contrast with our previous classification.

The greater part of the additional demand for food will be due to an *increase in population* which is practically inevitable. In 1965 there were approximately 1500 million people living in what are usually described as 'developing' or 'less developed countries'. About 60 per cent of the population in this zone live in Asia, in the densely populated belt stretching from West Pakistan to South Korea. The rest are in Latin America, Africa and the borderland between Asia and Europe commonly known as the Middle or Near East. The distribution of the world population in 1965 shows somewhat over 1000 million inhabitants of the economically developed countries of Europe (including the Soviet Union), North America and Japan; somewhere around another 800 million for the communist countries of Asia; with 1500 million people living in Zone C. The world total amounts to about 3300 million.

By 1985 the population of the rich countries is projected to increase by nearly 25 per cent; that of the developing countries is expected to approximate 2500 million, i.e. a billion more, with an increase of about 60 per cent. This implies that over the period of twenty years, 1965 to 1985, for every 100 additional people, 85 will be in developing countries, many of which are already 'overburdened' by the size of their populations.

The 'population effect' alone in Zone C would therefore require an increase of 80 per cent in food supplies over the period 1965–85, mainly to *maintain* existing nutrition levels and patterns of consumption. 'Maintain' would imply 'stagnation' both in calorie intake and in quality of the diet.

But there is to be considered also an 'income effect': the success in raising the levels of income per caput in developing countries would mean that the demand for food per caput would rise. The 'population effect' tends to simply multiply the demand for each product by a common factor: the additional population. The 'income effect' implies that – as income rises – the 'structure of demand' also changes. For instance, demand for cereals for human consumption is projected to double by 1985. But the demand for meat, fish, eggs – as a group – is projected to 'increase' by 250 per cent, and milk by 230 per cent, assuming that relative prices remain unaltered.

The 'population effect' and the 'income effect' together give a projected increase of demand for food in developing countries from 1962 to 1985 of about 140 per cent, i.e. an annual increase of 3·9 per cent.

At the same time the F.A.O. 'indices for food production' in developing countries show an increase of only 2·7 per cent per annum for the ten years 1955–7 to 1965–7. For the first six years of the 1960s the figure of 2·7 per cent fell to 2·4 per cent. If food production increases at the rate of 2·7 per cent per annum in the future, the production retained for consumption would be only 84 per cent above the 1962 level, whereas the projected demand for food would be 142 per cent over the 1962 level. This is approximately the magnitude of the 'food deficit'.

7. NEED FOR A FASTER GROWTH OF CEREAL PRODUCTION

A number of factors have retarded technical progress in raising cereal yields: limitation imposed by climate, inadequate irrigation and drainage systems, high returns of 'competing' industrial and export crops, institutional and structural constraints – in particular share cropping tenurial systems where landlords provide no imports; the ceiling placed on yield by physiological inability of traditional cereal varieties to respond profitably to the application of modern technology and in particular to high doses of nitrogen fertilizer. A major problem in tropical countries of Africa, south east Asia and Latin America – where wheat cannot be grown – is to influence dietary habits towards the consumption of cereals *ecologically* adapted to those regions.

If cereal yields continued in line with past trends, an additional 68 and 26 million hectares would have to be added to the 1985 areas required for cereals in the Asia and Near East and the North Africa regions respectively, in order to achieve the 'production objectives' proposed in the provisional Regional Studies of F.A.O. This would mean approximately 50 and 100 per cent *more land* coming under cereals, *at the expense of other crops and livestock*.

An alternative would be to *import*. In 1965 exports to *all* countries in Asia, Africa, Latin America and the Near East totalled 22 million tons, compared with a world total of 104 million tons, of which 65 million tons came from North America and Australia. Of the total cereal imports of 101 million tons, Zone C took approximately 35 million tons and European countries 47 million tons.

To cover the shortfall in domestic requirements Asia would require net exports of an additional 70 million tons of cereals; the Near East/North Africa would require 22 million tons more. The financial burden on the importing developing countries would be crushing: no less than United States $7.4 billion in 1985, at constant 1962 prices. It follows that a breakthrough in cereal production will have an overwhelming psychological, nutritional and economic importance. Cereals are the main staple of the diet, the main source of calories and protein. A faster rate of growth of cereal production could also release land, especially where pressure on it is heavy, and create a dynamism for the crop sector as a whole: especially massive increases in 'feed supplies', required to meet the livestock objectives.

8. IMPROVING THE COMPOSITION OF THE DIET

The magnitude of the food deficit must increase, if we take into consideration another aim. Much of the world's population is not only 'underfed' in terms of calories, but also 'badly fed' in respect of the 'composition' of the diet. Malnutrition in respect of proteins is a particularly serious problem. Protein deficiency can cause not only disease symptoms, but also irreversible effects on the mental health of children. So a special priority has to be given to measures to increase protein supplies from all sources more rapidly than in the past. But the supply of milk and meat from ruminants – the bulk of animal protein – has a slow potential for expansion, because of the long reproductive cycle. Pulses – the main sources of high quality vegetable protein – have a very low yield per hectare.

A particular emphasis, therefore, has to be put on the following:

faster expansion of pig and poultry production, as well as on developing supplies of vegetable protein; breeding higher protein cereals;
raising the output of high protein crops; increasing ruminant livestock production with control of disease and improvement of
nutrition; vertical integrated milk production and processing projects; developing the fishery potential. Protecting both children
and nursing mothers of the lower income groups are inescapable
lines of action.

Even on the basis of a relatively high growth-rate of production –
2·9 and 3·8 per cent, for the periods 1962–75 and 1975–85 – gross
import of no less than 5 million tons of meat and 34 million tons of
milk would be required for Zone C to fill the gap between domestic
production and essential economic demand by 1985. The cost of
imports could be approximately 4·2 billion dollars per year, at
constant 1962 prices.

9. EMPLOYMENT PROBLEM AGGRAVATES THE 'DEFICIT' CONSEQUENCES IN DEVELOPING COUNTRIES

The low levels of productivity in agriculture – which at the moment
characterise most developing countries – are partly due to the prevalence of traditional standards of farming; partly to more people
being on the land than are really needed to farm it. They stay there
because in the absence of adequate employment in the towns they
are at least reasonably sure of some food, of housing – no matter
how primitive – and of the protective care of the family which takes
the place of a whole range of social services.[2]

In the developed countries the problems of an excess of peoples on
the land has been solved by movement of farm population into other
sectors, accompanied by the increasing use of modern technology
in agriculture. Fewer farm workers have been able to produce more
and better quality food for the non-agricultural population and,
in some cases, even surpluses for export. In developing countries the
farm population has no escape into the non-agricultural economy.

In Asia – taken as a cast study – the non-agricultural population
is projected to grow at 3·8 per cent a year, compared with an increase of 2·5 per cent in the total population. Since the growth of
'non-agricultural' population starts from a *relatively small base* (250
out of 833 million), the difference in the rate of increase will not be
enough to 'absorb' all of the extra people. So nearly half of the
additional people would need to be 'absorbed' between 1962 and
1985 in the agricultural sector. The consequences are a very slow

growth in income per head (1·4 per cent per annum) – in spite of the rapid improvement in agricultural technology and of the rapid expansion of the monetary market – and a widening of the gap between non-agricultural and agricultural incomes.

The problem of providing employment in agriculture would be greatly eased, if the economy could absorb 'non-agricultural population' at a higher rate. The critical factor, however, in this higher rate of increase in off-farm employment is the *cost* of job creation. In order to face such a cost, a much higher rate of growth of gross domestic product would be necessary than is usually considered attainable, for instance a yearly average increase of 7·7 per cent against a recent trend of 4·3 per cent. Unfortunately an increasing proportion of national resources has to be used to provide minimum essential services for an 'escalating population' in areas already settled. So – if population growth continues at its present rate – there is likely to be a deepening crisis of poverty and underemployment, throughout the developing world.

Also the process itself of transforming traditional agriculture is hardly feasible in an economic situation where capital accumulation is frustrated by high rates of population growth, as such a process requires considerable capital expenditure in irrigation, mechanisation, other investments, as well as a massive increase in credit for the purchase of annual cash inputs, more and better trained technicians for research and other services.

Under these circumstances the best hope for raising levels of standard of living (from farming in most developing countries) lies in population control and increasing output through more intensive use of physical resources.

10. NEED FOR POPULATION CONTROL NOT ATTENUATED

No doubt the world could feed many times its present population.[3] As Mr. Abercrombie pertinently reminds us in his recent article[4] there is still unused but potentially usable land to be opened up in many parts of the world. There is still much scope for the intensification of production in the developing countries. In addition to higher crop yields, there are considerable possibilities in the humid tropics and sub-tropics for multiple cropping per year. World fish supplies could be increased, stocks can be scientifically managed and the sea 'farmed' rather than 'hunted' as at present. Man's ingenuity will also continue to devise sources of food, especially of protein. But the vast 'ultimate potential rate' of the world's agricultural land has not overcome great difficulties in increasing food supplies *fast enough* to meet rapid population growth in many countries. It would be most unfortunate if the recent evolution in attitudes to population control were reversed by a rather erroneous belief that the battle against hunger is already won.

11. A SECOND STEP: CONCERT AMONG GOVERNMENTS

Population control is indeed only one of the ingredients in any policy aiming at filling the gap between population and subsistence: a necessary ingredient, but not a sufficient one. Having ascertained the consequences of overcrowding on the land, it is not possible to believe that, even with a decisive reduction in world population, the problem of the economic and social development of a certain country – or even the food problem alone – could be solved. As we have already mentioned, steps must be directed towards an 'increase in subsistence'. Here, however, the problem becomes complicated. A decision on population policy can be taken unilaterally by a single government. A decision on production and trade becomes difficult, as it interferes with the economic policies of various governments, responding to an entire range of *interests* frequently conflicting with one another. It is necessary therefore for comprehensive collaboration, co-ordination and 'concert' among governments. And this is a really gigantic task.

12. PREFERENCE FOR THE STUDY OF TRADE PROBLEMS

Conflict and accord have marked the life of all peoples at all times. On the other hand, collaboration among governments for the protection of mutual interests is something that is only a little over half a century old.

It is a fact that international collaboration at the beginning of the century coincided with a marked interest of science in the exchanges of goods and services among countries, in the analysis of economic fluctuations, in the organisation of internal markets and stabilising mechanisms of national or international initiative. It was only later that the other problem – the even more fundamental problem of economic development of low-income countries – began to show up on the horizon of the international community.

c

13. THE GENEVA CONFERENCE (1964) AND THE NEW DELHI CONFERENCE (1968) ON TRADE AND DEVELOPMENT (U.N.C.T.A.D.)

As a matter of fact the prevailing current in literature and economic policy has been spreading. The Geneva Conference in 1964 and the New Delhi Conference in 1968, more than anything fit into this pre-occupation with trade problems. It is therefore necessary seriously to consider these problems and see what solutions can be produced.

At Geneva and New Delhi developing countries insisted on the theory of a 'fair return' to be ensured by high prices of primary commodities exported to the markets of industrialised countries. They emphasised that it was necessary for industrialised countries unilaterally to reduce obstacles to the importation of basic commodities, raw materials and industrial products from low-income countries. They suggested that industrialised countries should: (a) change their fiscal legislation; (b) channel the flow of capital to industrial activities to be developed in low-income countries in order to enable them to increase their export capabilities and, consequently, their ability to purchase on the markets of industrialised countries; (c) concentrate their activities on those industrialised sectors where technological progress was fastest. For these are the sectors in which industrialised countries might find adequate compensation for the losses suffered as a result of transfer of light industries to low-income countries.

14. LOOK AT THE FACTS

Liberalisation of trade granted unilaterally by the industrialised countries would intensify exports from low-income countries only to a modest degree. Agricultural trade barriers in the more advanced countries concern commodities and agricultural materials which in any case come from nations that are among the richest of the 'temperate zone': Australia, New Zealand, Britain, Uruguay, not to mention the United States and Canada. They are nations in a particularly advantageous situation to draw profit from any intensification of agricultural trade. They represent a good half of the international trade.

The other half comes from low-income countries. But tariffs applied by industrialised countries to tropical produce – tea, coffee, cocoa – are not very high. A survey by the GATT Secretariat shows that if in 1956 eight European countries had been able to abolish all internal taxation on the consumption of coffee and all customs duties on coffee imports, the export revenue of low-income countries would have risen by 2·5 per cent at most.

More recently a special report of the Third Committee set up by GATT for the expansion of international trade pointed out that the 'abolition of dues and levies of a fiscal nature, or a considerable reduction of their high rate, especially in the case of the above-mentioned countries, would favour increased consumption and thereby would make an extremely useful contribution to an improvement of the capacity of exporting countries to earn foreign exchange'. But this opinion of the report does not claim to offer a radical solution to the problem of fundamental imbalances in the balance of payments of low-income countries.

The same applies to the proposal that the industrialised countries of western Europe and North America should 'unilaterally reduce' their customs barriers and quantitative restrictions: (a) on agricultural commodities; (b) on raw materials – for instance cotton and jute; (c) on manufactured products – for example, products from countries with abnormally low labour costs, such as Japan; (d) on the products of light industries which the industrialised countries should transfer to developing countries. In all these cases it would be unrealistic to overlook the danger of profound disruption of national markets unless the more advanced countries proceed in this direction with great caution.

If an industrialised country gives up, at least partly, the production of certain industrial goods in favour of countries from which it can import them later on, its government must help the redundant industries by means of subsidies, of indemnities for the destruction of surplus equipment, of premiums for the modernisation of enterprises that carry on the work. It is essential for the government to help unemployed manpower either by relief benefits or by offering them ample opportunities for 'vocational retraining'.

Admittedly, in the long run, a process of modernisation in any country can give rise to more efficient production activities which require less protection. However, such a process takes time if developing countries are to be assured of lasting exports of new finished products.

15. THE SOLUTION OF FOREIGN TRADE PROBLEMS IS NOT ENOUGH FOR THE GROWTH OF LOW-INCOME COUNTRIES

One essential fact is that the study and even solution of foreign trade problems is not enough to ensure the growth of developing countries.

Unfortunately, prospects for exports to the markets of high-income countries appear unfavourable because competition from synthetics is growing, consumption of many commodities is nearing saturation point, and the population growth of industrialised countries is relatively slow.

It is also to be noted that the structure of the balance of payments in low-income countries has *already* undergone profound changes. With increased food aid granted to these countries, their exports to industrialised countries – even though they have risen in the past few years – have already been largely *exceeded* by imports of agricultural produce from industrialised countries.

Recent O.E.C.D. studies show that – if production in industrialised countries can grow at the present rate – it will be possible to export 'surpluses' (over and above internal demand) to low-income countries. However, these surpluses of developed countries will become more and more 'inadequate' to meet the needs of low-income countries, even if one adopts the hypothesis that demand for products will increase at the rate permitted by the lower increase of revenue and that food production will rise to the highest possible degree. The 'deficits' of developing countries are much greater than the export capabilities of industrialised countries.

Still other facts are that – in competition with low-income countries – the Soviet Union, eastern Europe and China have become large importers of food. Secondly, that the availability of food depends largely on sea transport, on ports and landing facilities, and on means of transport within low-income countries.

16. THE NEED FOR A POLICY OF STRUCTURE

The reality is that ensuring effective aid is neither a 'quantitative' question – a question of masses of dollars to be allocated – nor a question of trade policies only. The question is to choose carefully the points of attack of the problems facing the countries: 'emergency problems', 'stabilisation of prices and markets problems', 'structure problems': three categories of problems which can never be considered in isolation if *lasting* solutions are desired.

Too much importance has been attached, in the past years, to trade relations between industrialised and low-income countries. One has too often forgotten that behind the 'deficit' in the balance of payments there is an even 'more fundamental deficit'. There is a 'food deficit': a 'deficit' that shows that these populations can produce neither sufficient food to feed themselves, nor sufficient other goods and services with which they might obtain indispensable food.

The task of eliminating the 'food deficit' cannot be achieved by trade measures between industrialised and developing countries. The so-called 'deterioration of the terms of trade' to the detriment of low-income countries is not a commercial phenomenon; it is essentially a 'structure phenomenon'. Elimination of the gap between need and availability is entirely a question of raising the productivity of the agricultural sector.

In view of the size of the food deficit, as well as of the insufficiency of all food aid – even if one tries to increase it as vigorously as possible – and of the chronic disequilibrium in the balance of payments of low-income countries, it (the food deficit) can only be reduced by actions to be undertaken urgently by each country, in collaboration with other countries.

17. CAUSES OF THE INFERIORITY OF AGRICULTURAL INCOME

A 'policy of structure' should first of all identify the causes of inferiority of agricultural income in relation to the income of other sectors of production. These causes are: a marked disproportion among the production factors – for instance, surplus or shortage of manpower in relation to the land, capital and entrepreneurs; impossibility of introducing modern methods owing to economic conditions and limited size of farms; exclusion of part of the population living on subsistence farming from the economic circuit and thus from the marketing of agricultural produce; lack of land organisation to form 'viable units' of cultivation; lack of vocational training; inefficient organisation of productive groups; insufficient credit; destruction of crops by pests; waste of money due to excessive military expenditure; prestige projects; inefficiency of the public administration. These are some of the causes of inferiority.

18. REMEDIES

What are the remedies? First of all the causes of inferiority just mentioned must be eliminated. It must be realised that the possibility of raising real agricultural income does not lie in certain forms of customs protection, or price support, or export bonuses, or tax relief. The vicious circle must be broken.

In the second place, a 'structure policy' may aim at raising the yields per unit of acreage to increase production, *instead* of raising the acreage under cultivation. It might promote a more intensive use of fertilizers and pesticides on small and medium-size farms which, after all, predominate in the sector of food production where increases are most urgent. Certainly low-income countries could keep up non-food agricultural production for export, because – after mineral oil – these crops earn the largest part of foreign exchange. However, part of these foreign exchange earnings are used to import food, and the 'structure policy' must determine whether it is economically reasonable to continue using these earnings from non-food agricultural exports to finance imports of food; or whether, all things considered, it would be *more advantageous* to produce more food on the spot and use foreign exchange derived from exports to import equipment and intermediate goods which are absolutely indispensable for a higher rate of development.

Depending on the country, the policy of structure might aim at producing staple food to improve the quality of the diet, particularly — as mentioned before — grains and pulses, which have a considerable protein content. It might later aim as well at an increase of animal products as sources of protein and vitamin. The policy of structure, above all, should emphasise that shortage of food causes inflationary pressures, payment difficulties, increased production costs, reduction of investments in agriculture; so that the present situation in most low-income countries can only worsen, if food production does not grow considerably.

19. THE WORK OF F.A.O.

With adequate preparation, courage and spirit of sacrifice, F.A.O. has undertaken a task of long and exhausting labour. *Three* stages may be distinguished in it. *First* stage: projections for agricultural commodities in 1975 and 1985. *Second* stage: in the light of world projections, regional and subregional studies with suggestions which begin to give shape and substance to the policy of structure best suited to each region, and thereby to the Indicative World Plan. *Third* stage: in co-operation with the representatives of the countries concerned, the Organisation will have to start drawing up development projects, country by country in each region. Only this procedure can avoid disproportions of economic expansion among countries and assure each country in a region maximum development and integration with the economy of the others.

The 'Indicative World Plan' drawn up by the F.A.O. is not a plan in the true sense of the word. It tries to foresee – by means of projections – future phenomena: population, consumption, production, trade. It tends to promote a rapid expansion of the 'deficit sectors' of world agriculture. It formulates recommendations to achieve these objects.

Presuming that the population will increase each year by 2·6 per cent, in 1985 the developing countries will have – as we have already mentioned – one thousand million inhabitants more than today. In this perspective, the main objectives to which the Plan attaches the most importance are: (1) a much faster increase in *cereal* production, particularly in the first ten years of the Plan, in order to secure staple food supplies; (2) an integrated short-term and long-term programme to diversify the diet – in particular to increase the protein supplies, demand for which is expected to grow much faster than the demand for cereals, as a result of rising incomes; (3) more intense trade between countries, in order to achieve 'foreign earnings' through increased efficiency in production and marketing; more comprehensive commodity policies, and import substitution in order to save foreign exchange; (4) providing additional employment in the agricultural sector and helping to create opportunities for employment outside agriculture in agro-allied industries; (5) intensification of *land use* both in order to meet production objectives in countries where the population pressure is heaviest in cultivated areas, and to assist in the solution of employment problems.

20. CHARACTERISTICS OF THE INDICATIVE WORLD PLAN

The *first* characteristic of the Plan is that the projections, on the one hand, and the results of regional studies, on the other, complete and condition each other. No doubt it has been an advantage to identify beforehand the problems of certain agricultural sectors through the tracing of projections. In the light of these it has been possible to initiate regional studies. The result of the studies – proposals of directives, of policies, of 'sequences' – gives a practical and substantial content to the same complex of projections.

The *second* characteristic of the Plan – very rare today – is the absolute *independence* of the opinions on the situation of each country – a sort of 'technical objectiveness' which lies at the basis of a fruitful solution of the problems concerning low-income countries.

The *third* characteristic is its 'realism': namely an unceasing effort *not* to escape from factual situations. Realism for an exercise of this kind is indispensable in order to prevent more profound studies later on from being tied to hypotheses which have a slim chance of being put into practice.

Obviously we can criticise projections and regional studies. We can maintain, for instance, that in the absence of a considerable number of data, certain quantitative presentations appear to be ambitious. We can start out on numberless discussions on variables, parameters and every tool of methodology. In examining the Plan, we can – no doubt – conceive the possibility of an *ex ante*, of an *a priori*, criticism. We have nevertheless to bear always in mind that we can verify the soundness of our *ex ante* criticism, only at the end of the period considered by the Plan. During the period of the Plan operation, we can only introduce modifications on the basis of acquired experience and in accordance with the changing reality. The truth has never been revealed before to anybody.

Still – having said all this – we now can ascertain the usefulness of such a Plan – a usefulness which lies in the fact that, after the projections and the regional studies, the governments now find at their disposal a series of measures appropriate to realise objectives required for the development of a region or a subregion. These measures represent a remarkable outcome of studies and exercises. Above all they represent a 'turning point' in the possibility of granting really efficient aid to low-income countries.

We have so far shown our reluctance – in presenting some aspects of the world food crisis – to use big words and follow transcendent philosophies. Beyond prodigies, beyond myths, beyond land reform, industrialisation, gifts without limit, the few lines we have sketched may give a conception of more effective aid to low-income countries. Above all they allow developing countries to catch sight of the start and of the achievement of F.A.O.'s undertaking in a future that is no longer indefinite. The undertaking of F.A.O. and of international collaboration is the development which will have to enable the countries to help themselves and to reduce their dependence on industrialised countries; a dependence which should gradually shrink in the decades to come.

It is not superfluous to add that we have tried to underline some 'technical solutions' for gigantic problems facing all peoples of the world, whether in developed countries or elsewhere. However, the radical solution of all these problems lies in a far more complex and vaster field than the technical field. The radical solution of these problems lies in the moral field. Technology has its importance. But it is bound to represent a very small advance, unless the leading class of each country regards as an essential element of its success and survival the moral elevation needed to bring about justice and peace in the service of human beings.

Notes

1. Thompson, 'Population', in *American Journal of Sociology*, XXXIV 6 (May 1929) 959–75; *Plenty of People* (Lancaster, Pa. 1944); F. W. Notenstein, 'The Population of the World in the year 2000' in *Journal of the American Statistical Association*, vol. 45 no. 251 (September 1950) p. 355 ff.; F.A.O. 'The State of Food and Agriculture' (during the sixties).

2. F.A.O. Doc. 69, 4 vol. 3, p. 13.

3. Colin Clark, *Population growth and land use* (London, 1967) p. 153.

4. K. C. Abercrombie, *Population growth and agricultural development*, Monthly Bulletin of Agricultural Economics and Statistics (April 1969), vol. 18 no. 4; P. V. Sukatme and W. Schulte, 'Forecast of nutritional requirements and the expected level of demand for food', in *Proceedings of World Population Conference*, Belgrade, 30 August–10 September 1965, U.N. (New York, 1967) vol. III, p. 423.

DISCUSSION

Panel Members: Professor J. D. J. Hofmeyr, Professor F. X. Laubscher, Mr. T. C. Robertson

Professor Hofmeyr described the vicious circle of poverty in the less developed countries (L.D.C.s), and he drew attention to South Africa's experience in dealing with peoples at different levels of economic and cultural development and belonging to different ethnic groups.

Professor Laubscher took an optimistic view of food production. He contended that with the rapid growth in agricultural technology it would be just possible for food supplies to keep pace with, and even outstrip, the rate of population growth at least until the end of this century. In recent years tremendous improvements had been attained in the yields of cereals. Naturally the increase in yields must ultimately reach a physiological limit set by energy conversion potentials. But before such a limit was reached, it was quite possible that a growth-rate in production in excess of 4 per cent per annum could be reached. As far as production in the L.D.C.s was concerned, improved varieties of seeds seemed to offer the best line of attack, as the capital required for this kind of improvement was small.

In the developed countries great strides had been made in the amount of food produced, and these improvements were likely to continue. According to estimates by Roger Revelle (1966), by the year 2000 the United States alone would produce enough food for her own requirements, as well as for the economic demands of Europe and Japan, and, in addition, would still have a surplus sufficient to meet 20 per cent of the needs of the L.D.C.s.

Regarding the production of animal proteins, considerable improvement could be achieved by reducing the losses due to animal disease.

Mr. Robertson stressed the need for soil conservation and pointed out the danger that increased food production might result in increased water pollution. One had constantly to bear in mind the risk of the improved 'technosphere' destroying the 'biosphere'. *Mr. Oliver Kerfoot* emphasised that if any measure were to be economically sound it had to be ecologically sound.

Dr. Stephen Enke felt that there were greater possibilities of technological improvement in the developed world than in the L.D.C.s, and the problem might therefore be one of distribution rather than of production.

Mrs. Fatima Meer spoke of the need not only for a green revolution, but also for a moral revolution which would make the developed countries earnestly want to share with the less fortunate countries. One difficulty in bringing about the green revolution stemmed from the poor remuneration for agriculture compared with other spheres.

Dr. Papi commented on the need for dynamic, not static, models. In economic and social development there was a need for what Marshall called 'external economies'. Man must form the environment in which things would work. Economies within a region needed to be integrated.

4 The population explosion: Economic implications

JOSEPH J. SPENGLER

'It is an elementary fact . . . that among the varied materials which the human race requires for its growth and sustenance are many that are more or less readily interchangeable. . . . On the other hand, there are certain requisites that are irreplaceable, and therefore absolutely essential'

A. J. Lotka, in *Elements of Physical Biology*

'We are now, in a grim manner, thrusting against the absolute limits of human design on this earth.'

Georg Picht, *Mut zur Utopie*

'Long-run directionality tends to be in the beholder's eye, not in the materials themselves.'

R. A. Nisbet, *Social Change and History*, p. 284

Of the great disruptive periods in world history perhaps the most disordering is that elapsing since August 1914. Then began the first modern Peloponnesian War, to be followed by a second within twenty-one years. These destroyed the several-centuries-old hegemony of the European peoples who still formed about 35 per cent of the world's population in 1960 much as in 1900. While it was ideological cleavage and failure to subordinate national interests to western man's interests that destroyed his hegemony, it is the world's vital revolution that is converting this upheaval in world hegemony into what may prove the greatest watershed in mankind's politico-economic history. It is with this vital revolution and some of its implications that my paper deals.

1. DEMOGRAPHIC CONTOURS

World population growth did not accelerate until in the present century, which has seen the increment per decade rise from 90 million in 1900–10 to over 600 million in 1960–70 and perhaps to over 900 million in 1990–2000. Medium estimates of growth averaged 5 per 1000 population per year in 1750–1850 and 6 in 1850–1900. The rate of growth was somewhat higher in areas of European settlement than in Asia and Africa, falling short of 5 per 1000 per year in both Asia and Africa while in areas of European settlement approximating 7 in 1750–1850 and 11 in 1850–1900.

The present century witnessed the disappearance of this excess in areas of European settlement, in that for this region as for Asia and Africa the annual average rate was about 10 per 1000. There was of course considerable variation within each broad region, with rates in Asia ranging from 8 in mainland China to 14 outside the largest Asian countries, and with rates in the European sphere ranging from 6 in Europe to 20 in Latin America. These changes are reflected also in the movement of population in the more developed and the less developed parts of the world. In 1900–10 and 1920–30 population grew more rapidly in the more developed than in the less developed part of the world; but after 1950, as in the war-ridden decades (i.e. 1910–20 and 1940–50), the rate of population growth in the underdeveloped world rose above that in the developed world until now it is more than double that in the latter. Within a half-century, therefore, the ratio of the rate of population growth in more developed areas to that in less developed areas has fallen from 2·4 in 1900–10 to 0·5 or less.[1]

In table 4.1 I have assembled population estimates as of 1965, 1985 and 2000, together with estimates of the rate of growth as of 1990–2000. The data in parentheses are medium estimates as of 1963, and those outside parentheses medium estimates reported in Population Newsletter No. 7, of December 1969. The revised estimates are slightly higher for both more developed and less developed regions, though slightly lower for the Soviet Union and northern America. It is possible, therefore, that the rates of increase reported in the last column and based on the 'medium' projections as of 1963 may prove too low, should mortality decline further and natality fail to follow, as in earlier decades of this century. After 1910–20 the introduction of death control into less developed parts of the world greatly reduced mortality there, but without greatly influencing natality, with the result that natural increase rose markedly.[2] At present natality and mortality roughly approximate 40–41 and 16–17 per 1000 in the less developed regions, and 18 and 9 in the more developed regions. Whence natural increase in the former – somewhat over 2 per cent – is more than double that in the latter – slightly under 1·0 per cent. Despite the uncertainties respecting the paths which fertility and mortality will follow in various parts of the world, table 1.4 does provide us with orders of magnitude permitting analysis.

Perhaps the outstanding changes suggested by the 'medium' data projected in table 4.1 are these: (1) The more developed regions, which included 36·2 per cent of the world's population in 1920 and 32·6 in 1960 will include only 23·5 per cent in 2000 and might include only 10–15·8 per cent in 2100 should their numbers

TABLE 4.1   World Population Trends, 1965–2000

Region	1965	1985	Year (1985)	(2000)	% Increase 1990–2000
World	3289	4933	(4746)	(6130)	(18·2)
More developed regions	1037	1275	(1256)	(1441)	(9·36)
Less developed regions	2252	3658	(3490)	(4688)	(21·17)
East Asia	852	1182	(1105)	(1278)	(10·2)
South Asia	981	1693	(1596)	(2171)	(21·8)
Europe	445	515	(492)	(527)	(4·6)
Soviet Union	231	287	(297)	(353)	(11·7)
Africa	303	530	(513)	(768)	(30·9)
Northern America	214	280	(283)	(354)	(15·7)
Latin America	246	435	(436)	(638)	(28·2)
Oceania	18	27	(25)	(32)	(17·9)

and those of the less developed countries grow (say) 0·5 and 1·0–1·5 per cent per year, respectively. (2) The pressure of numbers on environment and resources will increase greatly. For example, abstracting from the impact of increase in average income and postulating a rate of world population growth of only 1·0 per cent per year in 2000–2100, world population will be about 100 per cent above the current level in 2000 and at least 450 per cent by 2100. Abstracting from changes in weights, should average output and consumption rise 1·75 per cent per year, aggregate pressure upon environment would be nearly four times as great in 2000 as in 1960, and about 60 times as high by 2100. (3) Population density, highest in Europe and Japan around 1960, will converge under the impact of differential rates of growth. For example, suppose that in 2000–2100 the population of Africa, Oceania and South America grows 2 per cent per year; that of Europe, 0·5 per cent; that of Asia, 1·25 per cent; and that of North America, 1 per cent; then by 2100 population per km^2 by continent will approximate 122 in Europe; 281 in Asia; 63 in North America; 184 in Africa; 172 in South America; and 28 in Oceania. These densities are of limited comparative value inasmuch as the ratio of cultivable to total land area – 0·24 in the world as a whole – varies considerably: Africa, 0·24;

Asia, 0·23; Australia and New Zealand, 0·19; Europe, 0·36; North America, 0·22; South America, 0·39; the Soviet Union, 0·14.[3] (5) The pressure of increasing numbers, together with that of industrialisation and growing dependence of most countries upon external sources for critical raw materials, may worsen international relations, particularly should international income inequality increase. This emerging situation could in turn make for improved relations among current and prospective members of the developed world, all of whom have a common interest in guarding the security of their relative economic situation.

2. SPATIAL CONTOURS

Of the migratory movements in prospect, the most significant will be that from rural to urban areas. For with the establishment of political sovereignty in all parts of the world and with the growing belief that only a limited number of international migrants could be absorbed compatibly with a nation's welfare, international migration on the pre-1914 scale ended, partly as a sequel to the First World War. Nor is it likely to be resumed even though international trade proves a much less effective substitute for international migration than economic theory suggests it can be.[4] Indeed, countries of potential emigration do not favour the outflow of their skilled personnel while countries willing to accept the latter are unwilling to accept large numbers of unskilled persons, the employment of whom is limited by the structure of the economy as well as by artificial constraints on employment (union rules, excessively high wage minima, etc.). As a result the relative magnitude of the international flow of migrants is small.[5]

Given modern transport, a high degree of industrialisation, and efficient agriculture, the movement of population out of agriculture and rural areas into urban centres proceeds until only small rural and agricultural populations remain. For example, 54·3 per cent of the population of the United States was rural in 1910 and only 22·1 per cent of the population lived in cities of over 100,000. By 1960 the rural percentage had declined to 37 while those living in cities over 100,000 had increased to 28·4 per cent of the population. Meanwhile the farm population continued to decline until by 1968 it constituted only 5·2 per cent of the nation's population; this fraction corresponds closely to the ratio of agricultural to total employment, namely, 0·05. We may say, therefore, that so long as a nation's agricultural population exceeds 20 per cent, or somewhat less, of its total population, movement out of agriculture and into urban centres and non-agricultural employment will continue. The ratio of the rural population to the agricultural population will vary in keeping with living patterns, tastes, largeness of cities and so on, though its magnitude will probably be governed primarily by the size of the agricultural population. In the United States, however, the total rural population, as defined in 1920, increased from 51·6 to 66·3 million between 1920 and 1960, though meanwhile the farm population declined from 32 to 15·6 million.[6]

While an urbanward drift has long been under way and was reflected in a rise in 1800–1930 from 1·3 to 11 in the percentage of the world's population situated in cities of 100,000 or more, it was long confined largely to the European area of settlement. In 1800 as well as in 1930 this percentage approximated 6 in Asia whereas in the European sphere it ranged from 18 to 29 in 1930 in comparison with 0·1 to 4·5 in 1800.[7] In 1920 only 8 per cent of the population of the less developed regions was urban and only 6 per cent lived in localities of 20,000 and over; in the more developed regions the corresponding percentages were 39 and 29. As late as 1950 only 16 per cent of the population of the underdeveloped regions was classed as 'urban' (a category that varies somewhat from country to country) and only 11 per cent lived in places of 20,000 or more; the comparable percentages for 1960 were 20 and 15. The corresponding percentages for the developed regions were 51 and 40 in 1950 and 60 and 46 in 1960. Change between 1920 and 1960 in the percentages living in localities of 20,000 or more inhabitants – 29 to 46 in more developed regions and 6 to 15 in less developed regions – indicates that urbanisation is effectively under way, though (as is noted below) it could proceed more rapidly *ceteris paribus* before 1950 when the overall rate of population growth was lower than after 1950, especially in less developed regions.[8]

As already suggested, Asia and Africa remained very rural as late as 1950, with only 14–16 per cent urban, and still quite rural in 1960, with 18–23 per cent urban. The corresponding percentages for Latin America, 41 and 49, were similar to the averages for the more developed major areas, 52 and 59, urban growth in Latin America having proceeded about 60 per cent faster in 1920–60 than that in the more developed areas.[9] By the year 2000 the expected urban fraction of the Latin-American population will approximate 80 per cent, the percentage anticipated for the more developed major areas. This fraction is double the 35–40 per cent expected in Asia and Africa in 2000. It is expected that by 2000 the overall fraction of the population in localities of 20,000 and over will approximate 55 per cent in Europe, 67 per cent in Japan, Russia,

Temperate South America, Australia and New Zealand, and 27–58 per cent elsewhere.[10]

When will the rural population of the less developed regions decline in absolute number? This did not happen in European countries, as a rule, until in the late nineteenth or early twentieth century, and in the United States until early in the present century. Should the population of the underdeveloped world grow 2–2·5 per cent per year, it will be very difficult to reduce the size of the rural population if, as Colin Clark asserts, increasing the non-agricultural labour force more than 4 per cent per year is virtually impossible to accommodate,[11] and the ratio of the non-agricultural labour force to the rural population is constant. This may be illustrated as follows, with columns U and R designating the urban and rural fraction of the population, initially put at 25 and 75 as in the underdeveloped world in 1970, and with the urban and total population T assumed to grow annually 4 and 2 per cent respectively. The column headed T′ is based upon the assumption that total population grows 1·5 instead of 2 per cent per year, while the column R′ designates T′–U as of the specified years. It is evident that the smaller the over-all rate of population growth, the more rapidly can the rural population be reduced and population redistribution stabilised. Given T′, together with U′ based upon an urban growth-rate of 3 per cent per year instead of 4 per cent, the rural population will grow as (T′–U′), but the rural population will not decline below 75 until the eighth decade.

Year	T	U	R(= T−U)	T′	R′	U′	(T′−U′)
0	100	25	75	100	75	25	75
20	149	55	94	135	80	45	90
40	221	120	101	181	61	82	99
50	269	178	91	211	33	110	101
60	328	263	65	244	−19	147	97

The rural population of the underdeveloped regions is expected to continue increasing into the twenty-first century, for while the urban population is expected to grow 3·8 per cent per year in 1970–2000, the total population is expected to grow 2·1 per cent per year and the rural population 1·3 per cent per year.[12] Even this rate of growth of the urban population will prove politically and economically feasible only if capital is formed rapidly enough both to increase urban jobs 3·8 per cent per year and to augment output per agriculturalist enough (i.e. 75 per cent, or about 1·8 per cent per year). Many decades will pass, therefore, before the distribution of population in space becomes relatively stable unless the rate of natural increase declines markedly.

3. GROWTH PROSPECT

Achievement of a stable spatial distribution of population would be facilitated by a high rate of growth of average output and the high rate of savings that would result if (say) something like 50–75 per cent of the marginal increment in average income were saved and invested. Even so, the absolute amount of savings per head would be low.

It would probably take a number of decades for average income in the less developed countries to approach closely to that in the more developed countries. Let us put the averages in these two sets of countries at 1 and 12 and suppose that these two averages rise 3 and 1·5 per cent per year.

Year	Developed	Underdeveloped	Spread
0	12·00	1·00	11·00
25	17·41	2·09	15·32
50	25·26	4·38	20·88
75	36·65	9·18	27·47
100	53·17	19·22	33·95
125	77·10	40·14	36·86
150	112·19	84·18	28·01

Under the conditions given, though the relative spread between the averages in the two sets of countries declines from a factor of 12 to a factor of 1·33, the absolute spread continues to widen and over 150 years must pass before the one average overtakes the other. In reality, of course, the relative as well as the absolute spread is continuing to grow. By 1961 national income per capita in 1958 United States dollars in non-communist industrialised countries ($1337) was 11·1 times that ($121) in the less industrialised countries, whereas in 1938 it was only 9 times as high.[13] Between 1955 and 1965 per capita gross national product rose about 1·33 times as fast in developed as in underdeveloped countries, with the increment in absolute income per head in the former about 14 times that in the latter.[14] Many factors contribute to the lowness of the rate of growth of average income in the less developed regions, but a number of these are associated with the high rate of population growth encountered in most of these countries.[15] These will be considered below.

So long as the labouring force is distributed between a modern sector, on the one hand, and a non-modern category, on the other, one composed of an overmanned, technologically inferior agricultural sector, and an undermechanised, craft-dominated sector, movement from the less modern into the more modern sector may serve to give an extra upward push to the set of forces elevating average output in particular sectors and subsectors. How output-augmentative such a movement can be turns in part upon the extent to which remediable unemployment – disguised or otherwise – exists outside the modern sector as well as upon the availability of capital, entrepreneurial capacity and other agents to augment employment within the modern sector.[16] The existence of these conditions, along with the opportunity to adopt methods much superior to those in use, must have contributed notably to the spectacular rise of average output in Japan since 1950.

4. OPTIMUM SPATIAL DISTRIBUTION

Growth of average income is subject to some acceleration through improvement of the distribution of population in space. In Section 2 discussion was limited to the movement out of the agricultural sector into other sectors. Here I have in mind the inter-regional and inter-urban distribution of population.

Today, at least in highly developed countries, a population has much more choice regarding where it will locate its activities than formerly. Forty years ago in the United States one person in four was directly dependent upon agriculture and additional numbers were engaged in serving those engaged in agriculture. A similar situation was found in other primary industry. A considerable fraction of the population thus was tied to resources. This is no longer true, today, with not much over 6–7 per cent of the population directly dependent upon primary industry. Freedom to locate is not, of course, free of constraint. Economies of scale and agglomeration dictate that complementary activities be concentrated and that therefore a nation's population be assembled around a large number of growth points. These points, however, may be variously distributed in space, subject of course to such constraints as flow from the networks of reciprocity into which cities organise themselves. Even so, there is far more freedom than ever before respecting location of activities.

American data suggest that the inter-state distribution of the population is sub-optimal. In the 10 most populous of the nation's conterminous 48 states lived 54 per cent of the nation's population, in the least populous, only about 3 per cent. In the 10 with the most dense population lived 36 per cent of the American people; in the 10 with the least dense population, just over 4 per cent. The states with the most dense populations rank roughly among the top third in average income whereas 9 of the 10 with the least dense population rank in the lower half of the 48 states ranked according to average income. While economic conditions have played a part in determining relative population density, it is highly probable that if the nation's population were redistributed and numbers became more dense in the sparsely populated states average income would rise there. Presumably, larger numbers would permit a better organisation of the economy situated within these states while a reduction of numbers in the densely populated states would probably permit an improvement in living conditions, if not in conventionally defined income.

Inter-regional distribution of population is dominated by the distribution of cities and the distribution of population among the cities, particularly after the urbanward movement of rural population has become strong and many small places or areas begin to lose population through net out-migration. In the past the pattern of distribution has been dominated by rail and/or water transport and the technology underlying production, distribution, and communication. As this technology changes, therefore, the range of locational options is modified and the locational pattern changes.

Change in technology has tended to relax at least some constraints on the distribution of economic activities over space. Diminution in size of optimum plant and hence in economies of scale makes possible smaller concentrations of population. Increase in the size of corporations augments the relative number of potential establishers of cities, since a large corporation can, by settling in a new or a small community, establish an urban base around which the ancillary activities constituting a city can be assembled.[17] For if corporations are small they are less free to locate undertakings otherwise than in the vicinity of going urban concerns which, unwittingly as a rule, bear some of the spillover costs and effects occasioned by 'Johnny come lately' firms and thus subsidise the location of the latter and tend to make cities too large. When, however, one or two corporations can establish an urban base around which ancillary activities settle as about a nucleus, it becomes more easy to internalise costs and returns and minimise adverse spillover effects. In general the more nearly costs and returns can be internalised within the establishments generating them, the more economically rational will be a city's organisation and the more nearly will its size be in keeping with what may be called laws of urban return.

In today's world, with the growth of discretionary income and time, many more persons than formerly set great store by amenities, at least some of which are space-oriented. Most of these remain more accessible when cities are not too large, or are situated very near to one another in what are usually compact ribbon-like patterns.

In these cities, moreover, pollution is less intense, *ceteris paribus*, since vulnerability to pollution tends to increase with urban growth. The actual pattern of urban growth sought in countries will vary, of course, with assessment of the trade-offs available.[18] For reasons calling for further analysis, the fraction of the urban population situated within the United States cities of 0·25–1·0 million increased about 16 per cent between 1910 and 1960 while that in larger cities declined by 2·2 per cent and that in smaller cities and towns declined only slightly.

5. COSTS OF POPULATION GROWTH

The costs of population growth fall under three principal heads: (*a*) age composition; (*b*) absorption of capital and (*c*) pressure on physical environment.

(*a*) When a population is growing rapidly, its age composition is less favourable to production than when it is growing slowly. Given an expectation of life at birth of 50 years, the ratio of those aged 15–59 – here supposed to reflect the number of productive age – to the total population rises from 0·509 when the gross reproduction rate is 3 to 60 when it is 1·5 and the population is growing only 3·9 per 1000 inhabitants. While increase in expectation of life at birth operates *ceteris paribus* to reduce the fraction aged 15–59 years, this fraction rises as fertility falls, whether life expectancy is high or low; thus, given a life expectancy of 70·2 years, decline in the G.R.R. from 3 to 1·0 is accompanied by a rise from 0·484 to around 0·585 in the fraction aged 15–59.[19] Turning to actual population structures we find that around 1965 the fraction of the population aged 15–64 was around 0·54–0·55 or lower in much of the underdeveloped world, or one-tenth or more below the corresponding fraction of 0·6 or higher in the developed world. Under *ceteris paribus* conditions, therefore, potential productivity per head is 10 or more per cent higher in the developed than in the underdeveloped world.

(*b*) Population growth absorbs inputs that might otherwise have been devoted to increasing productivity per head. How large an amount of input is absorbed and how much it might otherwise contribute to the growth of average output is not easily measured with precision, or put in terms of internationally comparable terms. When all the inputs absorbed by population growth are taken into account, however, it is not far off the mark to estimate them at 4–5 per cent, or perhaps more, of national income for a stable population growing 1 per cent per year. Such an amount invested at 10–15 per cent per year, a return realised by most leading American corporations,[20] would yield around one-half of 1 per cent, with the implication that *ceteris paribus* a population with 1 per-cent-per-year rate of population growth would have a per capita income increasing $x + 0.5$ per cent annually if a corresponding population with a 2-per-cent-per-year rate of population growth enjoyed an average income rising x per cent per year. This income spread might amount to 1 per cent, should one population grow 2 per cent per year more than the other. The adverse impact upon the rate of growth of income tends to be greater in so far as population growth depresses the rate of saving per capita, or as inputs have to be invested in activities yielding relatively low rates of return (for example housing, some infra-structure).

(c) The third cost, pressure of numbers upon physical environment, is associated with the change in aggregate size of a population consequent upon continuing population growth rather than with growth as such; it is the kind of cost Malthus and the classical economists generally had in view when discussing diminishing returns as well as the kind of cost Jevons contemplated when pointing to effects of depletion of Britain's coal supply. In general the composition of this cost changed as the environmental basis of the economy, together with the composition of gross national product, changed. This change is reflected in the ever-widening range of raw materials put to use, symbolised in the fact that today virtually all the elements in the table of elements are used whereas in the early nineteenth century only about 20 were used.

Pressure Π upon man's physical environment E arises both from population P and the average rate of consumption r. So we may write:

$$\Pi = E/Pr$$

In many of the world's countries increase in Π arises from the fact that P' the rate of increase of P, is high; in others, that r' the rate of increase in r, is high. Today, with both P' and r' much higher than in the past, the rate of increase in Pr, roughly $P' + r'$, is much higher than formerly. Even if P' declined to a low level by (say) 2026, r' would remain high, though perhaps not exercise as much pressure upon E as in the past, should demand become more oriented to services which embody relatively little of E. It is possible at times, of course, to reduce r by reducing the input of raw material per unit of output and by substituting more abundant raw materials for those which are relatively scarce.

While E is subject to depletion, as we note below, this depletion is offset in part. At any time, because of the state of technology and the composition of man's wants, only a fraction u of E is brought within the orbit of man's use, with the rate of this use conditioned by the relevant price-cost ratios. Overtime, particularly in the course of the past 75–100 years, the value of u has increased. The pressure Π of Pr upon uE, though often relieved, has seldom been relieved permanently; for even when P is growing slowly r is likely to be growing appreciably, with the result that $P' + r'$ keeps pace with the rate of increase in u, even supposing E to be constant instead of subject to depletion.

What has been said runs in world terms whereas economies, even when open, are nationally based, though engaged in exchange with other economies. The United States is a case in point, able to sustain a high $(P' + r')$ only because it draws a large fraction of its raw materials from outside its boundaries. Indeed, were uE drawn on at a rate comparable to that characteristic of the United States, the world Pr would be a number of times that found in the United States. International trade, therefore, serves to augment Π and r' for the world as a whole, though with little effect upon P or P'. While it may be true that a slowing down of population growth in the developed countries slows down the rate of growth in demand for raw materials and produce supplied by developing countries,[21] such slowing down is incident upon agricultural produce much more than upon raw materials.

Turning now to that which is drawn from the physical environment, we may divide its contribution into food and water, on the one hand, and non-food raw materials on the other. Regarding the potential food supply for the world as a whole, one may put this at something like 6–8 times the current supply obtained from the land plus protein and other food from the sea and inland waters amounting to several times what is obtained today. The propensity to develop the world's potentially arable but still uncultivated land – about 4·5 billion acres – is limited by the fact that little of it is found in low-income Asia (with 57 per cent of the world's population) or high-income Europe (with 13 per cent of the world's population) and much of it (2·9 billion acres) in Africa and South America (with 19 per cent of the world's population) and another billion acres in North America, Australia and New Zealand (with 8 per cent). While capacity to increase yields per acre is higher also in countries which are not short of food, the 'green revolution' now in process should permit a great increase in yields in many less developed countries.[22]

Even should it prove possible to increase the world food supply 500–700 per cent, population and average consumption could easily overtake the food supply. Given a rate of population growth of about one per cent per year after the year 2000, the world's population would be 8 times its 1960 size 170 years from now. Should per capita food consumption increase as little as 0·5 per cent per year and population grow 1 per cent per year after 2000, by the 2080s total food consumption would be 8 times what it was in the 1960s. At present agricultural production per capita is only about 3 per cent above its 1957–9 level in the less developed countries, but 15 per cent higher in industrial countries. Food production per capita has declined in some underdeveloped countries and risen very slowly in others, according to U.S.D.A. reports; this outcome reflects the double impact of population growth and the slowness with which the so-called 'green revolution' is proceeding.

Shortage of water will in time limit not only agricultural production but also other kinds of production and realisation of amenities. In the United States, for example, water use, now something like 350 billion gallons a day, is expected to total 600 billion by 1980, and 1000 in the year 2000. Yet the essentially unchanging supply of dependable fresh water is estimated at only 650 billion gallons. As a result, 'more and more, water will have to be re-used, and it will cost more and more to retrieve clean water from progressively dirtier waterways', especially when peak power consumption coincides with reduced water flow. Pollution and eutrophication will be accentuated.[23] In many other lands water shortage will make itself felt in manifold ways, though care in developing river basins and bringing into use larger fractions of the annual rainfall can cushion if not prevent the emergence of water shortage.

In time fossil fuels and other mineral and related resources will be exhausted, with the result that what we earlier called physical environment E is describable as subject to increasing economic entropy and contraction. Although minerals economically extractable from the sea can offset some of this environmental shrinkage, reliance must ultimately be put upon increase in the supply of energy through recourse to breeder reactors and fusion processes. For 'energy', according to A. M. Weinberg, 'can convert common materials – seawater, rock, air – into the materials needed by man', with 20 kilowatts (thermal) serving to maintain man's present average 'material standard'.[24]

The final resource in increasingly limited supply is suitably situated space, that is, space in and around cities. This limitation arises, as a rule, because too few cities are established, and too many activities are concentrated in the very limited area allotted to cities; for example, in the United States in 1960, 64 per cent of the population lived in places of 2500 and over, occupying about one-fifth of an acre of urban land per person, though in some cities this average approximated three-eighths of an acre. In consequence, the costs of congestion are likely to be high.

6. OFFSETS TO COSTS

Even as Toynbee discovered in the web of man's long history, challenge and response continually dominate man's affairs, economic and otherwise, less conspicuously in periods of stability manifesting the presence of something like a stationary state, and quite conspicuously when this state is disrupted. Increasing scarcity, whether the result of population growth or expanding average consumption, tends to provoke counter-response, initially in the form of efforts to increase the output of that which is scarce or make possible technological economy in its use.

There are two kinds of offsets to costs of the sort described in the preceding section, (a) compensating gains and (b) palliatives. Typical of the gains are increasing returns and advantages allegedly associated with population growth. Of these increasing return may be the more important as Adam Smith long ago implied in his analysis of division of labour. Until recently in much of the world and still in important parts (for example, Canada, Australia, New Zealand, parts of Africa and Latin America, the Soviet Union) of the present-day world, the substitution of larger for smaller populations has made possible greater specialisation and fuller exploitation of the newer, larger-scale technologies and the ever more diversified national productive apparatus that has continued to come into existence. Indeed, it has been estimated that a population of fifty or more million is essential to the full exploitation of this apparatus by a state,[25] though compatibly with a widely varying territorial extent; and it is evident that for this reason (as well as others associated with lack of diversified resources) only a minor fraction of the world's so-called sovereign states are of something like adequate or optimum size. Of course, should the development of technology no longer be so largely governed by exogenous forces, but instead be brought under the direction of scientists and engineers intent on miniaturising plants, factories, etc., and in general reducing the size essential to cost minimisation, it may prove possible to reduce the size of country and economy essential to full exploitation of the modern productive apparatus. Until the present, however, miniaturisation has not been emphasised, pressure for it has been almost non-existent, and what miniaturisation has been developed has been a virtually fortuitous outcome associated with increase in output per worker.

Allegations of the presence of increasing return, at least of increasing return associated with the development of larger populations, need to be scrutinised carefully. For when inputs are underestimated, or badly measured, residual unexplained output emerges, and this may be imputed to various sources, among them 'increasing return'. Given identification of all inputs, however, this unexplained residual may prove fully imputable to the inputs operative.[26]

Population growth as such is also described as rendering economies more efficient. It is said to facilitate the development of newer industries and the maintenance of optimum inter-occupational balance by providing a relatively larger number of workers to move into expanding industries and thus avoiding costs that beset inter-occupational transfer of workers. Population growth may correct errors in investment and in general sustain an optimistic set of expectations conducive to dynamic and effective management of an economy and its components.[27]

One may grant the existence of these positive offsets to population growth. There remains a question, however, one recognised by the classical economists, namely, do these offsets more than match the costs associated with population growth and increase in size of population? It has always been this issue to which proponents of optimum-population theory have sought to direct attention.

I turn now to what I called palliatives as distinguished from offsets. Population redistribution within countries may ease the pressure of numbers at particular points, improve the overall adjustment of a nation's numbers to its resource structure, and deconcentrate the incidence of pollution that is local or regional and hence susceptible of alleviation through both population redistribution and the curbing of pollution at its source. It may be noted parenthetically that, though much pollution is global or quasi-global in character, man's capacity for dealing with much of it remains handicapped by lack of knowledge as well as by lack of agreement respecting corrective action against forms of international pollution that are understood.

Since there is little scope for freedom of international migration, international trade constitutes a fairly effective substitute. It does this by allowing labour, in long supply in heavily populated countries to migrate by proxy in the form of labour-embodying imports. It is not to be expected, however, that international trade will ever be free enough to perform this function effectively. Moreover, countries highly dependent upon international trade, whether for imported raw materials (for example, the United States, Japan) or for other essentials, are always vulnerable to the interruption of this trade. Even more vulnerable are the economies most dependent upon international exchange, namely, those too small in population, territory, and variety of activity to realise economies of scale through domestic sales and use of domestic resources.

Palliatives need to be recognised for what they are, the incurring of particular costs in order to reduce the incidence of other and heavier costs. Had population not grown so much in a country resorting to palliatives, neither their cost nor the costs palliatives are designed to reduce would have been incurred and net average output would therefore have been greater.

As a rule, efforts to offset population growth beyond what may be called an optimum point or range, even when successful, usually entail costs. Man's response to food shortage has led him to use pesticides and herbicides that may contaminate the environment, to use fertilizer in such quantities as could reduce long-time natural soil fertility, and to over-use soils in such a manner as to bring about their deterioration. His exploitation of less rich mineral sources makes for the increasing accumulation of waste. Concentration of industrial activities and population accentuates problems of water supply, waste disposal and control of pollution. As was implied earlier, however, modern industry and affluent living are the principal sources of pollution, though increase in numbers intensifies pollution originating in industry.

7. WAYS OUT

About a century, not much more, remains, in the course of which man can solve the world's two demographic problems, population explosion and its corollary, population implosion, the speed of solution of which depends largely upon how low is the overall rate of population growth. For while some environmental components of man's diverse standards of life are relatively abundant or replaceable, others are in limited supply and not available, and these set limits to the augmentability of growth of population and average consumption.

Let G_i designate goods G_1 to G_n and let each good be reduced to terms of its physical environmental components E_1 to E_n. Suppose that environmental components E_1 to E_{100} are in short supply, non-augmentable in flow over a long period of time, or augmentable only at very rapidly increasing cost. Then if a nation's budget of wants G is dominated by, or heavily loaded with, goods G into which components E_1 to E_{100} enter in a marked degree, its population capacity will be far more limited, and much sooner reached, than if its budget consists largely of G into which E_{101} to E_n enter largely. The emergence and intensification of population pressure thus depends both upon population growth and upon the size and content of the budget of wants sought by a population. Within limits, therefore, population pressure can be eased through reorganisation of a society's tastes and expectations.

At the start of this paper the projections of the United Nations Secretariat were presented, along with indications of what continuation of population growth even at relatively low rates – say 1·0 per cent – might mean. It is possible, however, that fertility and the rate of natural increase may be reduced rapidly by the latter part of this century or the early part of the next century.[28] Should this happen and the world net reproduction rate approach zero early in the next century, it may yet be possible to hold world population at something like ten billion.[29] For while results to date respecting decline in natality have been disappointing, there is scope for much improvement in family planning programmes. Given a world population of ten billion, together with a zero rate of growth in most of the world, it should prove possible not only greatly to accelerate the urbanisation process but also to realise some relaxation of national barriers which no country can afford to relax at a time when population is growing at a rapid rate, especially in populations not well equipped for life in the modern world.

Should zero population growth come to prevail in the world and the expectations of peoples become adjusted to a zero rate of population growth and life in a state with a stationary population, the advantages long ago associated with such a stationary population by J. S. Mill could be realised in a modern setting. Populations might often be in excess of optimum size, and yet be able to enjoy close approximations to life under optimum conditions, among them greatly reduced military and related expenditures. Perhaps, given the bright image of an optimum population, men will be induced to seek establishment of an optimum and avert the dangers of increasing political instability associated with frustrations consequent upon increasing population pressure and making for increase in the probability of nuclear extinction.

Population does not tend to assume optimum size. Let $M = (A - O)/O$ where M designates population maladjustment and A and O designate actual and optimum population respectively. Unless M is quite large it is unlikely to affect the level of fertility significantly since it does not impinge directly enough upon man's expectations regarding his own welfare, and even if it does he will probably infer that his own behaviour cannot affect M. Only collective responses to increase in M will have any effect.

While the concept of a population optimum is useful on analytical grounds, difficulties surrounding its definition, measurement and translation into collective welfare terms limit its use for policy purposes. It is easier to build population policy upon the principle that the burden of proof is upon those who contend that further population growth is advantageous. Policy may, however, be directed toward modifying the trade-off between birth-rate and consumption with the object of directing the overall rate of population growth to some desired level.

Government intervention is essential also to secure improved distribution of population in space, among cities and within cities. Population settles where employment is to be had and there is access to amenities, so important in countries with much *discretionary* time and income. The transport system needs to be organised in such ways as to ensure a satisfactory distribution of population. Control of city size calls for the imposition of *all* costs on those whose activities give rise to costs of congestion, pollution, etc., and perhaps in addition for the collective ownership of land within and surrounding the environs of urban centres. The establishment of additional growth points is dependent mainly upon the activity of large corporations, sometimes supplemented by the state.

Notes

1. I have drawn on the following studies by the United Nations:
   The Determinants and Consequences of Population Trends (New York, 1953); *World Population Prospects* (1963) (New York, 1966), and *World Population Situation*, E/CN.9/231 (New York, 1968); J. D. Durand, 'World Population Estimates, 1750–2000', in United Nations, *World Population Conference, 1965*, II (New York, 1967) pp. 17–22; Milos Macura, 'The Long-Range Outlook-Summary of Current Estimates', in *World Population – The View Ahead*, ed. R. N. Farmer *et al.* (Bloomington, 1968) pp. 15–42; also Durand's comments, ibid., pp. 43–8.
2. On the state of mortality and natality in the world see *Population Bulletin of the United Nations*, nos. 6 and 7, United Nations (New York, 1962).
3. *The World Food Problem*, II, p. 434. This report, issued in 1967, is a Report of the President's Science Advisory Committee, Washington, D.C.
4. On the theory see W. P. Travis, *The Theory of Trade and Protection* (Cambridge, 1964) chap. 1; S. B. Linder, *An Essay on Trade and Transformation* (New York, 1961) pp. 15–19, 83–6, 100–9.
5. United Nations, *The Determinants*, chap. 6, and *Demographic Yearbook*, especially those for 1948 and 1966.
6. See W. S. and E. S. Woytinsky, *World Population and Production* (New York, 1953) pp. 116, 460, 462 for data somewhat comparable to the above data for the United States
7. Ibid., p. 118.
8. United Nations, *Growth of the World's Urban and Rural Population, 1920–2000* (New York, 1969) pp. 12, 31, 73.
9. Ibid., pp. 31–64.
10. Ibid., pp. 31, 71, 73, 124.
11. See Clark, *Population Growth and Land Use* (New York, 1967) pp. 258–60.
12. United Nations, *Growth of World's Urban . . .*, pp. 56, 71.
13. United Nations, *The Growth of World Industry, 1938–61* (New York, 1965) p. 194. See also L. J. Zimmerman, *Poor Lands, Rich Lands* (New York, 1965) chap. 2.

14. United Nations, *World Economic Survey 1967* (New York, 1968) pp. 18–19.
15. E.g. see *Population Bulletin of the United Nations*, no. 7.
16. On these matters there is an extensive literature going back to the writings of W. A. Lewis and others. E.g. see J. C. H. Fei and Gustav Ranis, *Development of the Labor Surplus Economy: Theory and Practice* (New Haven, 1964); Benjamin Higgins, *Economic Development*, 2nd ed. (New York, 1968) *passim*: M. Desai and D. Maxzumdar, 'A Test of the Hypothesis of Disguised Unemployment', *Economica*, XXXVII (February 1969) pp. 39–53.
17. See my 'Drift to the City: Way Out?' in *South Atlantic Quarterly*, LXVII (1948) pp. 611–26.
18. E.g. see Lloyd Rodwin, *Nations and Cities: A Comparison of Strategies for Urban Growth* (Boston, 1970); also my 'Population Pressure, Housing and Habitats', in *Law and Contemporary Problems* XXXII, Part I (Spring 1967) pp. 191–208.
19. United Nations, *The Aging of Populations and Its Economic and Social Implications* (Population Studies, no. 26) (New York, 1956) pp. 26–7. More detailed tables are given in A. J. Coale and Paul Demeny, *Regional Model Life Tables and Stable Populations* (Princeton, 1966).
20. See *Monthly Economic Letter* of First National City Bank of New York (April 1970) p. 41.
21. J. R. Hicks, 'Growth and Anti-Growth', *Oxford Economic Papers*, XVIII (November 1966) pp. 265–6, 268.
22. For data on food-output prospects see *The World Food Problem*, II, esp. chap. 7; Lester R. Brown, *Seeds of Change* (New York, 1970); National Academy of Sciences, *Resources and Man* (San Francisco, 1969) chap. 4.
23. G. Bylinsky, 'The Limited War on Water Pollution', *Fortune* (February 1970) pp. 103 ff.
24. Weinberg's and other papers on natural resources appear in a forthcoming volume edited by S. Fred Singer. See also National Academy of Sciences, *Resources and Man*, chap. 8.
25. E. A. G. Robinson, ed., *The Economic Consequences of the Size of Nations* (London, 1960) pp. xiii–xxii.
26. See D. W. Jorgenson and Z. Griliches, 'Explanation of Productivity Change', in *Review of Economic Studies*, XXXIV (July, 1967) pp. 249–84, reprinted with an examination of the major issues involved by E. F. Denison, in *Survey of Current Business*, XLIX, Part II (May, 1969), 1–27. See on alleged evidence of increasing return, Colin Clark, *Population Growth and Land Use*, chap. 7.
27. See ibid., chap. 7.
28. E.g. see J. L. Simon, 'Family Planning Prospects in Less-Developed Countries and a Cost-Benefit Analysis of Various Alternatives', *Economic Journal*, LXXX (March 1970) 58–71.
29. See Thomas Frejka, 'Reflections on the Demographic Conditions Needed to Establish a U.S. Stationary Population', *Population Studies*, XXII (1968) 379–97.

COMMENTS*

H. M. Robertson

The paper by Professor Spengler is short, yet remarkably comprehensive; it deals clearly with complicated issues; it adds new insights on problems which might have been regarded as by now already thoroughly explored; its claims to our attention are enhanced by the fact that it does not claim too much. It is striking, too, that Professor Spengler's paper links so interestingly with other papers prepared for this conference, particularly, perhaps, with those of Professor Sadie, Professor Papi and Professor Enke. His opening statement for instance, that 'World population growth did not accelerate until in the present century . . .' is exemplified in Professor Sadie's graph no. I.I.

But another feature which makes the current 'population explosion' stand out in history is not only that it is the first one to have developed upon a world scale, but it is the first one to have developed more particularly in the less developed areas of the world. In all previous periods of accelerated population growth, this had chiefly been manifested in the economically (and politically) more developed regions.

In the past urbanisation and rural migration into towns has always been a feature of a period of accelerated population growth. So it is at the present day; but Professor Spengler has very clearly pointed out that the very scale of the present demographical upsurge, particularly in countries still largely agricultural and of comparatively low agricultural productivity, with low investment in farming capital and less advanced agricultural practices, poses great difficulties in the way of the necessary transformation. The rate at which urban development can successfully take place depends, on the one hand, upon increased productivity in agriculture both per man and per unit of land. Agricultural output must be made adequate for the needs (both for food and for industrial processing) of a larger non-agricultural population; yet it must be secured out of an area of land, devoted to agriculture, which cannot be augmented at will. Yet, on the other hand, it also depends upon the opening up of enough opportunities for urban employment, the provision of adequate amounts of housing, factory building and necessary

* Professor Robertson, who was to have led the discussion of this paper, was unable to be present. He submitted these written comments for circulation at the conference.

urban amenities, and the development of adequate means of communication. All of these are very greedy of capital; but a very rapid rate of population growth may hinder the rapid accumulation of capital. There will be greater demands upon resources for consumption purposes and an age-composition of the population less favourable to productivity per head of the total population.

In an elegant discussion of 'optimum spatial distribution', Professor Spengler poses the interesting yet perhaps controversial suggestion that the large business corporation can have a discretionary ability, through siting of branch factories, with employee housing and amenities, to create new cities of adequate size, yet small enough not to suffer the congestion which has become characteristic of the overgrown metropolis. By having this discretion to plant a city 'nucleus' where it wants, a large and wealthy corporation can be a founder of a type of city which can serve human needs both better and at lower cost. There is almost an echo here of a rather different suggestion of Richard Cantillon, who argued that the landed proprietor of independent means had a similar special discretionary power. Perhaps Cantillon was really 'the first of the moderns'.

Yet before this is accepted, with the possibility that the idea might be carried perhaps a stage further, to encourage policies of nationalisation of large corporations, on the grounds that the power so to promote optimum units of urban growth ought not to be privately exercised, the matter would require much lengthier argument and not all of it would be strictly relevant to the particular theme of this conference. I am reminded of a discussion in Lord Keynes' Political Economy Club of some forty-five years ago, when Keynes was scoffing at the ideas of the 'optimum population' theorists, and arguing that at all times and places, a reduction in numbers would be beneficial to the remainder. The Secretary of the Club tried to counter with the old Greek argument that a city ought neither to be too small nor yet too big. 'Tell me', said Keynes, 'just how big it ought to be.' 'Well', said Secretary Barber, 'It ought to be as large as Cambridge, but not as big as Oxford.' Now I know that the Cowley works were more a piece of discretionary siting on the part of Lord Nuffield than an attempt to grasp 'external economies', yet I cannot see why there might not be accretions to a business corporation-founded city nucleus, which would clearly upset its earlier optimum balance, because of the later-comers who were attracted by the very features which would be destroyed by their coming in over-large numbers.

In the section upon the costs of population growth, where the succinct argument bears reading and rereading, an interesting corollary of Professor Spengler's argument, which is not made in he paper, is perhaps worth noting here. This is that should a rapid change of social attitudes supervene, creating a notable limitation of births in an area till then one of high fertility, and having a larger proportion of children in its population, such a country would quite soon enter a phase of having a particularly favourable ratio of those reckoned to be in their most productive years. The large army of children would within a few years become adult; they would not be replaced with similar large numbers of new babies. It would be a passing phase, yet during this phase there would have been a sort of compound effect in which a course of economic development could have become established.

In discussing the pressure of population upon man's physical environment, Professor Spengler points out that this pressure increases (a) as there are larger numbers to be fed and housed and clothed, and also (b) as consumption per capita increases. There are, on the other hand, offsets, such as occur when things come to be produced with greater economy in the use of resources; when demand switches more and more to demands for services rather than goods; when new resources are discovered and new uses for resources are developed.

In this connection, Spengler has introduced a number of useful distinctions, one of them made by A. J. Lotka in the passage quoted at the opening of the paper; namely that some of the requirements of life are readily interchangeable, but that for others there are no possible replacements. As regards food supply (in forms already existing, from already known resources), Professor Spengler sees the Malthusian foreboding looming up as a *world* problem, within a period not very long on the scale of the world's history, even though still remote enough in the view of an individual's life span. Fresh water supplies and pollution of the environment in its various forms, he sees as even more immediate problems.

In his always careful analysis, Professor Spengler points out that the costs of population pressure can be offset, but in different ways. It can be offset either by (a) compensating gains or (b) palliatives. Historical experience has shown that compensating gains during periods of rapid population growth may be real and substantial. As most of the classical economists expected – but to an extent which would have astounded them – such offsets have proved substantial indeed in the 170 odd years which have elapsed since Malthus wrote his *Principle of Population*. Indeed it had become commonplace to suggest that increasing returns resulting from population growth had been of such a magnitude as to render the Malthusian forebodings insubstantial scarecrows. Yet Spengler makes the point that some of these 'increasing returns' may well have been illusory. They

D

may have resulted not from genuine increasing returns to inputs, but have depended to some extent upon the use of additional inputs not recognised as such – including, of course, the rapid depletion of resources stored up by nature over millennia of very meagre exploitation.

Other offsets Professor Spengler classes as not real offsets, but palliatives. However, in his own words: 'Palliatives need to be recognised for what they are, the incurring of particular costs in order to reduce the incidence of other and heavier costs.' Both the costs they are designed to reduce, and the costs of the palliatives themselves, result from a growth of population and a rate of population growth in excess of its optimum point or range.

Professor Frank Knight used to preface his lectures on economics with a reminder that the importance of economics tends to be over-rated – that the important deciding factors even in the economic sphere result from deeper forces than those of economic calculation. In this particular sphere of economic choice – choice between numbers and standards of life – it seems unlikely that economic considerations will prove paramount.

I remember once having read that there is only one universally valid principle of population, namely that one can be sure that whatever is being currently debated in academic circles will represent concern over past trends, and be quite irrelevant to the developing situation. There is some merit in this cynicism over fashionable academic debate. Malthus wrote upon the verge of a population explosion which would have seemed bound soon to have come up against his positive checks. Yet this did not occur in England which experienced an era of unprecedented economic growth accompanied by population growth during the nineteenth century (though Ireland, indeed, did not prove so fortunate). In my own academic experience I have lived through the period when the stage was held by the anti-malthusian bogey of an imminent danger of declining populations leading to economic stagnation; when Enid Charles, among others, warned about a frightening general decline in fertility which might be due to the spread of the habit of bathing, of the whole body, and to the spermicidal effects of soap.

This sceptical view of academic concern with population problems is not altogether unreasonable. It is extremely difficult to discern turning-points until well after they have occurred. This, indeed, is one reason why I prefer to be a historian and enjoy the luxury of using hindsight. But if there is anything in this inductive law of population, it is the best augury – indeed virtually the only good augury – for the future. For if we have now reached a summit of concern and a turning-point, and a reversal of trends which we do

not as yet clearly see is virtually already upon us, then Professor
Spengler may find his wholly admirable yearning for the stationary
population and the stationary state of J. S. Mill's imagination realised some time early in the third millennium.

DISCUSSION

Panel Members: Dr. C. Strauss, Professor Marcus Arkin

Dr. Strauss, in presenting Professor Spengler's paper,* said that the spatial distribution of activities was of considerable significance for South Africa with its dual economy, but owing to the fact that the developed sector was relatively well endowed with minerals, entrepreneurial skill and other factors, the problem of achieving an absolute decrease in the population of the backward sector might be less difficult to achieve here than in other less developed countries.

He pointed out that G. Zaidan (*Finance and Development,* March 1969), unlike Professor Spengler, argued that the movement of people from more to less densely populated areas was not related to the density of population. Columbia and Pakistan illustrated this point. While there might be sociological and psychological advantages in decentralisation, the economic advantages, especially of rapid decentralisation, were less certain. Zaidan stressed the proportion of investment necessary just to maintain the present level of per capita income with a growing population – 65 per cent in less developed countries, compared with 25 per cent in developed countries.

Professor Arkin said he found it difficult to offer constructive comments on Professor Spengler's paper, which covered a tremendous amount of ground, but in a somewhat haphazard manner and without any clear pattern of argument. Especially disturbing, he felt, was the use of symbols on pages 68 and 69 and on page 74, which seemed singularly unenlightening, particularly in the latter case where there was the dangerously misleading implication that concepts such as 'optimum' and 'maladjustment' could be helpfully thought of in terms of neat formulae.

The problem of what might be called 'chronological dynamics' occurred especially in the early sections of the paper. The author gave estimates of the shrinkage in the percentage of world population living in the 'more developed' areas between 1900 and 1965 with forward projections. But over these decades there had taken place notable shifts in the balance between 'more' and 'less' developed regions, and South Africa, for instance, had shifted from the latter to the former category. Similarly, in 1800 a town of 20,000, even in Europe, was regarded as something of a metropolis, whereas in South Africa today towns of such size were seldom even included in discussions of urbanisation. Thus there were dangers in looking at past and future population trends in terms of stationary concepts.

* Professor Spengler was not present for the discussion of his paper.

He asked whether there was not a tendency to overdo the barrage against pollution. Rachel Carson's message had got through, and in one country after another the more dangerous chemicals had come under tighter control, or had been banned altogether. By continuing to be over-pessimistic, more harm than good might be done, as a backlash might be caused. Progressively higher living standards in the west were resulting in greater interest being shown in the quality of the surroundings.

Professor S. P. Cilliers appealed to the economists to define 'population explosion' as a situation in which the rate of growth of population exceeded the rate of economic growth, as he believed that this would lead to more fruitful discussion. There was no danger in the foreseeable future of the world as a whole not being able to produce enough food, but consideration should be given to means of solving the population explosion, such as more trade and other means of redistributing food supplies.

Professor Sheila van der Horst quoted the Pearson Report to show that Professor Cilliers' proposed definition would in effect define the problem of the population explosion away, since underdeveloped countries were achieving increases in income per head. The problem, rather, was that per capita income was not rising as fast as people would like.

Dr. Strauss said that the problem of redistributing food supplies, raised by Professor Cilliers, was really a political problem, not an economic one. *Professor H. Pollak*, too, pointed out that it was politicians who made the decisions, and, due to their desire to remain in power, they were influenced mainly by short-term considerations, not the long-term factors stressed by economists. The Yugoslavian developmental programme was cited to illustrate this.

Professor G. Ugo Papi argued that what caused concern was not the size of populations as such, but the low standard of living. The central problem was thus the determination of optimum population growth.

Dr. J. M. Lotter said that prices of agricultural products had declined relative to manufactures, probably because manufacturing had superiority as a pressure group. Also, while it was easy to increase output of manufactures by, for instance, working more shifts, it was more difficult to increase agricultural production.

Dr. Strauss acknowledged the power of manufacturing and the labour unions, but said that more money was no solution unless there was a corresponding increase in the flow of goods and services. The problem in agriculture was not that incentives were inadequate, but that farming units were too small. International trade in agricultural products was restricted by the reluctance of countries, for strategic reasons, to rely on food imports.

Mr. H. M. Marsh commented that the papers presented failed to take into account the problems that all levels of government faced in providing housing, land and communications, due to the population explosion.

Mr. S. O. Eklund said that the distinction between urban and rural was unnecessary and the question of decentralisation was irrelevant. The pollution problem, he felt, was a transitory one, and by 1990 there would, as a result of planning, be no smog or river pollution. In Africa long-term planning could achieve a redistribution of population which would solve the problems of growing population.

Professor G. J. Trotter said that Professor Spengler did not explicitly refer to the increasing cost of providing educational facilities for a growing population. Such facilities could easily be sealed up. He also made a plea for more research into the significance of education in economic development.

Professor H. V. Muhsam, referring to a point raised earlier, said that Professor Spengler regarded the optimum rate of population growth as that which would maximise per capita income. To determine optimum growth, assumptions had to be made regarding technology and social and political structure, and the time period (whether short run, intermediate period or long run). In the short run (2 to 5 years) the optimum rate of population growth was zero. In the long run, however, when stability was reached in the population structure, the optimum rate of population growth, as defined, was negative. Did we wish to maximise our level of living under such conditions, he asked.

Dr. Strauss concluded the discussion by stressing the urgency of the problems of overpopulation and poverty, but quoted Arthur Lewis as expressing confidence in man's ability to sustain economic growth.

5 Social aspects of population and its control

H. V. MUHSAM

Whoever meditates upon social conditions affecting demographic behaviour and the prospects of its control or the social consequences of population trends and happens to have been present at the closing session of the last, London, meeting of the International Union for the Scientific Study of Population, cannot help remembering Bourgeois-Pichat's remark about what he called 'the present demographic revolution': 'After fertility has passed from the control of society to that of the individual', he said approximately, 'mortality is now about to cease to be the fate of the individual, and society has started to assume the responsibility of deciding who shall survive.' I cannot tell how far Bourgeois-Pichat expected his audience to take this statement in its verbal sense and how far he tried to express vague trends in a paradoxical way. Be that as it may, the thought expressed is worth being explored, if we want to appreciate the societal factor in population trends and control.

Let us start with considering fertility, which Bourgeois-Pichat claimed to escape societal control. How succeeded society in exerting its control on human reproduction, if it did so, indeed, for, say, half a million years of human life on earth? Well, I do not think that I tell you anything new – though some of you may never have looked at the matter in this way; man differentiated himself from his phylogenetic predecessor by imposing what was perhaps the first social control on reproduction: the incest taboo. Later interferences of society with human sexual behaviour had to be carefully circumscribed so as not to impair the power of reproduction.

Whenever they did the procedure was doomed to defeat itself rapidly! Any society which does not fully exploit its reproductive capacity – or at least nearly so – is bound to succumb quickly in the universal struggle of all against all for space under the sun. Thus society had to build institutions which permitted that marriage should be contracted early, that matches could be made for all girls and that subsequently they should be kept in the married state, as far as possible, up to the end of their fertile ages. And men had to be induced to dispense their favours to every and any woman who was capable of bearing children. Thus monogamy was introduced as a rule, and polygamy to take care of problem situations arising often after wars, hunting accidents and other cataclysms affecting the male sex.

This is not the place to enter into a full discussion of the social determinants of fertility in what are widely called 'primitive' societies, and underdeveloped or developing countries. The Davis-Blake analysis of the subject is too well known to require presentation here. What interests us now is whether, indeed, society has lost, is losing or can be expected to lose, control of the reproductive behaviour of its members. To the superficial observer it might easily appear to be so. Marriage is nowadays, in industrialised, or otherwise modernised societies, contracted upon what is assumed to be the free decision of the youngsters concerned, and children are conceived, or their conception prevented, as the case may be, in the privacy of bedrooms, where the couple concerned appear to be the only ones to have a say. I would like, however, to ask myself how the couple concerned arrives at its decision, or more exactly, what fundamentally determines this decision. Is it not their education, formal, i.e. through school, educational broadcasts, etc., as well as informal: youth groups and organisations, motion pictures and entertainment programmes on the radio and the television and finally the example of the neighbours – the Joneses everyone has to live up to – the élite or the 'reference group' as it should properly be termed? And if this is indeed so – what is there left to the free decision of the individual? Even the timing of births, the spacing of children is subject to fashions and thus largely socially determined. Brass concluded, on the basis of profound analysis of birth data in industrialised societies, that the primordial factor in determining an individual birth is chance. If this be true, the next strongest determinant is certainly social constraint of the type of conforming to social norms, fulfilling social aspirations and accepting social expectations.

Thus I cannot refrain from concluding that it is – to say the least – doubtful whether indeed fertility has moved from the realm of social determination to that of free discretion on the part of the individual.

But whereas I found it difficult to agree with Bourgeois-Pichat with respect to fertility, I concur with him widely regarding mortality. Indeed, death used to be the fatal accident, unforeseen and unpreventable, for half a million years of humanity on earth. But things are changing rapidly at present. And if there is any point on which I disagree with Bourgeois-Pichat, it is the period, the point of time, at which I would place the onset of this revolution. I have the feeling that the change started at the moment at which medical science transgressed a certain threshold of efficiency in curative and preventive medicine. You may place this threshold at the time of Pasteur and Koch, of Fleming or of Bernard. In any event, progress was gradual, and it is within this progress, and not through any specific event, that death is becoming more and more a socially determined event. This development is largely due to the interesting coincidence that, when society engaged in a sustained effort to promote the development of medical science, it took the liberty of determining who should have access to medical services. I do not need to remind you that the rich were the ones who were first enabled to afford medical services: as from Farr's classical studies, through Hersch's '*inégalité devant la mort*' to this very day the income differential in morbidity and mortality is the most stable demographic feature in both space and time. With the advent of the welfare state and, in particular, of health insurance as an element of social security being offered to those who, again according to a decision of society, are entitled to this service, the control of a society on health, disease and death has obviously been strengthened. Nowadays, society determines not only who shall have access to medical assistance, but also what kind of service will be rendered to him. The old method of permitting the individual to purchase medical service, or additional medical service beyond the ration apportioned to him by health insurance, obviously still exists, but it is hard to claim that this ' liberty' can be considered as a means of removing societal control from the access to medical assistance and thereby to health and survival.

It should be mentioned that in addition to these social controls which are specific to the circumstances under which health is being promoted in all countries, be they industrialised, developing or underdeveloped, health practices are as much determined by reference group behaviour as reproductive practices have already been shown to be.

Recent developments, particularly in curative medicine, are liable to strengthen the amount of say which lies in the hands of society, with regard to the decision 'who shall survive'. The recent developments to which I wish to refer now are connected either with very expensive treatments such as artificial kidneys or with rare opportunities to perform the treatments such as transplantations which are limited by the scarcity of suitable donors. Once this type of treatment becomes routine, some selection procedure must be developed to decide who shall enjoy the advantage. Obviously society will establish appropriate rules for this selection and supervise the compliance with these rules.

With these last remarks I have passed from the aspect of the impact of society on demographic behaviour and ensuing levels and trends to that of societal control. It is true that by allotting resources to medical services, research, health education and sanitation, society has exerted already for several centuries a certain amount of control on levels and trends of mortality. The present revolution consists of adding to the powers of society that of interfering with the fate of the individual.

This is clearly the position in the field of the control of death. But can we recognise similar trends in the control of births or, shortly, birth control? I think that we certainly can, only the basic socio-psychological situation is here largely different. For good and sane reasons, practically all societies place a positive value on human life and all members gladly accept social policy implying lengthening of life. Societal control acts therefore in the same direction as individual desire. With respect to natality the situation is much more complicated, because among different societies – or different strata within the same society – we encounter nowadays all four possible combinations of concurrent or opposing individual and societal desires; some societies are pro-natalist, while some of their members individually prefer large and others small families, and other societies have made their choice in favour of birth control, while some individuals still prefer to be fruitful and to multiply, and others prefer a small family. I cannot help but repeat that all these preferences are socially determined, although the individual or the group concerned may believe that its personal decision stems from its own economic, moral or religious considerations, its own understanding of national interests, or the traditions of its particular family; all these are basically dictated by society – I have discussed this matter earlier.

The term 'control' assumes therefore in connection with fertility the very special meaning which attaches to the term 'birth control'. It appears, in fact, to be directed against some 'laws of nature', or 'natural' inclinations of human 'nature', while death control appears to be in concordance with nature as well as human aspiration. That I fancy that the desire for individual survival is for men not just an instinct but, at least to some extent, a feature of social norms, is in this context of no consequence for our discussion. But it seems important to repeat that the preference for a certain number, or the order of size of this number, of children is certainly not an instinct but stems from social norms and fashions. The sexual drive is an instinct and it exists in societies and individuals who are not aware of its natural, biological consequences, as well as among those who are trying to avoid them.

Thus the term 'birth control', or preferably family planning, should apply to all situations where conscious attempts are made to determine the number of children born to an individual or a society. We have already discussed, that – and how – society determines the level of natality apparently desired by its members. When we talk now of 'control' we have to discuss the means by which society attains this goal. These means differ obviously in the four cases mentioned before. But before we look at them one after another, one remark may be needed. Society may wish to determine not only how many children shall be born, but also who shall bear them.

Only in the case where both society and individuals desire some kind of maximal number of children, does this latter question not arise. But as soon as either the competent social agency, government or other, decides to curb the number of children or individuals declare a 'birth strike', both questions arise simultaneously and should not be separated: how many children shall be born and who shall and who shall not bear them. It has been pointed out clearly by Kingsley Davis,* and others after him, that most national population policies have no clear aim regarding the ideal numbers of births or birth-rates.

Policies are stated in terms of either desired trends in the birthrate, without determining the ultimate goal, or actions to be taken: so and so many centres to be established, so and so many I.U.D.'s to be inserted, etc. But who will be the subject of I.U.D. insertions, and who is expected to be the clientele of the centres, i.e. who will be helped or induced to bear fewer children, this is a matter of clearly directed choice. In most cases efforts will be directed towards those strata of the population where the invested effort is expected to yield the highest return. This might be areas where population pressure is most strongly felt, i.e. where poverty is strongest, families largest, land resources scarcest – but often the inhabitants of these very areas are, at the same time, most difficult to reach both physically (in terms of transportation and communication) and mentally, because of their very backwardness, illiteracy and inclinations towards prejudice and against modernisation. Thus higher returns are often expected from action directed towards the urban middle class of developing countries, where, in fact, the apparent success of birth control campaigns often reflects partly trends which would have occurred as well in the absence of the campaigns. But this is a matter which is not of major concern to us here. I wanted only to draw some attention to the fact that not enough thought is given to the social implication of selecting the site of family planning centres: is it not at least as crucial a matter of social policy to prescribe who

* K. Davis, *Science*, vol. 158 (1967) p. 730.

shall bear and bring up the children of the next generation, as it is to interfere with the question of who shall survive?

In the case of the 'birth strike', to use again the German term, the situation is different, although the consequences are the same. Here again, the strikers select themselves as those who shall not have all the children they might beget and shall be relieved or prevented from educating and socialising them, and be permitted to take a smaller share in paying for bringing up the next generation.

But whatever the circumstances, as soon as either society or individuals interfere, or try to interfere, with 'natural' fertility society is faced with the social implications of differential fertility. If differential fertility is at least partly a consequence of a national population policy the policy-maker has to assume responsibilities for both causes and consequences of the differentials, and even if there is no such policy and only voluntary agencies or private initiative interferes with natural natality, society cannot escape its responsibility for dealing with its consequences. Finally, I might add that in fact *laissez-faire* is also a policy.

The case of a pro-natalist policy involves a different kind of problem, which I do not wish to discuss in detail here. But it is obvious that nobody has a moral right to encourage couples to have children without offering to the couples and, even more so, to the children all the services: baby clinics, crèches, schools, playgrounds, vacation camps, universities, which these children deserve.

Emphasis was placed on social implications of fertility differentials rather than on levels, because this aspect seems to me to be too often disregarded in demographic research, in establishing population policies as well as in family planning action programmes. It does not imply that the importance of the average level, or the trend of its development, may be disregarded, be it considered to reflect 'natural' circumstances, i.e. the absence of control or its effect. But the sociological reasons of high fertility as well as of the difficulties of controlling it have been mentioned shortly in an earlier context of this paper and extensively by very many authors.

To complete this review of social factors in population trends and its control, a few remarks should be devoted to population distribution and internal migrations as well as to immigration and perhaps to emigration.

Social consequences of internal distribution range from aspects of the organisation of social services, such as schools, medical assistance, etc. in sparsely populated rural areas as against urban patterns, to problems of residential segregation, slum areas, street corner societies and delinquency. Internal migration may alleviate or aggravate these problems, but control of internal migration is rarely used for these purposes. It is true that the clearance of slums is one of the main actions of social reconstruction, but geographical redistribution of the population is rarely a substantial part of such actions. Nowadays societal control is seldom imposed on internal migrations except, perhaps, in connection with residential segregation, in countries or areas in which importance is attached to this matter.

International migration may theoretically affect social conditions in countries of origin as well as of destination. And it is easy to cite striking examples of the fact. But today it is hard to find a country where emigration is large enough to affect social conditions and immigration has such a tremendous impact in the few countries which still absorb mass immigration – Australia, Canada, Israel and a few others – that any short description which I could give here and now would only distort the picture.

The control of immigration, as well as that of emigration, wherever it is practised, is largely aimed at maintaining social conditions as they are, or, in any event, preventing them from developing in certain undesirable directions which it is feared they might take if uncontrolled immigration was permitted. Obviously regulations of immigration – and emigration, wherever this applies – are made in view of the desires and interests of the society concerned. But again, a short discussion of these matters is liable to misrepresent the situation, rather than to throw light on it. On the other hand, it seems that international-relations implications are here more direct than in the fields of natality and mortality. But if this is really so there will certainly be an opportunity to come back to this subject at a later occasion.

May I summarise now my outline by stressing that all demographic behaviour – be it in natality, mortality or migrations – is socially determined and has tremendous impact on social structure and relations.

But this is in fact a tautology: populations form societies and societies are made up of populations. So that if we want to get at the forces which shape populations and determine societies, we cannot limit ourselves to the internal stresses, pressures, actions and relations; we have to look for impacts coming from the outside: climate and soil, economics and politics, anthropology and physical resources. . . . Fortunately, on the one hand, it is not my responsibility to expose these subjects and, on the other hand, other sessions of this meeting are devoted to these subjects.

DISCUSSION

Panel Members: Professor S. P. Cilliers, Professor H. L. Watts, Professor J. H. S. Gear

In presenting his paper to the meeting *Professor Muhsam* added two additional points:

1. If societies are to survive they must balance high mortality with high fertility. Population problems arise when high fertility persists even when mortality has declined.

2. It is necessary to emphasise that education is a further social determinant of fertility. Wherever secondary education exists, fertility declines. However, the interaction between education and fertility is a two-way process. High fertility and the resultant large number of children may impede educational programmes because of shortages of teachers and the inability to finance education.

Professor Cilliers:* 'Although there is no social demographic theory, it is clear that mortality, fertility and migration are affected by a number of variables, such as the stratification of society, kinship and family structure, religion, economic and political organisation, etc. If we view the host of theoretical and empirical propositions developed in social demography about these factors and relate them to the problem of population control, we may link up with the central theme of Professor Muhsam's paper. Societal control of mortality which, according to the paper, is being attained in most parts of the world, developed and underdeveloped, is primarily a function of changes in the structure of the political organisation of society and concomitant differentiation of functions. Put differently, changes in mortality rates and the extension of life expectation are basically a function of the assumption of responsibility for the life of the individual by public authority. The responsibility for creating for each individual the most beneficial opportunity for survival has become the primary responsibility of public authorities.

'The central question is whether this is possible with regard to birth, since public responsibility with regard to death has led to the current population explosion. Professor Muhsam argues convincingly that fertility has not passed from societal control to control by the individual; for the behaviour of the individual in this regard is subject to social norms and institutional control, and society maintains certain conceptions in regard to natality ideals. When these conceptions are expressed in population policy, the lack of a comprehensive scientific social demographic theory is of strategic significance in efforts aimed at practical effects comparable to those attained in the field of mortality.

* Prof. Cilliers submitted this verbatim text of his comments to the Rapporteurs.

'One question which has not been sufficiently stressed is whether the development of contraceptive techniques may not lead to effects on future population trends comparable to those following techno-logical developments which have resulted in a substantial decrease in death-rates. Modern contraceptive techniques have for the first time in history enabled man effectively to divorce his sexual be-haviour from his procreational behaviour. The strategic question, therefore, seems to me to centre around the question as to the cir-cumstances under which man can be expected to subject to rational control decisions in regard to procreational behaviour. In this field contemporary sociological theory on social change and modern-isation may be utilised fruitfully. Demographic changes in the western world over the past few centuries show substantial changes with regard to fertility patterns as a concomitant to the change to what Max Weber called the modern rational bureaucratically organised society. Applying these perspectives to the field of fertility it could be concluded that, while for the present agreeing with Professor Muhsam that fertility has not yet, for most of the world, moved from the realm of social determination to that of free dis-cretion by the individual, this may in future occur in view of recent developments with regard to modern contraceptive techniques.

'In short, with modern contraceptive techniques, procreational activities may become subject to conscious decision-making, the pattern of which would differ vastly between traditional and modern societies.

'In the history of the western world the change from a traditional to a modern rational mode of orientation was part of a general evolutionary process affecting all aspects of life. Since high popu-lation growth-rates mitigate against the large social, cultural and economic changes required to transform traditional societies, the question arises whether one could manipulate this area of decision-making, i.e. that concerned with procreation. I tend to be optimistic that it would indeed be possible, particularly in the case of women. The relief that modern contraception offers women from the perils, drudgery and pain of constant pregnancy and childbearing is indeed tremendous. I would therefore suggest for discussion the idea that birth control can and will be effected, even in traditional societies, if only effective means of communicating modern techniques of contraception, especially to women, can be obtained. In some re-spects this may therefore be primarily a question of communication.'

Professor Watts did not agree that government agencies could control fertility in the same way that mortality was controlled. Although methods of contraception had existed from time imme-morial (however ineffective) a clear distinction had not been drawn between sexual and procreative behaviour. He stated that a change in social norms would have to precede fertility control. Under-developed countries would not accept controlled fertility until industrialisation and the emanicipation of women had occurred. In the absence of such change only tyrannical methods on the part of a government would succeed in controlling fertility.

Professor Cilliers, in reply to Professor Watts, reaffirmed the belief in the possibility of educating people towards birth control methods by establishing new norms and expectations, without having to wait for a minimum degree of economic development.

Professor Gear pointed out that although advances in medical science had extended the life span of many, the reason for the in-crease in population was the tremendous drop in infant mortality caused by improved methods of public hygiene. He also denied that large families were necessary for the purpose of national security.

Dr. N. J. van Rensburg expressed disagreement with Professor Watt's view that industrialisation must precede fertility control. He argued that poverty itself would promote an interest in birth control. He also contended that no state had the right to regulate the individual's procreative behaviour, although the state might try to educate its citizens towards birth control.

Mr. Jean Bourgeois-Pichat pointed out that Professor Muhsam's paper paid inadequate attention to the international aspects of the problem. International governmental organisations and non-governmental organisations (e.g. churches) were also affected by the population problems and were in duty bound to assist in the solution of these problems.

Professor Munger warned that 'have-not' countries might view efforts in support of birth control and pollution control by 'have' countries with suspicion, because they were primarily concerned with solving the 'haves'' own problems. He stated that the import-ance of improving living conditions and human relations in under-developed countries could not be neglected.

Professor Muhsam cautioned that the preferences of societies were determined by their social norms and that this should be borne in mind. *Professor Davies* emphasised the need for rapid birth control, and he warned that the creation of social norms would be outstripped by the population growth itself. *Dr. Piek* said that the role of the family would have to change if fertility were to be successfully controlled.

Father L. J. Smith referred to church attitudes and expressed the view that the present papal position on birth control could not be justified by Catholic theology.

Mr. W. J. P. Carr stated that in South Africa black women

favoured birth control but not their husbands. He expressed regret that the South African Government had refused to allow birth control clinics to be operated for African women in white areas, where they would be most useful. Mr. Carr's view was endorsed by a speaker from the Cape Town Family Planning Association. She pointed out that the most successful family planning clinics were those conducted at factories.

6 National policies for population control

JEAN BOURGEOIS-PICHAT

The subject of this paper concerns the whole of demography. As soon as human beings decided a long time ago to live in groups of households which they called villages, towns, cities, etc., and to establish laws and customs to permit the development of individual life, they had to adopt policies which had, more often than not, a bearing on population growth. Inversely, the demographic evolution led, in the course of history, to the adoption of policies aimed at modifying this evolution. Interrelationship between demography and policies is, therefore, at the very core of human relations. Before coming to the modern shape of policies for population control, it is worth while discussing the case of people living under the so called 'natural' demographic conditions.

INVOLUNTARY POPULATION CONTROL

At this stage, the laws and customs influencing the demographic evolution might be classified into two categories: those having direct effects on this evolution and those affecting it indirectly.

In category one there are, firstly, all the rules adopted for the mating of human beings. All societies have adopted special regulations for the conclusion and breaking of marriages, and these regulations have obviously an influence on the reproductive capacity of the society.

Secondly, there are all the measures modifying the sanitary conditions: public health innovations, sewerage and water supply, and also medical equipment and hospitals. All these measures affect directly the level of mortality.

Finally, regulations concerning migratory movements affect the distribution of population in a territory and, when they are related to foreigners, affect also the number of people.

In category two, the relations between the factors and their effects are not so simple, each factor having generally an effect on all the components of demographic evolution.

Some of the rules concerning the formation of marriages deal with consanguineous unions. It is not rare to find a very high proportion of such unions, as high as 50 per cent, for example. The genetic stock of such populations is inevitably affected by this special way of mating. We do not know very well what can be the consequences on population growth. It is suspected that the capacity of reproduction and the level of mortality are affected, but we do not know in what direction. It is the task of the genetics of population, a relatively new chapter of demography, to study these phenomena.

When a couple is formed, the two parties do not have complete freedom in organising their marital life. This life has to comply with some requirements. First there are physiological restraints. In many societies mothers practise breast-feeding for a long time after each birth. Breast-feeding is linked to ovulation and sterilises at least some of the mothers. This increases the spacing of the successive conceptions and diminishes the reproductive capacity. Breast feeding has also an impact on infant mortality. The mother's milk prevents the child from contracting many diseases. But if weaning takes place too late, there is at that time a danger of high mortality.

Breast-feeding is mainly the result of a general consensus of the population, and one finds a great variety among populations. There are examples of societies living in similar economic conditions which adopt completely different policies about breast-feeding.

There are also in many societies some customs which prevent sexual relations for a while after each confinement. The lack of privacy due to certain forms of family life has the same effects. All these phenomena reduce the reproductive capacity of couples.

Infecundity is another component of this reproductive capacity. Almost every couple is able to have children when the spouses are young, and almost every couple is sterile when the wife is older than 45 years. In the meantime infecundity is gradually increasing. The rhythm of increase varies widely among societies. It seems to depend mainly on the spreading of general illness which itself depends on the degree of freedom given by society to sexual relations, a complete freedom being eminently favourable to such a dissemination. Prophylactic measures, creation of specific dispensaries and, more generally, every improvement of the sanitary conditions, which were listed above as having a direct effect on population growth by lowering mortality, appear here as having possibly also an indirect effect by diminishing the progression of infecundity with the age of the wife. It is probably possible to generalise even further and to say that any improvement in the condition of living, all other things being equal, has the tendency to increase the reproductive capacity of couples. To give only one example, it is certain that a pregnant woman who can rest during her pregnancy has a higher probability to give birth to a live child than a woman who continues her daily life without any modification.

Migration might also have important indirect effects on population growth in the country of arrival. Generally, migrants are people who are not satisfied with the conditions of living of their native country. Having broken their links with the society they left behind them, they feel no more obliged to comply with the laws and customs of this society and they consider they are free to adopt new ways of living. It is particularly easy when the immigrants are colonising new territories. The case of North America is a good example of what can happen. When European settlers began to come to North America, late marriage was customary in Europe and a high proportion of women were remaining single. On the American continent, the immigrants adopted a new pattern of marriage for almost everybody. Their reproductive capacity was therefore greatly enhanced. In addition, they found in their new territories an improvement in their conditions of living, and the favourable effects mentioned above on the infecundity of couples took place. The immigrants in North America were more fecund than the people staying in Europe.

CULTURAL AND MORAL IMPLICATIONS

It is essential to note that all these 'policies' affecting population growth were not established purposely for that aim. Even those influencing directly the course of demographic evolution, as for example the laws and customs relating to the conclusion and breaking of marital unions, were not all imposed in order to curb or to accelerate the growth of population. Transmission of property by inheritance, religious beliefs, as for example the necessity of having at least one son to take good care of the cult of the ancestors, and more generally a good organisation of the daily life in the household, including in particular a division of labour between male and female, were among the reasons leading to the necessity of having laws and customs for family formation. It was still more true for policies having an indirect effect on population growth. Their effects were not even known by people. They have been discovered only recently by demographers.

Another characteristic of all these 'policies' is that they have a tone of moral value. Not only did people accept the policies but they considered it was good to follow the rules and bad to transgress them. It was not so much a question of legality or illegality but rather a question of good or evil. This remark is important because we will see later that 'policies' aiming at population control in the modern sense will raise also some ethical problems. But before coming to modern times, it seems worth while to say a few words on the quantitative effects on population growth of the various 'policies' we have just reviewed. Let us say to begin with that these effects were very important.

AN ESSAY IN MEASURING THE QUANTITATIVE EFFECTS OF INVOLUNTARY CONTROL OF POPULATION

Table 6.1 summarises in quantitative terms the effects on fertility in five different cultural patterns of the past. The last column corresponds to the biological maximum, and comparison of one given pattern with this maximum permits us to estimate the extent of control of fertility achieved by the various 'policies' which are the constituents of the pattern.

On the first line, the length of the childbearing period is the difference between 50 and 15 years, i.e. 35 years. It is evidently the same for all patterns and for the biological maximum.

These 35 years cannot all be used for procreation because biological factors cause sterility. 6·6 years are lost for this reason. This is only a rough estimate. In fact, the progression of sterility with age for biological reasons is a phenomenon that biologists do not know very well. The data given in table 6.1 correspond to the lowest sterility so far observed in a group of human beings: the French Canadians of the eighteenth century. It has been assumed here that the sterility of French Canadian people was due only to biological reasons. It was probably not completely true and 6·6 years must be considered as a maximum.

Additional years are lost due to various factors indicated here under the general denomination of 'poor living conditions'. Variations from one pattern to another are very important: 3·5 years for the United States in the eighteenth century and 15 years in today's Black Africa south of the Equator.

Finally, a certain number of years are lost for procreation due to marital customs. Here again the variations are great, only 2·4 years in Black Africa south of the Equator where almost everybody gets married at an early age and 14·4 years in Sweden in the

TABLE 6.1 Determinants of 'natural' fertility according to various cultural patterns (assuming that there is no mortality between 15 and 50)

Determinants	French Canadians (early 18th cent.)	U.S. (18th cent.)	Sweden (mid-19th cent.)	Black Africa south of Equator (present time)	India (present time)	Bio-logical maximum
Childbearing period 15 to 50 years	35·0	35·0	35·0	35·0	35·0	35·0
Reducing factors:						
(a) Sterility due to biological causes (years)	6·6	6·6	6·6	6·6	6·6	6·6
(b) Infecundity due to poor living conditions (years)	0·0	3·5	3·5	15·0	6·8	0·0
(c) Loss of fecund life due to marital customs (years)	8·7	8·1	14·4	2·4	3·1	0·0
Total of reducing factors (years)	15·3	18·2	24·5	24·0	16·5	6·6
Fecund life remaining for procreation (years)	19·7	16·8	10·5	11·0	18·5	28·4
Average interval between successive births (years)	2·0	2·0	2·5	2·5	3·0	2·0
Complete family size (number of children)	9·9	8·4	4·2	4·4	6·2	14·2
Gross reproduction rate	4·83	4·10	2·07	2·14	3·03	7·00
Approximate crude birth-rate rate (per 1000)	66·0	48·0	32·0	33·0	45·0	82·0

mid-nineteenth century where many people remained single and where marriages took place at a relatively old age.

Finally, the number of years remaining for procreation goes from 11·0 to 19·7 compared to a biological maximum of 28·4 years.

Another component to be taken into account is the interval between successive births which varies from 2 to 3 years.

By dividing the number of years used for procreation by the mean interval between births, one obtains the complete family size. By multiplying it by the proportion of females at birth (0·49), one obtains the gross reproduction rate and, finally, the approximate crude birth-rate.*

Two conclusions can be drawn from table 6.1, particularly from data on the last line:

(a) Fertility control was achieved with great efficiency in the past due to the adoption of various 'policies' not aimed at this purpose.

(b) The results varied widely according to the various cultural patterns. Starting with a maximum biological crude birth-rate of 82 per 1000 the reality varies between 32 to 66 per 1000.

It has already been said that the demographic evolution of the French Canadians and the population of the United States in the middle of the eighteenth century gave a good example of the indirect effect of migration on fertility. Quantitatively the effect can be estimated as follows: In table 6.1, the case of Sweden can be considered as representative of western Europe in the past. It is therefore obvious from table 6.1 that European immigrants to North America (U.S. or Canada) had adopted a pattern of life different from the European way of living. They married earlier, they reduced the interval between successive births and, at least for Canada, they reduced the risk of infecundity. In leaving Europe the immigrants to North America were really adopting a new pattern of life. The decline of fertility in North America until the middle of the nineteenth century was mainly due to the return to the old European pattern.

It is more difficult to measure results obtained in controlling mortality. The agricultural revolution was probably a decisive step in this respect. Before it, the expectation of life at birth was very low. Numbers around 20 years are generally given by demographers. After the agricultural revolution, when the new way of life was well established, numbers around 30 years were quite common. The gain was important for population growth. First and quite obviously, population increased much more rapidly than before. It is probably at the time that the human species took real possession of vast regions of the earth.

But another consequence was the possibilities of appearance of diversified cultural orders. With an expectation of life at birth of 20 years, societies were obliged to have a very high fertility in order to survive. All the years fitted for procreation had to be used and

*The birth-rate is said to be approximate because it depends not only on fertility level but also, to a lesser extent, on mortality level, and the values given here correspond to an average level of mortality (expectation of life at birth equal to 50 years).

there was no place for 'policies' permitting some of these years to be lost. For example, patterns of life such as the European one represented by Sweden in table 6.1 could not exist in the pre-agricultural world. It became possible after the agricultural revolution. Societies have therefore built up through time various 'policies' which achieved an efficient control of population. But how have these societies passed from policies achieving population control to policies *for* population control? This is what remains to be seen.

WISHES AND NEEDS

To understand how the change took place it is worth while to consider a little why a society adopts a policy on a given subject. A society is composed of people accepting to live together, this way of living permitting them – at least this is what they think – to reach their goals more easily than if they were living alone.

These goals have not the same urgency. There is first a whole set of wishes that each individual would like to see becoming a reality. He knows that every wish cannot be fulfilled immediately. He is even ready to accept that some of these wishes are closer to the world of dreams than to reality. In this realm of desire, the individual does not wait for policies.

Another step is taken when a wish is so widespread among people that it becomes recognised as a need for each individual. It is the task of society to frame policies permitting the satisfaction of this need.

An action on population growth may then appear necessary for facilitating the satisfaction of the need, and policies for population control have to be adopted accordingly. Let us look at an example: betterment of living conditions of people in developing countries became so sought after by individuals after the Second World War, that these countries had an urgent need of economic development. To fulfil these needs, it very soon appeared that population growth was an obstacle, and some countries adopted policies aiming at fertility control. At this stage population control is not pursued in itself. It is practised as a means of reaching another goal. It is not generally the only factor to be taken into account for reaching this goal and it may not receive a high priority. For example, communist countries considered for a long time that it was much more useful to change the whole organisation of the economic system than to adopt birth control policies. They even considered that birth control would appear unnecessary as soon as the Marxist economic system was applied.

THE PASSAGE TO HUMAN RIGHTS

A much more explosive situation emerges when the wish, turned into need, is suddenly raised to the level of an individual right. The situation is explosive because people consider that the characteristic of a right is that it be exercised without any delay. Of course everybody knows that rights compete with one another; but it is precisely the task of the society to settle the conditions permitting the exercise of the various rights. For each right the society has to devise and to adopt a 'policy'.

The promotion to the level of a right demands of course that the condition necessary for exercising it appears feasible to the individuals. It would be unrealistic to claim that each individual has, for example, the right to choose the size of his family, if the mechanism by which this goal can be reached is not known. If it is so, it can be a wish, or may be a need for easing the economic development, but certainly not a right.

A right is also an entity which evolves in the world of values. It is good to help somebody to exercise his right: it is bad to hinder him. A right involves therefore inevitably some ethical implications.

In the example of policies mentioned above, the rights which were behind them were not related to demographic events. This explains why these policies were not for population control in itself, even if they had an effect on population growth, and we have seen that this effect was important.

Policies will be for population control in itself when the right they intend to regulate deals with demographic events.

THE RIGHT TO HEALTH

The first right of this kind which has been recognised in modern time is probably the right to health.

The recognition has been linked to the progress of medicine. It is obvious that it would be impossible to claim this right for each individual if medicine had remained what it was two hundred years ago. For a long time it has been a wish. To achieve a certain goal, it became later on a need. Economic development, for example, needs people in good health. It became a right when people had the feeling that good health could be reached by everybody. Societies were then obliged to adopt policies aiming at the exercise of the right. From this moment the human species considered that one of its goals was to fight against illness. And policies were gradually adapted for controlling one component of population growth: mortality.

In reaching the category of rights, the fight against illness took place in a new world: the world of all or nothing, the world of values. A virtuous man has to be virtuous in every respect; if he fails only once, he is no more a virtuous man. Similarly, a right can not be suspended and everything must be done to prevent it from not being exercised. This is the fundamental difference between a right and a need. The latter can be fulfilled to a certain extent, the former is a totality. Policies must, of course, first settle the conditions permitting the exercise of the right. Here society will build hospitals, organise the production of medicine, the teaching of medical art. But it has also to provide a way of dispensing treatment free of charge, or at least at a cheap price, and social security schemes are created. Policies must also solve difficulties which may arise when the right to health comes into conflict with other rights. Such conflicts are not rare. A social security scheme, for example, limits the exercise of the right to freedom. Everybody must be included in the scheme. They have no choice to accept or to reject it. In the name of the right to health, policies will also impose vaccination. Enlarging the concept of health and passing from physical to mental health, it has been sometimes argued that for a good equilibrium of mental health of the family, the number of children must be limited and some countries have adopted for that reason policies on birth control. But here again the control is not pursued in itself, it is only because it facilitates the exercise of the right to health.

More generally when a society claims a right, it has the secret feeling that this right will be exercised by people. Moreover, it is almost ready to consider that people ought to exercise the right and this is the source of new problems.

Let us look at a great smoker who has been informed that he takes the risk of getting cancer and who continues to smoke in spite of this warning. Is society obliged to give him the benefit of expensive treatment when he comes later on to be cured? The same is true for alcoholics. Most societies – i.e. each individual – are paying for illness due to over-consumption of alcohol, but what about mental illness in which the sick person does not bear the same responsibility as do those suffering the consequences of tobacco and alcohol? A question is inevitably asked.

Is the right to health equal for everybody? 'Maybe not' is the reply of today, and if the reply is negative, new policies will have to decide who will be treated and who not.

We used above the word 'expensive', and this notion of cost will raise new problems. When a society decides that every individual has the right to health it is assumed – probably unconsciously – that the amount of time spent by healthy people to enable sick persons to live would not reach a level compromising other basic requirements of life. To say this in monetary terms, it is assumed that the cost of treatment of sick people would not exceed a certain level. Medical techniques are becoming more and more expensive and the time is not far off when it will be no longer acceptable to give to anybody the benefit of the most modern treatment. A policy will soon have to be decided upon as to who will die and who will survive. On what criterion? It will be one of the most difficult problems which will confront us. We are now no longer in the world of science and technique. We are faced with a moral issue.

THE RIGHT TO CHOOSE THE SIZE OF THE FAMILY

Another right which has been claimed only recently by society and which deals with demographic events is the right for a couple to choose the size of the family. The situation is here more complex. The right is given to the couple and there is obviously place for a conflict if wife and husband do not agree.

In the past there have always been couples wishing to have less or more children, but as with many other desires they had no effective means of fulfilling their desire. Later on when it was realised that high fertility was an obstacle to economic development, the need for birth control policies became more and more obvious. But reducing fertility was not the only condition needed for helping economic and social development. Many other requirements were necessary and policies aiming at curbing births did not always receive high priority. For example, investment and formation of people appeared very often more profitable, and this position was reinforced by the relative inefficiency of the means available for contraception.

Then technical progress in contraceptive methods, popularised under the name of the pill and I.U.D., gave the feeling to society that mankind had finally at its disposal a real means of controlling fertility. Time was ripe to proclaim the right for women to choose the number of their children. This was done in 1968 in Teheran at the International Conference on Human Rights convened by the United Nations to commemorate the Human Rights Year.

And here again the simple recognition of this right changes completely the nature of the various problems involved. Here are some of the consequences which followed: first, governments could no longer avoid adopting policies on fertility control. The exercise of the right had to be regulated. Many countries follow this course, and soon countries without policies in this matter will be considered by the various international organisations as violating a basic human right. They will be condemned by other nations and threatened with sanctions.

At the same time the United Nations Organisation which thus far has been reluctant to take part in action programmes for fertility control will not have any reason to continue to adopt such an attitude. Moreover, from now on action programmes must be part of its activities. The Catholic Church itself accepts the new right; it only disagrees on the means to be used.

But all the consequences of the recognition of the right to family planning are far from materialising. We are only at the beginning, and there is much more to come.

First it has to be pointed out that family planning can be exercised in two directions. We generally think of people willing to reduce the size of their family, but there are also people who want great families.

To put efficient contraceptive devices at the disposal of people is not enough to permit them to exercise their rights. Let us consider a couple who want an additional child but who live in a flat too small for having this additional child. If one gives to this couple a contraceptive device to prevent the arrival of the child, one does not really give them the choice. If really the couple has the right to choose the size of their family, they must have the choice between contraception and a larger flat, and policies will have to be adopted accordingly.

Another right recognised by society is the right to justice, and the concept has been extended to social justice. In a market economy the monetary signs are given to the labourer in exchange for his work for himself and his family. The salary received corresponds to an average size of family, and it follows that people having a family larger than the average have a lower level of living than people having a family below the average. This is considered as socially unjust, particularly when the right to choose the size of the family is proclaimed. This choice, if it is really a choice, cannot have as a consequence the lowering of the level of living for the family, if a large family is desired. The logic of the system implies consequently the creation of family allowances and fiscal taxation taking into account the number of children.

When a right is proclaimed by a society, one must also recognise the right of the authorities in charge of the common good to make propaganda in order to influence the choice of individuals, if these authorities consider that certain choices would be damaging for the common good. In developing countries, for example, it is advantageous for the society as a whole that couples should choose to reduce the size of their family. But it might not be so in industrialised countries. In both cases society must have the right to favour small families in the first case and larger families in the second one. But this must be done without preventing a free choice. Persuasion is the only way to be used.

It was different before the proclamation of the right, when lower fertility was considered useful or even necessary to achieve economic development. It was then possible to impose some policies without paying too much attention to the individual opinion. But as soon as the right to choose the size of the family is proclaimed, policies must be settled more carefully than before. Each time individuals receive rights, society has less freedom.

POLICIES FOR POPULATION CONTROL. AN ESSAY IN MEASURING QUANTITATIVE EFFECTS

It is time now to examine what can be the quantitative effects on the population control of the exercise of the right to health and the right to choose the size of the family. Two centuries of fighting against illness gave spectacular results. In the most advanced countries, the expectation of life at birth passed from 30 to 75 years. Many countries have not yet reached the upper value, but nothing seems to prevent them attaining it in the near future. Some gains are still feasible beyond 75 years, but it seems however that without any drastic new discovery the human species is approaching a limit. We may hope that the limit will be provisional, but we cannot foresee how long it will take to pass beyond it.

On fertility the forecasts are more difficult. It is of course possible to imagine a population in which couples do not want any children. But even in countries where birth control is practised extensively, couples want children. What they want is to avoid having too many. Many surveys have been made in industrialised countries in order to find out the wishes of couples regarding the size of their families. On the average couples want to have a little more than 2 children. This corresponds to a crude birth-rate a little higher than 13 per 1000 just equilibrating the crude death-rate and leading therefore to a stationary population.

But it is not certain that the opinion of today will be the one of tomorrow. Time may come when the size of the family is determined in the same way as the consumption of goods: the higher the income, the larger the size of the family. Some signs of such a tendency appear already in the United States. It is difficult to know in these circumstances what the average size of the family wanted by a couple would be. It may well exceed the net reproduction on one level and then lead to a population increase creating difficulties in the long run. Society would then have to limit the exercise of the right to choose the size of family, as it is about to do for the right to health. Here again societies will be confronted with moral issues.

MORE RIGHTS TO COME

The right to health and the right to control fertility are not the sole human rights dealing with demographic matters. The right to work, the right to leisure and the right to retirement which are mentioned in the universal declaration of human rights have obvious direct bearing on the economically active population.

A right which has not yet been proclaimed but on which discussion has already begun, will have more insidious effects: the right to choose one's own economic activity. The right to free circulation of people is another example. Policies are in the making to organise the exercise of these various rights.

Conflict with certain goals of the society has been foreseen for the right to health and the right to control fertility. With the additional rights just mentioned the conflicts are already there. Rapid economic development is more often than not incompatible with full employment, early retirement, short daily working durations and long vacations. Conflict will still be more drastic with the right to choose one's own profession.

INTERNATIONAL OR NATIONAL POLICIES

Translation in a given cultural environment of universal individual rights into policies is not static. The policies vary inasmuch as environment varies. It follows that policies must be national. The rights are common to all, but each cultural pattern conceals its genuine policies.

Ethical issues raised by the practical application of these policies have also to find their solution in each environment. Here the problems are the same for all but the solutions inevitably differ.

Policies concerning population control do not escape the common rule. They ought to be national.

CONCLUSION

National policies for population control will therefore appear gradually in all societies. It is part of the logic of the world system. We have explained that there is a danger of the policies rebounding and threatening the individual rights they are supposed to support. In each case a moral issue is raised. It seems we are touching here a crucial problem for the future of the human species. Mankind seems to be relatively well equipped for solving the technical problems encountered on the road of evolution. It does not appear prepared to deal with moral issues.

DISCUSSION

Panel Members: Professor D. Haylett, Dr. E. Higgins, Dr. B. J. Piek

Professor Haylett said that as a biologist he found himself in agreement with Mr. Bourgeois-Pichat on the importance of involuntary controls of population. He had doubts, however, regarding the 'rights' of which Mr. Bourgeois-Pichat had spoken. These were man-made and flexible, and depended on community acceptance. The only 'rights' he could regard as fundamental were:

1. the right to preserve the species, and
2. the right to avoid death.

He suggested the possibility of controlling fertility in subtle and indirect ways by modifications in various aspects of a population's living conditions, rather than by the simple application of birth control methods, whether voluntarily or by force. He felt that the developed countries should aid the developing ones to achieve internal adjustments, but felt it necessary to warn that policies should not be based on 'generalisation', i.e. that particular communities should shape their policies according to their own particular situations. The South African population, for example, was heterogeneous, and a general policy for all groups was unlikely to succeed.

Dr. Higgins said that no rights existed absolutely. All rights of the individual, for example, were limited and circumscribed by social rights. Regarding population, specific planning was needed rather than philosophical speculation, and he for his part regarded 'policies' as deliberate enactments by authority, and found the use of the word by Mr. Bourgeois-Pichat confusing. Population policies should be national rather than international, and he was in favour of large-scale government assistance in family planning in South Africa, especially for the underprivileged. Voluntary agencies could not compete with a deliberate government policy, and it was duty to posterity that should weigh with authority, rather than short-term considerations. Population problems were not purely 'economic' or 'demographic', but more widely socio-political.

Dr. Piek thanked the main speaker for raising issues of fundamental importance, and for drawing attention to associated moral questions such as the criteria to be applied regarding medical services and the numbers of children people might have. He was grateful to Professor Haylett for drawing a distinction between fundamental and man-made rights. Mr. Bourgeois-Pichat had not sufficiently emphasised that obligations were always implicit in rights. Rights, he said, were always counterbalanced by duties.

Professor W. Brand commented that rights and obligations generally went together, and he was convinced that those who advocated rights would also in the course of time advocate obligations.

He said that it was unfortunate that Mr. Bourgeois-Pichat had not introduced into his paper the distinction between 'rich' and 'poor' countries. This was so because rights and duties could not simply be interpreted in universalistic terms without regard to the different circumstances in 'rich' and 'poor' countries. The rights formed the basis for demands which could simply not be realised in developing countries. Professor Brand asked whether it was not a preferable course to stress family planning policies worked out by individual countries to suit their particular requirements.

Professor J. D. J. Hofmeyr said he heartily endorsed the principle that population control policies should be nationally determined to take account of differences within particular nations. Although aid had a role, he felt that sight should not be lost of the self-respect of the receiving states.

Professor J. L. Sadie said he wished to raise the pertinent question of how successful national policies had been up to the present time. The answer was important, because if national policies were successful a great deal of the need for international aid would fall away.

Mr. Bourgeois-Pichat, in reply to Professor Sadie, said that there were not many countries which had launched national policies – some 10 or 15 – and so far minimal success had been achieved. The reason he felt had to do with contraception. Up till now the forms of contraception proposed took little account of local circumstances. But new methods would change this.

Father L. J. Smith felt that one aspect which was missing from the papers which had been read, and the discussion thereof, was the psychological.

Mr. Knowles-Williams said two factors in his opinion were contributory to an explosive situation in the world. The first was the resentment experienced by developing countries of the developed nations, and the second was 'the revolution of rising expectations'.

Professor Davies raised the question of implementation. He said it was easier to enunciate policies than to implement them. The lack of success of existing policies he said was due not to contraception, as suggested by Mr. Bourgeois-Pichat, but due to the planning involved. Who enunciated the policy and who applied it were more important than the actual form of birth control employed.

Dr. Higgins, in reply to a point raised regarding the responsibility of governments, said that he was completely pragmatic in his approach to governments. It mattered little whether the government was democratic or a minority government. He assumed such

E

government would consult scientists and proceed, for example, with family policies. In the final analysis, however, the authority lay with the politicians.

Professor M. H. H. Louw said that, in discussing the matter of rights in relation to population control, one had to remember that procreation was a personal act. What governments could do, he said, was to establish incentives and disincentives. Governments might, for example, start by defining an 'optimum population'. What the structure of such an 'optimum population' was nobody knew, but it would certainly be a dynamic thing. For example, the 'optimum population' of the seventies would not be the same as that for the eighties. Returning to the question of rights, Professor Louw said this was a very complicated matter. He pointed out that parents were taking decisions for persons who would have rights of their own. There was also the fact that rights were stated in individualistic terms. But was it not possible to have differentiated rights, for example between men and women?

Professor Haylett wound up the discussion with the observation that there appeared to be a positive attitude towards birth control. He reasserted his belief that the fact that rights had obligations should not be lost sight of; and, secondly, that national policies were preferable to international policies, because the former could be suited to particular national circumstances.

7 International migration

C. A. PRICE

INTRODUCTION

In view of the general theme of the Conference this paper pays little attention to matters outside the effects of the population explosion on international relations, though such matters usually loom large in discussions of international migration. First, this paper says little about demographic problems of measurement, analysis and lack of comparability between national statistics. It is sufficient to note that statistics are often deficient (France, Canada and the U.S., for instance, keep no comprehensive records of emigration), frequently contain cumulative errors (as in Europe where countries of emigration tend to underestimate loss and countries of immigration tend to overestimate gain),[1] and invariably require careful interpretation (as in Australia where statistics show 3590 'former Italian born settlers departing' 1959–69 whereas closer study suggests at least 38,000 such departures, or nearly 25 per cent of Italian settlers arriving). It is most unwise to relate published migration statistics to statistics of population growth, food production, gross national product and the like without careful examination to see whether the migration statistics really mean what they suggest, and are strictly comparable between countries.

Second, as the population explosion is primarily a post-war phenomenon, this paper touches only briefly on the migrations of earlier centuries and decades; it is sufficient here to note that these were predominantly movements of Europeans to the Americas, Africa and Oceania, with lesser movements of Chinese and Japanese to other parts of Asia, the west coast of America, and parts of Oceania and Brazil, and of Indians to Malaysia, Africa and smaller countries such as British Guiana, Mauritius and Fiji.

Third, the paper pays little attention to post-war migrations which, though important in themselves, are not closely related to the population explosion. Notable here are refugee movements. Though the 1,039,000 refugees moved by the International Refugee

Organisation, 1947–51, and the 850,000 more moved by I.C.E.M. (Intergovernmental Committee for European Migration) 1952–70, covered most European refugees, some still remain in Europe while over 30,000 new ones appear each year asking for resettlement. (To these should be added nearly 1,000,000 persons repatriated to France from Africa.) Similarly, though many of the 25,000,000 Asian refugees of 1945–56 (Indian–Pakistan 12,000,000, Japanese 5,000,000, Koreans 4,000,000, Chinese 1,500,000, Arabs 1,000,000) have been resettled – with the notable exception of the Arabs – many more have appeared: 1,000,000 in Vietnam, 60,000 Tibetans, 675,000 Jews (now settled in Israel) and an unknown number in Laos, Cambodia and other parts of south-east Asia. In Africa numerous refugees exist, in and from many African countries, estimates ranging from 1,500,000 upwards. In Latin America, Cuban refugees are still moving to the United States and Spain while uncertain political conditions in several Latin American countries make further refugee movements likely and sudden. All such movements, though political in origin, represent considerable shifts of manpower and skill but are not closely related to the population explosion, except perhaps in places such as Hong Kong where the population has increased from about 1,000,000 before the outbreak of the Second World War to some 4,000,000 at present, largely by refugee immigration.

The other form of international migration having little connection with the population explosion is the growing movement of professional and skilled 'wanderers'; persons in the academic, commercial and highly-skilled worlds who take jobs for a few years in one country and then move on to another, maybe returning to their country of origin for retirement having spent part of their working life in anything up to a dozen different countries. This movement, which operates mainly between highly developed countries, is almost impossible to measure as it is statistically inseparable (except by special survey) from two other movements – the brain-drain from developing countries and the brain-loan to developing countries – which are both closely connected with the population explosion. All we need say here is that the 'wanderer' movement is considerable and important, reflecting easier exchange between academic and scientific institutions and the spread of international concerns with policies of moving trained managerial and technical personnel between those countries wherein they have branches or subsidiaries.

Other current migrations are much more directly connected with the population explosion and they, and the international relations connected with them, are the main concern of this paper. Before tackling them, however, it is necessary to emphasise certain matters referred to in other papers but which have particular relevance to international migration. First, the population explosion, and the pressures on resources deriving therefrom, are much more severe in some places than others; much more so in the developing countries of Asia, Africa and Latin America than in Europe, North America, Australasia, Japan or other places with relatively well-developed economies and well-established practices of population restriction. Second, though internal redistribution of population can provide relief for some countries it cannot help small overcrowded countries such as Malta, Hong Kong, Singapore, Mauritius, the Netherlands, Puerto Rico. Moreover, developing countries still possessing relatively empty territories do not use internal redistribution as much as they could. Both the Philippines and Indonesia, for instance, have seen some movement from the overcrowded to the emptier islands, but not on a scale sufficient to solve the basic problem. Third, the most effective solution, industrialisation, is limited in many developing countries by scarcity of capital, management and skill and by restricted access to overseas markets. The governments and peoples of such countries, therefore, not unnaturally sometimes turn their attention to the possibilities of emigration; this, after all, being the traditional method of relieving severe population pressure, as with the small habitation districts of Greece which, since Classical days, have periodically eased mounting population pressure on resources by colonisation in Africa, Asia and Europe or by less formal resettlement in more distant parts of the world.

EMIGRATION PROVIDES SLIGHT RELIEF FOR POPULATION PRESSURE

Sometimes such emigration takes place quite easily, as between Malta and Australia, or between parts of Latin America and the United States, and the international relations involved are usually amicable and comfortable. At other times countries under pressure find emigration prevented or curtailed by the restrictive immigration policies of other nations; international relations may then become raw and angry, as sometimes between Australia and the Philippines.

In general, emigration from countries with severe population explosions is relatively slight, partly because so many neighbouring countries are in the same situation and impose severe restrictions on immigration (thus Singapore, Malaysia, Thailand, Hong Kong, Taiwan and the Philippines have policies which restrict permanent settlement to the overseas-born families of citizens and to very small quotas of other aliens)[2] and partly because countries able to absorb immigrants are of a different ethnic composition and have, for longer or shorter periods, implemented immigration controls designed to preserve that ethnic composition; as with Australia, Canada, New Zealand, South Africa, the United Kingdom and the United States, and their historic policies of favouring European immigration.

In practice some of these countries have lately been easing their restrictions against non-Europeans, especially since the 1940s. New Zealand officially abolished all racial discrimination in immigrant control, 1944–52, until now entry rests entirely with the discretion of the Minister for Labour and Immigration, theoretically to be exercised on the grounds of economic and personal suitability. In practice this discretion limits the number of non-Europeans entering the country (except for natives of Western Samoa, the Cook Islands and other favoured Polynesian islands, now totalling some 2,000 a year) and Asian immigration has risen from a net gain of 400 a year 1959–63, only to 800 a year, 1966–9.

Australia, though reluctant to change its traditional 'White Australia' policy too rapidly, has in practice been admitting considerably more non-Europeans. In 1949 the government allowed wartime refugees from Asia and Oceania to remain permanently and in 1956 allowed non-Europeans to become naturalised and bring in families. Restrictions on persons of mixed blood were eased in 1964 and in 1966 non-Europeans with special skills, or who had been earlier in Australia and shown their ability to 'integrate' with native Australians, were allowed in for permanent residence. As in New Zealand, conditions of entry are not laid out by statute but rest with the discretion of the Minister of Immigration; a system which not infrequently causes public outcry both in Australia and Asian countries of origin because the principles upon which the Minister decides any one particular case are not always clear. Nevertheless this discretion has been so exercised that net gain of non-Europeans, principally Asians and Eurasians, has risen from 4500 a year, 1958–62, to 12,500 a year, 1967–9 (this includes a substantial increase in immigration from Lebanon and Turkey from 400 a year, 1958–62, to nearly 3000 a year, 1967–9).

Canada also eased its restrictions in the late 1940s, later made bilateral agreements with India, Pakistan and Ceylon and then, in 1962, abolished all racial discrimination in favour of a system of giving priority to persons with needed skills and to the close relatives of Canadian citizens. This last, however, produced such an influx of unskilled relatives that in 1967 the government decided to restrict free sponsorship to wives, children and aged parents, and to allow sponsorship of other relatives – close or remote – only if these attained certain standards of skill and education. The 1962 policy change lifted non-European immigration substantially: Asian immigration rose from 3500 a year, 1959–62, to nearly 20,000 a year, 1966–7; West Indian immigration from less than 2000 to 8000 a year; and Latin American from less than 1000 to 2500 a year. It is too early, however, accurately to assess the policy change of 1967.

The United States whittled away its exclusionist policy from 1944 onwards, until the new immigration law of 1965 abolished all racial and other quotas in favour of a system of priorities based on skill. This, plus special measures to help Hong Kong, resulted in an increase of Asian immigrants from 21,000 a year, 1959–65, to 59,000 a year, 1967–8. There was also some increase in immigration from Polynesia and Melanesia, presumably much of it from American Samoa, but little increase in immigration from Africa, excluding the United Arab Republic. Traditionally, the United States has always been kinder to Latin American than to other non-European countries. Even so, the effects of the new policy are noticeable: Mexican immigration has risen from an average of 28,000 a year, 1959–60, to 43,000 a year, 1967–8; Central American and Caribbean (excluding Cuba) from 8500 to 35,000; South American from 11,000 to 19,000; and Cuban, with special provision for refugees, from 7500 to 70,000 or so.

The exceptions to this easing of restrictions on non-European immigration lie principally in the United Kingdom and South Africa. The latter feels unable to increase its non-European element, already growing rapidly by natural increase, still further by immigration. The United Kingdom, having tried to maintain its tradition of free entry for all British nationals, was compelled by public unrest at the large number of arrivals from the West Indies, India, Pakistan and Africa – reaching 60,000 or so in 1960 – to pass the Commonwealth Immigrants Act 1962–5, which restricted entry to visitors, students, new settlers with employment vouchers and the wives and children of resident settlers. With this, and restrictions on the entry of aliens, the net migration of non-Europeans has now fallen to 15,000 or so adult males (1969), but 30,000 or more women and children are still arriving to join their menfolk already established.

These various policies, and their modifications, are at present enabling traditional countries of settlement to absorb nearly 350,000 persons a year from the developing countries of Asia, Africa and Latin America. Though this is not nearly enough to hold the population explosions, it does provide some relief, especially as most immigrants are of young working age, i.e. the very persons who would not only be seeking jobs in their own countries but would also be producing children, so adding to the strain on the resources of the country of origin. Moreover, the emigration is selective and eases the strain for certain places more than for others. Small countries such as Hong Kong, the Cook Islands, Jamaica, Barbados and Puerto Rico have undoubtedly found some relief through such emigration, as have certain districts, within larger countries, which have long traditions of emigration and a steady drain of families abroad, as for instance parts of the Gujarat and Punjab provinces of India.

Though restrictive immigration policies have often caused international friction they have rarely caused a major breakdown in international relations. The truth is that countries most anxious for emigration, and therefore potentially most resentful of restrictions against their nationals abroad, normally have stringent restrictive policies themselves; as with Asian countries anxious to see further easing of Australian restrictions. Indeed, some such countries have occasionally taken steps not only to prevent the influx of further numbers of their own ethnic minorities, but also to encourage many of them to leave; as for instance the Sinhalese with their Tamil minority, the Indonesians with their Chinese minority, the Malays with their Chinese and Indian minorities and so on. Arguments rarely arise, therefore, on the principle of restriction but rather on the particular form of restriction (for instance, complete exclusion on racial grounds where numerical controls or education, age or occupation would be acceptable) or on the administrative procedures (unreasonable separation of families, for instance). In practice it is plain that one reason for Canada, Australia, New Zealand and the United States easing their restrictive policies has been their awareness of foreign annoyance at the rigidity of the policy or the mode of administration; but the concessions have been relatively minor, and in accord with changing attitudes in the countries themselves, and in no sense a surrender of the sovereign power to control immigration.

The main case in recent years where it might be argued that a restrictive policy caused a major diplomatic quarrel was the United States' exclusion of Japanese in the early twenties – after the Japanese, disposed to look upon the United States as their elder brother and leader into the modern world, had been carefully observing the 'gentleman's agreement' on migration between the two countries. Some have argued that Japanese fury at this 'loss of face', at this unnecessary 'betrayal', was a contributory cause of Pearl Harbor.

EXPLOSION IN REVERSE

The general picture, then, is one where most countries of population explosion find little relief through emigration, mainly because other countries cannot or will not take immigrants in sufficiently large numbers. There is however one curious reverse effect, viz. in Australia where wartime fright at the attempted Japanese invasion has continued as a strategic fear of the exploding Asian populations to the near north; this fear, together with a desire to develop resources, has led most Australians to favour increasing their own population as rapidly as possible, if necessary by planned immigration. Since 1945, therefore, Australia has aimed at a population increase of 2 per cent a year, 1 per cent by natural increase and 1 per cent by a net immigration brought about by a vigorous programme of recruiting and assisting new settlers.

In the long run the programme has achieved slightly less than this, over the mid-year period 1947–9 averaging a net immigration of some 87,600 or 0·88 per cent a year. Because of a steady loss of native Australians, about 8000 a year, net settler migration has been higher, 95,700 a year (2,105,600 in all, over 60 per cent of whom have been assisted with passage costs by the government). These two million souls, together with their children born in Australia, have provided well over half the country's 4,716,000 increase from 7,580,000 in 1947 to 12,296,000 in 1969; at present one Australian in five is either a post-war settler or the child of one.

The ethnic composition of this considerable influx has changed every few years. Over the whole period, 1947–69, about 43 per cent have been of British stock (now netting some 70,000 a year, 1968–9), 11 per cent German, Dutch and Scandinavian, 15 per cent eastern European, about 25 per cent southern European, about 3 per cent other Caucasian (U.S., etc.) and 3 per cent non-European. This represents a considerable shift from Australia's pre-war emphasis on British immigrants but, with the exception of Malta, the Netherlands and Greece, is providing little relief for countries of high population pressure.

The international relations involved have been relatively easy. Apart from formal migration and settlement agreement with international agencies such as I.R.O. and I.C.E.M. (of which Australia has been a contributing member) and the United Kingdom, Germany, Italy, Malta and the Netherlands, Australia has had informal migration agreements with Austria, Belgium, Greece and Spain (through I.C.E.M.) and special agreements emphasising employment rather than settlement with Yugoslavia and Turkey.

Main points of disagreement have been Australian reluctance to recognise overseas trade and professional qualifications or provide reciprocal social services but here, as European migrants have become scarcer, Australia has had to make concessions. These agreements and discussions involve considerable international negotiation and it is interesting comment on the importance of immigration to Australia that some overseas posts have been opened by migration officers and only later staffed with full consular and diplomatic personages.

In a sense South Africa's re-entry to the field of immigration since 1965 reflects the same fear of being overwhelmed by large numbers of non-European populations round about. Present net intake is about 25,000 Europeans a year, including families from Canada, Australia and the like.

EUROPEAN MIGRATIONS

Population explosions in Europe are, generally speaking, much less severe than elsewhere. Nevertheless parts of the continent, notably Spain, Portugal, southern Italy, Greece, Yugoslavia and Ireland have long suffered pressure of population on resources. Industrialisation and internal redistribution (as between southern and northern Italy) have eased some of the pressure but considerable relief derives from emigration of two kinds: emigration to traditional countries of settlement overseas and internal migration within Europe itself.

The three major countries of settlement overseas are now Australia, netting over 80,000 or so Europeans a year, Canada, netting perhaps 100,000 a year and the United States, netting perhaps 100,000 a year. (These last two figures are rough estimates as emigration statistics do not exist.) South Africa, netting some 25,000 a year, and New Zealand, netting less than 10,000 a year, are less important, as are now the countries of Latin America. (In the early fifties Latin America was netting some 185,000 Europeans a year but this fell away sharply during the sixties until in 1969 it was probably less than 5000.)

This European emigration overseas, still averaging over 350,000 a year net, consists primarily of persons intending or contemplating permanent settlement abroad; hence the relatively large number of women and children. There is however a substantial minority who either return to Europe or migrate on to other countries: Canada, Australia and New Zealand lose between 15 per cent and 25 per cent of gross settler intake and the United States probably between

10 per cent and 15 per cent. In recent years (1967–9) the main countries of emigration have been: the United Kingdom, over 130,000 a year; Italy, over 50,000; Greece, nearly 30,000; Yugoslavia, over 20,000; and Spain and Portugal, about 25,000. Dutch emigration has fallen to less than 10,000 a year but German emigration, though relatively slight now to Australia and Canada, is still maintaining an appreciable level to the United States, perhaps 25,000 a year in all.

European migration within Europe is rather different, and more difficult to estimate. A recent analysis suggests that during the period 1960–6 Germans gained nearly 230,000 Europeans a year, France 77,000, the Netherlands 3000, Belgium 17,000, Switzerland 43,000, Sweden 15,000, and the United Kingdom 23,000 a year: conversely Italy lost nearly 65,000 a year, Spain 85,000, Portugal 25,000, Greece 33,000, Malta 2000 a year, Yugoslavia 23,000 and Ireland 15,000 a year.[3] Moreover, the census figures show very high masculinity ratios (for instance, 844 males per 100 Italian females in Germany in 1961) and numerous men separated from their wives (57,000 such Italian husbands in Germany in 1961).

From these statistics three things are clear. First, that there has been a large-scale movement of single men, or married men leaving families behind them, to take advantage of extensive industrialisation in north-western Europe. Second, most of these men derive from the less developed areas of southern Europe and Ireland. Third, families desiring permanent settlement abroad prefer remoter continents, and here persons from the United Kingdom are as prominent as those from southern Europe. In other words the areas of population pressure in southern Europe are finding relief by both long-term emigration overseas and short-term migration within Europe while British families prefer more permanent settlement overseas, leaving their jobs and homes to be taken by Irish, West Indians and Asians.

The international relations arising from these movements, though complex and detailed, rarely produce basic difficulties. In Europe itself, countries within the Common Market normally have reciprocal social service agreements and encourage private industries to provide adequate accommodation for single men, with regular paid holidays home, or adequate quarters for married workers with families. To some extent Spanish, Portuguese and Turkish workers, while not in the Common Market, benefit from similar arrangements. One bone of contention here is citizenship, the Swiss practice of requiring 15 or so years of residence before naturalisation being obnoxious to some immigrants familiar with the shorter periods of residence required elsewhere.

THE BRAIN-LOAN AND BRAIN-DRAIN

Clearly connected with the population explosion is the temporary loan of skill and management by developed countries to those countries suffering from rapid population growth. Indeed one of the essential parts of international and national schemes of assistance to such countries is that gifts and loans of equipment and capital be accompanied by persons trained to use and manage them. Additionally there are persons with capital, entrepreneurial experience and technical skill who are quite willing to leave their well-developed countries and settle permanently in a developing nation if opportunity is given for capital gain and job security.

Developing countries are well aware of their need for such skill and experience but usually oppose permanent settlement, partly through suspicion of 'neo-imperialism' and partly because they want such jobs and rewards to go eventually to their citizens. Thus Singapore, Malaysia and the Philippines all encourage 'pioneer industries', by taxation and other concessions, but all take strict measures to ensure that local talent is given first choice of suitable jobs and that when foreign skill and management is required it comes in under temporary permit only.[4]

It is difficult to assess numbers here and, even more so, the outcome. In general it seems that while international and national assistance programmes are little affected by such controls the inflow of private talent and capital is considerably handicapped; in this sense slowing down industrialisation and that method of controlling the population explosion.

The reverse movement – the brain-drain from developing to developed countries – is better known. The United States is the major attraction here, drawing nearly 450,000 professional and technical persons 1947–67, many from countries of population pressure. Official statistics of immigrants by occupation show that in recent years the United States has been drawing over 7000 professionally and technically skilled persons from Latin America each year, about 2000 from southern Europe and some 6000 from Asia.[5] Canada has also been drawing appreciable numbers, 1000 a year from Latin America, for instance, while even remoter countries such as Australia have attracted some; the 1966 census showed 10,000 professional and managerial Asians resident in Australia. The United Kingdom has drawn heavily from India and Pakistan, about 25,000 such persons during 1962–5 alone,[6] while France, Germany and other western European countries have attracted from Africa as well as Asia.

Unfortunately accurate statistics do not exist, partly because such settlers are included, both in census and migration statistics, with skilled persons intending to return to their country of origin or to join the growing bank of international 'wanderers'. There is no doubt, however, that the drain is considerable.

Frequently, it is argued that such a loss aggravates the effects of the population explosion as developing countries are losing precisely those persons best able to help with industrialisation, administration and population control policies. This oversimplifies the problem. First, some developing countries have been overproducing skill in terms of jobs available; hence the recent efforts of the United Arab Republic to persuade Canada and Australia to take its temporary surplus of young specialists (agricultural scientists and so on) and the inability of Colombo Plan countries such as Indonesia always to find jobs for engineers returning from training in Australia. Second, the attractions of life in highly developed countries are inevitably great, not only because of higher living standards but because there exist so much more specialised and sophisticated equipment, so many more knowledgeable colleagues, all of which greatly increase a skilled person's chances of professional advancement. Third, such migration is exceedingly difficult to control, and here we enter once more the field of international relations.

On one side are the developing countries, most of whom dislike trying to restrict the emigration of their skilled citizens, partly because it lays them open to charges of unprecedented and illiberal actions and partly because it is difficult to enforce without restricting temporary movement. On the other side are the countries of settlement, most of whom dislike imposing controls on the admission of skilled persons from developing countries, partly through fear that they be accused of racial or other discrimination. Thus Australia for long justified its insistence that non-European students should return to their countries of origin, on the grounds that they were needed there, only to be accused of doing so simply to stop the permanent settlement of Asian families. With countries such as Japan, Singapore and Hong Kong, which have periodic surplus of certain skills, the accusation has point but with many other countries the Australian case has merit. Lately Australia has eased its restrictions somewhat, not primarily because of international pressure but because internal attitudes have been changing and also it could see that many of its former Asian students did not return to settle in their homelands but took jobs in Canada and the United States. It is highly doubtful whether countries of settlement will ever impose controls on skilled immigration simply to save developing countries the trouble of restricting the emigration of local talent. The problem is clearly one for international negotiation, but is unlikely ever to produce major international friction.

SECONDARY EXPLOSIONS

There is one curious by-product of international migration: the temporary transfer of population explosions from developing to developed countries. A classic case here is Japanese settlement in California, 1890–1920, when the introduction of numerous women and children, with higher fertility patterns than those of native Americans, caused a rapid growth of American-born Japanese and American fears of being 'out-bred' by the 'yellow men'. Though demographers have shown that such fears were groundless – in that immigrant populations composed largely of young married couples are bound to have a relatively high crude birth-rate, and that before long the Californian Japanese began to adopt American family patterns – public outcry was great and played some part in the exclusion of the Japanese from the American immigration quotas of 1924. A similar situation may well be developing in the United Kingdom where there is evidence of relatively high fertility among Pakistani and West Indian settlers.[8] This may well cause public fear of a 'coloured fertility explosion' in the United Kingdom, further race friction and strong demands for further immigration restriction.

CONCLUSION

Here we must end this necessarily sketchy survey of complex international movements. The main conclusions are, first, that while migration between countries is occurring on a considerable scale it is more between countries of relatively high development than from countries experiencing population explosions; i.e. the populations that have most to gain from large-scale emigration have the least predisposition or opportunity to emigrate. Second, it is clear that while existing migration involves much international discussion it is not, in itself, a major international issue. Third, it is unlikely that migration will, in itself, ever become a major source of international friction, at any rate so far as the population explosion is concerned; the sovereign right to control immigration is as important to countries of population pressure as to countries of settlement, and they will not lightly surrender it. If trouble comes it will be on side-issues (rigid exclusion as opposed to controlled intake) or in particular places, as when a powerful country thinks that it can with impunity force a weak neighbour to accept immigrants; but here it will be political opportunism, not general principle. In short, international migration is clearly related very closely to the population explosion; but there are few signs of it becoming as yet a key matter in international relations.

Notes

1. Edith Adams, *International Migration Trends Affecting Europe in the 1960's*, I.U.S.S.P. Conference (London, 1969) A9.1 p. 2.
2. R. T. Appleyard, *Immigration Policies and Economic Development in South-Eastern and Eastern Asia*, I.U.S.S.P. Conference (Sydney, 1967) pp. 799–800.
3. Edith Adams, op. cit., p. 14.
4. R. T. Appleyard, op. cit., pp. 802–3.
5. The Committee on the International Migration of Talent, *Modernization and the Migration of Talent, A Report from Education and World Affairs* (U.S., 1970) pp. 24–7.
6. C. A. Price, *International Migration*, Proceedings of the I.U.S.S.P. Conference, (Sydney, 1967), p. 126.
7. Dorothy Thomas, *The Salvage* (University of California, 1952).
8. E. J. B. Rose and associates, *Colour and Citizenship, A Report on British Race Relations* (Oxford University Press, 1969) p. 113.

DISCUSSION

Panel Members: Professor B. J. Roux, Professor H. P. Pollak, Dr. C. J. Jooste

Professor Roux said he agreed with the following points raised by Professor Price:

(*a*) In view of scarce resources less developed countries would like to get rid of their least skilled individuals, but these are precisely the individuals not wanted by the developed countries. Conflict often arises as to which persons governments are prepared to accept and which they refuse.

(*b*) Migration between homogeneous countries is the least problematical.

(*c*) At present international migration cannot offer a solution to the population pressure of individual countries. Population problems should be tackled on the spot and cannot be exported.

He disagreed with Professor Price on the following points:

(*a*) The brain-drain is an important loss to the developing countries. The developed world should not rob the developing countries of the 'cream' of their populations.

(*b*) It would be preferable if Professor Price could have identified the '... other forms of migrations [that] are more directly connected with the population explosion ...' more clearly, and if he could have dealt with them separately.

(*c*) The statement '... the most effective solution, industrialisation ...' should be qualified. It is not industrialisation that is needed in the L.D.Cs; certain types of industrialisation can create problems. In addition Professor Roux pointed out that the relationship between migratory labour and international relations needed more attention. In Rhodesia and South Africa, for example, where large numbers of foreign workers were found, uncontrolled migration could have serious effects on international relations. Ideology might interfere where migratory labour was present, and could create resentment. In Ghana with its 2·5 million persons of foreign nationalities, the policy changed from *laissez-faire* to one of expulsion. Changes like these could evoke retaliation and could lead to border incidents and friction between countries.

Professor Price replied that

(*a*) he agreed that migratory labour should receive more attention;

(*b*) the 'other current migrations' he referred to were actually those discussed later in his paper; and

(*c*) the 'brain-drain' did have important effects on the countries of origin, but it was difficult to see how it could be controlled.

He also pointed out that sensible industrialisation was the best solution there was to the problems of over-population.

Dr. Jooste underlined Professor Price's view that international migration could not be seen as a remedy for the over-population problem of less developed countries. The main problems remaining were those of the distribution of food resources and industrialisation. Ideally the migration of skilled labourers should be beneficial to both the country of origin and the receiving country. Less developed countries, however, would have to be fairly developed in order to 'export' people, and by the time they were, they usually tended to restrict emigration.

It had to be remembered, he said, that countries should solve their own population problems and solve them nationally. No nation could plan the use of its resources fully if it had to rely on foreign manpower. Migratory labour was frequently used to supplement the existing labour force, but this type of labour was a less stable part of the working force. Furthermore, a reduction in migratory labour might have international repercussions. In recent times, countries with fewer restrictions had modified their policies to become more restrictive. He differed from previous speakers in that he felt the 'brain-drain' not to be a very significant factor.

More attention, he felt, should be given to the problem of assimilation. Immigrants usually did not cut the bonds with their native countries, and this implied that strains could arise in the receiving country.

Professor Pollak stated that international migration had come to mean the reshuffling of qualified workers from one part of the world to another. Current policies had the advantage of careful selection, and this would lessen problems for future generations.

Professor Pollak added that international migration could create international tensions. This had occurred in the relations between the Republic of South Africa and India over the treatment of Indian nationals, and tension had arisen also over the present expulsion of Asians from Africa. She emphasised, too, the impact of migratory labour on international relations. There were, for example, 650,000 foreign Africans employed in the Republic of South Africa, and cordial relations should be maintained between the Republic and the countries from which these migratory labourers originated.

Professor Pollak commented on the dichotomy which frequently existed between government attitudes to migratory labour, and those of the people in the receiving country. She cited Switzerland as a country in which the government favoured migratory labour, but the Swiss people in a plebiscite voted for restricted use of such labour.

She considered that refugee problems warranted further discussion, as they often create further long-term international tensions.

Professor A. F. K. Organski said that although international migration was not in the forefront of international politics today, it would be so in future. Selective and ethnic migrations would in future create problems in international relations.

Professor Roux concluded the discussion by stating that there was a consensus of opinion that international migration took place on a small scale, and that it could be helpful to certain countries. Through international migration new ideas could be disseminated in less developed countries, but it could not serve as a permanent relief to population pressures. Migratory labour could be regarded as a lifeline between developed and less developed countries, but both migratory labour and international migrations could create tensions.

8 International economic and financial implications of the population explosion

STEPHEN ENKE

SUMMARY

Much international trade and its associated international payments are based on comparative population differences. Differences in population 'density', as reflected in different ratios of available labour force to existing usable land, result in different factor prices, hence different product prices and hence different international trade movements. A less obvious cause of trade is differences in population growth-rates, and especially in fertility rates, as these last affect the age distribution of the population and labour force, the relative availability of capital again, and resultant per capita incomes. Per capita income differences in turn occasion different rates of saving, as represented both by domestic capital accumulations and net export balances. Moreover, nations with high fertility rates cannot compatibly aspire to high rates of improvement in per capita income, so that if they borrow abroad for their economic development they are less likely ever to repay these debts. While high fertility often results in high population density, especially in lands of ancient culture, this is not always so. Moreover, while the public recognises that high population density can sometimes be a cause of poverty, it less clearly recognises that high fertility is always an economic handicap regardless of the relative availability of natural resources.

BASIC DEMOGRAPHIC-ECONOMIC RELATIONS

Among the nations of the world, as among classes of people within a country, low per capita incomes tend to be associated with high human fertility, both as cause and effect. This relationship is more universal than any occasional relationship between population density and human poverty. (And the typical personal poverty that results from high fertility rates affects international trade and finance patterns in ways described later.)

The high fertility rates of less developed countries (L.D.C.s), reflected in crude annual birth-rates as high as 40 or even 45 births per 1000 population, are no longer matched by almost as high crude death-rates. These last have been falling to levels of 20 and less per 1000.[1] Consequently, rates of natural increase of 2·5 per cent a year are not uncommon in the L.D.C.s, resulting in a doubling of population every 28 years.

Viewed very approximately, a doubling of population (P) every 28 years would not *depress* per capita incomes if the gross national output of goods and services (V) were to double also in the same time period.

Such a doubling of V, neglecting the 'state of art' (technology) temporarily might well occur if the national stock of capital (K), the national employed labour force (E), *and* available national resources including arable land (R), were all to double also within 28 years. But 'land' as defined by economists is in fixed supply and cannot ever double. Hence, R being fixed, K and E must more than double (still forgetting technology) if V is to double.

The size of E unfortunately does not depend only on the size of the available labour force (L). There is a greater tendency for involuntary unemployment (E < L) the smaller is the stock of K relative to that of L. An increase in the K/L ratio not only tends to raise the E/L ratio towards unity, but also raises the marginal product of labour, because workers become better equipped with labour-saving devices.

Nor is the ratio of L to P a constant. On the contrary, and most importantly, a decline in age specific fertility rates has the demographic effect of making the age distribution less young. A country with a crude birth-rate of 4 per cent or more a year may have 40 per cent or more of its population under 15 years of age. While these children are certainly consumers, they hardly count as producers. Thus a reduction in fertility causes the work-age population (e.g. age 15 to 55 years) to increase relative to the child dependent population (e.g. under 15 years).

Hence if E/P is to increase, with E more than doubling say in 28 years, it is necessary that fertility rates decline and/or that savings from gross national product are sufficient to more than double K in 28 years.

A doubling of K within a given time period requires more annual aggregate saving of course as K itself increases. In some L.D.C.s current K is so low relative to V that rather small investments, whether borrowed from abroad or saved at home, would meet the requirement. Thus, if K is and remains twice V, a 5 per cent rate of saving from V each year will double K in 28 years if V also doubles in this period. Considering usual situations, such a doubling of K seems altogether feasible, which would maintain the E/L ratio.

The value of a nation's annual saving, and hence its domestic investment, unless it transfers funds abroad on loan account, is probably related positively with its V and negatively with its P. Thus, as between two nations with the same V but very different Ps, one would expect the smaller P country to have larger aggregate annual savings (S). Other things being equal, high fertility rates reduce savings rates, and retard real economic development.

However, even if E and K doubled exactly in the 28 years of our example, this would not be enough to prevent a fall in V/P if 'land' natural resources (R) became scarcer with twice as much P, E and K existing in the country. If R is scarce and becoming scarcer, there must be diminishing returns to E and K taken together. A doubling of E and K will not result in a doubling of V – unless technology comes to the rescue.

In many L.D.C.s it is a slow but steady 'modernisation', or improvement in technology (T), that enables the standard of living to improve, as reflected in an increasing V/P, even though R cannot and E can barely keep pace with P. This technology factor is hard to estimate. But it is probably enough to permit a given stock of E and K to provide from 0·01 to 0·025 greater value of goods and services each and every year.

These basic relations existing within a nation have been described elsewhere in more detail and schematised after the manner of figure 8.1. They have been programmed for a computer and the resultant TEMPO model has been applied to a number of advanced and less developed countries. In all cases a decline in specific age fertility rates contributes significantly to the rate at which V/P improves annually.[2]

L.D.C. ASPIRATIONS AND 'DEVELOPMENT' BORROWINGS

The above analysis suggests why it is that most L.D.C.s – *all* of which have high fertility rates and population growth-rates associated with their poverty – cannot expect more than very modest annual improvements in their V/P ratios. As a result, most seek and many receive transfers of funds, as so-called development loans and grants, from the more advanced countries. In a few recent years

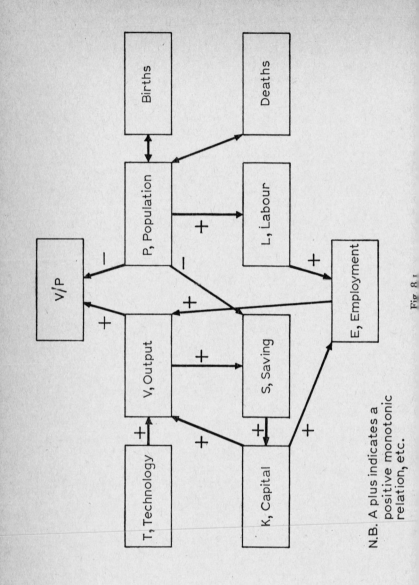

Fig. 8.1

N.B. A plus indicates a positive monotonic relation, etc.

such official transfers have approached 10 billion dollars a year. These capital transfers, and the merchandise flows they record, are due to 'development' needs that essentially have their source in differential poverty. The cause and effect of this poverty are high fertility and natural increase rates.

The 'need' for such assistance, in the form of domestic capital investments, is greatest where L.D.C.s have high fertility and natural increase rates and economic developments are incompatibly ambitious. Many L.D.C. governments and peoples expect and demand improvements in income per head of 5 per cent and more per year. What the achievement of such aspirations means, in terms of foreign assistance in capital accumulation, can be calculated by a demographic-economic model programmed to reflect the interactions depicted in figure 8.1.[3]

Thus table 8.1 is based on calculations for a representative nation called Developa, which has an initial population of 10 million and an initial income per head of $200 a year. For *each* of several *constant* aspirations, i.e. annual improvements in income per head, there are shown: (1) the number of years before the international capital flow reverses, (2) the total debt including accrued interest at

TABLE 8.1 L.D.C.'s need to borrow and ability to repay (for different aspired rates of G.N.P. per capita improvement)

Aspired annual growth, in G.N.P. per capita	Year when repayment of principal can begin		Year when loans completely repaid		Maximum debt when repayment begins (c) (millions)	
	Fertility		Fertility		Fertility	
%	High	Low	High	Low	High $	Low $
1·2	3	(b)	5	(b)	12	(b)
1·5	8	3	12	5	98	16
1·8	18	6	23	9	506	100
2·0	32	7	45	11	2038	174
2·2	(a)	9	(a)	14	(a)	300
2·5	(a)	13	(a)	20	(a)	674
2·8	(a)	18	(a)	28	(a)	1502
3·0	(a)	22	(a)	40	(a)	2680
3·2	(a)	(a)	(a)	(a)	(a)	(a)

(a) Debt never repaid.
(b) No foreign debt required.
(c) As compared with an initial G.N.P. of $2000 million.

the date of reversal and (3) the number of years before all debt service is completed. The essential contrast between a Developa with 'high' fertility (which means no change in the present gross reproduction rate of 3·025) and a Developa with 'low' fertility (which means a reduction in gross reproduction rate from 3·025 to 1·479 during the initial 25 years).

The relations summarised in table 8.1 assume Developa to have a labour output elasticity of o·6 (so that o per cent more employed labour occasions 6 per cent more G.N.P.) and a capital output elasticity of o·35 (so that 10 per cent more capital stock means 3·5 per cent more G.N.P.). The productivity of labour and capital increase by 1·5 per cent a year because of exogenous improvements in technology. The nation's annual savings equal 20 per cent of its G.N.P. less $30 per head of population. Interest on outstanding foreign loans is at 4 per cent compound a year. At time zero there is a zero foreign indebtedness. *All* of the proceeds of foreign loan debts are supposed to be translated into *net* domestic capital investment.[4]

There is a variable and implicit grace period in that loans are repaid exactly to the extent that domestic saving exceeds the necessary domestic investment to maintain the stipulated annual improvement in per capita income.

In all cases a high aspiration rate of V/P improvement means more assistance, and a longer delay in completing debt service when this is feasible. Thus a 2 per cent annual improvement in V/P means total accumulated borrowings of $2·038 billion (or 1·02 times initial V) with high constant fertility, as against $0·174 billion (or 0·087 initial V) with a declining and eventually lower fertility. A more ambitious improvement goal would require foreign capital assistance in amounts that could never be repaid with or without interest by high fertility Developa. This is because there is never a sufficiently high V, and hence domestic savings, to provide the ΔK needed to maintain an annual 2 per cent improvement (and meet current interest changes on the outstanding foreign indebtedness).

Also significant is the inability of the high fertility country to increase its V/P by more than 2 per cent a year with the help of foreign assistance it can *repay*. The declining or 'low' fertility country can legitimately attain a 3 per cent rate. This is because it can repay borrowings that accumulate to a maximum of $2·68 billion.

The above calculations, combined with still other circumstances, explain the difficulties some L.D.C.s will have in repaying with interest the development loans they have received directly and indirectly from western Europe and North America. Rescheduling of debt service has already been necessary for several L.D.C. borrowers. Prospects for more general defaults in the seventies are ominous.

A great deal of multi-national and national lending has been for 'infra-structure'. Much of this infra-structure is of a kind that provides services free of charge or at subsidised rates. As a result the real worth of roads, bridges, sewers, canals, airports, etc. cannot usually be determined. Thus a lot of unsound investments have probably been financed on the easy and unverifiable rational of so-called 'external economies'. In other words, the loans have resulted in legal obligations for debt service, but not in capital assets of commensurate productivity.

It may be supposed that the productivity of particular development loans does not really matter because they are underwritten by the government of the borrowing L.D.C. And such governments have taxing authority – but in local currency only. Can there be (1) enough domestic economic saving plus (2) enough increment in export earnings to finance and transfer these debt service obligations?

The record of high fertility L.D.C.s in promoting exports is not encouraging. For many of them the ratio of exports to gross national product (V) is declining. This is especially so where there is high population density also.

Incentives for some L.D.C. governments seriously to attempt external debt service are diminishing. In a few cases the yearly flow of new loans is no longer greater than the opposite flow of debt service. Also, the internal political sanctions of not taxing voters to repay foreigners not being exactly serious, the temptation to default on payments becomes considerable.

During recent years development grants and soft loans, some of the latter with long grace periods, have tended to replace hard loans. In effect these grants, financed by the taxpayers of advanced countries, have facilitated continued service on hard loans owned by governments and *private* investors. But how long hard loans and grants will be made after grace periods on soft loans expire, and there are some defaults, is surely questionable.

The ability of L.D.C.s with high fertilities and population densities to save and transfer debt service adequately, quite apart from their willingness to do so, appears increasingly doubtful.

CLASSIFYING NATIONS BY DEMOGRAPHIC CHARACTERISTICS

For purposes of economic development and international trade analysis, the discussion above suggests a gross demographic classification of nations, on the basis of two characteristics. First, and most important but less obviously so, is human fertility as represented by gross reproduction rates.[5] The second is population density, or the size of population relative to usable natural resources.

With these characteristics a 2 × 2 classification yielding 4 cells can be used, namely:

	High Fertility	*Non-High Fertility*
High Population Density	(1) 'INDIA'	(2) 'JAPAN'
Non-High Population Density	(3) 'BRAZIL'	(4) 'CANADA'

With each of these four cells the name of a prototype nation appears in quotation marks. Instead of 'India', the country in Cell No. 1 could have been China, Pakistan or the island of Java. Instead of 'Japan', the country in Cell No. 2 might have been the Netherlands, Belgium or even the United Kingdom. Instead of 'Brazil', almost any other Latin-American or sub-saharan country would have served as well. Australia, and perhaps the United States even, could be a substitute for 'Canada'.

TRADE PATTERNS AMONG NATIONS BASED ON DEMOGRAPHY

The effects of demography on trade patterns should not be exaggerated, for much else also determines what goods and services countries export or import. Climate is clearly of great importance, as it affects what can be grown, besides influencing the health and resourcefulness of peoples. Geographic location is important because it influences the transport costs that exports and imports must pay. The existence or absence of exchange controls and other government restrictions has for some countries been an important factor ever since the Second World War. Nevertheless, with these *caveats*, human fertility and population density affect trade patterns in several ways already touched upon.

The most pervasive effect of high fertility rates upon international trade patterns is through its association with poverty. Countries with high specific age fertility rates tend to have low per capita incomes. And from this many consequences flow.

The most striking is probably the relative scarcity of capital and superfluity of labour that result, with extensive unemployment in industry and underemployment in agriculture, and hence low wage rates. Moreover, the labour that is employed tends to provide little more than muscle power, because it is so often poorly equipped with capital. Thus countries with high fertility tend to specialise, in so far as they engage in international trade at all, in labour intensive productions, the exact nature of these products depending on climate, exploitable mineral reserves, location, etc.

People who are poor have a different consumption mix than people who are not. Food and clothing feature more predominantly in the budgets of poor families and nations. Hence high fertility countries are less likely to export food (unless they have a very marked comparative advantage) and are more likely to import it (given purchasing power). This tendency is especially marked if high fertility is also associated with high population density, as in 'India' compared with 'Brazil'.[6]

Nations with high fertility rates have relatively 'young' labour forces that are not very experienced. Moreover, because poor countries can afford less technical training of their youngsters, their employed labour forces tend to have limited applications. These are the countries, especially if land densities are not too high, that export sugar, coffee and tea, semi-luxury products that are labour intensive and cannot be grown by the advanced countries well outside the tropics.

ADDITIONAL FRUSTRATIONS FROM HIGH FERTILITY

L.D.C.s are not only frustrated because of their inability to improve V/P by domestic capital accumulation. They also resent the trade patterns that seem to be 'imposed' upon them by neo-colonialism. They find themselves unable to educate their children so that their labour forces can compete through exports having a scientific or technical base and content.

Much resentment over international trade patterns takes the form of allegations about worsening terms of trade. Spokesmen for L.D.C.s not unreasonably would prefer their countries to have more varied exports. But more varied exports often require a more varied domestic consumption mix, which requires more income per head, which in turn requires a reduced fertility. Many exports that suffer relative price declines depend on cheap agricultural field labour. Through international commodity markets, young and poorly trained workers of different L.D.C.s compete to their own disadvantage. What attracts attention all too often are such obvious consequences as low export commodity prices. But fundamental causes, such as high fertility and population density, usually escape attention.

These same countries' governments are well aware of the importance of general and technical education. Many of them have grandiose education programmes. Nevertheless, although the percentage of school-age children in school is increasing in most L.D.C.s the absolute *number* of children *not* in school is probably *increasing* throughout the so-called 'Third World'. The education authorities cannot provide enough extra teachers and schoolrooms to keep pace with the increasing number of children.

Poor countries tend not only to be minor participants in world trade, as distinct from richer countries having similar-sized populations, but they also find it more difficult to develop net exports for a 'favourable' current account.

One reason is that a positive (favourable) current account ordinarily indicates that purchasing power is being lent abroad. This foreign investment has its source in domestic saving. And, as between two nations with the same gross national product, the one with the larger population will usually consume more (including some imports) and thus save less.[7]

When fertility rates are *not* high, the situation is very different, even when there is serious population density. The higher per capita incomes that a lower fertility permits result in more schooling and technical training. Scientific management is combined with industrial labour that is well disciplined and relatively cheap because there is an insufficiency of land to provide a significant agricultural alternative. Thus 'Japan' can export high-technology items in exchange for raw materials and food imports.

Major food exporters, actual and potential, are countries with low populations relative to cultivatable land, a high technology and capitalisation, and often locations in the temperate zones. Their technological productivity in agriculture tends to increase rapidly too. For these and other reasons it is the 'low fertility with low density countries' that most significantly provide others with wheat, rice and other food grains.

Thus high fertility rates, especially when combined with high population density, have many adverse international trade and lending implications. Participation in world trade is lessened and the choice of practical exports is reduced. Development loans can be productive but high fertility occasions credit unworthiness. High fertility and associated poverty erode an L.D.C.'s potential gains from being part of a world economy. The fundamental remedy is reduced human fertility through voluntary but effective birth control programmes.

Notes

1. Crude death-rates in L.D.C.s are almost as low as in advanced countries, despite higher specific age mortality rates, because of the relatively 'young' age distributions that result in L.D.C.s from their high fertility rates.
2. 'Birth Control for Economic Development', in *Science* (16 May 1969), and 'Effect of Fewer Births on Average Income', in *Journal of Biosocial Science* 1 (1969) 41–55. In these models a modified Cobb-Douglas aggregate production function has been used to represent the domestic economy. Typically employed labour and capital elasticities of output have approximated 0·6 and 0·35 respectively.
3. This programme is available through TEMPO, General Electric Center for Advanced Studies, located in Santa Barbara, California.
4. In reality there can be substitutions, with an L.D.C. releasing more foreign exchange for consumption import and taxing less to achieve public savings, because of hard currency borrowings from abroad for specific domestic capital investments.
5. The gross reproduction rate is the number of live births women who survive their childbearing years will typically have.
6. However, in the case of clothing, mass production economies and relative absence of arable land may lead to exports of cloth, shoes, etc., to neighbouring countries that may be equally poor but have lower populations densities.
7. The exception to these statements is to be found among nations that have significant exploitable assets – very often minerals – or which by virtue of climate perhaps have a special ability to grow or produce (rather than extract) something for which there is a real export demand (often in the advanced nations). Development loans, including private investments, are then usually made and in time repaid. This 'colonial' pattern of financing and trading continues for good and sound reasons. The countries thereby 'exploited', and which often experience obvious economic development as a result, tend to participate actively in international trade, and later evolve export surpluses, although they may have high fertility rates and even high population densities.

DISCUSSION

Panel Members: Professor L. H. Samuels, Professor C. de Coning

Professor Samuels agreed that an increase in population could offset or more than offset, the contribution to economic prosperity which all the factors could make, whether created by technical progress by the discovery of new natural resources, by economic aid from abroad or by the removal of foreign trade barriers.

In countries where fertility rates were high, a large proportion of savings must be allocated to supplying the increasing population with houses, 'infra-structure', machinery, stocks of goods, etc. On the basis of Kutznets' and Goldsmith's empirical investigations, one might guess that the investment needs of a 2 per cent yearly increase in total employment would amount to 5 per cent–10 per cent of the gross national product (a considerable part of net investment in countries such as Australia and South Africa). In countries with a fairly stagnant population (e.g. Sweden) nearly all of the net saving increased the capital per unit of the working population and should, therefore, result in increasing productivity and higher standards of living.

Professor Samuels felt however that Dr. Enke had overstated the importance of high fertility rates, and considered that a useful distinction could be made between population increases due mainly to a decrease in infant mortality without an improvement in health at a later age, and increases due to better nutrition (for all age groups), better education, better sanitation, etc., which enabled children to survive to a healthy and productive adult age.

He furthermore criticised the lack of definition of 'less developed countries'. Were these countries which were poorly endowed, or were they countries, however poor at present, which had good potential prospects of either supporting the present population on a higher level of living, or of supporting larger populations at a not lower level of living? The second definition Professor Samuels considered the more sensible; it included all countries with future potential regardless of whether they had high or low present per capita incomes.

He felt Dr. Enke should also have paid attention to domestic policies which made some countries poorer than they needed to be. Among such policies Professor Samuels mentioned the inflationary policies, characteristic of many L.D.C.s, which arbitrarily distributed the direction of investment, generated waste, reduced incentives to efficiency, directed talent and personnel from production to speculation, etc.

Finally, Professor Samuels was sceptical of Dr. Enke's use of various production functions relating output to labour and capital in some fairly fixed ratios. The variables in Dr. Enke's model were created as if they were endowed with a single characteristic, varying only in quantity and degree. In a world of rapid change in tastes, resources and technology, there was no reason to expect the set of relationships in Dr. Enke's model to subsist, nor any reason why, if there was a change, such change should follow a definite and predictable pattern.

Professor de Coning circulated six tables reflecting the results of surveys he had helped to conduct in two South African urban areas. Tables 1 and 2 showed how per capita income decreased with rising family size, and table 3a (when read with table 1) showed how little saving there was in low income urban families – sometimes even an excess of expenditure over income. Table 6 confirmed Dr. Enke's contention that the poor had a different consumption mix from the rich – the poor spent more on necessities, but also on tobacco and alcoholic drinks. The poor lacked *discretionary* purchasing power and especially could not afford durable consumer goods. In developed countries new wants were continually created, thus complicating the demand patterns. Contact with developed societies and mass communications media passed these wants and demand patterns on to poor peoples who could not afford to satisfy them. Envy and frustration were bound to result.

Conversely, relatively primitive economic communities were self-sufficient in their immediate environment. There was little saving of goods or money, and the incentive either to save or create surpluses was lacking.

Professor S. P. Cilliers accepted Dr. Enke's conclusions and felt that the motivation to reduce fertility rates was to hand, namely the universal love of mothers for their children. It only needed to be communicated to mothers that family planning was in the interests of the children they had borne.

Dr. A. Sauvy felt that Dr. Enke's conclusions were not borne out in all cases in real situations. In the nineteenth century France alone in Europe had a very low birth-rate and low rate of population increase. On Dr. Enke's argument, France should have had a much faster growth of G.N.P. than the rest of Europe. This had not been the case. Population size and growth were not the only factors to be considered. During the same period, Argentina had had a very low fertility rate and Mexico a very high one. Yet it was Mexico that had the faster national income growth. The same was true for Europe, if one compared, say, Sweden with Holland.

Mr. Bourgeois-Pichat emphasised that any plea for a zero population growth-rate by A.D. 2000 was impossible of realisation; at most a new reproduction rate of *one* could be achieved by that date.

Professor S. S. Brand urged the need to disaggregate the variables being used. 'Capital' and 'foreign aid', for example, were so complex that to treat them as aggregates was to deprive them of all meaning.

Miss S. Hall maintained that it was not the overall level of education and experience of the labour force which determined its productivity. In South Africa it was found that, where proper entrepreneurial know-how and managerial ability were present even completely illiterate and inexperienced workers could rapidly become a highly productive labour force using modern technology

Father L. J. Smith asked the conference to consider the aesthetic moral dilemmas (especially for doctors) inherent in any policy of abortion – if abortion were to be allowed it must be at the earliest possible stage of pregnancy and only in a crisis.

In his summing up *Professor Samuels* emphasised, *inter alia*, that even overpopulated countries might benefit from immigration, if the immigrants were people with special skills, especially in the managerial and entrepreneurial field. This was one example which showed the importance of not dealing with aggregates. He ended on a hopeful note: human ingenuity is at its best when faced with pressing problems.

Note: As a result of illness, Dr. Enke was not able to be present for the whole of this session and to reply to points raised during the discussions.

9 The political implications of the population explosion

W. B. VOSLOO

The influence of demographic factors on the political sphere is one of the most intractable facets of political analysis. If one thinks of politics as the process of making governmental policies for a particular society, then the political implications of population factors must be sought in its impact on the formulation and achievement of domestic and foreign policy goals.

This task is complicated by the fact that it is difficult to establish a direct and constant relation between demographic factors and politics. A glance into history shows that this relation is somewhat erratic. It is conditioned by intervening variables such as natural resources, the availability of capital and entrepreneurial talents, cultural values, social organisation, living standards, levels of educational and technological attainment and also psychological determinants.

The rate of population growth in today's world, however, has reached such dramatic proportions that demographic factors have emerged as extremely critical on the global political scene. Mounting population difficulties are increasingly intermingled with political tensions and instabilities both nationally and internationally.

For the purposes of this analysis, the political implications of the 'demographic revolution' will be considered in terms of a few major facets: the magnitude and distribution of population increases, domestic implications and international implications.[1]

1. MAGNITUDE AND DISTRIBUTION OF INCREASES

After many centuries during which the world population stagnated for long periods, recurrently suffered catastrophic declines in particular regions, and increased very slowly in the long run, the trend abruptly reversed during the twentieth century in a veritable 'population explosion'. Demographic estimates put the world's

F

Graph 9.1   World Population from A.D. 1 to 2000

approximate population totals at about 0·25 billion early in the Christian era; just over 0·3 billion in the A.D. 500; around 0·4 billion in the year A.D. 1000; around 0·5 billion in 1500. The turning-point came apparently during the seventeenth century, because by 1800 it stood around 0·9 billion; in 1900 it was around 1·5 billion; 2·5 billion in 1950; and if current trends continue there is a prospect of well over 6 billion earth-dwellers by A.D. 2000.[2]

More significant than the increase in total number is the accelerating rate of increase. If prevailing estimates for the world's population be accepted, the total population approximately doubled between the first century A.D. and 1650. It approximately doubled again in the following 200 years. It more than doubled during the next 100 years (1850–1950). Currently the estimated doubling time is less than 35 years (see graph). A continuation of the world's population growth along these dimensions must inevitably create pressures of numbers on environment and resources to the point of a global crisis. Not only is man's ability to expand his *Lebensraum* essentially limited, but there is abundant reason to be pessimistic about the possibility of greatly increasing the average world level of living during the remainder of this century.[3]

A close analysis of the phenomenal population growth reveals great variations in different parts of the world. The most significant aspect is that a disproportionate share of this accelerating population growth is occurring in the underdeveloped, poor and non-industrial countries in Asia, Africa and Latin America. (See tables 9.1, 9.2, 9.3.)

TABLE 9.1   Population trends: 1900–2000 (million)

Dates	World	Asia	Europe (+ Soviet Union)	Africa	North America	South America	Oceania
1900	1550	857	423	120	81	63	6
1950	2497	1380	574	199	168	163	13
2000	6267	3870	947	517	312	592	29

TABLE 9.2   Estimated percentage population increase per quarter-century 1900–2000

Dates	World	Asia	Europe	Africa	North America	South America	Oceania
1900–1925	23	19	19	22	56	57	57
1925–1950	31	35	14	35	33	65	36
1950–1975	53	60	31	52	43	86	59
1975–2000	64	75	26	71	30	95	40

TABLE 9.3 Percentage of total world population by continent: 1900–2000

Dates	Asia	Europe	Africa	North America	South America
1900	55·3	27·3	7·7	5·2	4·1
1950	55·2	23·0	8·0	6·7	6·5
2000	61·8	15·1	8·2	5·0	9·4

Source: (with modifications) United Nations, *The Future Growth of World Population* (Population Studies No. 28, New York, 1958).

The most crucial aspect of this disproportionate population growth lies in the serious and growing imbalance between resources and population. As indicated in the paper read at this conference by Professor W. Brand of the University of Leiden, the 'poor regions' of Asia, Africa and Latin America (in contrast to the 'rich regions' of Europe, North America, Oceania, Japan and the Soviet Union) contain approximately 70 per cent of the world population, but possess 58 per cent of the land, 54 per cent of the arable land, 58 per cent of the meadows and pastures, 53 per cent of the forested area and 66 per cent of the livestock. Moreover, they produce only 48 per cent of the cereal production, 18 per cent of the milk production, 15 per cent of the gasoline production and altogether only 15–16 per cent of the world's goods and services embodied in the national products of states for the period 1960–70.[4]

2. DOMESTIC IMPLICATIONS

(a) Demands on governments

One of the most significant impacts of population increases on to-day's government is the enormous expansion in the number, variety and complexity of its functions. Peoples everywhere, and most especially those in the less developed countries, are anxious to achieve higher standards of living, and there are no limits to the services which the government is called upon to perform. The traditional definition of governmental functions in terms of providing internal order and external security has been enlarged to include the promotion of the well-being of the members of society – with all that higher living standards imply. Governments have taken upon themselves the responsibility for the direction and utilisation of manpower, natural resources and the fast-growing technology of the modern world for the creation of an environment conducive to widespread economic and social well-being. Less and less are the rank and file resigned to live lives of poverty, hunger, illness, ignorance and idleness. More and more, particularly in developing areas, the governments are looked to as agencies to meet these urgent demands.

There are of course great variations in the functions assumed by modern governments. These variations grow out of dissimilar national traditions and philosophies, as well as out of great disparities in national resources and methods of utilising them. A modern government may act as the director, entrepreneur or stimulator of private initiative, or indeed in all three capacities. In a completely socialised state, practically all organised effort is placed in the public sector and its entire management becomes the concern of the public service. Other countries, for reasons dictated by their history, value system and resources, are committed to reserving the largest possible sphere of activity to private enterprise and local initiative. But even in these countries vastly increased functions have been given to government. The concept of the 'Welfare State' (sometimes euphemistically called the 'Service State') in various forms and based upon various definitions, has been almost universally accepted as the chief instrument to achieve the widest possible diffusion of welfare. Measures such as public education, old-age pension schemes, public housing, social insurance, schemes for full employment, health services and redistributive systems of taxation are now regular items on the agenda of most governments.

In virtually all countries the vast expansion of governmental functions generated by population increases has resulted in a serious administrative lag. It is manifested by a serious imbalance between the needs to be met and the adequacy of the administrative machinery to carry them out. Demands for basic utilities such as adequate water supply, drainage, sanitation, highways and transportation, power and fuel and communications networks swamp most public services. In each of these fields success or failure depends increasingly on the efficacy of the public services. To an ever-increasing degree it requires careful planning, continuous attention to reform, high standards of leadership and a growing commitment in terms of men, money and material.

The problems created by population pressures are particularly urgent in developing countries as a result of the divergence between national goals and national means. Since the colonial era the image of western countries provided the standards and models for the new states of Asia, Africa and Latin America. The western standards of 'development' have to a substantial degree become the accepted ideological commitment in the developing countries – irrespective of variations in political tradition, socio-cultural background and capacity for success in the attainment of these standards. As a result a 'revolution of rising expectations' has been superimposed upon a compound of transitional problems: social disorganisation, economic depression and administrative confusion. In the face of severe handicaps, the inexperienced new governments are confronted with expectations and demands which even advanced nations find difficult to fulfil. The resultant political pattern is one of instability, uncertainty, discontinuity and extra-legal change.

The political instabilities in developing countries resulting from pressures upon governments to meet increased popular demands raise questions about the most appropriate governmental system in such situations. The crux of the problem is that demands can be met only after a long series of stringent steps requiring deprivations in the form of delayed satisfactions and enforced savings for capital accumulation and investment. These conditions seem to tip the scales in favour of authoritarian rather than democratic governmental systems.[6]

(b) Urbanisation

A direct result of population growth is the accelerating rate of urbanisation. In the economically advanced nations of the world, urbanisation is both an antecedent and a consequence of technological advance and a higher standard of living. In the underdeveloped nations, however, urbanisation represents instead the transfer of rural poverty from the countryside to a mass urban setting. The prospect for individual nations, while variable, is in general the same – one of explosive urban growth.[7]

Although metropolitan areas have their individual problems, they share several pathological ones in common. Their difficulties accumulated because most of them 'just grew' – inadequately planned or arranged for the tasks confronting them. Today it is a rare city that does not have wretched slums; excessive noise, pollution and overcrowding; traffic congestion and insufficient open space; and inadequate housing, transportation, schools, hospitals, water sanitation and police protection. Apart from these more or less physical implications of urbanisation, the process also involves profound socio-cultural transformations and problems of metropolitan governmental organisation.

Rural communities are usually characterised by their organic social structures. This implies a high degree of homogeneity and social solidarity, informal and intimate inter-personal relationships, a rigid attachment to traditional values and modes of life, and a strong resistance to change. Migration to the cities involves profound socio-cultural transformations. Urban societies are characterised by their atomistic social environments, heterogeneity, fluidity in social relationships, specialised division of labour and diffusion of cultural values. Adaptation to these conditions is universally a slow and painful process. Its most important manifestations are problems of social disintegration, inter-group tension and political conflict.

In most countries, city government is generally a ramshackle affair. The reasons for this inadequacy are not hard to find. Most cities have grown in a haphazard fashion, rapidly assembling, but not always assimilating, their populations from rural and immigrant elements. They are commonly equipped with inferior governing power, financial resources and facilities. They are usually obliged to contend with dispersed and overlapping multi-tiered units of local government dating from earlier times. The remedy for such ills calls, among other things, for larger, one-tiered, all-purpose units of urban government, a balance between central control and local self-government, a sound basis for municipal financing and far-sighted programmes of planning and modernisation.

(c) Inter-group conflict

Especially in heterogeneous societies, differential population growth lies at the root of most political cleavages and tensions. Sub-national groups in diverse societies are particularly sensitive about threats to their identities and their relative power positions *vis-à-vis* rival groups. These sub-national rivalries may be based on race, ethnic identity, language, caste, religion or region.

As a result of the widespread phenomenon of cultural pluralism in parts of Asia, Africa and Latin America, the very survival of the present state system is at stake in many countries. Available evidence suggests that 'progress' and 'modernisation' are not necessarily correlates of national integration, despite the widely held assumption of such an automatic relationship in much of the literature of development. Sub-national solidarity patterns are growing stronger as modern communications and education penetrate and the self-enclosed, small-scale, rural subsistence communities are progressively eliminated.[8]

The South African situation provides a good example of the impact of demographic factors on the political system. As a result of the numerical preponderance of non-whites, the attitudes of the whites are pervaded by a not unfounded fear of being swamped culturally and politically. In consequence a policy of 'separate development' has been introduced which aims at the gradual disentanglement of the various ethnic groups, making it possible for each group to exercise political rights and enjoy unhampered economic opportunities within its own territories, and to develop into an independent state.

(d) Population policy

The demographic situation is also closely related to population policies. Some measures contribute directly or indirectly to population growth. Other measures are deliberately designed to retard population growth or to curtail its ill-effects.

Examples of legislative and administrative measures favouring population growth include the development of public health and medical services which reduce death-rates, incentives offered to encourage large families through tax provisions for dependants and assistance to regions stricken by droughts and other natural disasters. Paradoxically these measures can encourage rapid population growth, even in the absence of rising living standards and the other accompaniments of economic progress. These services are part and parcel of normal modern governmental operations. The provision of such services is a function of the political process in every country.

Measures designed to deal with population growth, however, are much more troublesome. Basically there are two ways of coping with the population problem. The first is to take the rate of population growth as given and to try to cope with its effects. The other is to try to alter the rate of increase itself.[9]

If the first approach is used exclusively, it is usually because various religious and ideological reasons make any attempt to curb population repugnant to those in power. In such cases the efforts are directed towards *effects rather than causes*, and in particular to the common problem of growing unemployment. Under these conditions employment-creation becomes a goal of national policy. The implementation of such a policy usually includes decentralised community development projects where the unemployed are involved in rural public works programmes, the stimulation of labour intensive decentralised industries, the control of pollution and the preservation of natural resources (e.g. food, rich crop-land, fossil fuel, etc.), and the stimulation of research in agricultural and technological development.

The second approach is directed towards lowering the rate of population increase, usually through various campaigns to reduce the birth-rate. The specific measures include: campaigns favouring family planning, legalising abortion, improvement of contraceptive technology, modification of income-tax provisions for dependants, and changing social attitudes through education towards having fewer children.

Generally speaking, however, there are few reasons for optimism that commitment to the second approach will gain ground. The main reasons for this conclusion are ignorance, the lack of public interest, the substantial opposition to birth control in official quarters in most countries, and also the persistent opposition on ideological and religious grounds (e.g. doctrinaire communists and Catholics). Moreover, more information is needed to convince decision-makers of the necessity of intelligent and realistic plans.

3. INTERNATIONAL IMPLICATIONS

(a) *Effects on national power*

(i) Military potential

In the early days of the European state system, and well into the twentieth century, military power depended in large measure upon the size of the national population which supplied army recruits and paid taxes to equip them. Hence Voltaire claimed that 'God is always on the side of the heaviest battalions'. The efficacy of an army was largely proportionate to the number of its soldiers rather than to its fire power. Thus at the Congress of 1815 a committee provided an estimate of the populations of German areas in order to distribute them among Prussia, Austria and Russia and thus maintain the balance of power.[10]

However, population was not a measure of power when Europeans encountered peoples of different technology and organisation. Cortez, in the sixteenth century, conquered several million Mexicans with four hundred Spaniards equipped only with guns and horses. Similarly the British were able to win control over India with small forces in the eighteenth century. In the nineteenth century European countries overran a China containing ten times their combined populations. In the twentieth century a small but well-equipped, dedicated and disciplined Jewish army overran the armies of Arab countries containing more than twenty times the population of Israel in the 'Six-Day War' of 1967.

History, therefore, seems to indicate that demographic strength has been a factor of military power only where there was a convergence of the social, economic and financial conditions needed to maintain, equip and command the armies. In the contemporary world, military power seems even less closely related to population than it was earlier as a result of the industrialisation of war.[11]

Despite these considerations, population is bound to remain an important military asset under specified conditions. As a *defensive weapon* a large population, together with a large area, permits defence in depth, makes possible industries capable of producing weapons, assures sufficient personnel for maintenance services, and makes unlikely total annihilation in time of war. Also as an *offensive weapon* population size is by no means obsolete. Modern weapons vastly augment the fire power and destructiveness of the individual soldier, but to the extent that they permit any reduction in the number of men needed at the front, they substantially increase those required for service and supply in the echelons. Therefore, it is not likely at all that the day of the mass armies has passed – either as a defensive shield or as a psychological weight in aggressive strategies.

(ii) Economic potential

Possession of economic power allows a state to exercise command, influence, control and even coercion in international affairs. The connection between population growth and such economic power is implied by the very term 'manpower'. It confirms the importance of labour as a basic factor of economic production.

Over the long course of history, until fairly modern times, population growth has been the major source of general expansions of economic output. This was because labour, assisted by a minimum of tools and working in essentially traditional ways, was unquestionably mankind's greatest productive asset. A growing population almost invariably leads to an increasing total output, but it also makes for a greater number of persons among whom this output must be divided. Increases in total output are qualified by per capita output. Whether the net effect of population growth on a society's economic potential is positive, neutral or negative, will thus depend on the particular pattern of population increase and on the context within which it occurs.[12]

The examples of western nations such as France, Great Britain and Germany since the Industrial Revolution show that population increase stimulated production, and that industry would not have developed so rapidly had not the surplus rural population provided an abundant supply of industrial manpower. Similarly the industrial development of the United States was enhanced by the influx of millions of immigrants in the period 1820 to 1920. Likewise, the large labour force in Japan made it possible for industrialists to keep salaries and costs low and thus to compete with European products on the markets of the world.

Economic development, however, is not a function of demographic factors alone. An abundant supply of manpower is useless without natural resources, technology, capital and entrepreneurial talents. There must be some balance between population and resources which permits a society to generate an economic surplus over and above the subsistence level before it can start on the long road to economic development and industrialisation.

It is precisely in this context that the contrast between the highly industrialised and the 'underdeveloped' countries is sharpest. The characteristics of the underdeveloped state are, indeed, the very opposite of those required for economic development. To make matters worse they tend to perpetuate abysmal circumstances in a 'vicious circle'. The poor, being poor, save little above what they need for subsistence. They are ignorant because they cannot afford schooling. Being ignorant, they cannot learn the skills of more efficient production. Lacking efficient production, they cannot raise their own living standards or contribute to the capital necessary for industrialisation. In large parts of Asia and Africa, moreover, they are trapped in ancestral patterns of family structure, community life, caste distinctions and feudal relationships, which emphasise conformity to ancient ways and discourage initiative and independence without which no significant economic development can take place. Under such circumstances, population growth is not a stimulant to development, but a depressant.

The connection between population increase and economic development leads one inevitably to the concept of overpopulation. It refers to a situation in which there is sufficient pressure of population on resources to cause a reduction of living standards or to retard their improvement. Famines, pestilences, unemployment and extensive emigration are typical symptoms of overpopulation of this kind – as has long existed in large parts of Asia. But an improvement in technology may make it possible for a given area to sustain a larger population at a higher standard of living than was possible at a lower level of technology. Germany, with 30 million people in the mid-nineteenth century, experienced population pressures as shown by low living standards and wholesale emigration. However, with 60 million people in the mid-twentieth century, it was no longer overpopulated, for the industrialisation of the country had intervened. One can therefore only properly speak of overpopulation in relation to numbers, resources, technology and standards of living.

The political significance of 'relative' overpopulation lies in the fact that it can become a discordant element in international relations when the peoples concerned are conscious of it or when they associate the observed fact of overpopulation with that of unequal living conditions. This awareness of the growing disproportion between population and resources and the differences in economic progress between 'have' and 'have not' nations is likely to be enhanced by the development of information media and is bound to provide a serious cause for international tensions, discordant alliances and international violence in the decades to come.[13]

(b) External effects

(i) Migration

Throughout history the migration of immigrants and temporary workers has often played an important role in domestic and international politics – sometimes as the cause, and sometimes as the occasion of disagreements or conflicts. The large-scale migration of such persons from Europe to other parts of the world, particularly the Western Hemisphere, began in the sixteenth century and has persisted ever since. Migration from the Far East did not begin until the nineteenth century, increased rapidly soon thereafter, but cannot compare with the massive displacements of European populations that had taken place between the 1870s and the First World War.[14]

Most migration has moved from thickly populated to thinly populated areas. The principal motive of migrants has apparently been their desire to improve their economic status or to escape from a situation in which population pressed upon resources. Some have also sought to get away from what they regarded as oppressive political regimes.

What are the major effects of migration on the countries of origin? From the point of view of the European states that furnished the largest contingents of emigrants it could be said that it mitigated the excessive population density in agricultural regions and reduced the evils of unemployment in industrial regions. In this sense it provided an outlet for potential political malcontents. It also provided the mother country with a means of spreading its views or influence and to develop colonial territories as prosperous markets.

We turn next to the major effects in the receiving countries. In the Western Hemisphere, where 95 per cent of European emigrants went, the great migration vastly contributed to economic development. Its social and political effects, however, were more troublesome. Wherever the influx of foreigners reached any considerable proportion, it tended to create alien minorities which became a threat to national unity and hence a source of political instability. The problem arose in the United States by the end of the nineteenth century when waves of Italian and Slav immigrants were not as readily assimilated as earlier German, British and Scandinavian groups. These groups tended to preserve their own language and customs. Similar problems were created by the Indians in Natal and all over east Africa and by the Chinese immigrants in Indo-China, Indonesia, Siam, Burma and Malaya. Receiving countries for various reasons such as cultural homogeneity, fear of being overwhelmed by alien populations, fear of competition for jobs and fear of infiltration by alien doctrines or religions, do not want large numbers of immigrants or even migrant workers from countries suffering most from population pressures.

In quite a number of instances waves of migration led to international disputes and armed conflict. It was the cause of controversy and conflict in the Transvaal prior to the Anglo-Boer War (1899–1902), in Manchuria prior to the Sino-Japanese conflict of 1931, and in Palestine since the advent of the Zionist 'Homeland' policy.

Generally speaking, migration scarcely seems to provide an easy answer to the problem of overpopulation.

(ii) Expansionist aggression

Professor Kingsley Davis expressed the view that '. . . excessive population growth seems to intensify the struggle for scarce raw materials, to build explosive migration pressures, and to encourage *Lebensraum* wars . . .'[15] In this context, one automatically thinks of Japan, Germany and Italy in the 1920s and 1930s when the population thrust was often advanced as one of the arguments in favour of territorial expansion.

Closer analysis of the historical evidence raises the question, however, whether or not real value must be attached to the demographic argument. It is generally known that in all three cases, the demographic policy had its basis in a political programme: its purpose was to assert hegemony through demographic superiority. In propaganda efforts a higher birth-rate was represented as a national duty and a sign of prosperity and vitality. Large families were subsidised. By encouraging population growth, these governments were, in effect, deliberately creating 'population pressures'. Simultaneously they pointed to their population explosions to justify their programmes of territorial expansion.[16]

Whether or not the demographic argument is used by leaders to conceal their ambitions to power, it seems reasonable to expect population pressures to set off aggressive programmes of territorial expansion in various parts of the world including Japan. India, Pakistan and China are not apt to remain frustrated in their efforts to attain a higher standard of living without noting the relatively sparsely settled areas in south-east Asia and Africa.[17]

Global effects
(i) Ideological conflict

The success or failure of underdeveloped areas of the world in raising their standards of living in the face of their explosive population growth has profound implications in terms of the so-called 'war for men's minds'. The burning question is whether the free world approach is more effective for achieving economic development.[18]

It is generally agreed that communism is making its greatest conquests precisely in the impoverished and crowded countries. One must therefore be particularly concerned about the impact and appeal of communism in these areas in contrast to that of the capitalist type of economic organisation.

In the communist propaganda the problems of overpopulation and underdevelopment are generally presented as the fault of former colonial powers and the reflection of the inability of the capitalist economic system to satisfy basic human needs. Furthermore, advocacy of control is described as a capitalist trick to keep Asian and African countries weak. The communists also argue that the 'socialist' recipe provides rapid improvement of living conditions compared to the slower progress in 'capitalist' economies. The comparison between India and China is frequently cited to persuade the peoples of underdeveloped areas to adopt at least the economics, if not the politics of communist states. In this connection Sondermann suggests that it may be well to reflect that in 1937 communism controlled 170 million people, or 8 per cent of the world's population, while 20 years later it controlled 1 billion people, or 37 per cent.[19]

The chief weapon of the free nations, apart from the example of their free way of life, is undoubtedly the provision of assistance to the less developed nations to help them achieve their economic goals and to encourage private capital to invest more heavily in those areas.

(ii) Balance of power

The tensions and political instabilities caused by explosive population growth have a special significance with regard to the balance of power in international politics. Although the world's political scene is still dominated by the two super-powers, the structure of world politics has been fundamentally changed by the declining influence and prestige of both the United States and the Soviet Union. The structure of world politics has in recent years tended to shift from bi-polarity towards multi-polarity. The two super-powers are not likely to remain much longer, as they have done for most of the post-war era, virtually alone on the pinnacle of power.

One arena where the United States and the Soviet Union are losing influence is Asia. The power vacuum created by this trend is likely to be filled by Japan and China. Japan has already become the world's third-ranking economic power. This power will give Japan growing influence over its Asian neighbours, and economic aid plus a regional military role will probably become inevitable within this decade. Its major rival is China with its gigantic population, centralised government, revolutionary ideology and nuclear power.

China has already been involved in various conflicts in neighbouring areas (Korea and Indo-China) and along its borders (with India and Russia). Although its domestic economic problems are likely to make its foreign policy more flexible in the immediate future, China is bound to cast a large shadow on world politics in the long-range future.

In the rest of the underdeveloped world, population difficulties and political instabilities are so intermingled that they constitute, in the words of Irene B. Taeuber, 'virtually insoluble problems'.[20] In most areas within this category – including the Middle East and North Africa, middle Africa and southern Africa, south-east Asia, India and Pakistan, and to a lesser degree Latin America – the problems created by population pressure are compounded and aggravated by the diversities among their peoples. The prognosis for their future is generally a period of anarchy and instability, of *coups* and counter-*coups*, of widespread suffering and of the gap between the 'have' and the 'have not' nations increasing rather than decreasing.[21]

CONCLUSION

From this analysis it appears that population is only one of the many factors that account for a nation's power. The influence of a country's population on its capacity to formulate and achieve desired domestic and foreign political goals can only be properly assessed in terms of the reciprocal relations between population size, growth-rate, natural resources, type of socio-cultural organisation, standard of living and also its levels of educational and technological attainment.

For many generations a large and fast-growing population was regarded as an indisputable measure of national power. It was held that population size determines the reservoir of productive power, the potential advantages of scale to be gained from mass production and mass distribution and the proportion of personnel available for military service. Today, however, it is clear that a huge and growing population can be a source of weakness rather than strength if it exceeds the capacity of a country's productive resources to support it, or if it impedes the efficient development of those resources. Furthermore it is clear that in the world-wide state system of today, which includes nations of varied technology, culture and organisation, military power is less closely related to population than it was in the European state system from the sixteenth to the twentieth century.

It should be clear, however, that pressures generated by the current explosive population growth are bound to lie at the root of many political crises in the coming decades. If mankind does not succeed in stemming the population tide through rational programmes of family planning and economic modernisation on a global scale, the looming crises will be resolved irrationally by violence and starvation. But we do have reason to believe that the problems can be solved by a world fully alert to the dangers and willing to devote serious quantities of resources and energy to attacking them.

Notes

1. See W. C. Olson and F. A. Sondermann, *The Theory and Practice of International Relations* (New Jersey, Prentice-Hall, 1966) p. 153.
2. Derived from United Nations publications: *Demographic Yearbook; The Future Growth of World Population* (Population Studies No. 28, 1958); *World Population Prospects* (1966).
3. P. M. Hauser, *Population Perspectives* (New Jersey, Rutgers University Press, 1966) pp. 8–9.
4. W. Brand, 'World Resources, their Use and Distribution', Paper read at Conference on the 'Impact on International Relations of the Population Explosion', the S.A. Institute of International Affairs, Johannesburg, 1970.
5. E. Shils, *Political Development in New States* (The Hague: Mouton & Co., 1962) p. 10. See also R. Bendix, *Nation-Building and Citizenship* (New York, John Wiley & Sons, 1964) p. 300.
6. This trend is emphasised by Sondermann, 'Political Implications of Population Growth in Underdeveloped Countries', in Olson & Sondermann, op. cit. p. 157.
7. Hauser, op. cit., pp. 20–2.
8. K. W. Deutsch and W. J. Foltz, *Nation-Building* (New York, Atherton Press, 1963) p. 6.
9. R. T. Gill, *Economic Development; Past and Present* (New Jersey, Prentice-Hall, 1967) pp. 97–8.
10. Q. Wright, 'Population and United States Foreign Policy' in *Population and World Politics*, ed. P. M. Hauser (Glencoe, The Free Press, 1958) p. 266.
11. Ibid.
12. See R. T. Gill, *Economic Development: Past and Present*, pp. 4–5.
13. P. Renouvin and J. Duroselle, *Introduction to the History of International Relations*, translated by M. Ilford (Oxford, Pall Mall Press, 1968) p. 28. See also Q. Wright, *The Study of International Relations* (New York, 1955) p. 364.
14. For a survey of the history of intercontinental migration see Renouvin and Duroselle, op. cit., pp. 33–52.
15. K. Davis, 'The Other Scare: Too Many People', in *New York Times Magazine* (15 March 1959) p. 114.
16. Renouvin and Duroselle, op. cit., pp. 31–3.
17. W. Thompson, *Population and Progress in the Far East* (Chicago: University of Chicago Press, 1959).
18. Hauser, op. cit., p. 27.
19. Sondermann, op. cit., p. 158.
20. I. B. Taeuber, 'Population and Political Instabilities in Underdeveloped Areas', in P. M. Hauser (ed.), *Population and World Politics*, op. cit., p. 237.
21. S. Kuznets, 'Regional Economic Trends and Levels of Living' in Hauser (ed.) op. cit., pp. 79–117.

DISCUSSION

Panel Members: Professors M. H. H. Louw and E. S. Munger

Professor Louw said that overpopulation gave rise to the question: How do you subtract and whom do you subtract? This was the political problem, and the politician had to take the ultimate decision. The problem for the politician was to identify what was involved. He thought the main paper had focused on the essential problem for the decision-maker; one of reducing or increasing or even restructuring the population. It had also shown that the magnitude and disproportion of increases placed the solutions far behind the problems. Government had to deal with conflicting demands. Its task was to find and to legitimate the consensus on solutions: namely, viable and realistic policies. Government must be served by other disciplines to build integrated viable policies to deal with the problems in relation to values. The relevant values had yet to be determined. Decisions as to the values must carry authority, and thus international consensus was necessary, for no one state or group of states could prescribe for others.

Professor Munger said that, very unfortunately, the existence of different races tended to complicate problems of overpopulation. The United States, for example, had changed from a melting-pot to a pressure-cooker. Attempts to limit population cross-racially readily brought accusations of genocide, especially if the proposer was a white nation. He proposed:

(*a*) That the Conference should go on record as accepting *quality* rather than the sheer numbers of population as constituting the basis of decisions in international institutions.

(*b*) That institutions such as the World Bank should recommend aid on the basis of population control.

(*c*) That borrowing from international institutions for the purpose of granting old-age security be facilitated, in this way easing or removing the reliance on large families.

Professor Marcus Arkin deplored the political attitude which equated urbanisation with expansive economic repercussions. This was true during the period leading up to and attendant upon the Industrial Revolution of the eighteenth and nineteenth centuries, but was not so today.

Mr. Gordon Lawrie ridiculed the concept of idealism in political motivation. The welfare of the people received mere lip-service from ruling cliques for the most part; the prime objectives of most politicians – either singly or operating as a group – were connected with survival, and any benefits accruing to the population which they governed were largely fortuitous.

Professor H. V. Muhsam disagreed with Professor Munger's suggestion that aid to countries with exploding populations might be weighted against their capacity to control birth increase. 'No control, no aid' was not a logical approach and, in any case, would be almost impossible to rationalise. *Mr. Jean Bourgeois-Pichat* supported this argument, pointing out that policy in the several countries was so diverse that it was difficult for any kind of yardstick to be applied.

Mr. Alf Stadler considered that no relationship between politics and population growth had yet been established. Decision-making was based upon a whole complex of factors, and population growth might merely be incidental to political attitudes.

Mr. M. Nupen regretted that politics had been ignored for so long at a conference whose major theme had strong political connotations. What right had the affluent nations to apply their own policy guide-lines to the exploding poor? This was merely conceit and the acme of egocentricity, and such policy might not be to the structural benefit of the less developed countries in the long term, however effective it might be among the 'haves'.

Mr. O. Kerfoot gave a 'hawkish' biological criticism of both economists and politicians. Man's political and economic destiny must be dependent upon fundamental biological laws, and it would be a sorry plight if man's future were to be controlled by the expediency of politicians. The whole theme of the Conference was basically an ecological one, and the population explosion, urbanisation and attendant facets were symptomatic of man's disastrous attempts to divorce himself from an environment which had become increasingly entropic.

Dr. N. J. van Rensburg maintained that governments could only initiate a degree of motivation to birth control. No enforcement was possible as conception was to the ultimate degree a private and individual matter, essentially one of personal choice.

In reply to the floor speakers, *Professor Vosloo* agreed that a variety of interpretations and shades of meaning could be applied to the word 'politics'. Nevertheless, he believed that the population explosion was a crucial variable in political analysis. However, policymakers needed as much information as they could get from all sources before coming to decisions.

10 Effective population as a source of international power[*]

A. F. K. ORGANSKI
(with the assistance of ALAN LAMBORN)

I

Ever since the time the modern quickening of population growth was first observed, the facts of population have been the facts of life in world politics. The reasons why Europeans – not Africans or Indians or Chinese – have dominated world politics lie rooted in part in population changes that occurred at a strategic time. Asians hope that things will change, that somehow, some day, 'east wind will prevail over west wind'. Such hopes rest in part upon demographic actualities and upon projected future trends. At the same time, one of the most serious obstacles to the realisation of these hopes (and, indeed, to the hopes of all the underdeveloped world for greater power and wealth and esteem) is likely to be the timing and composition of their population increases.

It is a foolish statesman and a more foolish scholar who would overlook the important role played by the demographic variables in shaping national power, prosperity and prestige. The relationship has long been recognised. Yet it is not easy to relate with precision exactly of what that relationship consists. Part of the difficulty lies in inexact definitions of national power and in a lack of independent measures of the relative power of different nations at different times. Another difficulty lies in tracing through the effect of population changes upon all the myriad factors that in turn affect the distribution of world power, wealth and prestige.

Let us confine ourselves here to a detailed analysis of the effect of population (specifically the effect of population size and rate of growth) upon the distribution of world power.

In general terms, there is substantial agreement that national

*This paper is a research offshoot of a larger programme of research on politics and development in the Comparative Political Studies in the Latin Cultural Area, which is supported at the University of Michigan by a Ford Foundation grant. The authors would like to express their public thanks to the Foundation and to the Center for Political Studies at the Institute for Social Research for making this piece of work possible.

power is the ability of one nation to influence the behaviour of the government and of the people of another nation. This power is most dramatically exercised through military coercion but is also exercised in the daily workings of international politics through economic pressures, both governmental and private, through the offering and withholding of political rewards and punishments, and through simple persuasion. There is also general agreement that national power is in large part determined by population size, by level of economic development, and by the political effectiveness of the national government, as well as by a number of lesser determinants. Not only does each of these factors affect directly the power of a nation, but they affect one another in intricate and significant ways.

In demographic terms, national power depends primarily upon the number of people a nation can tap to make a contribution to national goals and upon its capacity to aggregate the individual activities of its nationals into national pools. To gain some knowledge of a nation's power one must ask three questions. How many people does a nation have? How motivated, skilled and productive are they, or in other words, what contribution are they capable of making to the pursuit of national goals? And how successfully can their individual contributions be organised and aggregated?

II

The importance of population size as a determinant of national power is relatively obvious, for people constitute a nation's most precious resource. They are the soldiers, the workers, the consumers and the carriers of a nation's culture and beliefs. Population size sets crucial limits to a nation's power, whatever its other characteristics. There are in fact no major world powers with populations under 50 million. Even 50 million may not suffice for grandiose ambitions. Charles de Gaulle's dream of a new role for France was a delusion because France was simply too small compared to giant America and the Soviet Union.

The distribution of population among the 221 political units of the world is interesting (see table 10.1). As in the case of many other resources, the 'haves' are few and the 'have nots' are many. Furthermore, the differences are vast. It is clearly a world of Gullivers and Lilliputians, and this uneven distribution is a major source of stratification in the international political system.

More than one-third of the world's population lives within the boundaries of the 2 largest nations, more than two-thirds within the 13 nations that have populations of 50 million or more. The remaining third is scattered among 208 different political juris-

TABLE 10.1   Distribution of population among nations*

Category by millions of population	Number of countries in category	Sum of population in millions	Percentage of world's population†
0–9	171	342	9·8 ⎤
10–19	22	314	9·0 ⎟
20–29	7	163	4·7 ⎬ 31·4%
30–39	7	230	6·6 ⎟
40–49	1	47	1·3 ⎦
50–59	3	158	4·5 ⎤
60–69	2	124	3·6 ⎟
70–79	0	0	0·0 ⎟
80–89	1	88	2·5 ⎟
90–99	0	0	0·0 ⎬ 32·5%
100–199	3	324	9·3 ⎟
200–299	2	439	12·6 ⎟
300–399	0	0	0·0 ⎟
400–499	0	0	0·0 ⎦
500–599	1	524	15·0 ⎤
600–699	0	0	0·0 ⎬ 36·0%
700–799	1	730	21·0 ⎦
Total	221	3483	100·0%

* Mid-year, 1968.
† Does not add up to 100% because of rounding.
Source: United Nations, *Demographic Yearbook, 1968* (New York, 1969) tables 2 and 4.

dictions, the vast majority of them very small (148 of them with populations of less than 5 million), and a substantial number of them (75) not even politically independent.

Even among the largest nations, the differences in population size are immense; China is 39 per cent larger than India, which in turn is more than twice the size of the Soviet Union or the United States, which in turn are roughly twice as large as Indonesia, Pakistan* or Japan, which in their turn have almost double the population of Nigeria, West Germany, Britain, Italy or France. Brazil falls between the last two clusters (see table 10.2).

III

Total population size, however, is somewhat misleading as an indicator of national power. No matter what its census declares its size to be, a nation, for power purposes, is no larger than that portion of its population whose activities can be aggregated into national pools to be used to further national goals. This is the effective population.

* Before Bangla Desh revolt.

TABLE 10.2 Nations largest in population*

Nation	Population in millions
China	730
India	524
Soviet Union	238
United States	201
Indonesia†	114
Pakistan	110**
Japan	101
Brazil	88
Nigeria	63
West Germany‡	61
United Kingdom	55
Italy	53
France§	50

* Mid-year, 1968.
** Before the Bangla Desh revolt.
† Including West Irian.
‡ Including West Berlin.
§ France in 1968 had 49·9 million people. She has since joined the 50-million-plus group.
Source: United Nations, *Demographic Yearbook, 1968* (New York, 1969) table 4.

The exact size of the effective population of a nation is extremely difficult to identify. Small children do not belong to it. Even some of the older students may not, although they are preparing for future participation. Certainly the hippie drop-out does not, for he has dropped not only studying but also working, fighting and a large part of his national loyalties and national identity. Many old people have left the effective population though others continue to be economically and politically active. Some of the physically and mentally ill do not participate. Neither does the peasant villager who works all his life to provide only his own subsistence and who forms part of no larger group than the one he meets face to face in his daily life.

The concept is a valid one: that part of a nation's population contributes to its power while another part does not, but it is fraught with difficulties. In actuality there is a continuum of contribution. Nearly every adult makes some minimum contribution, if only through the taxes that are extracted from him. People may contribute in one area and not in another: teenagers and peasants may be drafted, the unemployed may be politically active, the politically disaffected who neglect even to vote may be economically productive. Also, we must be careful not to equate personal worth or general usefulness with contributing to the national interest, or to equate the national interest with increasing the nation's power. Our concern here is with the contribution population makes to national power, but there are, of course, other and more important personal and national goals. Finally, we must guard against an unconscious bias that the only activities increasing a nation's power are those in support of the national government in office. True, the national government does co-ordinate and focus the activities of its nationals in international affairs, but its policies may be misguided. It is difficult to see how resisting the draft could contribute to a nation's international power, but it is perfectly possible that protesting in order to convince the government to withdraw from a lost war with grace could do so.

With these cautions in mind, it seems useful to apply the idea of effective population when considering the relative power of nations. The concept is particularly useful in distinguishing between the influence of population size in a modern, industrial nation like the United States or the Soviet Union and that in an undeveloped country that is a 'nation' in name only, with only the thinnest network of political control and the rudiments of a national economy. Cambodia, for example, has a total population of six and a half million, but her effective population is only a tiny fraction of that, and she has collapsed in the face of military attack as one would expect a tiny nation to do.

To measure the contribution to national power of every citizen of any nation is obviously methodologically unfeasible, but it should be possible to devise a relatively accurate index of effective population. Unfortunately, no such index exists at present. The idea of effective population is a new one, presented here for the first time, so far as we know, and no one has as yet devoted to it the time and attention required for the construction of an index that is on the one hand valid and on the other hand made up from data readily available on a wide range of countries, including underdeveloped countries.

The indicator we propose to use is very crude: the number of economically active non-agricultural workers. About the best that can be said for it is that it eliminates a good portion of the ineffective population: children, the aged, the unemployable. By eliminating peasants it roughly separates the modern sector of the nation from the non-modern sector. Unfortunately, it also eliminates the very modern and nationally integrated farmers of nations like Denmark and the United States, though the distortion here is not too great, as such nations have a low percentage of workers in agriculture anyway. It also distorts the contribution of women by eliminating all who are not in paid employment. Though it is not considered here, the whole question of women's contribution to national power deserves consideration.

The purpose of this paper is to suggest a new concept. The indicator used is too inaccurate, but crude as it is, it will indicate the usefulness of the idea. Table 10.3 lists in order the nations with the

TABLE 10.3 Nations largest in effective population

Nation	Number of non-agricultural workers (in millions)*
United States 1960	57·3
China 1958	56·9
Soviet Union 1955	52·3
India 1961	38·0
Japan 1955	29·4
United Kingdom 1966	24·2
West Germany 1961	20·2
France 1962	15·0
Italy 1961	13·9
Indonesia 1961	8·6

* Figures are for males and females combined.
Source: United Nations, *Demographic Yearbook, 1964* (New York, 1965) table 9. Figures for China from John Emerson, *Non-agricultural Employment in Mainland China, 1949–58* (Washington, D.C., U.S. Government Printing Office, 1965) p. 128.

Warren W. Eason, *Soviet Manpower: The Population and Labor Force of the U.S.S.R.* (New York, Columbia University, microfilm, 1959) tables 9, 11, appendix tables K1, K2.

General Register Office, London and Edinburgh, *Sample Census 1966, Great Britain Economic Activity: Tables Part I* (London: H.M.S.O., 1968) table 15.

largest effective populations as indicated by the number of non-agricultural workers, both male and female. Listing nations in order of effective population size, rather than total population size, produces some significant changes in their ranking. Nations of 50 million or more still head the list, but China shrinks to one-thirteenth of her size, dropping below the United States, while India shrinks to one-fourteenth of her total size, which puts her well below the Soviet Union. Indonesia also drops, while Pakistan, Brazil and Nigeria disappear from the top group altogether (compare tables 10.2 and 10.3). Interesting comparisons can also be made among the smaller nations. While South Africa and the Congo do not differ greatly in total population size (South Africa is a little larger), South Africa has an effective population at least 4 times as great as that of the Congo. In the Middle East, the United Arab Republic has a total population 11·5 times as large as Israel's, but her effective population is only 5·5 times as large.

It should be clear that to rank nations by size of effective population is not the same thing as to rank them by power, although it approximates it more than total population size does. The effective population indicates the number of nationals that make up the 'nation', for purposes of international power, but it does not truly indicate the effectiveness of their contribution. It shows that they are in modern occupations, but it does not indicate the level of their skills or the capital goods they have at their disposal to increase their productivity. Secondly, the measurement of effective population used here is fundamentally an economic measurement. It makes no allowance for effective political mobilisation as distinct from economic effectiveness. Let us consider these missing factors, beginning with economic productivity.

IV

Even a middle-sized nation may achieve considerable international power if its population is highly productive economically. Economic efficiency means that military forces will be armed with modern weapons, that civilian workers are prosperous and healthy, and that they produce the abundance of goods and services that enable their nation to exercise economic power over other nations. Population expansion lay behind the surge that sent western Europeans forth to colonise and conquer most of the non-European world at the peak of European power, but it was economic (and military) efficiency, not superior numbers, that enabled them to subjugate the native populations they encountered. The compensatory effect of economic productivity can also be seen in modern power relationships. Though large, the United States and the Soviet Union are not the largest nations on earth.

The combined effect of size of effective population plus level of economic productivity is hard to measure but can be roughly approximated by gross national product (or gross domestic product), providing the best index of national power as yet devised.* Such an index reflects not only the size and the economic skills of the effective population. It also reflects how effective the economic system is in aggregating the economic output of individuals. Productivity is a

* For extended discussion of this idea, see A. F. K. Organski, *World Politics* (New York, Knopf, 1968) chap. 9.

function of the efficiency of the system; it is the system that makes the individual productive.

Applying the measurement of G.N.P. to the examples already considered gives a clearer indication of the relative power of nations, while comparison with rankings by total population and by effective population shows the role of population size.

In table 10.4 it can be clearly seen that nations ranking higher in

TABLE 10.4 Power as indicated by G.N.P., total population, effective population

Nation	G.N.P.* (billions) $	Rank in total population†	Rank in effective population‡	Rank in G.N.P.
United States	804	4	1	1
Soviet Union§	—	3	3	2
West Germany	121	10	7	3
France	116	13	8	4
Japan	116	7	5	5
United Kingdom	109	11	6	6
China§	—	1	2	7
Italy	67	12	9	8
Canada	57	26	13	9
India	44¶	2	4	10

* 1967 G.N.P. at market prices. United Nations, *Statistical Yearbook, 1968* (New York, Statistical Office of the United Nations, Department of Economic and Social Affairs, 1969) pp. 591–3.
† Mid-year, 1968. United Nations, *Demographic Yearbook, 1968* (New York, 1969) table 4.
‡ 1955–66. For sources, see table 3.
§Ranked on basis of 1965 G.N.P.
¶1966.

G.N.P. than they do in total population or in effective population have made up the difference through high economic productivity. Japan and the western European nations are conspicuous examples. Nations ranking lower in G.N.P. than in total population or in effective population (for example China and India) are characterised by low economic productivity and owe their power in large part to their size.

Consideration of economic productivity also sheds light on the confrontation between Israel and her Arab neighbours. Though we have observed that the United Arab Republic has 11·5 times the total population and 5·5 times the effective population of Israel, Israel is manifestly more powerful. Much of the discrepancy is explained by economic efficiency, for Israel, with her far smaller labour force, produces almost as large a G.N.P. (see table 10.5).

TABLE 10. 5 Relative power of Israel and the United Arab Republic

Nation	Total population* (millions)	Effective population† (millions)	G.N.P.‡ (billions) $
United Arab Republic	31·7	3·2	4·7
Israel	2·8	0·6	3·4

* Mid-year, 1968. United Nations, *Demographic Yearbook, 1968* (New York, 1969) table 4.
† 1960–1. United Nations, *Demographic Yearbook, 1964* (New York, 1965) table 9.
‡ 1965 G.N.P. in current market prices. United States Agency of International Development, *Reports Control No. 137, Estimates of Gross National Product*, 1967.

V

The case of Israel, however, serves as a reminder of a determinant of national power that G.N.P. does not reflect. It is also the factor most often overlooked in political estimates of the power of other nations. We refer to political efficiency.

Looked at from the point of view of the individual citizen, national political efficiency means a high level of political participation as an informed and concerned citizen, as a voter, a party worker, a campaign helper or a public official, as a propagandist for the national ideology and the national goals, as a willing taxpayer, a willing military recruit, a willing accepter of such sacrifices as wage and price controls or rationing in times of crisis.

Looked at from the government side, political efficiency means a high level of political mobilisation, of efficient governmental organisation in aggregating the political actions of its individual citizens.

From a demographic point of view, political efficiency means that a large proportion of the total population has joined the effective population in political as distinct from economic terms.

The missing factor to account for Israel's military success is her extraordinarily high level of political participation and political mobilisation.

We are used to assuming that high levels of political participation are present whenever nations are highly developed economically, and in a general way this is probably true. No adequate measure of political participation exists, but studies of the percentage of voters show fairly high voter participation for most (though not all) of the economically developed nations (see table 10.6).

Nevertheless, the two factors may operate independently (and apparently do among the economically underdeveloped nations). The case generally overlooked is one where a high level of political

TABLE 10.6   Political participation and economic development

Highly developed nations	Economic development as measured by per capita G.N.P. $	Percentage voting among people of voting age
United States	2577	64·4
Canada	1947	74·2
Switzerland	1428	28·0
Luxemburg	1388	71·1
Sweden	1380	83·1
Australia	1316	85·3
New Zealand	1310	86·4
Belgium	1196	87·6
United Kingdom	1189	78·0
Norway	1130	78·8
Selected underdeveloped nations		
Guatemala	189	27·5
Albania	175	94·6
Nicaragua	160	92·7
South Korea	144	31·3
Egypt	142	0·0
Indonesia	131	92·0
Liberia	100	82·9
Bolivia	99	51·4
Nigeria	78	40·4
India	73	52·6

Source: All data from Bruce Russett *et al.*, *World Handbook of Political and Social Indicators* (New Haven, Yale University Press, 1964) pp. 84 ff., 195 ff.

participation unexpectedly accompanies a very low level of economic development. In such an instance a good deal of national power may be generated, though it differs from the kind of power generated when economic modernisation is also present.

Most of the major miscalculations in international politics and the subsequent unexpected outcomes of military confrontations have been at bottom failures to take into account the level of force that can be generated simply by developing a political network that mobilises a peasant population. Consider the experience of the United States in fighting the Chinese in Korea. Two years earlier, mainland China had been in a state of collapse, exhausted by civil war, her armies disintegrated, her new communist government just beginning to assume control. Yet in 1951 Chinese soldiers crossed the Yalu River and fought the United States to a draw. Geography, resources, population size, economic productivity, nearly all the things we think of as contributing to national power, were the same.

Only one thing had changed; China had a political system that had mobilised a large fraction of her population. The results were dramatic. The United States should have learned for the future.

Or consider the relative strengths of North and South Vietnam. Their population size and level of economic development do not differ greatly, but there is an impressive difference in their level of political mobilisation. The North Vietnamese have successfully built a political network that has tied millions of peasant villagers into a formidable force capable of resisting successfully the military efforts of first France and then the United States for a period of twenty-five years. South Vietnam's government, on the other hand, does not even exercise political control over many of the people within its boundaries. Its effective population is extremely small, and its political efficiency in mobilising them is low.

It is interesting to note some of the differences in the kinds of power generated by population size, political efficiency and economic productivity. Population size alone, if large enough, apparently generates an obstacle to conquest by foreigners (for example China and Czarist Russia), though it is not insurmountable (for example India). Political efficiency generates stronger defensive strength which may even carry over into aggression against immediate neighbours (for example North Vietnam). But economic productivity is apparently necessary to dominate other nations at a distance. All of the great colonial powers were highly economically developed for their day, and the most powerful nations today are all industrial nations as well as being large in size.

The whole area of political efficiency, political mobilisation and political participation requires much more study. Measures for international comparison are sorely needed. It is this lack, more than any other, that prevents the formation of a truly valid index of national power. If a means could be found of accurately measuring the political and economic contribution made to a nation by its citizens, the concept of effective population would provide a better index of national power than any that now exists.

VI

Up to this point we have considered population size as a static characteristic of nations. The present period of history, however, is characterised by dramatic and continuing changes both in total population size (the population explosion) and in the effective population size (economic and political modernisation). These changes brought western Europe to its peak of power, produced the present predominance of the United States and the Soviet Union, and will produce whatever power distribution characterises the future.

The effect of population growth on power has not been the same, however, throughout this period. The differential population growth of the past few decades – and the behaviour of the demographic variables responsible for it – differ in many respects from western European experience.

Population growth was an important component of the massive power advantage that the western European countries gained over the rest of the world in the seventeenth, eighteenth and nineteenth centuries. It was an asset to the United States and the Soviet Union, and it could continue to be an asset to some of the highly developed countries. For example, such nations as Israel and Australia would certainly gain in power if they could be assured of additional population.

It is doubtful, however, that many of the presently underdeveloped countries are gaining in power from the additional increments to their populations. There are a number of reasons for this. First of all, many of these nations are already much larger and more densely populated than the western nations were when they embarked upon their economic and social modernisation. Second, their population growth is much more rapid. No modern western nation had rates of increase higher than 2 per cent per year during its period of modernisation, but rates as high as 3 or 3·5 per cent are common in the developing countries today. It is difficult for any nation to absorb such an increment without economic and social disruption.

Third, and even more important, the increases in population are badly timed. In western Europe, rapid population growth was accompanied by a rapid rise in economic productivity. This is not the case at present in large portions of the world where the levels of population increase are highest and economic productivity is quite low.

It should be noted that the demographic variables, fertility, mortality and migration, respond to different environmental stimuli. Changes in mortality are more likely to respond to structural changes within the society. When governments start or terminate wars, establish sanitary facilities or institute health programmes, the effects upon mortality are likely to be both immediate and dramatic. Often citizens have no choice whether or not to participate. Governmental action, then, may have an immediate, visible effect upon mortality.

Fertility patterns, on the other hand, are influenced by widely shared social values that are implemented by repeated individual choices. That changes in social values are not easily brought about by governmental action is attested by the very indifferent results of governmental programmes to raise birth-rates (in the thirties) or to lower birth-rates (in the fifties and sixties).

Migration lies somewhere between fertility and mortality in its susceptibility to governmental manipulation. Though initiated by individual choice, it can certainly be directed or prohibited by governmental action. International migration, in particular, can be sharply diminished by decree.

It is therefore demographically significant what pattern of modernisation a nation pursues. In western Europe high levels of political participation and political mobilisation (and accompanying governmental programmes) that had the effect of reducing mortality were not achieved until after relatively high levels of economic and social modernisation had been sustained for a considerable period. Thus fertility as well as mortality dropped, with a gap between them large enough to assure substantial population growth, but the rate of growth was not so high as to be unmanageable, and the increase in total population came at a time when it could be absorbed into economically productive labour.

More recently, in the Soviet Union, in China and in much of the underdeveloped world the transitional period from underdeveloped to developed status has been signalled by the achievement of high levels of political mobilisation, while levels of productivity, urbanisation and social mobility remain low. In part because levels of political mobilisation are relatively high, effective governmental programmes to reduce mortality achieve impressive results far in advance of the rises in economic productivity, urbanisation and social mobility. It is mobility, productivity and urbanisation that generate the constellation of values favouring lower fertility. The result is low mortality combined with high fertility, resulting in faster, longer-lasting and ultimately larger population growth: the contemporary population explosion. If economic and social modernisation can nevertheless proceed without too long a time lag, as they did in the Soviet Union, the result is a rapid increase in national power. But if they do not, rapid population growth may impede economic development and disrupt political unity.

The relationship between population growth and economic development has been treated so many times by so many distinguished economists and demographers that there is no need to elaborate it here. Briefly stated, the problem is one of assuring that increments to the total population are absorbed into economically useful roles and thus join the effective population. To add additional people to the population of an underdeveloped nation that cannot use efficiently the people it already has is simply to compound the problems of economic development.

Rapid population growth may also impede the political development of an underdeveloped country. Political mobilisation of the previously unmobilised is often best achieved by raising expectations, often by suggesting that increased participation in political activities or in government sponsored activities will result in material improvements. Failure to meet such expectations results in disaffection, disruption or even revolt. A case in point is the inability of the Chinese to absorb into the modern sector of the economy tens of millions of high-school graduates. For this and other reasons, millions of urban youths were resettled in the countryside. One can only wonder if the anger and disruption caused by the Red Guards was in part a response to unfulfilled expectations.

High rates of natural increase may also disrupt a political system where a nation is divided along class, religious, ethnic or racial lines and where the disproportionate growth and internal migration of one such group is viewed as a threat by the others. The recent mass migration of American Blacks from high fertility, low opportunity areas into the northern cities provides an example.

Fourth and finally, population growth does not increase the power of nations today as it did in the past because there are no longer empty continents into which to dump their surplus population. Growing Europe could export her criminals, her religious fanatics and her economic failures. And she found through her colonial conquests new farmlands, new resources and new sources of international power. Today, the empty lands are largely filled and the natives who were not exterminated have learned to defend themselves. Colonial conquest and free international migration have passed away.

The population growth we see today is the continuation of a pattern that began more than 250 years ago. The curve has been almost exponential. As nations have begun their economic and social modernisation at different points of their population increase, the effects of additional people upon their national power have varied. Nations that added industrialisation to their early population growth have gained tremendously in power. Those that are today experiencing rapid population growth but have not yet developed economically will not gain much in power from their population increases. Thus the population explosion of today is not likely to alter much the international distribution of power. Rather it will confirm it. The strong will become stronger and the weak will be left further behind.

Future changes in the international distribution of power will not come primarily from population growth. They will be much more influenced by increases in economic productivity and in political mobilisation. They will come not from changes in total population size but from changes in the size of the effective population.

DISCUSSION

Panel Members: Professor B. Cockram and Dr. S. Enke

Professor Cockram regretted that the present discussion could not come after all the regional topics. Regarding Professor Organski's new concept, he wished to stress the effectiveness of efficient agricultural population such as that of the United States. Only true peasants should be excluded from the effective population. Commenting on the current strategic situation, he said population increase beyond resources would be likely to reduce living standards in underdeveloped areas. Disappointment of expectations, especially among the urban unemployed, would lead to pressure on governments who, unable to solve internal problems, would turn to xenophobia. The rich countries would continue to give aid to the poor ones. The problem would become more serious, tempting the strong powers to remove the threat from the others at all costs.

The fact that the confrontation would be largely on racial lines (with the United States and the Soviet Union co-operating more closely) would make the prospects of peace less favourable. He was sceptical of the power of the United Nations to solve the problem.

He noted the decline of the United States and the Soviet Union relative to China, Japan and Germany, the escalating costs of military expenditure, nuclear proliferation, the location of wars since 1945 in overpopulated Asia, the reluctance of major powers to use ultimate weapons, and predicted an end to the cold war through ideological disillusionment with both east and west.

Dr. Enke said the establishment of indices of war potential was an impossible task. Agricultural labour could be as important as industrial labour, for example in Australia. Per capita output extractable for war purposes might be informative, but wars varied very much and factors such as technology, 'guts' and social homogeneity made the task a hopeless one. Professor Organski had, however, made the useful point that population size was not equivalent to power.

Professor Organski explained that he did not interpret strategy in terms of war. The Black people of the United States were not able to contribute politically, socially and economically before now. In regard to major problems he argued that there was always talk about weapons, technology and nuclear bombs. These, he felt, were not as important as was generally assumed. By way of explanation he mentioned two examples:

(*a*) *The Vietnam War.* Vietnam was a small country, not well developed and scoring low on all important customary indicators. The one indicator scoring high was that having nothing to do with

G

war: the political system that was able to mobilise the peasantry when attacked in their own homes.

(*b*) *The Korean War*. In 1949 China collapsed. Two years later she took on the United States army and fought it to a standstill. What had changed? The difference was in politics: an effective political machine to send soldiers to the battle and keep them there.

We should not think in terms of 'guts'. We should rather consider the difference made to men by training and organisation.

Mr. Radford Jordan said his difficulty was that the speaker's balance was onesided. It considered only assets, not liabilities. If there was an unproductive element one had to subtract it in computations. The marginal productivity of agricultural labour in some countries was approximately nil. Automation could reduce the marginal productivity of the rest of the economy of the United States. Countries who could find additional jobs for additional hands were likely to become better off and those threatened by alienated proletarians from without or from within were likely to become worse off.

Professor S. P. Cilliers agreed with the speaker's conclusion that the population explosion would not alter the power distribution. He submitted that population was the most important resource only if other resources were present as well. He granted that Canada could be better off with more people, but not the Netherlands. The population explosion prevented many parts of the world from reaching the stage of modernisation take-off.

Professor W. Brand said that on the second page of Professor Organski's paper it was assumed that power was affected by three factors. A rather vague phrase 'effectiveness of government' had been used, and it seemed that ideology or aggressive spirit or 'guts' was meant. He had to criticise the indicators for measuring the power potential. On the third page and after, it was alleged that population size crucially limited a nation's power and that because of population growth Europe was forced to expand overseas.

He did not think that this was true. At the end of the sixteenth century, the Netherlands had one million people. She had no other resources and it was this, not over-population, that sent her colonising. It seems to have been 'guts' that sent the Netherlands overseas, but the indicators in the paper gave no idea as to what these 'guts' were.

He would also say that in Indonesia, with most of the population engaged in agriculture, it would be meaningless to calculate an 'effective population' that excluded agricultural workers.

Professor Organski said that he was only repeating what other demographers had said. There were, he argued, two kinds of colonial expansion. Europeans went out as traders in the seventeenth century. In the eighteenth and nineteenth centuries they went as conquerors and this was related to their population growth.

Dr. A. Sauvy stressed that there was another factor. Resources for power depended on population, productivity and frugality or low consumption per capita. He provided a table in support of the concept that low consumption per capita would enable a country poorer in numbers to achieve national power close to that of a well-populated one:

Population	Production per capita	Nat. Income	Proportion	Resources for Power
800	3500	280	15	42
240	1800	430	11	47
200	3000	700	8	56

Mr. Deon Fourie observed that a large population seemed to have a subjective psychological or non-rational impact. On the one hand, the United States had come to rely heavily on nuclear weapons in defence against the large Russian conventional forces. On the other hand, belief in the value of numbers encouraged adventurism in the sense that Mao had said that after a nuclear exchange between the powers, there would still be 300 million Chinese against the odd few million Americans, British and others.

Professor Organski agreed that the Chinese believed in their importance because of their numbers, and it was true that this was a matter for concern to the United States. The United States relied on nuclear weapons because it considered it was cheaper to do so and because research institutions proved these weapons to be acceptable. However, no nuclear wars had had to be faced.

Professor H. V. Muhsam pointed out that the conference was not concerned with politics and strategy, but with the effect of the population growth on them. He briefly criticised the model Dr. Sauvy had described. Non-productive age groups should be taken out of the model. Permanent occupation of women with childbearing and rearing made it impossible for them to replace male manpower for strategic purposes. Population growth ate up part of the national income for demographic investment which would not be available for a high percentage of use for power purposes.

Dr. Enke said that, considering the effects on international relations, there was the prospect of chronic charity for the future. The issue was whether this was preventable or not, and the most important need was that the international community should agree that the moral responsibility of a nation was to balance population growth and the ability to feed its population not by self-sufficiency but by exporting to pay for imports of food. The state intervened in motivations in diverse ways and in this manner could promote the control of population growth. It was, therefore, conceivable that governments could rid themselves of pro-natal policies and turn to birth control policies. The Conference should establish it as a principle that governments should ensure that they maintained and fed their own populations. The problem was for *each* nation to do so, not whether the *world* could produce enough food.

Professor Cockram concluded the discussion with three remarks:

(*a*) He agreed with the concept of 'guts' or the effectiveness of men only when this was linked to nuclear weapons. In history small nations made their mark in wars and dominated others for a while with new weapons or tactics. But without numbers they could not maintain their position. They could only be effective if supported by technology.

(*b*) He mentioned that the waste of war was not only of men, but also of weapons. Over the longer view Britain needed to conserve manpower; this signified the first signs of British decline from 1944. Thus not only the quality of men, but also of weapons was critical.

(*c*) Nuclear weapons had not been used, not because they were ineffective, but because no nation wanted to lose its nuclear virginity; this tended to be forgotten when nuclear power was written off.

11 Population factors in Latin America

As there was no main paper on this topic, the discussion was led by four panel members: Professor J. L. Sadie, Professor W. Brand, Professor E. S. Munger and Mr. M. Nupen. They each contributed brief statements, which are summarised below, before the discussion from the floor.* Professor M. H. H. Louw, also a panel member, made brief comments at the conclusion of the discussion.

Professor Sadie said that as a result of a birth-rate of 38 and a death-rate of 9 the population of 283 million in Latin America was growing at 2·9 per cent per annum, which was the highest regional rate of growth in the world. Two-thirds of Latin America's population was found in Brazil, Mexico, Argentine and Columbia. Only a few countries (Argentine, Chile, Uruguay, Cuba) had experienced transition to low fertility rates, and the rest, which contained 82 per cent of the region's population, had birth-rates from 40 to 49. The result was a youthful population, only 55 per cent being in the 15–64 age-group compared with 65 per cent in North America. More than half the population was urbanised, and the urban population in each country was usually heavily concentrated in one major city. 'Over-urbanisation' was a serious problem in this region. Very little had been done to promote family planning, but opposition to it was not as great as it was five or six years ago.

Professor Sadie said that taking as our frame of reference the ratio: Gross National Product to Population, which reflects, albeit inadequately, the average level of living, we might distinguish three categories of economies and, accordingly, ascribe three types of roles to population. In the first category there was a large amount of entrepreneurial talent generating a large G.N.P. In such countries there was economic development proper. These countries could cope with a reasonably rapid population growth, and such growth might indeed stimulate development. In the second group were countries which were also experiencing economic development proper, but the rate of population growth was so high as to act as an impediment to rising living standards. In the third group there was an absence of entrepreneurs coupled with a high population growth, so that the growth of the G.N.P. as well as population was unfavourable.

Latin America probably fitted into the second category, although

* Summaries prepared by Rapporteurs.

the economies were not very dynamic. Economic growth was a function of external events rather than endogenous entrepreneurship

The United States tried to co-ordinate aid through O.A.S. and A.I.D. The Common Market, established by six countries in 1958–9, reduced trade barriers and resulted in some co-ordination of fiscal policies, but this co-operation had begun to peter out. The Latin-American Free Trade Association hoped to establish a common market, but had not been very successful. Finally, Professor Sadie mentioned the political instability of the region, which he attributed in large measure to the population explosion.

Professor Brand maintained that no country conducted a real policy regarding births and deaths. The effects of efforts to lower the death-rate were difficult to assess; low mortality resulted from a variety of measures, but the effect of institutional arrangements was diffused so that improvement could not be attributed to any one factor. In the Netherlands no policy regarding fertility had been promulgated, and the birth-rate was considered as a datum not subject to manipulation, but some politicians and scientists now considered this to be an obsolete attitude.

Though Latin America had an average G.N.P. per capita of $400, higher than other developing regions, its economic growth-rate combined with its high rate of population increase had resulted in a slow rate of increase in income per capita. This did not mean that population growth as such had impeded economic growth, as some countries with a low population growth had done rather poorly economically. The high population growth-rates had placed a heavy burden on agriculture; no scope had been left for an improvement in diets or a decrease in the number of those suffering from malnutrition.

The housing situation had deteriorated in the region, he said. Latin America was also falling behind in the educational growth race. Concomitantly, the problems of wastage of manpower, unemployment and underemployment had increased. Patterns of landownership and income distribution seemed to be tending towards greater inequality. Population pressures had led to a further division, especially of smallholdings.

During the next thirty years the population of Latin America was likely to double, and to press severely on natural and other resources. Improvements in life expectancy, in infant mortality, education and the high rate of urbanisation, had so far not modified levels of fertility in Latin America, but there were wide variations. Surveys suggested that women were anxious to have fewer children. There was widespread concern about the effect of the high rate of population increase. The explanation of high fertility in terms of the

Roman Catholic Church's attitude to contraception, or as a result of the prevalence of a virility culture (*machismo*), he thought wanting. Fertility decrease was, of course, associated with the emancipation of women, but this concept was difficult to measure.

There were two schools of thought, he said: the first proposed that a higher rate of economic and social development was required to modernise Latin America and create a climate which would reduce the number of children. But there was bound to be a considerable time lag between economic changes and fertility decline. The second school of thought assumed that a demand for curtailment already existed and that positive government action would lead to a quick decline in fertility.

Generally he believed that in Latin America income growth was independent of population increase and that a lower fertility rate would raise income per capita. A birth control programme to bring down fertility would be many times less expensive than ordinary investment in achieving growth in per capita income. It would be rash to designate Latin-American countries in which such programmes would be feasible, but one should not underestimate the rapidity with which opinions change, and governments might become convinced that family planning deserved a place among other economic and social measures to alleviate human misery.

Professor Munger discussed the attitude of the Roman Catholic Church in Latin America towards birth control. He contended that it was wrong to view the Church as a force operating against birth control in this region. Church leaders had not emphasised the pronouncements of Pope Paul against birth control in Humanae Vitae; instead they had stressed the personal approach to marital relations embodied in the encyclical, which replaced the Church's traditional legalistic approach to marriage. Church leaders accepted that it was largely for the individual to decide whether to use birth control methods or not. While it was true that the Church did not promote birth control, it did not actively obstruct it. Professor Munger pointed out that most Church opposition to birth control had been caused by attempts on the part of foreign institutions to promote birth control, because such efforts, particularly from the United States, were viewed with suspicion.

Mr. Nupen emphasised the political factor as the greatest impediment to achieving a global equilibrium of development and population growth. He dealt firstly with the growth of an ideology of conflict and violence in Latin America, which was the main political result of unequal development. The Latin-American countries were deeply suspicious of the willingness of the developed world to assist them. The basis of this suspicion was Lenin's thesis that large sections of the underdeveloped world were victims of imperialism, of economic and political exploitation. The Third World was finding its identity in solidarity against all possessing powers. At a meeting of the Organisation of Latin-American Solidarity in Havana in August 1967, Moscow-line communists were subject to attacks no less intense than those made upon the United States. Leninist analyses of contradiction had long since given way to an ideological literature of hate, frequently irrational, frequently nihilistic, but vital because at its core lay a truth.

Secondly, Mr. Nupen developed Celso Furtado's thesis that 'United States hegemony in Latin America, by underpinning the anachronistic power structure, constitutes a serious obstacle to development for the majority of countries in the region'. The United States had not shifted from the view that, as Professor Wolfers put it in 1959, 'the most effective type of aid will be the aid that promises to give the greatest satisfaction to those elite groups who are eager to keep the country out of communist or Soviet control'. This was not a very constructive policy, and an overall strategy of aid had to be developed. The influence of a giant American corporation in the primitive conditions of Latin America was devastating. Attempts by Latin-American governments to restrain this influence invited retaliation from the United States, which had not been lacking.

Finally, Mr. Nupen argued that the political struggle was increasingly between the 'classes' who inhabited the cities and the 'masses' of disenfranchised peasants and labourers in the countryside. For the moment the cities tended to be areas of reform rather than revolution, but the level of urbanisation was approximately twice that of industrialisation and this was an explosive situation. If reform was to succeed it would be necessary to eliminate the 'class-mass' dichotomy at present building up. One of the indispensable steps towards this would be agrarian reform.

DISCUSSION

Father L. J. Smith congratulated Professor Munger on his exposition of the attitude of the Church in Latin America towards birth control. He also pointed out that St. Thomas Aquinas had advocated personalism rather than legalism in the marriage relationship.

Professor Brand conceded that there was a serious unequal distribution of income within Latin-American countries, but he disagreed with Mr. Nupen's view that the situation was therefore explosive. He suggested that a so-called revolution had become part of the accepted South American style of life in several countries. He contended that the threat of a 'communist take-over' in Latin America was exaggerated.

Professor S. P. Cilliers drew attention to the need to relate the issues discussed to international relations. He warned that the loss of faith on the part of the 'have-not' nations in the 'have' nations was a matter which had to be remedied urgently.

Mr. Nupen, in reply to a question, stated that although United States policy on economic matters had been well articulated, little attempt had been made to formulate the social and political goals of the United States in the Latin Americas. The enumeration of goals was a priority. Mr. Nupen also disputed suggestions made by *Professor Munger* (in discussion) that the United States private enterprise was withdrawing from Latin America and that the American Government was no longer so concerned about the type of government put into office in Latin-American states.

Professor Munger suggested that American withdrawal from South America left the continent open to United Nations assistance in the field of reform.

Professor Sheila van der Horst stated that an O.E.E.C. type organisation might contribute much to reform.

Professor Brand made the following further points during the discussion: the unity of Latin America should not be overestimated. There were great differences in income levels, economic potential and political and social development since the continent had acquired independence. Frictions and tensions even between neighbouring countries were more or less normal and the willingness to co-operate in a common endeavour was not really great. It was not generally true that Latin America was rich in natural resources; few rivers were navigable, the continent had few natural harbours and the quality of the soil in the tropical regions was deficient. There was a widespread belief among Latin Americans that theirs was a rich sub-continent, but this was an illusion.

When visiting Latin-American countries he felt one should suppress one's own values regarding justice, distribution of income, etc. The situation in various countries appeared rather unstable, but revolutions in his opinion seldom accomplished the results expected from them.

In conclusion, *Professor M. H. H. Louw* sketched some of the main population problems confronting Latin America: uneven settlement, migration and race regulations. He reiterated the need for the promotion of birth control, agrarian reform and economic development, but warned that benign authoritarianism was the most one could hope for in Latin America. Liberal democracy had little chance of success. He concluded that he foresaw no serious population problems for the Latin Americas, because of the growth of the middle class which carried with it smaller families.

12 Population problems in Europe and the Soviet Union

ALFRED SAUVY

For an easy exposition it is preferable to examine separately western Europe, taking as its boundaries the political frontiers, and the Socialist Republics of the east (Soviet Union and the people's republics).

1. WESTERN EUROPE

If one disregards the backward south, that is to say, Portugal, southern Spain and southern Italy, one finds the most homogeneous demographic zone in the world, both as regards birth-rate and mortality rate. As an average, the rate per 1000 inhabitants is respectively 16·5 and 10, which gives a rate of natural increase of about 6·5 per 1000. In fact the birth-rate varies from 14 per 1000 in Sweden to 21 per 1000 in Ireland and life expectation at birth is from 69 years in Ireland to 73·5 years in the Netherlands and in Sweden. At the moment the net reproduction rate nearly everywhere is slightly higher than one (usually between 1 and 1·25).

But as the demographic history of these countries has been somewhat different, their composition by age remains different, although these also show a tendency towards regrouping.

As a whole the populations of western Europe are old. The proportion of the over-sixty-fives is from 10 to 14 per cent, whereas it is only 3 per cent in underdeveloped countries. This ageing of the population is not the result of lengthening of life expectation, as is still widely believed, but of the earlier drop in the birth-rate.

Tendencies of birth-rate and of fertility
In the most advanced countries, there was a sharp drop in birth-rate and in fertility before the War which rose again during and after it. Since 1964 one can observe the opposite. The birth-rate has fallen by about 10 per cent and it has not yet been proved that this is due

to any marked behavioural change. We must ask ourselves two questions in this connection:

- Will birth-rate and fertility go on falling and, if so, in what proportions?
- If birth-rate and fertility go on falling will this bring in its wake economic and social difficulties? Could the drop in birth-rate and fertility bring about political repercussions?

The factors of voluntary fertility

That subject is still somewhat obscure. Not only has the rise in fertility from 1940–50 and even later still not been properly explained (leaving aside the 'catching up' of births which have merely been postponed and the drop in marriage age) but the causes of the reflux since 1964 have not yet been established. The following factors can be mentioned:

- Progress made in contraceptive techniques.
- The general atmosphere caused by open debates on this subject.
- Legalisation of abortion in some countries.
- Anguish regarding the overpopulation of the world.
- Fear of unemployment following automation.
- Working women.

The contraceptive pill has been used in Europe since about 1960. Although the use of the pill is not enough to explain the drop in fertility, its use must not however be seen as negligible. And above all, we must take into account that the commotion which has surrounded the pill, the public debates which it has provoked, have had a definite influence.

If the *clinical* effectiveness of the pill is complete, its effectiveness in practice is only partial. The loud campaign in England and in other countries in favour of legal abortion is sufficient proof of this and this pressure is part of the vast liberating movements sweeping the whole world, and especially in those countries where liberty is the greatest. The number of legal abortions in England is more or less 40,000 per year, but the drop in the birth-rate due to the new law should be less than this figure.

The influence of the anxiety caused by overpopulation in the world cannot be proved scientifically, at least not in an experimental way. The birth-rate is largely a phenomenon of *collective psychology* transcending the individual. We may however quote the Swedish professor who, in all candour, advised his fellow citizens to exercise moderation in reproducing themselves, saying that their descendants should make place for other more prolific populations and this conviction exists at the very centre of the unconscious.

Although one cannot speak of world solidarity in the direction of charitable duty, nor of a solicitude for justice, it seems certain that there is a confused and widespread fear, but once again its influence on the birth-rate cannot be proved.

The fear of unemployment

This is also part of a collective feeling. At the time of the Great Depression in the thirties, the birth-rate dropped not only in the families threatened by unemployment but also in the families of civil servants who were in sheltered employment. The feeling of man's uselessness weighed heavily in those days and found expression in those words often heard at that time, 'What's the use of creating out-of-works?'

The fear of machines adjudged to be job-eaters has always existed and has maintained itself, despite the fact that events have given the lie to it. Today this fear is particularly strong on account of the progress of automation.

What about the 'absolute weapon'?

The future lowering of fertility may be the result of a change in the behaviour of couples or of a greater efficacy of contraceptive methods.

What would bring the 'absolute weapon', the perfect contraceptive? We have two guide marks here. In the countries where abortion has been legalised (Hungary, Japan, Rumania) the reproduction rate at present has dropped to below 1. The case of Hungary (birth-rate from 1963–5 13·1 per 1000, i.e. 0·85 for the net rate of reproduction) is the most striking. Surveys in French maternity hospitals have shown a proportion of unwanted preganancies of over 40 per cent. This figure does not mean that the perfect contraceptive would bring down the birth rate by 40 per cent, for some unwanted pregnancies simply occurred before they were desired. Nevertheless one may suppose that the birth-rate would diminish considerably.

In other highly developed countries the proportion of unwanted pregnancies is undoubtedly lower than this figure; nevertheless it must be considerable.

Mortality: the prospects

The risks here are not so great, so much so that the forecasters often adopt only one hypothesis concerning mortality. Besides, life expectation at birth is not expected to increase as fast as it did in the past, now that the struggle against death is directed against endogenous causes. Already one can observe in certain highly developed countries like Norway a slightly rising tendency to a higher mortality rate, above 55 or 60 years of age. Life expectation at birth might only be 76 or 77 years in the year 2000, thus increasing by 4 or 5 years, whereas from 1940–70 it has increased by more than 13 years. Nevertheless there are some who think that by the year 2000 life expectation will be over 80 years of age. But even the eradication of cancer as a cause of death would not suffice to bring about a rate of increase such as was experienced in the last 30 years.

It is, however, possible that the process of ageing caused up till now solely by the lowering of the birth-rate will result from now on partly from a falling in the mortality rate.

The most delicate problem is that of the effort that society will agree to make to prolong the life of the sick and particularly the life of the aged. Even now most of the aged do not receive the care which would be given to them if they enjoyed strong financial resources or a high prestige, political or otherwise. This difficulty can only become more marked.

Possible consequences

Let us choose a pessimistic hypothesis. The birth-rate drops, whereas the burden of old age pensions and of sickness insurance becomes steadily higher under the triple influence of the cost of new therapeutical techniques, the increase in the number of the aged and the tendency shown by a socially insured population to demand more care. The risk then is of seeing old age preponderate in an ageing population which will no longer have sufficient resources to create and to invest, or even to react against a slow evolution; all this, of course, while postulating political stability.

But it is possible to oppose another hypothesis to that pessimistic one: relative stability in the behaviour of couples, or more exactly maintaining the size of the completed family at the level of 2·1 or 2·2 children. The evolution would then be much slower; it would entail a slightly more rapid growth of population and a less marked ageing process.

So far we have dealt only with *natural demography*. We must now consider migration. It gives to future perspectives a rather different look and leads us now to consider the active population.

In western Europe, the growth of education has brought about a certain disregard for manual trades, particularly those which are the lowest paid and the most arduous. To compensate for the shortfall, one calls in foreigners from less developed countries. This phenomenon is particularly marked in France, Germany, England and Switzerland.

When a rich man and a poor man find themselves in the same region, it is fairly natural and almost inevitable that the first should employ the second. Portugal, southern Spain, Algeria, Morocco and Tunisia are important reserves of manpower as the men find it difficult to get employment at home. Birth-rate in Algeria is near 50 per 1000, which will pose problems for a long time to come.

Without passing a value judgement on this exchange of manpower and without discussing the problems of justice that it raises, we must note that there are demographic consequences: in western Europe a greater heedlessness of the natural falling of the birth-rate, in north Africa an equal heedlessness of the excessive birth-rate. In western Europe this exchange of manpower may well give a solution to two problems: *that of the possible reduction in births* and, in part, *that of the professional composition* of the population. On the other hand, it also entails serious risks on the political and social level.

2. THE SOCIALIST COUNTRIES

The Marxist doctrine
Before we start describing how the Socialist countries are evolving, we must recall briefly the Marxist doctrine concerning population: it is less a true theory than the result of Marx's violent reaction against Malthus and his disciples. It has been said that in a socialist regime there can be no overpopulation; 'the table is laid for everybody to sit round' – an allusion to Malthus's fable of the banquet of nature where the men who are too many cannot find place. A little later, the Marxists have estimated that the drop in the birth-rate of the west was a specially '*bourgeois*' phenomenon, a result of capitalist materialism.

They broke away completely from the reformist socialists who stipulated a reduction in the births of the working class. Today, that doctrine is directed towards the 'Third World' and is expressed by a fundamental optimism about the ways in which we can master nature. An optimism which for these past few years has been somewhat less vigorous.

Mortality
There has been a general drop in the mortality rate, but it does not seem that this drop has been more marked than in other countries which have known sufficient economic development.

At birth life expectation is, however, nearly as high as in the west, despite the fact that the economic standard, properly so called, is lower than in the west. It is probably between 68 years (Albania, Yugoslavia) and 72 years (Soviet Union and Czechoslovakia). The male mortality is rather markedly in excess of the female. The result achieved by the Soviet Union is the more remarkable in that it applies to the whole territory, Asia included.

The drop in birth-rate since the First World War.
In all Socialist countries, even Albania, birth-rate has dropped since the war, particularly so in countries where it was traditionally high (Poland, Rumania, Yugoslavia and Albania). The rate per 1000 recorded or estimated in 1969 is as follows:

East Germany	14·3	Soviet Union	16·9
Hungary	14·9	Yugoslavia	18·7
Czechoslovakia	15·3	Rumania	24·0
Poland	16·3	Albania	34·0
Bulgaria	16·5		

East Germany offers various special characteristics:

- East Germany already had well-established contraceptive traditions.
- She lost a very high proportion of her population and of the best elements of the population by migration to West Germany until the sealing-off of Berlin; therefore the population is old which partly explains the low birth-rate.
- The East Germans only have recourse to abortion with great reluctance.

The reason for the drop in the birth-rate in other Socialist countries is two-fold, depending on whether it is examined at the social or the technical level:

- Couples' behaviour rather similar to that of the western couples.
- Spreading of contraceptive practices and especially the author-isation of abortion, which is practised in public hospitals and nursing homes – the rules differing from country to country and also varying from time to time.

Behaviour of couples
After a survey conducted in Moscow in various households in order to learn the reasons for the refusal to have second or third children, the most usual answers were: inadequate salaries, crèches too far or too few, lodgings too small to allow the granny (*babouchka*) to live within the household.

Work by women is widespread in the Soviet Union and accommo-dation is still very inadequate. Apart from the acceptance of shared accommodation, we find that the preoccupations of these households are very similar to those in the west. Hungary has adopted since 1965 certain social measures to raise the birth-rate, but Bulgaria has gone further and has granted, since 1968, substantial birth bonuses and monthly grants for the second and third child.

	Bonus	Monthly Grant
1st child	20 levas	5 levas
2nd child	200 ,,	15 ,,
3rd child	500 ,,	35 ,,
4th child and over	20 ,,	5 ,,

As a matter of comparison it should be mentioned that the average salary may be taken as 80 or 90 *levas* per month.

The consequences of these measures to encourage births are difficult to assess, as they were taken at a time when abortion was not so readily allowed (the birth-rate has gone up since 1968, while the measures were only applied at the beginning of this year).

Spreading and use of contraceptive techniques

In the Socialist countries abortion plays a bigger part than contraceptive techniques because the government can easily modify the rules governing its practices. Abortion techniques have been improved (namely, by aspiration) and the risks of death are very low. But it is noted in Hungary that babies born of women who have had at least one abortion weigh, on an average, less than the others.

In order to conform to the Marxist doctrine, government have announced that the spreading of birth prevention practices was not motivated by economic reasons. However the policy in Poland, in Yugoslavia and doubtless in other countries, has been, if not laid down, at least strongly inspired by the extent of demographic investments (factories, hospitals, housing schemes, etc.) made necessary by growth in population at the rate of 1·5 per cent or 2 per cent per year. In Marx's time, the view taken was static (overpopulation or not) while today it is dynamic, at least in the industrial countries (speed of development). On the other hand, in Marx's time, the average life span was about 40 years, which has now jumped to 72 years; the rate of survival at 28 has moved from 60 to 96. It would appear as though the birth-rate has increased by half in the absence of birth prevention practices. Conditions then are very different.

Abortion is used as a means to lift the birth-rate when this is found necessary.

The narrowing of the conditions of admission to abortion or even the raising of prices which must be paid by the women allow the birth-rate to be raised by a procedure which is more efficacious than social, since it produces unwanted pregnancies. Several countries have adopted this method: Czechoslovakia employs it as a regulating mechanism quite successfully, but Rumania handled it so clumsily in 1966–7 that the birth-rate jumped in one year from 14 to 39 per 1000 to drop back later. The consequences of this irregularity in the age pyramid will have repercussions for a long time (flooding school entrance, examinations, marriage, employment, etc., which will plague the generation born in 1967).

Anyway the procedure runs the risk of destroying itself in the long run because the couples or the women will have more and more recourse to contraceptives for fear of seeing the means of avoiding pregnancies withdrawn from them at the last moment.

Generally speaking social assistance plays a big part in these countries, but family allowances in cash are very low, except in Bulgaria for the second and third child (see above).

Projections

Projections have been made by the Census Bureau in Washington for different Socialist countries.

An increase in population is generally foreseen up to 1990, on all hypotheses for all countries, with the sole exception of East Germany (a drop of 1 per cent) in the most unfavourable of the hypotheses. In Albania, the forecast increase ranges from 57 per cent to 92 per cent.

But this increase will affect above all adult and elderly people. The proportion of over-sixty-fives will be higher than 10 per cent overall, a figure which is still below that for western Europe.

Situation in the Soviet Union

The drop in the birth-rate has been partly due to the arrival at marriageable age of the 'lost' generation born between 1942 and 1946. On the other hand, there has been at the same time a drop in fertility, but this is not very well documented because the statistics are incomplete and are made available very slowly. Speaking generally, the drop in birth-rate becomes less and less pronounced going from west to east and as economic conditions become more favourable. Here are the birth-rates in 1968 per 1000 population in some of the Republics:

R.S.S.F.R. (Europe)	14·2
Lettonia	14·1
Estonia	14·0
Azerbaidjan	32·3
Turkmenia	36·2

These Asiatic birth-rates correspond to only a very moderate use of birth prevention measures. The drop in the birth-rate is worrying the Soviet Union authorities* for economic reasons and doubtless also political ones, but they do not seem to be having recourse to a policy of family assistance.

In any event, demographic science is still in a rudimentary stage both for pure analysis and for the relationships between economic and demographic conditions. Hungary and Czechoslovakia are better provided for in this respect.

3. GENERAL VIEW

In spite of differences of regime, certain phenomena have been almost identical on either side of the political frontier, in particular the lowering of the mortality rate and of the birth-rate.

It is above all in the manner in which the difficulties are tackled that the two types of government differ. Comparing Europe with the other regions of the world, it is possible to forecast a *moderate increase of population* accompanied by *ageing*. The costs of sickness will climb and will present moral problems for medical practice.

It is difficult to speak of demographic pressure for any country or at least of over-population, the difficulties of the south of Europe being essentially the result of underdevelopment. The most marked phenomenon in western Europe is the immigration of foreign workers for manual tasks.

We have not dealt here with problems of quality: notably those of population genetics. These have not yet reached the stage of *population policies* beyond the traditional consanguinity prohibitions in marriage. But biological discoveries may well pose completely new problems.

* On this subject see an article by Dimitri Valentey in the review 'Population, March–April 1970', *Les problèmes démographiques de l'Union Soviétique.*

DISCUSSION

Panel Members: Professor W. B. Vosloo and Mr. Jean Bourgeois-Pichat.

Professor Vosloo saw the ageing structure of the population of western Europe as placing a strain on resources. He believed that migration carried with it political and social dangers. For the country of origin there were the economic benefits of relieving unemployment and the sending home of foreign currency, and workers would acquire new technical skills. However, migrants would also carry back new social and political ideas. The receiving country might experience over-foreignisation and pressure on basic services (housing, transport, etc.). There would be a heedlessness of falling birth rates and a growing disregard of the manual trades.

In the Socialist countries there were difficulties of insufficient and distorted demographic data. The discrepancy between Marxist theory and practice was interesting; both were changed according to circumstances. If one accepted Professor Organski's association of power with population, then the effect of Europe's declining population since 1964 must be significant.

Mr. Bourgeois-Pichat drew attention to the almost complete lack of interest in European demographic questions in Europe itself. The ageing of the population was significant because in a market economy basically the means to pay for goods and services were obtained by work. Immigration was also new to Europe which heretofore had been a continent of emigration. He drew a parallel with South Africa, and referred to the hypocrisy of the frontier.

Professors Sheila van der Horst and *Marcus Arkin* questioned the validity of the comparison with South Africa, since in Europe immigrant workers had freedom of choice. *Professor H. V. Muhsam* felt this choice was very limited in practice.

Professor S. P. Cilliers questioned Professor Vosloo's contention that migrant labour encouraged social change – he saw it as even dis-functional in this respect.

Dr. Sauvy saw benefits to both the sending and receiving countries in migrant labour, but he felt the balance was in favour of the receiving country.

He said further that the experience of different countries showed very different results. It had to be remembered, too, that when one spoke of migrants one was speaking of human individuals; some areas of Algeria would have died had it not been for migration to France. One had to think of the conditions of migration not simply as of a trade in goods.

Professor W. Brand suggested that disenchantment was a real but incalculable factor – disenchantment with regimes in eastern Europe and disenchantment with affluence in western Europe.

13 Population factors in the regional politics of Asia

KEI WAKAIZUMI

1. INTRODUCTION

Asia is a heterogeneous entity full of diversity and complexity. Politically unstable, militarily vulnerable, economically destitute, socially backward and culturally diverse, Asia is constantly beset with tension and unrest. To this list of major determinants affecting international relations in this part of the world one must today add another important factor. This is, namely, the explosive increase in population. The population of Asia, which at present already occupies more than one-half of the entire world population, is expected to grow at an even faster pace than ever. To put it bluntly, Asia is the problem area more than anywhere else in the world. What kind of implications does such a trend have, and what sort of impact will it have on Asian relations? In what way and to what extent is this problem an aggravating factor in the development of international politics of the region?

What follows are only some preliminary observations by this writer on the subject. It is hoped that the points raised will prove fruitful grounding for empirical research and general future studies in this area.

2. SURVEY OF POPULATION PROBLEMS IN ASIA

According to a United Nations assessment, the population of Asia as of 1970 is 1980 million, accounting for as much as 56·9 per cent of the estimated world population of 3480 million.[1] At present, the world population is estimated to grow by 60 million per year, of which nearly 40 million are Asians. In terms of annual rates of population growth, the 2 per cent average of Asia is exceedingly high in contrast to 0·8 per cent in Europe and 1·3 per cent in the United States. Furthermore, the growth-rate in Asia is expected to remain at a very high level until the 1980s so that *World Population*

Prospects, published by the United Nations, puts the Asian population at 2210 million by 1975 and 3870 million by 2000. The Asian share of the world population will have reached a high mark of 61·6 per cent by then.[2]

These figures indicate that Asia is now in an age of population explosion. What then are the causes of such a drastic increase in population? As already pointed out by experts in the field, the immediate cause is the discrepancy between the birth-rate and the death-rate.[3] In the years since the Second World War, progress in medical services and the extension of public health activities have contributed to a marked reduction in the death-rate in Asia, while at the same time the birth-rate has remained high. Apart from Japan, which has kept her birth-rate below 2 per cent and which, for that matter, is by and large an exceptional country in Asia, many countries of the region show an unusually high pattern in the birth-rate, over 3 per cent. Such high rates are in turn caused principally by the overall economic and social backwardness of Asian countries. Religious influences on society, illiteracy, matrimonial customs, more unique to rural communities and poverty in the broad sense of the term are among the major factors that lead directly to the high birth-rate and to the phenomenal growth of population in Asia.

What kinds of problems are evident in Asian countries that face this huge population, the growth of which will not abate? The first is that of 'overpopulation' and 'population pressure'. Overpopulation exists not where the man-to-land ratio exceeds a certain level, but where natural and economic resources and industrial productive capacity are not sufficient to feed the people.[4] In other words, the degree of overpopulation is largely determined by the relative level of per capita income and production of a given country.

Given this definition and the existing level of economy and industry in Asia, we find that most of the countries of the region are overpopulated. All the available data indicate that about 80 per cent of Asian countries have per capita national income of less than 250 U.S. dollars. Particularly noteworthy in this connection is the fact that both China and India, with populations of 750 million and 540 million respectively, have per capita incomes of less than 100 U.S. dollars. The situation is not very much different in Indonesia or Pakistan where populations exceed 100 million. Under the circumstances, it appears that the larger the population of a country, the greater is the population pressure. This pressure bears down on the nation with greater force because these countries are at present in a developing stage and lack the administrative capability of a modern sovereign state.

The second problem, arising from the first, is that of the 'survival' of Asian peoples. The rapid pace of population growth has most serious implications for the living standard of Asian peoples, who, already suffering a very low level of life, do not have a sufficient social and economic basis to support an ever-increasing population. Most serious in this respect is the food problem, having as it does a direct bearing upon livelihood.

D. R. Sen, Secretary General of F.A.O., warned at the Second World Population Conference in 1967 that Asia now faces a food crisis. Past performance indicates that the annual rate of increase in food supply is lagging behind the rate of population increase. Although some people make the optimistic projection that a break-through in food production technology, the so-called 'green revo-lution', will eventually solve the food problem – I wish that this would be the case – the existing gap between food and population should still be regarded as a portentous danger to the survival of Asia's people.

Judging also from the very premature stage of their economic and labour market, it is difficult to expect an early consolidation of internal economic and social institutions that could absorb a growing population. This leads to the problem of unemployment. Since an overwhelming proportion of the working population in Asia is in agriculture (50–90 per cent except for Japan, Hong Kong and Singapore), large increases in the population can hardly be trans-formed into an effective productive force. *An enormous population and the need to feed it is the most serious problem of all that confronts Asian countries, for their destiny depends on how it is solved.*

A third problem arises when we consider population policy. Population policies of Asian countries place the principal emphasis upon efforts to control high birth-rates, seeking more specifically the introduction and extension of family planning programmes. The net result of these programmes, however, has not been very sub-stantial so far, except perhaps in Japan. The fact that population control policies are less effective in those countries suffering from overpopulation eloquently shows how serious the population prob-lem is in Asia. Needless to say, Asian countries have not neglected population control policies. India, for instance, introduced family planning as a major national policy in the early fifties and in the past 15 years a total of 9 countries of the region have adopted similar programmes. What matters, however, is that the overall efficacy of these programmes, despite differences among individual countries, is unfortunately far from satisfactory. No matter what one's evalu-ation is, population control policies along these lines were strongly endorsed by the Asian Population Conference of 1963 and have received positive support and assistance from the various United

Nations agencies; and some experts, including Göran Ohlin, contend that these programmes have marked a new turn for progress since 1965.[5]

The population problem, as it now exists in Asia, is indeed extremely serious. All of the aspects discussed above still remain unsolved. In terms of individual nations Japan alone has to a greater or lesser degree achieved a successful solution. In terms of the region as a whole, however, policies remain to be tried and tested, for it is only in the very recent past that the importance and gravity of the population problem has come to be fully grasped.

3. IMPACT OF POPULATION PROBLEM ON ASIAN POLITICS

What is the impact of this enormous and alarming population growth on the international relations of Asia? What are its implications? Of the various approaches to this question, I will first look into the matter from the perspective of power politics.

The structure of world politics has recently shifted from bipolarity, characterised by the post-war dominance of the two superpowers, to political multi-polarity. Although little has changed in the overwhelming military balance between the United States and the Soviet Union, their political influence is no doubt on the decline. The fallen prestige and reduced leadership of the United States as symbolised by the Vietnam War, a similar decline in the Soviet Union's political influence within the communist world, and the intensification of the Sino-Soviet conflict are only several of the many political realities which clearly indicate a changing pattern in world politics. Naturally, portents of such change are visible also in the international relations of Asia: the political dynamics of Asia are breaking away from conventional cold war logic, and undergoing a new period of reshuffling now at the outset of the 1970s.

In addition to the United States and the Soviet Union, the major powers that will determine the future of Asian politics will be Japan and China. Both the United States and the Soviet Union have a common interest in maintaining the *status quo* in order to keep the system of peaceful co-existence on Pax Russo-Americana. In this regard, Japan has no objections to working within a political framework of peaceful co-existence. The problem seems to be China. From her revolution of 1949 through the recent Great Cultural Revolution, China has constantly been opposed to the *status quo* based upon Soviet-American predominance; she has been forced to isolate and has isolated herself from international community. The keystone of Chinese foreign policy is an anti-*status quo* policy based upon Mao Tse-tung's stragegy for national liberation. It is this China that has 750 million people today and is still increasing her already enormous population. The fact that China, with more than one-fifth of the world's population, is an anti-*status quo* country in an Asia beset with tension and turmoil will undoubtedly exert an extremely important influence on Asian politics. After all the Chinese comprise 40 per cent of all Asians, and they are tightly united. With the population factor in mind, the seriousness of the problem and the degree of its impact acquire an especially important dimension.

Needless to say, population alone is not today a decisive factor in determining the power of a nation. For instance, neither Pakistan nor Indonesia, despite their sizeable populations, can be regarded as big powers, largely due to their economic weakness and the unfinished process of their nation-building. But such is not the case with China. 750 million Chinese are regimented by a highly centralised government with a revolutionary ideology. Furthermore, China is the only nuclear power in Asia. As long as the balance of nuclear terror continues, although China would not run the risk of nuclear war, we cannot underestimate the psychological weight of a nuclear China upon her less powerful neighbours.

In terms of population growth, the countries of south-east Asia (average birth-rate 2·6 per cent) and south-west Asia (average 3 per cent) have higher rates of increase than China. However, what matters here is the enormous size of the Chinese population at present. If one examines international relations with regard to China, there have been a number of conflicts and sources of concern. For instance, China played both direct and indirect roles in the Korean War that embroiled Asia in crisis. Of course one must not forget the direct major military role played by the United States and the indirect role of the Soviet Union. For another example, in 1962 China came in conflict with India, another very large and populous country of Asia. China has cast her shadow on the Vietnam War, where again the United States plays a decisive role, and the final settlement of which is still difficult to foresee. The intensification of Sino-Soviet disputes will be a major problem for Asian politics for years to come. There are many other questions to be mentioned in this broad context. The sharp population imbalance between China and the rest of Asia thus exercises a considerably detrimental influence on the power balance in Asian politics.

I shall next approach the question of the impact of the population problem from the perspective of 'north-south relations'. The population explosion poses a very serious problem in that it causes sharp disparities between population and wealth. This point is vividly shown in a set of population and G.N.P. maps which Edwin O. Reischauer drew some time ago.[6] (Please refer to this set and to a per capita G.N.P. map designed by this writer on p. 207 below.)

On a population map Asia reveals itself to be drastically different from what it is on an ordinary Mercator projection. Namely, Asia is greatly enlarged. Particularly conspicuous also are the sizes of China, India, Indonesia and Pakistan. In contrast, the European continent is considerably shrunken, and Australia is reduced to a small island attached to Indonesia.

On a G.N.P. map Asia is again dramatically transformed. In contrast to the expanded sizes of Europe, the Soviet Union and the United States, Asia is reduced to a very small part of the world. Particularly impressive are the changes in size of China, India and Indonesia. Africa and Latin America are also reduced to almost negligible proportions. Japan alone does not show much change on these two kinds of maps.

Asia on a population map is one thing, and Asia on a G.N.P. map is quite another. This means that Asia, occupying first position in terms of population, has almost no place in the world in terms of wealth (G.N.P.). These maps clearly demonstrate how sharp is the imbalance between population and wealth in Asia. The per capita G.N.P. map drawn by this writer also underscores this point.

Economically, then, Asia belongs to the 'have-not' south. It is only Japan, now the world's third largest economic power, that belongs to the 'have' north. Due to the trend towards large population increases, Asia's economy has little prospect for growth and development. This is so because, as population experts indicate, there is an almost unavoidable correlation between poverty and population pressure. P. M. Hauser, for example, identifies a vicious circle in overpopulation and poverty and its impact on world politics.[7] In Asia, increases in population aggravate the poverty problem; acute poverty slackens economic and industrial development; the delayed pace of such development retards social and cultural progress, and this in turn prevents the effective control of population. If Asia is trapped in this vicious circle and cannot escape from it now or in the future, the continent will remain a 'danger spot', as J. O. Hertzler has aptly pointed out.[8]

Needless to say, the aggravation of the north-south problem is not only a minus factor for Asian relations; it also has a detrimental effect on international relations on the global scale. Obviously the population problem alone is not the cause of the grim outlook for Asian relations. But when intermingled with poverty and tension in this region, population pressures could have an extremely great impact on international politics in Asia. It is for this reason that the rich industrial nations of the north should pay greater attention to the realities of the population problems of Asia.

Next let us look into this problem from a broad ideological point of view. With few exceptions, Asian countries are newly emerging nations which gained their independence only after the Second World War. In order to maintain their political independence, these countries have advocated such ideologies as nationalism, anti-colonialism, socialism, communism and the doctrine of non-alignment. The role of ideology in Asian international relations is too important to be overlooked. None the less ideology alone cannot solve Asian backwardness. Heightened nationalism, for instance, is no panacea for population control. On the contrary, pressures and frustrations against the higher expectations, created by food problems, unemployment, the slow tempo of development, unused resources, etc., coming from population expansion, are more often than not by-passed by political leaders who seek external targets for disaffection. This tends to make nationalism all the more rigid, exclusive and dogmatic. Disaffection caused by domestic politics is made to seek scapegoats abroad, making the cry of 'anti-colonialism' harsher. At the same time, one can see the positive side of nationalism, which is the spirit of independence, self-respect and self-help. I consider this element to be *sine qua non* in tackling the population explosion in the process of nation-building. Also, as treated by Professor Vosloo's paper, there does exist an ideological conflict in terms of communism versus capitalism in Asia, and a meaningful comparison can be made between China and India in this context. Of course the population problem is not directly connected with ideology, but ideological orientations may well prove to be serious barriers or stimuli to steady efforts to solve the population problem. This is not without its implications for Asian relations.

It is also necessary to consider the racial implications of the problem, although this is as yet only a potential issue. Since Asia is racially heterogeneous, the possibility of conflicts between her races will become greater as populations grow. However, since the international flow of people and migration are much less active in Asia than in Europe and America, it is not likely that racial problems arising from population expansion will immediately cause serious conflicts on a nation-to-nation level. Certainly the problem of the overseas Chinese is not negligible, but it has not as yet become grave enough to have a decisive impact on international relations in this region. In addition to the racial aspect, problems of religion and language will also have to be considered in connection with the population problem.

4. PROSPECTS OF THE POPULATION PROBLEM IN ASIA AND SOME OBSERVATIONS ON POSSIBLE POLICIES

In projecting the future of the population problem in Asia it may be useful to review the past policies and performances of Asian countries. Let us take the case of India.

India, with an estimated population of 540 million, is one of the Asian countries that has made a most serious attempt to tackle the population problem. Yet it appears that India's achievement has been mediocre, if not a failure.

It is true that a sense of crisis over the population problem was already articulated in India before the Second World War. The first five-year plan, starting in 1950, identified concrete strategies for population control and family planning with a Malthusian orientation. This plan was followed by the second and the third five-year plans. At least we can be sure of the constant concern and eagerness of the Indian government over the population problem. But the Indian population has kept increasing at a rate even higher than the Asian average, and there is no sign that this trend will change. India's per capita national income is less than 100 U.S. dollars, making her one of the world's poorest countries. Furthermore, her food situation is getting more and more critical, as indicated by some reports of starvation.

What is then the cause of the failure of India's effort? In short, it is the social and cultural backwardness of India herself. Religious practices are tenaciously maintained; the caste system has been retained; as much as 70 per cent of the population is illiterate. Indian political life is also unstable, as seen in the split of the Congress Party. The very fact that, unfortunately, India still remains economically and socially underdeveloped is the decisive factor that makes it impossible to prevent the excessive expansion of the population.

Take the case of China for another example, and the picture is almost the same. Although no definitive data are available, an educated guess would be that her rate of population growth is over 2 per cent, i.e. an annual increase of more than 15 million. Agricultural production, on the other hand, may not expand as rapidly. This will probably impose a heavy burden upon the Chinese economy and society. Unlike India however, China, being a highly centralised totalitarian country, may be able to find a way out of this situation, depending on the kind of political leadership available to her government. T. E. Dow, in his analysis of the Chinese population problem, also suggests this possibility.[9] But it is yet uncertain whether China can effectively control her enormous population and whether the highly unfavourable effects of China's population pressure on Asian politics can be eliminated.

The United Nations' 'decade of development' has failed to achieve its original goals as far as Asia is concerned, where economic, social and cultural depression hinders prosperity and the forecast of welfare and future promise is bleak. This poses a threat to the peace of Asia. We cannot emphasise too much the fact that poverty and internal political instability are directly inter-related. As Robert S. McNamara points out in his *The Essence of Security*, insurgency is directly related to the economic conditions of the country where it takes place. Since 1958, 87 per cent of those poor countries with per capita national incomes of less than 100 U.S. dollars have suffered from major insurgencies.[10] This is generally the case with most of the poor nations of Asia, including India, Pakistan and Indonesia.

If economic destruction is one of the major causes of overpopulation, as pointed out by the Pearson Commission and many others, the Asian population problem must be attacked from a global point of view in order to help solve the economic poverty of the region. If Asia remains as poor as it is today, Asians will inevitably come to feel a strong sense of inequality and inferiority *vis-à-vis* the peoples of the rich industrial countries. Such psychological burdens alone, if not leading directly to conflict or war, would clearly obstruct the achievement of stable world peace.

What direction should solutions to the Asian population problem take? Let me suggest some feasible alternatives. First is an international approach to the problem. This would call for substantial assistance to and co-operation with those Asian nations suffering from overpopulation on the question of national programmes of family planning of all kinds, through government policies in the short run and through education in the long run as well as on the basic question of economic development and social modernisation. Contents of and procedures for assistance and co-operation should be carefully examined, so that they promote the self-help efforts of the recipient countries. In my view along these lines, multilateral channels of assistance are more desirable than bilateral arrangements. As is shown by the Vietnamese and other experiences, economic assistance may not necessarily lead to the development of the recipient country, depending on the political intentions of both donor and recipient. It may also be that assistance for soy sauce may sometimes be transformed into assistance for guns. In any multilateral arrangement it is desirable to make use of organisations which are not ideologically oriented. The United Nations is at present the most desirable kind of organisation. Specifically in Asia, more effective use should be made of such agencies as the Economic Commission for Asia and the Far East and the Asian Development Bank.

The above orientation however, signalling little more than a secondary approach to the population problem, cannot therefore provide a fundamental solution that goes to the heart of the problem. An alternative must be proposed: the self-help efforts of the Asian countries themselves. They should become more aware of the seriousness of the problem and intensify their determination to meet it. Assistance from outside can only become effective with such a spirit of self-help on the part of recipient countries. It seems to be clear that developed countries can encourage, motivate and help less advanced nations to *help themselves*, but developed nations cannot go much beyond that and do the work for them.

Unaware of the international implications of the population problem, many Asian countries under population pressure tend to regard it simply as their individual internal issues. It would be highly desirable if these countries, facing a common problem as they do, would promote as much regional co-operation as possible in order to introduce common policies and programmes. A long-range solution to the problem can best be found in this way.

Finally, let me add a few remarks on the kind of things we should be aware of in dealing with the population problems of Asia. Assistance to Asia, particularly in the form of co-operation by advanced countries for the solution of population problems, should be based on a full understanding of the diversity and complexity of Asia and the nationalistic feelings and aspirations of Asians. For instance, the kind of co-operative assistance extended to the Philippines ought to be different from that extended to Pakistan. The experiences of the advanced countries that have successfully controlled their populations cannot simply be copied in Asia.

What should be the extent of the Japanese contribution? While recently much has come to be expected of Japan because of her remarkable economic growth as well as her location in Asia, the practical area of feasible and effective Japanese contribution is much more limited than is commonly thought. As the Japanese G.N.P. is expected in the near future to become larger than that of all other Asian countries combined, I fear Asians will come to look at Japan more with an eye of envy than with one of respect. In the Asian Population Conference of 1963, the late Premier Nehru said: 'Many countries of Asia should learn from the experience of Japan which has achieved miraculous success in the harmonious development of population and economy'. In this sense Japan should not spare any effort for co-operation and assistance, not only in material terms but also in terms of moral support, as we Japanese have succeeded in rapid modernisation mainly through the national spirit of self-help and hard work.

Regarding China, the virtual isolation from international society of the nation having the world's largest population is highly undesirable, not only for international relations in Asia but also for the peace of the world at large. It is very unnatural that this country, with a population comprising one-fifth of the world's people, should not be represented at the United Nations; even though there may be difficulties in connection with all the ramifications of Taiwan's representation. When we think of the population problem in the context of Asian politics, the existence of 750 million people should not be treated lightly. It is fair to say that China's enormous population and the trend of international politics are critically inter-related.

The above observations may lead to the conclusion that the current situation, as well as the prospects for the Asian population problem, is much darker than is generally anticipated, and that its impact on Asian politics is and will become much greater than is usually thought.

We can at least be very certain that there is still considerable room for studies from these points of view. While this paper could not go much beyond a summary survey of the possible directions of solving the population problem in Asia, it is also obvious that there is no one answer. Finally, it should be emphasised that although the basic solution should be sought in the self-help efforts of the countries concerned, all avenues should be explored vigorously so that the population problem becomes an object of serious study from the wider perspective of international politics.

Notes

1. United Nations, *World Population Prospects as assessed in 1963* (New York, 1966); U.N., *The Future Growth of the World Population*, Population Studies No. 28 (New York, 1968).
2. *World Population Prospects*, op. cit.
3. Toshio Kuroda, *Analysis of Japanese Population* (Ichiryusha, 1968).
4. N. Doman, *The Coming Age of World Control* (New York, Harpers, 1962) pp. 258–9.
5. Göran Ohlin, *Population Control and Economic Development* (Development Centre of the Organisation for Economic Co-operation and Development, Paris, 1967) pp. 7–9.
6. Edwin O. Reischauer, 'New Maps of the World', *Chuokoron* (September 1965).
7. Philip M. Hauser, 'Population, Poverty, and World Politics', in *University of Illinois Bulletin*, vol. 62 no. 97 (June 1965) pp. 3–16.

8. J. O. Hertzler, *The Crisis in World Population – A Sociological Examination with Special Reference to the Underdeveloped Areas* (Lincoln, University of Nebraska, 1956) p. 110.

9. Thomas E. Dow, Jr., 'The Population of China', in *Japan–America Forum*, vol. 15 no. 7 (July 1969) pp. 34–5.

10. Robert S. McNamara, *The Essence of Security: Reflections in Office* (New York, Harper & Row Publishers, 1968) p. 146.

11. P. M. Hauser, 'Population, Poverty and World Politics', op. cit., p. 12.

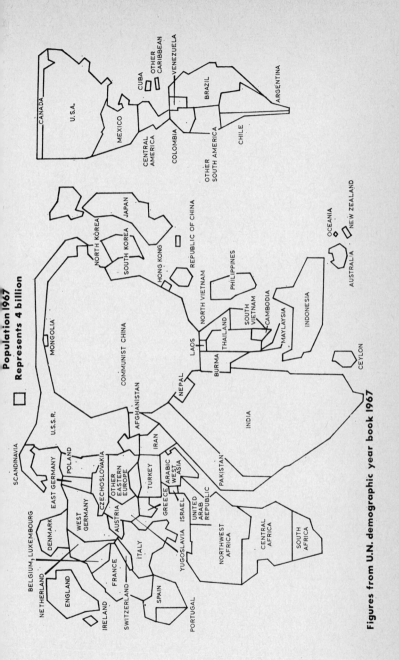

Population 1967

☐ Represents 4 billion

Figures from U.N. demographic year book 1967

H

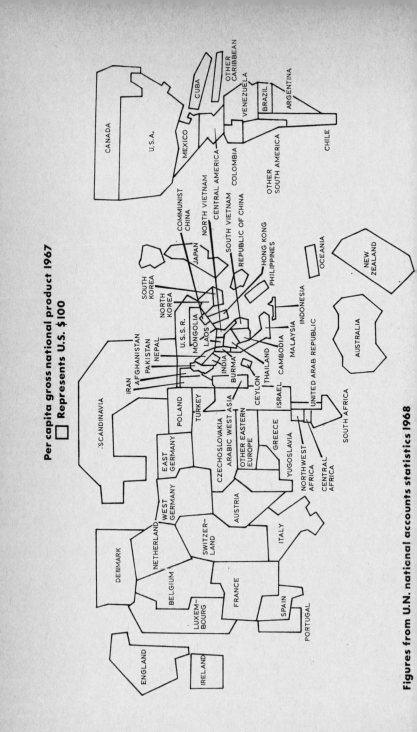

Per capita gross national product 1967

☐ **Represents U.S. $100**

Figures from U.N. national accounts statistics 1968

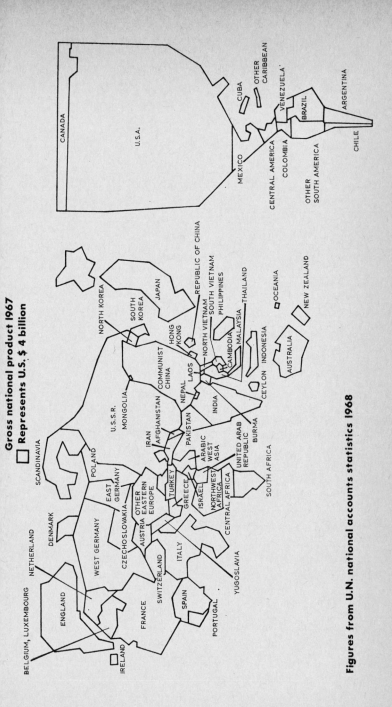

Gross national product 1967

☐ Represents U.S. $ 4 billion

Figures from U.N. national accounts statistics 1968

DISCUSSION

Panel Members: Professors C. A. Price, B. Cockram and W. Brand

Professor Price commented on a number of points:

(*a*) The heterogeneity of Asia. Asia was not a single part of the world which could be thought of in conglomerate terms. It fell into five groups:

- (i) Soviet Asia whose policies were those of the Soviet Union.
- (ii) Islamic Asia ranging from the Middle East to Pakistan.
- (iii) Indian Asia with its own peculiarly Hindu background and great diversity.
- (iv) China, a country about which little was known. China, he said, had a changing population policy which veered from the Marxist condemnation of population control at one time to policies which advocated family planning.
- (v) Island Asia with a variety of diverse lands in the Pacific and Indian Oceans.

(*b*) Japan, he said, had had considerable success in adapting to modern industrial trends. In addition to hard work and a spirit of self-help, Japan's advance was also due to its social values and social system which made it possible to reconcile its values with those of the west. One of the major problems in the rest of Asia was the changing of social values to raise achievement levels.

(*c*) India was faced with overwhelming problems. Many educated Indians believed that communism offered the only solution, as it was the only ideology ruthless enough to change traditions and weld the Indians together effectively.

(*d*) He questioned whether solving the population problems of Asian countries would obviate international friction. It was possible that many Asian countries would go through a militaristic stage in the same way as Japan had done.

(*e*) He agreed that regional co-operation was essential and that people who shared a problem should tackle it together.

Professor Cockram agreed with the main speaker's assessments of the dangers facing Asia. To these he would add:

- (i) China's entry to the nuclear club and the possibility that the future might demand of Japan that she look to nuclear weapons for herself as an alternative to adapting to United States policies.
- (ii) India did not have the prospect of the American nuclear umbrella. Because of her feud with Pakistan she might turn to nuclear weapons before Japan.
- (iii) Japan's and India's mutual interest in containing China might lead to defence co-operation between them.

(iv) United States policy towards south-east Asia was likely to be re-formed around Indonesia to encourage the anti-communists there and to hold the off-shore line from Japan to Singapore. The United States might prefer the Straits of Malacca to the Cape route as an entry to the Indian Ocean.

Professor Brand thought that the economic development of Asia was subject to misrepresentations, and he wished to add the following points:

(*a*) Countries such as Taiwan, Hong Kong, Singapore and Malaysia had a higher G.N.P. growth-rate than any European country or South Africa.

(*b*) From what was known the growth-rates of India and China were almost the same over the periods 1949–66 for China, and 1947–66 for India. However, India's difficulties were better publicised than China's, but China was not developing any better than India.

(*c*) The differences between Asians and Europeans had perhaps been overemphasised. They were alike in their wants, and the differences arose because of Asia's greater population problems and limited economic opportunities.

(*d*) Racial problems in Asia required further emphasis. In some countries racial minorities were the focus of considerable conflict.

(*e*) Japan might be forced to assume a military position towards China because of China's size and influence in Asia, coupled with the distance between Asia and the United States.

Professor Wakaizumi replied to Professor Brand's comment about Japan's military role in Asia. He said the Japanese were concerned overwhelmingly with self-defence, and though some wished for nuclear weapons there was a strong sentiment against them. Predictions were however difficult, especially as China's intentions remained a mystery.

Mr. A. J. Karstaedt suggested that by 'self-help' Professor Wakaizumi meant that population questions were a national matter. South Africa, for example, did not want 'international' advice.

Mr. Radford Jordan desired more discussion of the Soviet Union and especially of the Sino-Soviet conflict, including the possibility of a *rapprochement* between Japan and the Soviet Union.

With regard to 'self-help' *Professor Wakaizumi* felt that international advice and encouragement were very important. With regard to the Soviet Union, he considered that the Soviet Union and her deteriorating relations with China played an important role in Asian politics, as did also the peaceful coexistence of the Soviet Union and the United States.

14 Africa: Economic and other implications of population growth

G. M. E. LEISTNER

INTRODUCTORY

1. In Africa, as in other less developed parts of the world, the population explosion of the past few decades profoundly affects all aspects of human existence. This paper analyses and interprets a few outstanding features of these developments in so far as they can be discerned at present. In Part 1 the changes recorded in recent years in Africa's population, food resources and incomes are analysed. The more important consequences of the observed trends are discussed in Part 2 with regard to education, employment, urbanisation, migration, the refugee problem and related matters. In Part 3 family planning and other measures to obviate further worsening of man–resource ratios are dealt with. The foregoing provide a basis for an evaluation of current and prospective trends in internal politics and their impact on international relations in Part 4.

2. Our discussion focuses mainly on east, west and central Africa or what is commonly called black Africa. Unless the context indicates otherwise, north and southern Africa* are excluded, the former because it is more usefully treated as part of the Middle East, the latter because the economic and political structures of South Africa, Rhodesia, Angola and Mozambique would necessitate more qualifications than can be accommodated in this paper, which must of needs remain at a fairly high level of generalisation.

---

* For practical reasons, the division into 'sub-regions' as defined by the Economic Commission for Africa (E.C.A.) and other U.N. bodies is being followed here. Their definition of southern – or as they call it, 'Other' – Africa includes only South and South West Africa, Botswana, Lesotho and Swaziland, whereas in South Africa, 'southern Africa' is commonly understood to embrace also Rhodesia, Zambia, Malawi, Angola, Mozambique and – sometimes – Madagascar.

1. CHANGES IN POPULATION AND RESOURCES

POPULATION DENSITY

3. Outside the teeming principal cities, black Africa's plains, forests and mountain highlands generally appear to be under rather than overpopulated. With an average density of about 12 people per km², black Africa is indeed sparsely inhabited compared with western Europe's 148 persons per km² or India's 156. In fact, Africa's low average density figure hides a diversity ranging from 1 person per km² in Botswana and South West Africa to over 120 in Rwanda and Burundi, and much higher figures in particular regions. The Lowlands of Lesotho with a *de jure* population of 278 persons per km² of cultivated land are representative of many rural areas that are seriously overpopulated given their present pattern of resource use.

POPULATION GROWTH

4. Until a few years ago the view prevailed that Africa was under-populated, and that except for a few intensively settled areas no population pressure existed. This view dated from colonial days when estimated population growth was in fact as low as 0·6 per cent a year for 1900–30 and 1·3 per cent from 1930–50. In British East Africa the growth-rate for the decades after 1920 was put at about 0·5 per cent, whereas today that of Kenya is at least 2·5 per cent per annum and is expected to rise to 2·9 per cent in 1975–80 (see table). During the past two to three decades death-rates have fallen considerably, with the result that current rates of natural increase are four to five times as high as before. In respect of 1965–70 average annual growth-rates for the major regions were: central Africa 1·6 per cent, east Africa 2·2 per cent, southern Africa 2·3 per cent, west Africa 2·6 per cent. In several countries, such as the Ivory Coast, Upper Volta, Niger, Cameroons, Zambia, etc., the rate is put above 3 per cent and may well be equally high in many others still believed to have a lower figure.

5. By all indications, these high growth-rates will continue for some appreciable time. Africa is believed to have the highest fertility among the world's major regions. Its estimated crude birth-rate is 46 per 1000 (in 1960–6) which is well above the world average of 34 per 1000. As between African countries, birth-rates range from about 40 to 60 per 1000. Mortality rates, on the other hand, aver-aging 23 per 1000, are still the highest in the world and compare with a world average of about 16 per 1000. Regional averages range from

17 per 1000 in southern Africa to 27 per 1000 in western Africa. Within a decade or two Africa's falling death-rates are likely to lead to growth-rates surpassing those of Latin America. Whereas the 1960 population of total Africa has been put at 279 million and that of black Africa at 178 million, the estimates for 1980 are 457 million and 291 million respectively (see table). Forecasts for the year 2000 for total Africa range from 684 million to 864 million, those for black Africa from 294 million to 473 million.

LAND RESOURCES

6. These prospective population increases would cause less concern if Africa disposed of vast reserves of unused and fertile land. In fact soils are generally poor, and liable to wind and water erosion; the thin topsoil is rapidly destroyed; rainfalls in many parts are very low and/or highly erratic; natural water resources are very unevenly distributed; only insignificant areas of cultivable soil are not yet in use; crop and animal husbandry are mostly of the subsistence type and cannot support the fertilisers, insecticides, implements and capital works needed to raise the feeding potential of the land.[1]

7. Even today, the areas of highest fertility and most favourable climate are those most overcrowded with men and overstocked with livestock. According to tentative estimates by William A. Hance,[2] 142 million people in the whole of Africa were inhabiting areas experiencing population pressure in 1966. Of these, about 57 per cent lived in urban or in high density rural areas, about 32 per cent in areas of moderate density, and the remaining 11 per cent in areas of low density with very low carrying capacity. In Africa south of the Sahara, 38 per cent of the area and 32 per cent of the population are estimated to be in regions of pressure.

8. Already large areas of arable and pasture land have been seriously eroded and depleted by ever-growing populations attempting to eke out a livelihood from a shrinking acreage by means of the primitive technologies evolved for a nomadic or semi-nomadic form of life. (On the island of Ukara in Lake Victoria, though, highly effective methods of cultivation, including irrigation, stable feeding, use of manure, etc., have been developed in response to a worsening man-land ratio.) Serious repercussions on food supplies are bound to result from a continuation of these trends.

FOOD RESOURCES

9. On the whole, hunger is not a significant feature of African life. What is serious however is malnutrition, mostly in the form of protein deficiencies. Again generally speaking, this reflects ignorance or traditional prejudices (for example, in respect of eggs, milk and fish)

and religious views (notably in respect of cattle), rather than poverty. To some extent the lack of an efficient distributive system is to blame. Whereas in western Europe around 50 grammes daily of animal protein were available per head of population in 1960–2, the corresponding figure for black African countries typically lay between 5 and 12 grammes. Even though fat requirements differ in warm and cold climates, an average of 130 to 150 grammes of fat per day in western Europe contrasts with roughly 20 to 50 grammes in Africa.[3]

10. If production figures compiled by the F.A.O. and by the United States Department of Agriculture respectively are a true reflection of actual developments, per caput food production in black Africa is declining. Thus the total output of cereals, starchy roots and pulses in east Africa has increased by a mere 5·9 per cent during the four-year period 1961–5 whereas the population grows by well over 2 per cent every year. In central Africa the output of these products appears to have fallen in the aggregate. Per caput meat production in east Africa has dropped from 11·3 kg in 1961 to 10·8 kg in 1965. According to E.C.A., per caput agricultural output for Africa was lower in 1962–3 than five years earlier, whereas food production per caput was estimated to have declined by about 4 per cent, and may in fact have gone below pre-war levels.[4] Whatever the reliability of these estimates, there is nothing to suggest that the unfavourable trends noted have been arrested in recent years. Growing imports of food from abroad reduce the foreign exchange required to buy machinery and other capital goods for industry.

INCOMES

11. Gross domestic product (G.D.P.) per head of population in Africa (excluding South Africa) is very low – roughly one-tenth and one twenty-fifth respectively of what it is in western Europe and North America. According to the E.C.A. Secretariat, per caput G.D.P. at constant 1960 prices has risen on average by 1·1 per cent per annum during 1960–66 in north, east and west Africa respectively, whereas it fell by 1·5 per cent per annum in central Africa, and showed an annual increase of 3·2 per cent in southern Africa. Total increase in real G.D.P. for the whole of Africa was estimated at 3·4 per cent per annum for 1960–6. In individual countries growth-rates naturally may be higher or lower than these averages. Tanzania, for example, achieved a growth-rate of about 5 per cent per annum at current prices under the 1964–9 development plan (as compared with the planned 6·7 per cent). Since population grew by 2·7 per cent per annum (against an estimated 2·2 per cent) and

prices rose by at least 2·5 per cent a year, real per caput income has fallen or at best stagnated. Tanzania's predicament is typical, for in many – if not most – African countries population growth appears to be higher than was commonly accepted until quite recently.

2. SOME CONSEQUENCES OF RISING POPULA-TION PRESSURE

YOUTHFUL POPULATION

12. Black Africa's rapid population growth is largely due to falling infant mortality. As a consequence, no less than 43 per cent of its population is below 15 years of age as compared with only 25 per cent in Europe and 30 per cent in North America. The African percentage is equalled by Latin America and surpassed only by central America (45 per cent). Mali and Togo lead in Africa, 49 per cent and 48 per cent respectively of their populations being under 15 years whereas Gabon's 36 per cent is the lowest on record. 13. These percentages imply a high dependency ratio, that is, relatively few economically productive people have to provide for many unproductive ones. In poor countries where the majority are living close to subsistence levels, and where consequently only low rates of saving and capital formation are attainable, this preponderance of consumers over producers impedes economic progress seriously. Resources that could otherwise be applied to raising the overall living standard must be used to combat its tendency to fall. Expanding medical and health facilities are the main agents lowering death-rates, and in the weak economies of black Africa expenditure on health services may threaten the sustained growth of these very services by contributing towards a lower income per head.

EDUCATION

14. More than anything else, the black Africans' almost universal desire for literacy and education is a tangible expression of their quest for change generally and a higher living standard in particular. Everywhere on the continent, parents (and children too) make considerable sacrifices for education, hoping that it will be the key to a better future. Governments also accord high priority to education. This is underlined by the following statistics for 1965, showing public expenditure on education as a percentage of national income: Ghana 4·6 per cent, Ivory Coast 5·9 per cent, Kenya 5·6 per cent (of G.D.P.), Malawi 5·1 per cent. If private expenditure is added, these figures rise still further. Even so, they compare well with

countries such as France (4·8 per cent), West Germany (4·5 per cent), and the United Kingdom (6·4 per cent).

15. However, the target of universal primary education by 1980, as formulated at UNESCO conferences for Africa in 1961 and 1962, is overtaxing financial and manpower resources. In recent years public spending on education has actually declined or remained practically unchanged in the Ivory Coast, Kenya, Niger, Tanzania, Togo and Uganda. Quantitatively at least, secondary and higher education generally are progressing at the planned rate but there is much criticism of its quality, enormous unit cost and practical relevance. Whereas primary school enrolment in Africa as a whole was to have grown by 5 per cent per annum, a mere 1·8 per cent was in fact achieved during 1960–5. The battle against illiteracy is being lost because the rate of enrolment growth is outstripped by far by population growth.

16. Other results too have gravely disappointed the expectations that led to heavy spending on primary education. Firstly, the mere in-increase in literate people has not so far helped to raise national output and productivity, notably in agriculture. Secondly, the inordinately high cost per pupil raises doubts as to the priority universal literacy should receive in the allocation of national re-sources. Apart from the serious waste due to very high percentages of 'drop-outs' and 'repeaters', the large majority leave after three or four years at school and commonly relapse into complete illiteracy through lack of practice. Thirdly, those who complete their primary (or secondary) education have not been trained for, and generally are not inclined to return to, agricultural pursuits. Other practical training is woefully inadequate, nor is there much demand for it. Fourthly, the conflicts leading up to the Nigerian civil war have shown that in present-day Africa, education easily aggravates rather than eliminates tension between tribes and regions because there simply are not sufficient resources to ensure real equality of oppor-tunity.

UNEMPLOYMENT

17. Until the Second World War, the labour scene in Africa was characterised by complaints about the lack of workers for mines, plantations and works. Today, the diverging growth-rates of popu-lation and employment opportunities are acknowledged to be one of Africa's most ominous problems. Lack of uniform definitions as well as of statistical data make it difficult to substantiate the general impression that not just underemployment but true unemployment is increasing significantly. According to estimates prepared by James N. Ypsilantis of the International Labour Office, average

annual growth-rates of population will be well above the corresponding rates for employment during the decade 1970–80. The respective rates for the major African regions are put as follows: north 3·00 per cent against 2·75 per cent; west 2·86 per cent–2·55 per cent; central 2·00 per cent–1·70 per cent; east 2·21 per cent–1·80 per cent; southern 2·68 per cent–2·05 per cent. These growth-rates lead Yves Sabolo (I.L.O.) to expect 8·8 million unemployed persons in black Africa in 1980, that is, 7·1 per cent of the economically active population, as compared with 8·7 million unemployed in 1970, equal to 8·5 per cent of the economically active population.[5]

18. Judging by the experience of a country such as Kenya, these projections appear optimistic. There, only about one-quarter of the 1964–8 increase in the adult population, or 15 per cent of new labour market entrants, was absorbed in some form of paid employment – and even this is an avowedly sanguine figure. Under the ambitious targets set by the 1968–74 Development Plan, nearly two-thirds of new entrants to the Labour force are to become self-employed in agriculture (or unemployed!), and less than one in five can expect non-agricultural wage employment. As regards the latter employment, it has been pointed out that the capital cost of creating one new urban job in Kenya is ten to fifteen times as expensive as it is in (say) western Europe, when the unit of measurement is G.D.P. per head of population.[6] In Dakar, capital of Senegal, only 2212 persons were placed in employment during 1968 as compared with 40,503 applicants having some form of general, vocational or technical training, no less than three-quarters of the applicants even being skilled workers.[7]

URBAN POPULATION

19. Africa's urban population of approximately 48 million was equal to 15·4 per cent of its total inhabitants in 1965. In 1960 it was estimated at 13 per cent, which compares with 19 per cent for east Asia, 33 per cent for Latin America and 58 per cent for North America.[8] Though still comparatively low in absolute figures, urbanisation in Africa proceeds at a high rate, namely, two to three times as fast as aggregate population (see table). If, as in nineteenth-century Europe, this rural-urban exodus was due to the push of rapidly increasing agricultural productivity on the one hand and the pull of urban industrialisation on the other, it would not pose insurmountable problems. In fact, however, it is not primarily an economic but a demographic problem.

20. Mounting population pressure in the rural areas, unaccompanied by rising output and alternative employment opportunities, induces large numbers of black Africans to seek a living in towns and cities.

There they swell the mass of unemployed or underemployed who somehow exist on occasional work, illegal or criminal activities, and the help of more fortunate family members, friends, etc. Even though traditional bonds are much more resilient in the urban milieu than is generally assumed, it is clear that a shiftless proletariat of de-tribalised, unskilled and ill-nourished individuals is arising in all the major centres. Many school-leavers and others whose education and training could not provide them with suitable work merge into this class, rendering it a potentially explosive factor. Unemployment, crime, drunkenness and illegitimacy are of necessity rising at a fast rate. Opportunities being few, it is understandable that traditional social restraints break down in the struggle for survival, and that bribery and corruption flourish.

21. Governments naturally seek to ensure at least minimum accommodation, sanitary and health conditions as well as transport in order to contain the threat posed to health and social peace by this urban explosion. Apart from such a threat, politicians must also reckon with trade unions and other politically influential urban groups. Considerations of national prestige also affect urban planning. The result is that urban housing, water supplies, health and other social services absorb a share of available capital and recurrent funds out of proportion to the returns thereon. Investment aimed at raising agricultural and industrial output, as well as the competitiveness of exports, is diminished correspondingly. Marketable surpluses of food production are not keeping pace with urban population growth. There are also instances where surpluses are available but fail to reach the cities because of the poor system of transport with the result that food must be imported. Already in 1965 food imports constituted 8·7 per cent of total west African merchandise imports as compared with 7·5 per cent, 5·9 per cent and 16·5 per cent for east, central and north Africa respectively.[9]

22. About three-quarters of the unemployed in African cities are under the age of 30. Hence the following outline of the urban problems of young people, formulated by a senior E.C.A. official, is to the point here:

. . . unemployment, low-paid jobs, lack of skills, lack of basic education, lack of vocational training opportunities, poor housing conditions, insanitary conditions, overcrowding, lack of recreational facilities, frustration and loneliness, restlessness and instability, feeling of neglect and being unwanted, insecurity, and often lack of understanding from responsible authorities. Many of the personal problems . . . arise out of the inability of the young person to adjust himself to urban patterns of living based on a new social order, new habits and values.[10]

MIGRANT LABOUR

23. The flow to the cities is by no means a one-way traffic, nor is it the only major population movement in Africa. Very large numbers are in urban employment for brief spells of a few months or perhaps years, after which they return to their rural homes whence the need for cash to buy food, clothing and other essentials or to pay taxes may again drive them to seek short-term wage earning. All over the continent, but with a few regional focal areas, millions of men and – to a lesser extent – women are on the move in search of means to sustain or perhaps improve their material existence. About ten years ago, 5 million people were tentatively estimated to be involved, 2 million in respect of South Africa alone.

24. In South Africa the mines and industries of the Witwatersrand complex and other industrial areas and agriculture at any given time employ roughly 600,000 Bantu workers from outside countries, especially Lesotho, Mozambique and Malawi. In 1960 probably around 700,000 male and 150,000 female Bantu were temporarily absent from the South African Bantu home areas. In west Africa south of the Sahara, from Senegal to Cameroons, seasonal migration is taking place on a vast scale from the more poorly endowed inland countries to the plantations, ports and commercial centres near the coast. Up to the early 1960s, large seasonal movements played a role in harvesting cloves in Zanzibar and Pemba, sisal in Tanzania, cotton in Uganda, diverse crops in Kenya's White Highlands and elsewhere. The present position is not clear.

25. Basically, these population movements – within or between countries; seasonal, short-term or permanent – reflect the economic and social imbalance between traditional areas of settlement and areas with modern economic activities. Before the advent of the colonial powers, inter-tribal warfare and slavery kept millions constantly in motion and, together with diseases and natural factors, helped to preserve the ecological balance between man and environment. Peace and public health measures have upset this balance and led to the movements outlined above. Continued population growth together with the poor showing of agriculture will enhance the pressure on the few focal points of modern commercial activities.

EXPELLEES AND REFUGEES

26. Until a few years ago, migration across borders was a matter of course. Now that the recently independent states are struggling to establish a national consciousness and identity and to satisfy the expectation of rising levels of living in the face of a population explosion and a host of economic odds, the workers and traders from

other countries are increasingly drawing unsympathetic attention.
27. In Ghana, for instance, the 1960 census established that foreigners constituted 12 per cent of the total population of about 7 million, and that further immigration was taking place at the rate of 5 per cent and more a year. Migration is commonly skill- and initiative-selective, and many of the more than 827,000 foreigners, notably Yorubes from Nigeria, had become well entrenched in retail trading, diamond mining and other lucrative activities. When the economic débâcle of the Nkrumah regime and other factors caused widespread unemployment, the government of Dr. Busia felt constrained to act against foreigners without residence permits. An estimated 30,000 to 50,000 Nigerians and tens of thousands from Togo, Upper Volta, Niger and Mali were compelled forthwith to leave Ghana, which many had made their permanent home.
28. Similar developments, though on a smaller scale and less publicised, appear to be taking place all over Africa. Even though the number of expellees may not generally be as large as those from Ghana, it may yet seriously affect the precarious economic and/or political balance in the receiving countries. The expellees (or refugees) not only swell the ranks of the unemployed but, more significantly, many of them have lost important and well-paid or otherwise lucrative positions, the like whereof they have little chance of regaining. This is a distinctly unstabilising element, and gives cause for concern to the host governments.
29. This applies in particular to those political refugees from South and South West Africa, Rhodesia and the Portuguese territories who have set up their headquarters in Lusaka and Dar-es-Salaam whence they direct guerrilla activities against their countries of origin. The frequent admonitions and threats of the host governments concerning their in-fighting and intrigues clearly indicate that their militancy is by no means directed exclusively against the 'white south' but to a significant extent against those whose hospitality they enjoy as well as against fellow-refugees from other tribes. Political refugees from other black governments are a constant source of distrust and friction between the countries concerned. This is a not insignificant impediment to closer inter-African economic co-operation – one of the primary prerequisites for the continent's economic progress.
30. In early 1964 the total number of refugees in Africa south of the Sahara was put at 400,000, more than half thereof being Angolans staying in the Congo (Kinshasa). In subsequent years the total was as follows: 1965: 535,000; 1966: 625,000; 1967: 735,000; 1968: 800,000. In January 1967, the principal countries of asylum were the Congo (Kinshasa), with 357,000 refugees (including 300,000

from Angola), Uganda, with 156,000 (including 68,000 Rwandese and 55,000 Sudanese), and Burundi, with 79,000 (including 54,000 Rwandese). More recent detailed figures are not available. It may be noted though that Tanzania harboured an estimated 50,000 refugees in early 1969 as compared with 33,300 in 1967. According to United Nations estimates, at least 160,000 southern Sudanese people have fled their country whereas 'hundred of thousands more' are said to be unregistered. Groups of refugees are to be found in almost every African country.[11]

31. Between 1962 and 1967, between £15 million and £20 million is estimated to have been spent on immediate aid to refugees as well as to their rehabilitation in new settlements. The major portion of the funds comes from diverse international organisations. However, the host governments also incur expenses by providing shelter, food, schools, etc., and thus experience yet further pressure on their limited resources.

3. AN ESCAPE FROM THE IMPASSE?

32. Given the plausible expectation that death-rates in Africa will continue to fall in the foreseeable future, a worsening of the man-resource ratio and all the attendant problems can be averted only by either a decline in birth-rates or by economic growth-rates exceeding those of population or by a combination of both. The available evidence gives little ground for optimism because progress in either respect is impeded by deeply-rooted human values and social institutions. Time alone will answer the crucial question as to how fast and in what direction these values and institutions will change. Forecasts are largely speculative.

FAMILY PLANNING

33. In his book *False Start in Africa*, Rene Dumont states that if Africa rejects colonialism, birth control and large-scale efforts to develop economically, it has only one way out, that is, 'to send away all the doctors, and re-establish a high mortality rate'.[12] Others have given similar warnings. Yet the fact is that so far Kenya is the only black African country with an official policy aimed at reducing the rate of population growth. This policy was first enunciated in 1965 and emphasises the welfare of the family and the individual rather than the effects on aggregate economic development. Outside black Africa, the governments of the United Arab Republic, Morocco, Tunisia and Mauritius have shown concern over population growth.

34. In the other anglophone countries, the import and manufacture of contraceptives is permitted and family planning clinics have been established, notably in Uganda, Nigeria and Ghana. However, with the exception of Kenya, the organisations concerned are voluntary agencies that are handicapped by lack of funds and trained personnel, by inadequate publicity and doubts about official approval. Most francophone and the former Italian countries still have laws prohibiting or restricting any form of contraception or family planning, and there are no family planning clinics.[13]

35. The reasons for the general lack of governmental interest appear to be four-fold. Firstly, a large population is widely believed to enhance a country's power and international standing. Secondly, politicians are reluctant to propagate measures impinging upon old-established views and customs. Thirdly, there is sheer ignorance, and lastly, there is the common human fault of refusing to face inconvenient facts. Some countries, such as Somalia and Ethiopia, consider themselves underpopulated and welcome population growth as contributing to a fuller exploitation of their economic potential, and providing a larger internal market.

36. The common desire of black Africans to have many children and the underlying needs and motives, have been widely dealt with in scientific studies. Viewed in historical perspective, it is clear that clans and tribes ever-threatened by human enemies, wild animals, drought and disease, must have numerous children if enough are to survive into adulthood and at least to reproduce the group. In fact, the average African woman, if she lives to the age of 50, is estimated to have 6 live-born children, though there are countries where the average is 7 or even 8.

37. Even though the ravages of tribal warfare, disease, etc., have receded since colonialism brought black Africa into closer contact with the west, the old reproductive pattern has remained essentially intact. There are many plausible reasons. Where no comprehensive system of old-age pension and social security generally exists, numerous offspring can afford protection and care for those unable to look after themselves. In an economy with very low levels of capital investment, children are a welcome addition to the labour force. Where man lacks both the knowledge and the means for the physical control of his environment, he tends to consider himself at the mercy of ancestral spirits and other supernatural powers. This in turn profoundly influences his thinking on the chain of life linking his own being with the deceased and the as yet unborn, and the role of his own progeny in keeping this chain intact and ensuring the perpetuation of his existence beyond death. Lastly, numerous children enhance the social status of father as well as mother.

38. Many experts believe that social and economic modernisation will modify these attitudes, and that consequently family planning campaigns are superfluous, whereas others disagree. J. G. C. Blacker, for instance, regards this view as 'absolute nonsense'. According to him the indications are that in Africa rises in the level of living and other forms of economic development may well result in rises – rather than declines – in fertility.[14] Caldwell's studies in Ghana, on the other hand, indicate that birth-rates in the four major towns 'are probably about one-ninth lower' than in the rest of the surrounding regions.[15] He suggests 'a continuum of socio-economic change from the rural areas to the highest socio-economic division of the towns accompanied by a continuing reduction in fertility levels'.[16] In Caldwell's view, increasingly delayed female marriage is principally responsible for this decrease. (A deferment of marriage from under 19 to over 23 years may reduce the size of the completed family by as much as a third.)[17] Deliberate efforts to prevent pregnancies within marriage appear to play a minor role. Both delayed female marriage and attempts to prevent pregnancy are positively associated with extended education. They are also associated with second generation town living and membership of the upper and middle classes.[18]

39. Ohadkie's investigations in Lagos bring him to the conclusion that urban areas are likely to take the lead in any fall in the birth-rates but he also stresses that 'for some time' African populations will continue to be predominantly rural with all the connotations of traditional values and high fertility this implies.[19] In view of the relatively low level of urbanisation, the significance of extended education as a factor decreasing fertility stands out even more prominently. However, as indicated in paragraph 15 above, explosive population growth is increasingly reducing the share of national resources available for education in many African countries.

40. No other group of black Africans has been exposed more intensively and over a longer period of time to industrial and urban conditions, or has attained higher average levels of living and education than those in South Africa. On the whole, their attitudes favouring a large offspring are the same as elsewhere in Africa. However, very many Bantu women deliberately restrict or space out births by means of modern contraceptives, mostly the pill, in order to be better able to provide for their families, notably the health and education of their children. Generally, their husbands show little interest or are against family limitation. In the middle and upper social strata, the men also favour some restrictions. About 2 years ago, 90 per cent of a group of 200 Bantu university students, 70 per cent thereof from urban areas, declared themselves in favour

of birth control in marriage, and 96 per cent stated that from an economic viewpoint a smaller family could meet its obligations more easily than a larger one. 92 per cent were unwilling to marry a spouse unable to have children, but all wanted children, preferably 4.[20]

41. The Bantu's desire for higher living standards is of the utmost significance in shaping their attitudes towards family planning. Quality clothing, kitchen and living-room furniture, a radiogram, a second-hand car – these and other items pertinent to 'keeping up with the Khumalos' have become social and economic factors the full significance of which is not yet adequately understood even in this country. Although more noticeable in the urban areas, the same forces are operating in the countryside, too.

42. There can be little doubt that only a change in the socio-economic environment can lead to falling birth-rates. The extent of such change need not be large but what is needed is the awakening of the recognition that some improvement in material living conditions is (a) desirable for the individual, (b) socially acceptable and (c) actually within the individual's capability to achieve. All three conditions are essential but the last one, i.e. that higher levels of living must be *within the individual's reach*, is critical. In fact, it may be the key to all efforts at uplifting less privileged societies.

PROSPECTS FOR ECONOMIC DEVELOPMENT

43. By present indications, we must expect black African birth-rates to remain high, and death-rates to fall further for some time. What are the prospects of economic growth offsetting population increase? The data concerning real incomes (cf. Part 1) portray the slow rate of economic change. One may hope that the high growth-rates envisaged by current development plans can be realised. However, a comparison of planned and achieved rates compiled by the E.C.A. last year gives little ground for optimism.[21]

44. Of 24 unspecified countries, only 4 realised the target growth-rate of G.D.P. in recent years whereas 14 (or more than half) did not even realise 60 per cent of the planned rate. Only 5 of 19 countries for which data were available achieved the planned rate of growth of the agricultural sector, while 12 performed at less than 50 per cent of the planned rate. Only 3 of the 19 attained their targets of industrial growth, and 4 performed at less than 50 per cent of the planned rate. The mode for industry was 60 to 79·9 realisation ratio. Bearing in mind that the export sector is critical to most African economies, it may be noted that 4 out of 16 unnamed countries realised their export growth targets whereas 7 (or almost half) failed to achieve even half their target.

45. The same E.C.A. document leaves no doubt regarding the sombre prospects for future performance. After referring to the problems posed by external economic factors beyond the African countries' control, the report states that 'internal impediments' appear to be even more important as an explanation of the poor results sketched above. It adds: 'Faculty plan design and implementation are generally characteristic. Problems of implementation have often proved to be the result of contradictory political directives.'[22] Lack of professionally and personally qualified personnel, weak governments, tribal tensions, small and fragmented markets in Africa, unstable markets overseas – all these will not change significantly in the foreseeable future. At the same time, populations are growing at an accelerating pace.

4. POPULATION PRESSURE AND POLITICS

46. Two basic conclusions emerge from the foregoing. Firstly, black Africa's rate of population growth is outstripping the rate at which resources are being mobilised for economic development. Secondly, there is no reason to believe that a sustained worsening of the man-resource ratio will be averted in the foreseeable future either by voluntary individual restraint on births or by measures to accelerate rises in aggregate output.

47. The pattern of urbanisation, rising unemployment – notably among school-leavers – the losing race against increasing illiteracy, the prevailing and possibly worsening extent of malnutrition, these are the most immediate and striking features of what may be summed up as falling average levels of living. The observable and prospective consequences for political life will be briefly discussed under five headings below.

SOCIAL CLIMATE

48. As the British sociologist Andreski points out in his illuminating study, *The African Predicament*,[23] economic distress fosters parasitic tendencies and institutions, and stimulates strife and disorder which in turn aggravate the economic difficulties. Since relief cannot be found in attacking external enemies, internal predation is the only way out. Energies are turned to the struggle for survival and for power and its fruits rather than to the building of viable economic structures. Andreski, significantly, heads one of his chapters, 'Kleptocracy or corruption as a system of government', and points out how the prevailing uncertainty impedes planning, saving and investment.

TRIBALISM

49. Tribal hostilities that were forcibly suppressed by the colonial powers and, later, were deliberately put aside in the striving for independence, are increasingly reasserting themselves today. Apart from deeper causes, such as the very long collective memory of African peoples, this recrudescence is strongly aided by politicians jockeying for power. Where there are so very few opportunities for economic gain as in the black African states, political power or a senior position in the public service is the surest road to wealth. Once out of these positions, a man becomes a nonentity. It is only natural that those struggling to attain or stay in high office mobilise those groups to which they are bound by origin and blood – groups which, in turn, can rightly expect to benefit in various ways if their candidate is wielding power.

50. At a juncture when economic and political exigencies require that the multifarious tribes of Africa amalgamate into self-confident nations forging their destinies with a powerful concentration of all their human and physical resources, these would-be nations are increasingly paralysed by tribal in-fighting. Dearth of resources and tribal rivalries thus tend to reinforce and perpetuate each other.

IRREDENTISM AND SEPARATISM

51. The factors just outlined, on the one hand, and the anxious efforts to establish national unity on the other, cause much restiveness among the many tribes that have been divided by the arbitrary boundaries drawn in Berlin in 1884–5 and confirmed at the Brussels Conference of 1890. These tribes either agitate for independent states of their own or for the incorporation of tribal fragments into the country harbouring the majority. Examples are the Somalis in Kenya and Ethiopia; the Ewes of Togo and Ghana; the Azandes of the Sudan and the Congo (K.); the Bakongo of Angola and the two Congos. Border conflicts trouble the relations between Ghana and the Ivory Coast, between Nigeria and Cameroons, between Rwanda and Burundi; in fact, most of Africa is afflicted by irredentist or separatist movements. The most tragic instance of the latter is of course the Biafran war.

ACTIONS AGAINST OTHER RACIAL GROUPS

52. Reference has been made above to the eviction of Nigerians from Ghana. Where it is non-black groups that draw the envy of the dominant groups, steps to deprive them of coveted jobs or their property are much less likely to cause embarrassment in

inter-African councils such as the Organisation of African Unity (O.A.U.). Thus persons of Indian origin in Kenya, and to a lesser extent Tanzania, Uganda, Zambia and Malawi, have been the victims in recent years.

53. Numerous individual whites have been expelled in the name of Africanisation, but even though the desire to take over their work or their farms, or to inherit their 'power', has probably been the motive in most instances, one should guard against facile generalisation. Large overseas investments have been nationalised or brought under effective government control on the stated assumption that this would provide more employment opportunities, especially in the higher ranks, for local people, and would also lead to a greater portion of earnings being invested locally instead of being transferred overseas. So far, however, the principal effect of these measures has been to frighten away private overseas investors. Steps aimed at alleviating social and economic pressure thus achieve the very opposite.

TOWARDS A LATIN-AMERICAN PATTERN?

54. Between January 1963 and January 1970, no fewer than 21 successful *coups d'état* have taken place in 12 black African states, 5 in Dahomey alone. Almost a hundred *coups* have failed. It is a question what role, if any, has been played respectively by personal ambition, by tribalism, the wish to eliminate corruption, and – underlying these – economic want or greed. Several *putsches* have been made by army officers, avowedly to stamp out corruption, and 11 black African states are at present governed by the military. It is a hopeful sign that in Ghana these officers have voluntarily handed back control to civilian government.

55. Some observers point to similarities between the African and Latin-American situations – very low average incomes, heavy dependence on a few products subject to wide price fluctuations, cliques of venal politicians determined to enjoy the spoils of power, the handy bogeyman of imperialism and neo-colonialism. However, one could readily list numerous significant differences, notably in respect of land tenure and the absence in black Africa of feudal landlords. The role of the Catholic Church hierarchy in Latin America and religious life in Africa are worlds apart; African tribes have no meaningful parallel in Latin America either. Latin-American countries have vigorous and in several instances highly cultured élites indisputably committed to western culture. In Africa, the élites are torn between their desire to modernise on the one hand and their inability, on the other, to break away from a tribal background dominated by magic and ancestral spirits. Hence, despite many

features common to both, one should beware of seeing in Latin America a prototype of what lies in store for Africa.

5. CONCLUSION

56. Given the continued fall in average levels of living, the most explosive factors are firstly, the growing number of unemployed and impoverished young men, and secondly, the tendency of political and social conflicts to crystallise around tribal interests, thereby accentuating tribal differences. In the large urban complexes, though, these tribal cleavages tend to merge so that the one way is open for the emergence of a true proletariat. Contrary to the popular belief of non-Africans, the often staggering discrepancies between the earnings of the élites and those of the masses are not yet a cause for a widespread discontent because of the extent to which next-of-kin and hangers-on share in the fruits of privilege. However, growing individualism and the weakening of tribal bonds threaten this system of redistribution and hence social peace.

57. One can only agree with Chou En-lai who concluded during his 1964 visit to east Africa that there is an excellent revolutionary potential on this continent. Even though the subject matter of this paper may call for a discussion of communist penetration as well as of other aspects of Africa's relations with outside states and forces, this could be done more usefully in a separate paper. Only this: despite the many setbacks suffered by the communist states in their diplomatic, aid, trade and other dealings, this should not blind us to the fact that 'creeping communism', as it has been called, is noticeable everywhere in Africa. One cannot gauge the extent to which communist doctrines are being absorbed by young Africans. All we can be sure of is that the worsening man-resource ratio is promoting the climate in which these doctrines flourish.

58. To the non-African, our analysis may be conclusive proof that for several decades black Africa inevitably will experience deepening economic misery, social disruption and political chaos. Indeed, there is enough of all this. However, Africa has its way of confounding the confident predictions of those who base their prognoses on analogies borrowed from Europe and elsewhere.

59. In an age dominated by the calculating and impersonal approach of western science and technology, it is all too easy to overstress the emotional, social, educational and other shortcomings of the black Africans, and to overlook their as yet largely dormant dynamism, their subtle understanding of human nature and relations, their resourcefulness and resilience. Notwithstanding the ominous facts

presented in this paper, these qualities still inspire, in Leonard Barnes's words, 'a surprising confidence, a kind of tranquil trust, in the latent genius of the African peoples'.[24] This may sound like cheap optimism. However, how many of us realise that a mere forty years ago, the Ibos were generally considered the most primitive of all Nigerian tribes? Yet, as Dame Margery Perham recently wrote, these very people 'have flourished under external stimulus with a quick exuberance which has matched or even surpassed the growths of the older and more developed societies.'[25]

60. It is all too easy, too, to overlook that millions of whites on this continent are not 'settlers' and hundreds of thousands of people of Asiatic origin are not 'aliens' but white and brown Africans respectively. Any reflection on the future course of events in Africa must take this into account.

Notes

1. Joy Leonard, 'The Economics of Food Production', in *African Affairs*, vol. 65 no. 261 (London, October 1966) p. 317–28. See also United Nations, *African Agricultural Development*, by René Dumont, 66.II.K.6, New York: United Nations, 1966.

2. William A. Hance, ''The Race Between Population and Resources. A challenge to the view that Africa need not worry about population pressure', in *Africa Report*, vol. 13 no. 1 (Washington, D.C., January 1968) pp. 6–12.

3. United Nations, Food and Agriculture Organisation, *Production Yearbook 1968* (Rome, F.A.O., 1968).

4. See, among others, F.A.O., *Production Yearbook 1968;* F.A.O., *The State of Food and Agriculture 1968* (Rome, 1968); U.S. Department of Agriculture, Economic Research Service, *The African and West Asia Agricultural Situation. Review of 1967 and Outlook for 1968* (Washington, D.C., 1968), and *Indices of Agricultural Production 1959–68 in Africa and the Near East* (Washington, D.C., 1969); United Nations, Economic Commission for Africa, *Survey of Economic Conditions in Africa 1967*, E68.II.K.4 (New York, 1969).

5. Y. Sabolo, 'Sectoral Employment Growth: The Outlook for 1980', in *International Labour Review* vol. 100 no. 5 (Geneva, November 1969) pp. 445–74.

6. Emil Rado, 'Employment, Incomes Policy: Kenya's New Development Plan', in *East Africa Journal*, VII 3, (Nairobi, March 1970) pp. 13–20.

7. *I.L.O. Panorama* No. 4 (Geneva, March–April 1970) p. 20.

8. United Nations, Department of Economic and Social Affairs, *Growth of the World's Urban and Rural Population, 1920–2000*, Population Studies No. 44, E.69XIII.3 (New York, 1969) p. 53.

9. U.N./E.C.A., *Survey of Economic Conditions in Africa 1967*, op. cit., p. 54.

10. United Nations, Economic and Social Council, Economic Commission for Africa, *Problems and Needs of Youth in Africa*, E/CN.14/SW.25 (5 September 1969) p. 8.

11. Sven Hamrell (ed.), *Refugee Problems in Africa*, (Uppsala, Scandinavian Institute of African Studies, 1967) pp. 9–25. It may be mentioned that at a conference on refugee problems held in the U.S. late in 1969, the total number of refugees in Africa was given as 5·2 million – a figure more than 6 times as high as the U.N. estimate quoted in the text of this paper.

12. René Dumont, *False Start in Africa*, (London, 1966) p. 96.

13. Göran Ohlin, *Population Control and Economic Development* (Paris, Development Centre of the Organisation for Economic Co-operation and Development, 1967) pp. 100–1; Leonard Barnes, *African Renaissance* (London, 1969) pp. 82–3.
14. J. G. C. Blacker, 'Population and Economic Development in Africa', in *The Role of Family Planning in African Development* (London, International Planned Parenthood Federation, 1968) p. 7.
15. John C. Caldwell, *Population Growth and Family Change in Africa. The New Urban Elite in Ghana* (Canberra, Australian National University Press, 1968) p. 213.
16. Caldwell, loc. cit.
17. Ibid., p. 172.
18. Ibid., p. 213.
19. Patrick Ohadike, 'The Possibility of Fertility Change in Modern Africa: A West African Case', in *African Social Research*, No. 8 (Manchester, December 1969) pp. 613–14.
20. C. J. Botha, 'Houdings ten opsigte van die huwelik onder universiteitskollege-studente'. ('n Voorlopige verslag) (Pietersburg: University College of the North, 1968) (mimeographed).
21. United Nations, Economic and Social Council, Economic Commission for Africa, 'Structural Development and African Planning', E/CN.14/POP/7 (23 May 1969).
22. U.N./E.C.A., 'Structural Development', p. 13.
23. Stanislav Andreski, *The African Predicament. A Study in the Pathology of Modernisation* (London, 1968) p. 25 ff.
24. Barnes, *African Renaissance*, p. 15.
25. Margery Perham, 'Reflections on the Nigerian Civil War', in *International Affairs*, vol. 46 no. 2, (London, April 1970) p. 235.

United Nations estimates and projections concerning the populations of main African regions and countries

Region and country	Total population					Urban population*				
	Mid-year estimates		Density per km₂	Average annual growth		Total	As % of total population		Average annual growth	
	1960 millions	1980 millions	1967 Persons	1965-70 %	1975-80 %	1965 millions	1965 %	1980 %	1965-70 %	1970-75 %
Africa total	278·9	457·3	11	2·4	2·7	48·0	15·4	21·3	4·7	5·0
North Africa	66·0	114·0	9	2·7	3·1	20·4	27·4	35·5	4·7	4·6
West Africa	85·9	147·0	17	2·6	2·9	12·4	12·8	18·8	4·8	6·1
Nigeria	48·6	88·8	67	3·0	3·1	8·3	14·8	20·3	3·8	6·2
Ghana	6·8	12·0	34	3·0	3·1	1·2	15·1	22·6	6·1	5·8
Upper Volta	4·5	6·6	18	1·7	2·3	0·2	3·1	7·3	10·8	7·6
Mali	4·1	6·5	4	2·0	2·7	0·3	5·5	8·4	7·6	4·1
Ivory Coast	3·5	5·4	12	2·0	2·6	0·5	14·0	25·5	8·4	6·3
Guinea	3·2	5·1	15	2·2	2·8	0·3	8·5	14·6	7·0	5·9
Senegal	3·3	4·7	19	1·6	2·2	0·9	24·1	30·2	5·1	3·4
Niger	3·1	4·9	3	2·1	2·8	—	1·5	4·5	12·5	12·2
Central Africa	28·5	41·6	5	1·6	2·4	2·9	9·3	14·3	5·3	4·9
Congo (K)	14·6	22·2	7	1·8	2·8	1·7	10·9	16·0	5·1	4·8
Cameroon	5·1	6·7	12	1·2	1·7	0·4	6·5	9·4	3·7	4·4
Chad	3·0	4·4	3	1·6	2·2	0·2	5·8	13·0	8·8	6·6
Burundi	2·9	4·5	120	2·1	2·4	0·1	1·9	3·1	5·9	6·6
Central Afric. Rep.	1·4	1·8	2	1·1	1·8	0·2	12·6	22·0	6·8	5·1

East Africa	65·4	14	2·2	2·5	4·5	6·2	9·7	5·5	5·4
Ethiopia	20·8	19	1·8	2·0	1·0	4·4	6·1	4·2	4·3
Tanzania	10·3	13	2·7	2·8	0·5	4·3	8·3	6·1	7·4
Kenya	8·4	17	2·5	2·9	0·6	6·4	11·0	7·0	6·5
Uganda	6·9	34	2·0	2·3	0·2	2·2	3·8	3·8	7·7
Madagascar	5·5	11	2·1	2·9	0·6	10·0	12·2	2·9	3·5
Malawi	3·5	35	2·7	2·9	0·1	2·6	5·3	10·4	6·1
Zambia	3·3	5	2·8	3·1	0·9	23·2	30·2	6·1	4·4
Rwanda	3·0	126	1·3	1·5	—	—	0·8	—	—
Southern Africa	33·0	8	2·3	2·5	7·8	21·3	26·0	4·0	3·8
Rep. of South Africa	15·8	15	2·7	2·7	6·2	35·0	38·4	3·5	3·5
Mozambique	6·4	9	1·6	1·8	0·3	4·9	9·0	6·0	6·0
Angola	4·9	4	1·2	1·4	0·4	7·9	14·2	5·3	5·3
Rhodesia	3·6	12	3·3	3·5	0·7	16·0	17·1	4·0	3·9
Lesotho	0·9	29	1·6	2·0	—	—	2·8	—	7·0

* In towns of 20,000 and more inhabitants

Source: Economic Commission for Africa, Document E/CN.14/Pop/6–17 April 1969; *Demographic Year book 1967*, table 2.

DISCUSSION

Panel Members: Professor E. S. Munger, Dr. P. Smit, Mr. Otto Krause

Professor Munger drew attention to the dramatic changes that had taken place in South Africa over the last two decades with regard to the knowledge of and interest in conditions in other African countries. He referred in particular to the pioneering work of the Institute of Race Relations to further knowledge with regard to those countries, and to the more recent work of the Africa Institute.

In regard to the population explosion in Africa, he referred firstly to the apathy of African leaders towards the implementation of birth control policies, and secondly to the instability caused by the large number of ethnic groups, a problem that had been aggravated by the existence of arbitrary political boundaries.

Dr. Smit regarded the increasing unemployment in some African countries as one of the most important consequences of the rapid population growth. Investigations showed that South Africa's neighbours would be threatened by more and more crises because of the inability of their economies to provide employment for their rapidly growing populations. South Africa would be forced in future to follow a policy that would radically affect the labour structure of the whole of southern Africa. Decentralisation of industries to areas within or near the borders of Bantu areas, the greater role that Bantu Homeland authorities would be playing in respect of labour matters, and the anticipated decline of the gold-mining industry would inevitably jeopardise the position of the foreign Bantu in South Africa.

At least 600,000 foreign Bantu from the countries of southern Africa were employed in South Africa. This alleviated considerably the pressure on the natural resources of neighbouring countries. In the period 1936–51, Lesotho, for example, rid itself of virtually its entire natural population increase through migrant labour to South Africa.

Mr. Otto Krause stressed the importance of studying political systems in Africa. There was an ominous imbalance in the world with the rich getting richer and the poor getting poorer – a world dominated by the developed nations, with the backward nations becoming ever more resentful in their poverty.

The backward world quite rightly tried to emulate the developed world. The problem was that ideas took root faster than ability was acquired. If there was to be an attempt to solve the ugly problems of Africa – the twin problems of population explosion and slow economic growth – then they had to be approached from the point of view of government. In looking at the quality of a government one considered its continuity, stability and strength. In order to attain this in the African context, he wished to suggest something quite heretical, namely government by the privileged classes. The west had revolted against government by the élite. In Russia, however, this revolt merely led to a substitution of one privileged group by another, viz. the aristocracy by the party élite. Today members of the party were the privileged group.

He suggested that African countries should not necessarily regard the western forms of government as best suited to their particular circumstances.

Professor F. R. Tomlinson stressed the importance of agriculture in the South African economy and criticised the attempts of some commentators to minimise the role of agriculture. He further felt it was a duty to assist other countries in southern Africa to solve some of their agricultural problems, and quoted figures of the qualified technical and other staff working in this field in South Africa.

South Africa had a comparative advantage over Europe and North America in being more conversant with the natural environments of African countries. Assistance was already being given in varying degrees to Lesotho, Botswana, Swaziland, Malawi and Madagascar, and South Africa was willing to go further north if asked to do so.

Professor Tomlinson also commented, in reply to questions, that one could not teach modern methods of agriculture to Africans directly. One must work through their leaders. The problem was to detect the leaders in a community, both European and African.

Professor Muhsam (in a written statement handed afterwards to the Rapporteurs) said: 'The problem of the reliance on traditional leaders for introducing efficient methods of agriculture or family planning has both internal and international aspects. It is obviously easy to use traditional leaders to introduce new techniques, and it may be impossible to introduce these methods against the opposition of traditional leaders. But new methods of agriculture should bring about, together with family planning, health habits, etc., a general process of modernisation which gradually replaces the traditional leadership by a new style of social structure, where the physician or nurse is the "leader" in matters of health and family planning; the agricultural instructor is the "leader" in agriculture, etc. The same applies to international relations. It is hard to see who the "traditional" leaders in this respect are, but it is surprising that most independent states in Africa easily accept advice and technical aid from the former colonial powers: France in the previous French colonies, Britain in the previous British colonies. It seems to me important to consider how the "traditional" international leaders can be replaced by new leaders. Israel has been mentioned, but in view of its small size and remote geographical situation seems not to be more than an example. But I have a feeling that the role of South Africa and its multiracial structure should be understood in this frame.'

Professor H. Pollak emphasised that specialists in the behavioural sciences could make the greatest contribution to family planning, and added that better use should be made of persons educated in those fields.

Professor Munger said that South Africa had a tremendous contribution to make to the states further north in Africa, and felt it was a tragedy that the great expertise of South Africa in various fields could not be used in those states. He suggested that better results might be obtained if non-white specialists were sent to other African countries.

Professor L. H. Watts supported the views expressed by Professor Pollak. He favoured the multi-disciplinary approach. When patterns of settlement and land tenure were changed, one had to realise the wider implications of such efforts.

Dr. Ellen Hellmann said too much emphasis was placed on tribal leadership. In African countries it was very important to have different leadership in different situations. She felt there was room for modern, educated and elective leadership for people who preferred to be free from the shackles of tradition.

Dr. B. Unterhalter commented that there had been no success in reducing the fertility of the non-whites substantially, and that there was still a problem of differential infant mortality. The coloured infant mortality rate was 128 per 1000, and the African rate might very well be higher, particularly if the first five years of life were taken into account.

Mr. M. Nupen, referring to Mr. Krause's views, warned against the danger of an oligarchical élite as a form of government. In the Soviet Union, he said, economic development was slowing down. The greatest danger was the emergence of an urban class taking over the traditional role of the agricultural sector.

15 International action on the population explosion

MICHAEL H. H. LOUW

1. INTRODUCTION

International action on the population problem rests on the assumption that it is a global problem and thus legitimately the concern of international society. Because there is at present no world government to provide laws or rules regulating the activities of all states and individuals on population matters, it devolves upon the spontaneous and fortuitous perception and action on the part of existing international institutions and individual countries to establish such action programmes as are possible under the circumstances. There is a widespread concern with the population problem today; many qualified observers have in recent years pointed out the dimensions of this problem and the dangers that might face mankind as a whole if it is not resolved in time. The words 'demographic revolution' and 'population explosion' are today common words in the international vocabulary.

The world population problem consists essentially of two irreconcilable elements: on the one hand, an accelerating population growth-rate (due to increased longevity, a decline in mortality, and an increase in effective fertility, all three due largely to improved health measures and better material living standards), and on the other hand, limited availability of food and resources and, eventually, of space, to make life for this population worth while or even tolerable. The problem is further compounded by an unequal distribution among nations of resources, of population and of the technologies to improve the use of resources and thus absorb higher population increases. The developed nations have a high capacity to use, improve and protect resources, whereas the underdeveloped nations have relatively undeveloped technologies and a low capacity to absorb additional population. In previous centuries fertility and mortality about equalled each other but through man's conquest of disease and famine, the death-rate has dropped and the birth-rate has risen to such an extent that the rate of population increase today on a global scale amounts to close on 3 per cent. In order to maintain reasonable levels of living for this increased population, the necessary resources for living at a certain minimum tolerable level would have to be made available. There thus seem to be three interrelated aspects of the population problem which require attention today: population (in numbers), resources (and technology) and values, i.e. the standards of living possible with certain ratios between the other two.

The solutions for the population problem generally proposed today are: reduction of the rate of population increase through reducing the birth-rate, increased investment for economic development, which would provide greater resources with which to sustain a bigger population (or a stable population at higher levels of living), diversification of the economy and developing the skills of the people so as to provide a greater capacity for producing resources and improve distribution of income. In the non-material sphere may be mentioned an emphasis on the values of individualism and self-choice which would free a parent from having to conform to group or cultural pressures prescribing a large number of children.

However, modern thinking on the population problem does not see a solution so much in merely limiting or reducing population, but rather emphasises the search for an 'optimum population' for a country, in terms of both numbers and structure, which would ensure that the resources are rationally used, produced and distributed, so that reasonably high and rising standards of living for all the members of the population are ensured. This means that an 'optimum population' policy should be related to available resources and economic conditions (and the people needed for developing them), as well as to the value systems and preferences and the demands for improved levels of living among the population. Other solutions have also been mentioned from time to time, for example, migration to other countries and the settlement of empty spaces, but these are today generally considered to be marginal solutions.

2. POPULATION AS A WORLD PROBLEM

The population problem may be considered to be global in the sense that with the uneven distribution of populations and resources, the population pressures in overpopulated countries might create social unrest which could affect other countries. This unequal distribution of population and resources also creates a widening gap, for example, it is estimated that between 1975 and 2000, while the rate of population increase in North America will average 1·2 per cent per year, and that for Europe 1 per cent, the rate for Asia will be 3 per cent, that for Africa 2·8 per cent and that for Latin America 3·8 per cent.[1] Taking the case for Asia: to achieve a per capita income equal to that of North America in 1950, while experiencing its present population growth, Asia would have to increase her aggregate income by 35 times by 1975 and 62 times by the year 2000.[2]

The second main reason for an international interest in the population problem derives from the realisation that as there are now no self-activating mechanisms (such as wars and famines through the centuries) to maintain a 'natural' population equilibrium, the present accelerating population growth would within generations press upon available world resources and space to such an extent that levels of living would be intolerably lowered. But preventive action will have to be collective and integrated action by all countries of the world and built on a generalised world view of the problem.

A world view is especially supported by the ecological approach to the population problem. Various observers are emphasising that the earth, with its surrounding space, is one integrated 'ecosystem'. Man's ability to survive and to maintain a satisfactory level of living on this planet within this ecosystem is dependent on how he behaves in it. From the ecological perspective, political boundaries are irrelevant because the oceans and the atmosphere, the weather and the water cycle make the planet an integrated whole. This is already implicitly acknowledged by a number of existing international measures, for example, the various agreements on the radio waveband, on the ocean floor and its exploitation, on the Antarctic and on the atmosphere and outer space. There is also a growing realisation today that measures will have to be taken for protecting the global environment through the international control of pollution, especially by chemical effluents and by oil discharged accidentally or purposely into the oceans.

A third major consideration is the assumption by the international community that great differences in wealth and living standards between the wealthy and the poor peoples of the earth (differences which are directly related to population), are undesirable for both humanitarian and political reasons. From the humanitarian point of view it is now considered a moral duty of the wealthier countries to assist (the present 'suggested' rate of such assistance is expected to be around 1 per cent of the G.N.P. of the donor) the less developed countries in improving their standards of living. From the political point of view it is considered that an awareness of these differences,

I

especially among peoples who have high expectations of improving their own levels of living, would give rise to frustrations, social unrest and eventually political instability, revolutions and civil and even international wars.

In the absense of an international legislature or other law-making body, it devolves upon perceptive and enlightened diplomacy and upon the United Nations and its associated specialised agencies, to articulate this international concern and to find the solutions for the problems of man's adaptation to his global ecosystem. This includes of course regional arrangements for a rational control of parts of the ecosystem.

However, if international concern with the population problem is legitimate, international action would be appropriate only if it is based on certain essential premises. These are: first, international action must be international and relevant to the problem, i.e. it should be action complementary to that of individual states. It should support or assist action by national governments and not supersede, duplicate or substitute such national action. Second, international action can only enter the operational context to the extent that it flows from internationally formulated and financed programmes and does not infringe the sovereign rights, the interests, the values and the policies of individual national states. International action can therefore be directed only to national governments, which remain the final decision-makers regarding action directed towards their citizens for the solution of the population problem. Third, international action must concentrate on the international context; it represents or takes as its special point of departure the international context and must therefore present and maintain the global international perspective. This is uniquely its contribution as against the national contributions of individual states. The value of international action lies essentially in its global point of view, its total as against the partial or particularised perspectives of states or groups of states.

It should be remembered, however, that international action also has certain limitations. First, it can only emanate from a consensus among participating member states and this consensus represents a minimum rather than a high level of agreement. It can therefore not operate beyond this basic and minimum common agreement because of the danger of conflict with the value systems, religions or policies of individual states. On delicate and private matters, such as family planning, this has often been shown to be of the utmost importance. Second, international action cannot be on any larger scale than the available resources, voluntarily contributed by states, will permit.

3. PROBLEMS OF OVERPOPULATION

Some of the major problems may be briefly outlined.

(a) THE MALDISTRIBUTION OF POPULATION AND RESOURCES

Hauser indicated some major gaps between developed and less developed countries. First, the difference in per capita income, which he estimated to be as great as 20 to 1 between these countries. Second, the availability of non-human energy which he considered as perhaps the best single measurement available of differences in capital investment, know-how and technology which account for the great differences in productivity and, consequently, in the size of the aggregate product available for distribution among the population. He estimated that the non-human energy consumption in North America was 10,000 kilowatt hours per capita per year, in contrast to that in Asia of less than 300. The report of the United Nations Conference on the Application of Science and Technology for the Benefit of the Less Developed Areas stated that 'the present very uneven distribution of the world's peoples and natural resources is accompanied by even greater maldistribution of capital, knowledge and skills among the different peoples, and hence there are wide disparities in levels of living'.[3] The problem therefore lies not so much in absolute population figures as in the relationship between population on the one hand and the capacity to carry a population on the other hand.

(b) OVERPOPULATION GENERALLY LOWERS LIVING STANDARDS BY DIVERTING INVESTMENT

With a disproportionately large child population investment is of necessity directed to the rearing of children (food, schooling, buildings, health programmes, etc.) which could have been used for productive investment to increase the general productivity of a country. This child dependency reaches 40–50 per cent in some of the developing countries. The effects of too many children on the individual family can also be very tragic: the very quality of life is threatened by the quantity of life, human dignity is degraded, and the possibilities of improvement of the welfare of parents and children are submerged by sheer numbers. As U Thant has said, 'half of those living and two-thirds of those still to be born in this century face the prospects of malnutrition, poverty and despair'; he added that 'there is no right more basic to humanity and more important to each individual than the right to enter this world as a wanted human being who will be fed, sheltered, cared for, educated, loved and provided with opportunities for constructive life'.[4]

(c) EXCESSIVE URBANISATION

A typical phenomenon in the less developed countries of the world is that of increasingly large proportions of the population which leave the rural areas on account of pressures and poverty there, and move to the larger urban areas. But whereas normal urbanisation is related to industrialisation and economic development generally, this type of urbanisation in developing countries is merely uncontrolled migration and represents instead, in Hauser's words, 'the transfer of rural poverty from an overpopulated and unsettled countryside to a mass urban setting'. He adds that 'in the economically underdeveloped areas of the world, urbanisation is outpacing economic development and the city is more a symbol of mass misery and political instability than of man's conquest of nature'.[5]

(d) POLITICAL INSTABILITY

There are various aspects to this problem: first, with an increasing awareness of the higher standards of living enjoyed by people in other countries, those in the underdeveloped countries might, with a feeling of increasing frustration, express their dissatisfaction in various forms of civil unrest, which may have repercussions in other countries. The possibility of military action by countries from overpopulated lands moving into 'empty lands' is not taken seriously today, largely because of the high cost of war and the settlement of colonists in foreign territory.

Another political complication might result from large spontaneous migrations of people from one country to another, where employment opportunities are more attractive. This often results in the settlement of large foreign communities within a country, and often, while remaining separate and aloof from the indigenous inhabitants, nevertheless compete with them for employment and economic opportunities. Such spontaneous migration in previous generations has in many countries created problems of large foreign minorities within countries, for example, Asians in Kenya and Tanzania, Chinese in Indonesia and Malaysia and Nigerians in Ghana, which have given rise to unrest, friction and serious diplomatic confrontations.

4. THE NATURE OF INTERNATIONAL ACTION

First, international action on population problems is by its very nature limited to its international context; it cannot deal directly and freely with individuals whose voluntary personal decisions bring about an increase in the population in the first place. It should be remembered that the act of procreation is a deeply personal and private affair, linked to family, social and cultural values and recognised as a personal right. For example, rights to a family are stated clearly in the Declaration of Human Rights in Article 16 (i): 'men and women of full age, without any limitation due to race, nationality or religion, have the right to marry and to found a family. They are entitled to equal rights as to marriage, during marriage and at its dissolution', and in Article 16 (iii): 'the family is the natural and fundamental group unit of society and is entitled to protection by society and the state'. Another important provision is contained in Article 25 (ii): 'motherhood and childhood are entitled to special care and assistance. All children, whether born in or out of wedlock, shall enjoy the same social protection.'

These basic rights were further emphasised by the World Leaders' Declaration on Population, signed by heads of state or prime ministers of 30 countries, which was presented to the United Nations on 11 December 1968, on the occasion of Human Rights Day. In this Declaration the signatories expressed their belief that the population problem must be recognised as a principal element in long-range national planning 'if governments are to achieve their economic goals and fulfil the aspirations of their people'; 'that the opportunity to decide the number and spacing of children is a basic human right; that lasting and meaningful peace will depend to a considerable measure upon how the challenge of population growth is met; and that family planning, by assuring greater opportunity to each person, frees man to attain his individual dignity and reach his full potential'.[6]

But on this occasion the United Nations Secretary General, U Thant, also said that population planning was seen today not only as an integral part of national efforts for economic and social development, but as a way to human progress in modern society, and added: 'there now exists in many countries an express desire to limit the size of families'. Continuing, he said that any choice with regard to the size of the family must irrevocably rest with the family itself, but 'this right of parents to free choice will remain illusory unless they are aware of the alternatives open to them'.

Second, international action on population can reach individual persons only through their respective governments. Any concrete and direct action on the demographic problem is the responsibility of the government concerned. But in the final analysis, because the nature of procreation is private, such enforcement measures or incentives and disincentives are inappropriate, except as they operate through the decisions of the participating persons. Such decisions depend on their motivation, which in turn may be effected by outside influences or persuasions emanating from the government or from private associations interested in establishing birth control attitudes.

Third, international action derives from such consensuses as can be attained in the international bodies which debate the measures and make decisions on population control. However, it should be borne in mind that among these member states there are wide differences as regards their approach to population problems and policies and these are naturally reflected in the positions they take regarding proposals for international action. To mention three major examples: a first group of countries, viz. France and the Soviet Union, follow expansionist policies regarding population. France has had a falling birth-rate in recent years reaching a point of natural decrease of population. The main policies which the government and private associations have found it necessary to establish are those of promoting immigration and encouraging larger families through various governmental measures, especially the landmark *code de la famille* of 1939. Under this law various birth control practices were discouraged and family allowances for larger families provided. This resulted in a slight increase in the birth-rate beginning in 1946. The Soviet Union follows a positive population policy on the argument that it has vast undeveloped resources and huge areas which are underpopulated and for the exploitation and settlement of these larger populations are needed. In the second group of countries are those which actively practise restrictive policies designed to lower the birth-rate, of which India and Japan are the outstanding examples. Both have developed extensive measures to limit population growth through education and orientation programmes, the provision of clinical services, and research and guidance on family planning programmes and fertility controls. The third group of countries, represented by Sweden and the United Kingdom, follow stabilisation policies in population matters. The policy of stabilisation is intimately related to the maintenance of a satisfactory level of welfare in the nation, which would be to the benefit both of the family and of the nation as a whole and would ensure that the population at least maintains itself by replacing itself.[7]

International action on the operational side is therefore limited to the provision to governments of the necessary basic knowledge regarding population and its effects, the training of demographic experts, the calling of attention to population problems in a global context through population conferences and debates in international bodies, and to the publication of important studies and reports on population problems and especially their effects on economic development and standards of living.

The key to effective international action is therefore to establish good working relationships between operational international organisations and individual governments on population matters. At its tenth session in 1959, the Population Commission defined its mandate and its relationship to member governments as follows:

> It is not the Population Commission's task to suggest the policies that any government of any member state should pursue. Its interest lies in doing all that it can to see that the knowledge of population trends and their interrelations with social and economic factors is widened and deepened and that this knowledge is brought to the attention of the governments. Each government, the Commission believes, has a responsibility to study the inter-relations between population growth and economic and social progress as fully as possible on its own initiative, and to take the results of the study of these matters into account in formulating and implementing its policies. This responsibility is particularly heavy when a fast rate of population growth is occurring under conditions of widespread poverty.[8]

5. UNITED NATIONS ACTION ON POPULATION

(a) THE GENERAL ASSEMBLY

The major role of the General Assembly is to establish the basic principles, policies and guide-lines on which international operational programmes on the population problem can be based. Its most important act was the well-known Resolution on population growth and economic development (1838-XVII of 18 December 1962). This Resolution represented a recognition by the international community of the existence and of the seriousness of the world population problem. Prior to the Resolution, however, important work had already been done in the population field, for example, the establishment of a Population Branch in the Secretariat, a Population Commission (a group of government representatives meeting every two years), the holding of a World Population Conference in Rome in 1954, and the encouragement of the Regional Economic Commissions in Asia, Latin America and Africa to devote special attention to the population field. The United Nations had also organised regional demographic research and training centres in Santiago, Bombay and Cairo to provide advisory services to the countries of these cities.

The Resolution was designed for specific action of various kinds. First, the Secretary General was requested to conduct an inquiry among member states 'concerning the particular problems confronting them as a result of the reciprocal action of economic development and population changes'. This idea demonstrated a basic premise of the General Assembly that there is a relationship between economic development and population and that this should be carefully explored and understood for purposes of economic and social planning.

Second, ECOSOC was asked (in co-operation with Specialised Agencies and Regional Economic Commissions and the Population Commission) to 'intensify its studies and research on the interrelationship of population growth and economic and social development with particular reference to the needs of developing countries for investment in health and educational facilities'. This meant additional research and activities in demographic work and parallel studies in education and health by UNESCO and the World Health Organisation (W.H.O.). Third, the United Nations agencies were asked to assist governments, especially in the less developed countries, 'in obtaining basic data and carrying out essential studies of the demographic aspects as well as other aspects of their economic and social development problems'. Also, the World Population Conference scheduled for 1965 was requested to pay special attention to the 'interrelationships of population growth with economic and social development, particularly in countries that are less developed'. Finally, the United Nations should give technical assistance as requested by governments for national projects and programmes dealing with the problems of population. It was this section which was widely interpreted as calling for United Nations assistance in the actual implementation of family planning programmes (including birth control), and which had earlier caused a great deal of disagreement between countries on the advisability of the United Nations providing technical assistance on birth control.

It is interesting to note here the role of the United Nations in its various institutions as an international forum, where the concern of the international community regarding the problem of population could be articulated. Opinions were expressed which indicated completely different points of view. One group of countries, for example, advocated the introduction of birth control measures because of the grave problems for economic and social development created by uncontrolled population increases. Another group of states denied that the population problem was so serious, and for many reasons, including religious and political ones, were strongly against officially supported birth control programmes. A third group felt that the population problem was not very urgent and action on it could be postponed for some years. A fourth group, the

Communist countries, denied that a population problem actually existed, and were of the opinion that it was based on 'neo-malthusian fallacies' and that its existence was the result of the malfunctioning of the capitalist system. In their view it was merely a matter of organising the economy to overcome what problem of population there might be. (There are indications that the Soviet Union has now come round, for various reasons, to a new view of the population problem more in line with the western view.)

It should be noted that these Resolutions represent in effect internationally sanctioned guide-lines for policy in executing national population programmes. As such, they represent a legitimation of certain assumptions with value components, for example, most important, birth control, and also other assumptions, such as that (a) advisory services on family planning were not to be regarded as a substitute for energetic action to increase production and investment and to reduce unemployment and underemployment; (b) nations had the sovereign right to determine their own population policies; (c) the responsibility and exclusive right of parents to decide the size of their family was respected; and (d) a strictly professional and scientific approach was applied in dealing with population problems.

Attention to the population problem was also given by the General Assembly Resolution of 17 December 1966 (2211-XXI), which expressed concern over the growing food shortage in the developing countries, due in many cases to a decline in the production of food relative to population growth. It recognised the need for further study of the implications of the growth, structure and geographical distribution of population for economic and social development, including national health, nutrition, education and social welfare programmes carried out at all levels of government activity. It stated, as its belief, that demographic problems required the consideration of economic, social, cultural, psychological and health factors in their proper perspective, and recognised that in these matters the sovereignty of nations in formulating and promoting their own population policies, with due regard to the principle that family size should be the free choice of each family, should remain unquestioned.

(b) UNITED NATIONS OPERATIONAL UNITS AT THE
    HEADQUARTERS LEVEL

Apart from the General Assembly, which approves resolutions for the general guidance of other United Nations organs, ECOSOC and the *Population Commission* also fulfil important functions of policy-making on the United Nations commitment in the population field. On the operational side, the units concerned with demographic matters are: *The Population Division*, the *United Nations Trust Fund* (later *Fund for Population Activities*), the *Unit for Population Programmes and Projects*, and the *Sub-Committee on Population of the Administrative Committee for Co-ordination*.

Initially the major activities of the United Nations in the field of population were concerned with the development of technical manuals on methods of population analysis and population estimates and projections. These were used widely by countries in developing their own economic and social development programmes. After the Resolution on population growth and economic development in 1962, these activities were increased. In 1964 an *ad hoc* committee of experts was convened by the Secretary General and it recommended an amplified and long-range programme of United Nations work in the population field, especially the improvement of demographic statistics; the intensification of research and technical work on such priority topics as fertility, mortality, internal migration and urbanisation and on the demographic aspects of economic and social development; and work on the programme of technical assistance and conferences in the population field.

The United Nations also organised various population conferences, viz. one in Rome in 1954, in Belgrade in 1965 and an Asian Population Conference in New Delhi in 1963. These conferences served as forums for the exchange of views and experience among experts in demography and related disciplines. The proceedings and the technical papers presented were subsequently published by the United Nations and provide very useful reference material on the present state of demographic knowledge.

After 1965, with the adoption of Resolution No. 1084 (xxxix) and 1347 (xlv) of ECOSOC as well as General Assembly Resolution No. 2211 (xxi), a new trend was set for population work by the United Nations, viz. emphasis on technical assistance to governments in all fields of population, including family planning. As a result of these Resolutions, the various Specialised Agencies now have full mandates concerning fertility and family planning and these were subsequently formalised in Resolutions by their respective governing bodies. United Nations technical assistance on birth control measures had thus become legitimate.

From the operational point of view the work carried out by the Specialised Agencies and by United Nations Headquarters presented new problems of co-ordination. In 1968 an Inter-Agency Meeting on Population was established under the Administrative Committee for Co-ordination (A.C.C.); this is in effect a body with continuous responsibility for co-ordination of United Nations work on population matters.

A new type of training course to prepare Population Programme Officers for the United Nations to work on field assignments in developing countries was started in New York on 14 January 1969. The participants attended about seventy sessions and the course was designed to help them in their work of preparing governments to identify population problems and to develop action projects that might qualify for United Nations aid or other external aid. These officers were subsequently sent to over thirty countries. The course was financed by the United Nations Fund for Population Activities.

The United Nations also sent teams of specialists in family planning to have consultations on the family planning programmes of various governments and on the success which these have had in reducing fertility. Such teams were sent in 1969 to the United Arab Republic and to India.

At Headquarters a special unit for Population Programmes and Projects was established to provide for planning in this field and for backstopping activities for field projects. These field projects are being handled, like other technical assistance projects, through the Resident Representatives of the United Nations Development Programme (U.N.D.P.). Other divisions in the United Nations Headquarters departments have also become involved in some of these activities in the population field in so far as they are relevant to their own fields, for example, social development, public administration, economic development, human rights, the status of women, etc.

Among the new projects envisaged are the establishment of additional regional demographic centres to include family planning programmes among their activities, and a proposal for the establishment of an International Population Institute to deal with all the inter-disciplinary components of research, training and advice on family planning. In its research programme the United Nations has given as priority areas recommended for study by the Population Commission the following five topics: fertility, family planning, migration, urbanisation and the demographic aspects of economic and social development.

The work of the United Nations in evaluating basic population data and preparing projections of future population trends has been of special importance, as such projections have an important bearing on the national development policies of governments.

To ensure that its publications on population are more widely studied, the United Nations will now consider every two years a special report to be presented by the Secretary General on the world population situation. The United Nations has also started publishing a *Population Newsletter* and various pamphlets on population for mass circulation.

One could therefore summarise by saying that the United Nations has by now developed a fairly wide, representative, differentiated and integrated machinery to handle population problems. There has also been a remarkable response on the part of member states of the United Nations to the population problem, first, in approving the population programmes and even some of their more sensitive components such as family planning, and second, in making financial contributions to the United Nations Fund for Population Activities.

(c) THE REGIONAL ECONOMIC COMMISSIONS

Programmes of varying kinds on population have also been adopted by the *Economic Commission for Africa* (*E.C.A.*), by the *Economic Commission for Europe* (*E.C.E.*), the *Economic Commission for Latin America* (*E.C.L.A.*) (which established the Latin-American Demographic Centre – C.E.L.A.D.E.), and the *Economic Commission for Asia and the Far East* (*E.C.A.F.E.*).

A word might be added about the work of C.E.L.A.D.E. The Centre operates under a Fund to which contributions are made from U.N.D.P. and from the United States Agency for International Development (U.S.A.I.D.), as well as from other organisations. It provides regular training programmes in specialised work of a demographic nature and carries out research on certain aspects of population and evaluations of family planning programmes. Up to the end of June 1969 a total of $3,501,752 had been contributed to the Fund.

The major activities of regional economic commissions in technical co-operation have been services of an interregional, regional and national advisory type. Various regional advisers were appointed to advise countries on family planning policies. Advisory missions in family planning were sent to Pakistan and India to make evaluations of the regional demographic training centres and research centres, and various seminars and meetings were organised, for example, a seminar on the evaluation of family planning programmes in Bangkok in December 1969.

6. UNITED NATIONS ACTION ON THE HUMAN ENVIRONMENT

(a) THE GLOBAL ENVIRONMENT

Turning now to the *environment* of the globe within which 3·5 billion people live at present (expected to increase to 7 billion by the end of the century), note should be taken of international action, especially action under the aegis of the United Nations, in this all-important area which is so directly related to population; population is a recurrent theme in the problem of environment. During recent years, numerous observers have drawn attention to the deterioration of the human environment (partially caused by the demands of population increases and of higher levels of living), such as the pollution of air and water, and other disruptions of the ecological balance of the globe as a whole. This deterioration has clear international ramifications, because world-wide pollution of the 'biosphere' (the layer of the earth where land, air and water meet and where life can exist) means that the very survival and the quality of human life on the whole planet are being threatened.

In the Swedish memorandum on the environment which was submitted to ECOSOC in 1968, it was pointed out that man's survival depends on an infinitely complex system of relationships and balances among countless living organisms, existing in or on the extremely thin crust of the earth, or just above it; it pointed out that 'the system has a remarkable capacity for adaptation and regeneration; but nature's patience has a limit'. And although modern technology is indispensable for economic and social progress, it could also set off a reaction of 'unforeseen harmful effects'.[9] The Secretary General, in his report, noted that 'if current trends continue, the future of life on earth could be endangered', and that it is urgent to focus 'world attention on those problems which threaten humanity in an environment that permits the realisation of the highest human aspirations'.[10] After pointing out the complexities of environmental deterioration, he concluded that three underlying causes of the environmental crisis may be identified: accelerated population growth, increased urbanisation and new and expanded technologies – all these being associated with increased demands for space, food and natural resources. As a result, all areas of the earth's surface have been to some degree modified by man, for example, many millions of acres of arable land have been lost through erosion and salinisation, two-thirds of the world's forests have been rendered unproductive and an estimated 150 types of birds and animals have become extinct as a result of human action.

A special aspect of environmental pollution, viz. the effects of atomic radiation or pollution of the atmosphere resulting from atomic bomb tests by nuclear powers, was handled at an earlier stage within the context of the disarmament negotiations. In 1963, the Soviet Union, the United Kingdom and the United States reached agreement on the text of a treaty banning nuclear weapon tests in the atmosphere, in outer space and under water. The treaty was signed by their Foreign Ministers in 1963 and entered into force on 10 October 1963, at which time the original signatories had ratified it and 98 other United Nations members as well as 7 non-members had signed it. Even before that, i.e. in 1955, the General Assembly had established the Scientific Committee on the Effects of Atomic Radiation. This Committee is making a continuous study of the radio-active contamination of the environment due to the testing of atomic and nuclear weapons. It gave special attention to radiation from radioactive debris, how this entered into the food-chains of various animal and marine species, and how it may ultimately be lodged in man, on whom it could have certain genetic and other physiological effects.

The Secretary General's report classified environmental problems into three categories: (a) human settlement problems affecting local areas and requiring action mainly by local and national authorities, such as rapid urbanisation and the decline of rural settlements; (b) territorial problems of land areas and non-oceanic and coastal waters, which must be safeguarded by governmental action and by regional arrangements among states; and (c) 'global problems affecting all countries and requiring international agreement and joint action'. As examples of problems which one state cannot solve alone, were mentioned river basin pollution (which might involve a region of various states) and oceanic pollution, which requires international agreement. The report advocated an integrated approach at the national level and an overall view at the international level on environmental problems; it pointed out that the considerable scientific and technical knowledge now available to deal with environmental problems was not being sufficiently used. Further research was also needed on global physical and biological phenomena, socio-cultural factors, non-pollution techniques, and rational and conservation-oriented use of resources. The report concluded that a major area for international action would be in world-wide or regional legislation, standardisation and conventions dealing with these problems.

The report suggested that a United Nations conference on the human environment be held to exchange information and experience on the concrete problem of action programmes by public authorities to plan, manage and control the environment. It emphasised the global nature of the problem: 'no nation can any longer be isolated from these global pressures . . . we all live in one biosphere within which space and resources, though vast, are limited.'[11] The report added that policies of environmental preservation must be viewed as part of the long-term and sustained development of resources for economic and social progress and not as a restriction upon progress.

The General Assembly, at its twenty-third session, unanimously adopted a Resolution (2398-XXIII of 3 December 1968) calling for a United Nations Conference on Human Environment in 1972 to be held in Stockholm.

The Advisory Committee on the Application of Science and Technology to Development produced a report in June 1969, for presentation by the Secretary General, in which it was noted that radically new attitudes and concerted political, economic and social action by both developed and developing nations will be needed to meet the 'looming crisis' of the human environment. It pointed out that portents of the crisis were apparent in the explosive growth of human populations; the unforeseen impact of new and powerful technologies on the environment; unplanned urbanisation with its problems of slums, disease, crime and inadequate educational facilities; the loss of space and agricultural land; and the impending extinction of many forms of plant and animal life. It expressed the opinion that if current trends were to continue, the future of life on earth could be endangered.

(b) THE SEA-BED

The significance of the sea-bed from both the population and environment points of view lies in its importance as a source of food (especially protein) and industrial materials, as an area for oil exploration and in its vulnerability to pollution. There are also the military aspects, viz. the possibility that the sea-bed and the deep sea could be used by some powers for military purposes. In addition, in many fishing areas fishing was being carried out by some countries on such an intensive scale that it could endanger existing fish populations. In 1967 the General Assembly established a Committee on the Peaceful Uses of the Sea-bed and the Ocean Floor beyond the Limits of National Jurisdiction, which was empowered to make studies and recommendations on certain legal and economic questions as well as to study political matters in regard to disarmament related to the sea-bed and the ocean floor. It also adopted resolutions on safeguards against pollution, on marine conservation, research and exploration, and exploitation of marine resources.[12] The Committee later reported that some form of international regime will have to be established to ensure fair development of the ocean floor by all countries. In 1968 the Assembly also called for action by appropriate international bodies in relation to meteorological aspects of ocean science, mineral development and educational programmes. This is related to the World Weather Watch and the Global Atmospheric Research Programme, both of which are run by the World Meteorological Organisation (W.M.O.).

An interesting aspect of the sea-bed regime was the legal basis on which it could be established. There is still a dispute on the definition of the sea-bed and the ocean floor beyond national jurisdiction. One line of thought is the concept of the common heritage of mankind, containing the notion of trusteeship, while another view is the concept of *res communes*, which requires only the internationally accepted test of 'reasonable use'. An interesting aspect of the principle of common heritage is the concept of indivisibility, which means that the area could be used only for peaceful purposes and for the benefit of all.

7. ACTION ON POPULATION BY THE UNITED NATIONS SPECIALISED AGENCIES

In 1962 the General Assembly considered for the first time the issue of population growth as related to economic development. The purpose was to ascertain the role which the United Nations should play in assisting governments to implement programmes aimed at moderating population growth to rates more compatible with the rate of economic progress. The Assembly recognised that 'the health and welfare of the family are of paramount importance, not only for obvious humanitarian reasons but also with regard to economic development and social progress, and that the health and welfare of the family require special attention in areas of relatively high population growth', and further that 'it is the responsibility of each government to decide on its own policies and devise its own programme of action dealing with the problems of population and economic and social progress'.[13] In 1964 ECOSOC, in a unanimous resolution, called for the intensification of United Nations efforts to assist governments of interested developing countries with advice to cope with the population problem confronting them. In 1965 the Council affirmed the authority of the Secretary General to provide such advisory services.[14] In 1966 the General Assembly unanimously endorsed an expanded programme of United Nations activities in the population field, including the provision of information and advisory services on family planning (General Assembly Resolution 2211-XXI).

Although family planning programmes were intended to be included in the general assistance to be rendered to requesting countries, they had important technical aspects for which specialised knowledge and action were necessary which would most appropriately be provided by the various Specialised Agencies. As a result of the resolutions of the General Assembly and of ECOSOC the various

Specialised Agencies were also authorised to give special attention to the population problem. Some of their activities are mentioned briefly.

(a) THE WORLD HEALTH ORGANISATION (W.H.O.)

Acting on the authorisation of the General Assembly, the World Health Assembly passed resolutions to give W.H.O. a broad mandate to work on the health aspects of the population problem and more specifically on human reproduction, family planning and population dynamics. The W.H.O. philosophy is not to endorse or promote any particular population policy but rather to see that the problems of human reproduction involve the family unit as well as the whole society. In conformity with the prevailing United Nations philosophy, it also emphasises that the size of the family is the free choice of each individual family and reaffirms that all families should have the opportunity to obtain information and advice on problems relative to family planning. W.H.O. provides various types of advisory service and technical assistance on family planning from requesting states to which they send experts to assist their governments in their own national programmes of family planning. W.H.O. also provides, within its existing programmes, training focused on family planning for public health physicians, nurses, midwives and auxiliaries. It also stimulates, co-ordinates and supports research in the biological and clinical aspects of human reproduction, of family planning and of population dynamics. This includes work on the psychological aspects of human reproduction and family planning within its ongoing epidemiological studies.

(b) THE FOOD AND AGRICULTURE ORGANISATION (F.A.O.)

The work of F.A.O. on population problems lies mainly in two areas: first, policy-oriented research into the implications of population trends for agricultural development, rural employment, current and projected levels and patterns of long-term demand and supply for agricultural products, levels of food consumption and nutrition, levels of living, the effects of food and nutritional factors on fertility and mortality (particularly among the young), and on other demographic variables; second, it gives attention to the development of an educational approach to assist in integrating family planning into a comprehensive and better family living programme. It accordingly carried out research on various aspects of these problems and brought out annual reports on trends in food production and population, and in its report *Indicative World Planning for Agricultural Development* it reviewed the problem of agricultural development against the background of expected trends in population up to 1985. This report concluded that rapid population growth in rural areas stands in the way of increasing agricultural productivity, and hence of raising the incomes and levels of living of the agricultural population, by making it difficult to get a productive sectoral distribution of the labour force between agricultural and other occupations.

In general the F.A.O. programme objectives are to assist governments to foster among their people an awareness of the relation between rapid population growth and hunger, malnutrition, ill-health and low levels of living; to effectively integrate educational programmes in planning for better family living into comprehensive plans for national development; and to study ways in which educational and field programmes in home economics, nutrition and related fields can be used in solving the food/population dilemma. An interesting innovation of F.A.O. in this regard is the Planning for Better Family Living Programme which emphasises the entire family as a unit and the need to give continuing attention to the whole family throughout its life cycle, i.e. from the time a couple expects to establish a new family unit, through the years when the family is enlarging in size, until it diminishes during the later stages of life. The purpose is to develop a process whereby a nation can provide for all its people the opportunity to acquire the knowledge, skills and attitudes that will enable them to make sound decisions with regard to all aspects of family size, including marriage, parenthood and number of children.

(c) THE UNITED NATIONS EDUCATIONAL, SCIENTIFIC AND CULTURAL ORGANISATION (UNESCO)

In interpreting its mandate in the population field, UNESCO saw its functions as covering: a long-term programme of studies, including some cross-national analyses, concerning the reciprocal relationship between levels of education and population; the promotion of demography as an academic discipline; the training of demographers at university level and the creation of opportunities for post-graduate demographic research; the dissemination in schools of knowledge about population data and problems; and finally the introduction of population material into adult education programmes. UNESCO's General Conference approved the following co-ordinated programme within the field of UNESCO's competence: within the field of education, the development of teaching materials, curricula, adult education and the study of pilot projects on family planning in the experimental literacy programme; within the social sciences, studies on different aspects of population and family planning, so as to establish 'the intellectual base for understanding the complexity of family planning in the context of different cultures'; and within the communications field, studies of ways and means for the establishment and operation of efficient programmes within the fields of population and family planning and the provision of relevant information and documentation. An example of a project in the latter field was the Seminar on Mass Media and National Family Planning Campaigns in Paris, 23–28 June 1969.

(d) THE UNITED NATIONS CHILDRENS FUND (UNICEF)

UNICEF has in recent years been concerned with the effects which a too rapid and unplanned population growth can have on the welfare and health of children, as well as on their preparation for subsequent productive participation in society. In this regard it should perhaps be remembered that there are approximately one billion children under 15 years of age living in developing countries, with their number growing at 2·5 per cent annually, and that the percentage of young people under 20 ranges from 45 per cent to as much as 65 per cent of the populations in these countries. Some implications of this situation may be noted: such large numbers of children and young people increase the dependency ratio of the population, i.e. there are many more consumers than producers in the economy, a condition which increases the burden on existing limited resources and the cost of raising young people. UNICEF tries to relate its programmes to assistance in the strengthening and the extension of maternal and child health services, including family planning, encouraging a fuller consideration by governments of the effect of population growth on planning and providing services for the development of the young. UNICEF regards as one of its first concerns the quality of the life of the child in the family and it therefore regards its support of family planning and population limitation activities as one of the ways in which to improve the health and well-being of the child, the mother and the family. In general UNICEF, while leaving it to requesting countries to develop their own population policies, promotes greater awareness of the demographic factor in planning for the development of the young, particularly as it bears on the protection as well as the preparation of the younger population.

(e) THE INTERNATIONAL LABOUR ORGANISATION (I.L.O.)

The particular concern of I.L.O. with the population problem lies in its interest in the influence of rapid population growth on the employment, training and welfare of workers, with special reference to developing countries. It is therefore interested in the adoption of appropriate population policies, including family planning and manpower plans. I.L.O. carries out, as a long-term goal, the World Employment Programme, which is intended to contribute to the achievement of the highest possible level of productive employment in the developing countries of the world. This implies that the governments concerned have to be persuaded to introduce full employment as a major objective of economic and social development planning and policies. This involves studies of the labour force and projections of the labour force as well as labour productivity, which in turn are related to the total population structure. I.L.O. attempts to create understanding among employment authorities, employers, trade union leaders and academic circles in recipient countries of the serious obstacles posed by rapid population growth in the attainment of development goals. It also provides assistance to governments, trade unions, employers and interested institutions, in orienting workers on matters of family planning.

8. OTHER INTERNATIONAL PROGRAMMES

International programmes on population may be of various types: first, within the official context there are multilateral and bilateral programmes in which states are involved; second, within the private context there are also multilateral and bilateral programmes, but these may be between private international associations on the one side and governments or private national associations on the other side. In addition to these there are also the programmes of the Organisation for Economic Co-operation and Development (O.E.C.D.), and especially its Development Centre, which have in recent years taken an interest in population affairs and organised a first population conference in December 1968.

The international organisations, both official and private, offer a variety of programmes. These can be grouped into two main categories, those directly and those indirectly related to the population problem.

PROGRAMMES DIRECTLY RELATED TO THE POPULATION PROBLEM

As indicated in previous sections, the population programmes carried out by the United Nations organisations specially created for this purpose, viz. the Population Commission, the Population

Division in the Secretariat and the Fund for Population Activities, are mainly focused on information and orientation for policy purposes. These programmes include the collection and analysis of demographic data; research and the gathering of technical information on demographic and population problems; training of population personnel; interchange of technical information through international conferences and direct technical aid to requesting countries on population policies; as well as evaluative studies on family planning programmes in various countries, including motivation. The basic purpose of such information is to assist the countries in making population planning an integral part of their national economic development plans. The Population Commission stated in its 1961 report that

> the principal object of the demographic work of the United Nations should be to help governments in the technologically less developed areas to understand the nature and evolution of their demographic situation and to utilise knowledge of the connection between demographic factors and social and economic change in deciding and carrying out their development policies . . . while national governments must make their own decisions, it is the task of the scientist, including demographers, and of the United Nations and other bodies concerned with the welfare of mankind, to supply the policy-makers with the relevant facts about the demographic situation and to draw attention to current trends and their consequences.[15]

PROGRAMMES INDIRECTLY RELATED TO THE POPULATION
PROBLEM

(a) The United Nations Development Programme – U.N.D.P.
Of these programmes, probably the most important one is the United Nations Development Programme (U.N.D.P.) under which a large number of different programmes in many fields are carried out. The basic purpose of the U.N.D.P. is to attain an accelerated overall socio-economic development in underdeveloped countries, which in effect means increasing the capacity of such countries to absorb more effectively the burden of additional population without an undue lowering in the standard of living. The key purpose here is to maintain the pace of economic growth at a higher level than that of population growth, so as to prevent the standard of living from falling.

The U.N.D.P. is currently engaged in helping the governments of 150 countries and territories to carry out more than 3000 projects in agriculture, industry, education, health, public utilities, development planning and social services. These projects range from the provision of experts' services and fellowship grants to assistance in executing major pre-investment undertakings. The accomplishments of the U.N.D.P. (its predecessor before 1966 was the U.N.T.A.A.) over the past seventeen years have been quite impressive. These include the attraction of over $1000 million in capital investment; the development of agriculture, power, mining, manufacturing, transport, communications and forest industries; the training of nearly 250,000 men and women in vitally needed productive skills; the development of effective new methods for farming, fishing, forestry, manufacturing and construction; and the encouragement of the use of local raw materials and new low-cost products for domestic consumption. However, socio-economic development is a slow and complex process and must in its deployment carry the burden as well as resolve the problem of overpopulation. The Pearson Commission's sombre finding is relevant: 'No other phenomenon casts a darker shadow over the prospects for international development than the staggering growth of population.'[16]

(b) Science and technology
Closely related to the U.N.D.P. programmes are the scientific programmes of the United Nations Advisory Committee on the Application of Science and Technology to Development. This Committee was established after the United Nations Conference on the Application of Science and Technology for the Benefit of Less Developed Areas which was held in Geneva in February 1963. This world conference was unique in that it touched on a broad range of scientific disciplines and their role in modern life, including natural resources, human resources, agriculture, industrial development, transport, health and nutrition, social problems of development and urbanisation, the organisation, planning and programming for economic development, international co-operation and problems of transfer and adaptation of scientific knowledge, training of scientific and technical personnel, and communications. The conference was designed to focus world opinion on the practical possibilities of accelerating development through the application of science and technology. More particularly it was intended to bring home the need for a reorientation of research to meet the requirements of the developing countries and, at the same time, to emphasise the importance to those countries of utilising scientific knowledge and techniques which were already available. In general however, the role of science and technology in regard to the population problem has been to reduce the death-rate and increase the rate of sur-

vival as well as general life expectancy. As the Conference Secretary General put it: 'the course of the world's population has been closely linked with the advance of scientific knowledge and technology; man's control over environmental factors – his capacity to provide food, clothing, shelter and other necessities, control disease and protect himself from the natural elements – has improved more or less continuously and in recent times at a remarkable rate.'[17]

In order to give practical effect to the findings and recommendations of the Conference, an Advisory Committee on the Application of Science and Technology to Development was established in January 1964; it consisted of eighteen members appointed on the basis of their individual qualifications rather than as representatives of governments, and they included specialists in agriculture, atomic energy, biology, medicine, scientific research, etc. In its second report, the Committee identified eight problem areas which it believed to be of special significance to a large number of developing countries, and which lend themselves to a large-scale attack in which the developed countries might co-operate with the developing countries. These were: food supplies, improvement of health 'a more complete understanding of population problems', more effective exploration and utilisation of natural resources, industrialisation, better housing and urban planning, improvement of transport and communications, and the raising of levels of education, including new educational techniques. In its third report the Committee proposed a World Plan of Action with four main objectives to build up the scientific infra-structure of the developing countries, and it presented specific recommendations, among others, on the wider application of existing knowledge on certain problems of contemporary importance, and these it identified as water, the expansion of the supply of edible protein, the more complete understanding of population problems, exploration and utilisation of non-agricultural natural resources, acceleration of industrialisation and the development of new educational techniques.

(c) Food programmes
(i) The Food and Agriculture Organisation (F.A.O.)
The Food and Agriculture Organisation keeps under constant review the world food situation and agriculture situation. In a report in 1965 entitled *The State of Food and Agriculture*, it pointed out that while the developing countries achieved impressive gains over the ten previous years to 1965 in the production of food and in the export of agricultural products, these advances 'were in the main wiped out by the rapid growth of population, and the rising volume of trade signified little in the face of falling prices'. It further showed that the

production of food per person in 1964–5, compared with the average of the years 1952–3, rose by 14 per cent in developed countries but by only 1 per cent in the developing countries. The Director General also pointed out that the technical means for coping with the world food situation were available, but that the problem could not be solved unless 'the leaders of the nations are alive to the issues at stake, and are prepared to devote a large share of the world's resources to meet the looming crisis'. He thought that it was a considerable achievement that it had been possible to cope with the population explosion without widespread starvation resulting from it, but it was imperative that 'mankind should accept collective responsibility for the elimination of hunger and malnutrition'.[18]

(ii) The Freedom from Hunger Campaign
In 1960 F.A.O. launched a Freedom from Hunger Campaign which was supported by private citizens and was intended to stimulate world awareness of hunger and to create a greater general determination to deal with the problem. Under this programme, numerous projects have been carried out in land reclamation, land use, agricultural education, nutrition education, home economics, etc.

(iii) The World Food Programme (W.F.P.)
The joint United Nations/F.A.O. World Food Programme formally started operations in 1963 and by 1965 had established 115 projects for economic and social developments, including feeding programmes in 55 countries, committing more than $60,000,000 of the total of $94,000,000 pledged by the members of the United Nations in cash, commodities and services. Under this programme, food is used in low-income countries as a partial substitute for cash wages paid to workers on development projects, or it may be provided to the families resettled for developmental purposes until the harvest crops on their new lands are reaped. Food supplied under the programme is also used for emergency relief in cases of disaster such as earthquakes, floods and volcanic eruptions.

The W.F.P. is an interesting innovation in that it provided for contributions from countries in the form of food, cash and shipping services. Its basic idea is to use the food as 'subsistence capital' or as a wages fund to finance labour-intensive projects such as rural public works, road building and minor irrigation, afforestation and community development projects. The programme received about $94,000,000 from 71 contributors, including 40 countries of the Third World as well as Romania and Cuba. In 1965, at the end of the experimental period, the United Nations and F.A.O. decided to continue W.F.P. indefinitely and a target of $275,000,000 was set for the three-year period 1966–8.

(iv) The World Food Congress (W.F.C.1 and W.F.C.2)

The first World Food Congress (W.F.C.1) was held in Washington in June 1963, and the second (W.F.C.2) was held from 16 to 30 June 1970, in the Hague. The idea is based on a resolution of W.F.C.1 to hold a world food congress periodically 'to review a world survey, presented by the Director General of F.A.O., of the world food situation in relation to population and overall development, together with a proposed plan of action'.

The first Congress was primarily concerned about the imbalance between food and population. It drew attention to food and population problems and tried to stimulate wider support for action to support agriculture and rural development. The second Congress had a somewhat different mandate. Due to the development of new, high-yielding varieties of certain staple foods, plus increased investment and better planning for rural development in many countries, the food situation is at present somewhat easier but still serious. However, attention was given especially to changes in social investment priorities. The agenda of W.F.C.2 included two out of five panel discussions which were devoted to population growth in relation to economic development and conservation of man's environment.

(v) Other food assistance

The world's food situation has in recent years given general cause for anxiety, especially in view of the rapidity of population growth in the underdeveloped areas as compared with their ability to feed the population. This is shown by the gaps in nutritional levels (i.e. the daily food intake in terms of first, total calories, second, total protein and third, animal protein) between the less developed countries, North America and the European Economic Community. These are: for the less developed countries 2184, 55 and 11, for North America 3090, 91 and 64, and for the E.E.C. 2910, 87 and 46 respectively.[19] Wightman points out that if action to limit population growth on an overall basis in the world were to succeed, it would probably be stretched over a relatively long period and it must therefore be assumed that the growth in demand for food will continue to increase. For most countries growing at 2·5 per cent, a target growth of 5 per cent per annum in total income, for example, implies that food supplies should increase at close to 3·75 per cent. On a world scale, the underdeveloped world has actually produced less in the period 1958–63 than in the period calculated 1953–63, viz. 2·9 as against 3·0, while the E.E.C., for example, has increased its production from 2·3 to 3·2 and North America from 1·8 to 2·0. The result is that there is a growing dependence by many less developed countries on food imports from the developed countries.

(vi) The United States Food Aid Programme

One partial solution to this overall food shortage was the United States Food Aid Programme which was based on the export of agricultural products on concessional terms, i.e. food aid, which began in 1954 and was authorised under Public Law 480 (known as PL480). These exports were made possible because of bumper harvests in the years 1952–3 and also in 1953–4, when the total wheat stocks in the United States alone reached a peak level of 38 million tons. From 1954–66, food shipments under PL480 averaged about 13 million tons a year at a total export value of about $15·4 billion, accounting for about 40 per cent of the total net aid from the United States.

The programme provided for three types of food exports: first, bulk sales for local currency, which was then used for the local expenses and local currency commitments of the United States government; second, donations for famine and disaster relief and for programmes to combat malnutrition, especially among children; and third, food which was donated to voluntary welfare agencies and to intergovernmental organisations such as UNICEF as well as food which was bartered for strategic materials for United States stockpiles. In 1959 a fourth type of food aid was added, viz. dollar sales to governments on long-term and favourable credit terms.

By the mid-1960s however surplus food stocks had practically disappeared in the United States and the government had to put back into production part of the reserve idle crop-land which had been taken out of production over the previous years. In 1966 the whole food aid scheme was modified and the new PL480 requires that applicants for food aid demonstrate that they are making adequate efforts to increase agricultural productivity and to improve food shortage and distribution facilities in their own countries; sales for local currency would also be phased out by 1971 in favour of dollar, cash and credit sales, although on fairly generous terms. Food donations are retained for relief, school feeding, work-creation projects and voluntary agency relief.

This programme has been criticised in recent years on the grounds that it has been used for political reasons, for example, in the case of the United Arab Republic and Algeria, two countries to which food shipments were cut off because of their international behaviour.

SUMMARY

It may be instructive to note the extensiveness and the high degree of sophistication which the various international programmes on population, especially those of the United Nations family, have reached since the initiation of action on population problems in 1962. The insights of the Population Commission as to the requirements of effective international action are instructive: the Commission takes the position that its work programme should be flexible and effective and that there is need for inter-disciplinary, inter-agency and inter-regional co-operation and co-ordination in population programmes. The underlying principles in its approach are, first, that the population programmes are so vast and complicated that it is essential that many agencies participate in them, and in differentiated programmes and projects; second, that special attention should be given to the work and advice of experts in the field of population; and third, that greater emphasis should be placed on action programmes at the regional and country level. The Commission also foresees continuing and increasing requests for assistance in family planning, 'which are becoming an accepted element of developmental policy in many developing countries'.[20]

9. BILATERAL PROGRAMMES

(a) THE UNITED STATES AGENCY FOR INTERNATIONAL DEVELOPMENT (A.I.D.)

After some initial difficulties the A.I.D. programme on population began in 1962, with a major statement by the United States representative in the United Nations offering assistance to countries which wanted to have technical assistance on matters of birth control. A.I.D. assistance to population and family planning programmes in developing countries has increased from $2·1 million in 1965 to $ 34·7 million in 1968. A.I.D. gives high priority to programmes designed to limit excessive rates of population growth and to the increase of food production.

The programme operates on the following fundamental principles of policy: help is given to country programmes in response to specific requests. Such help is intended to stimulate and supplement a requesting country's own efforts. Programmes eligible for assistance are those in which individual participation is wholly voluntary, and in which each individual is free to choose, from among available methods, those methods of family planning in keeping with his or her beliefs, culture and personal wishes; A.I.D. does not advocate any specific population policy for another country, nor any particular method of family planning. Its aim is to provide needed assistance upon request, so that people everywhere may enjoy the fundamental freedom of controlling their reproduction, health and welfare as they desire. These policies were eventually formally stated in title X of the Foreign Assistance Act of 1967, which came into operation in 1968.

The major activities of A.I.D. are the following:

(a) Grants for projects and programmes of qualified private and voluntary organisations in order to enable them to expand their clinical, educational and pilot programmes, for example, to the International Planned Parenthood Federation (I.P.P.F.), to the Population Council, and to the Pathfinder Fund.

(b) Grants to universities for their Population Centres in which programmes are operated on a multi-disciplinary approach to population problems.

(c) Support for the United Nations programme on population, including $500,000 for the Secretary General's Trust Fund for Population Activities.

(d) Grants to individual governments to assist them in their family planning programmes, for example $5 million to India, $1·4 million to Korea, $1 million to Pakistan and $1 million to the Philippines.

(e) Support for research to develop better methods of fertility control.

(b) THE DANISH GOVERNMENT

The Danish assistance under bilateral programmes is mainly concerned with family planning. It covers bilateral assistance to India for a pilot study on contraception devices and to the United Arab Republic for the operation of family planning clinics.

The multilateral assistance consists of grants to the I.P.P.F. and to the United Nations Trust Fund for Population Activities.

(c) BRITISH AID

British aid is relatively small (£120,000 in 1968–9) and also consists of bilateral and multilateral components. Its multilateral contribution included grants to the I.P.P.F. and to the United Nations Trust Fund for Population Activities. It has provided for advisory visits to various countries, assignments of experts and training on family planning practices.

(d) SWEDISH AID

The Swedish government gives high priority to population control, especially through family planning. Its approach to the international problem emphasises the following objectives: to focus attention on the population problem as a global problem; to support efforts of international organisations on family planning; to provide financial resources to governments and organisations in the execution of family planning programmes and to provide, where necessary, commodities and education in connection with family planning.

The multilateral aid provided by the government was about half and bilateral aid about half of the total of about $9 million. Its multilateral aid was to the United Nations Trust Fund for Population Activities, to W.H.O., and to UNICEF. Its bilateral aid went to a few selected countries, viz. Ethiopia, Kenya, Tanzania, Tunisia, India and Pakistan. This aid also covers aid to family planning programmes and to the provision of commodities connected with family planning.

10. PRIVATE ORGANISATIONS

(a) THE INTERNATIONAL PLANNED PARENTHOOD FEDERATION (I.P.P.F.)

This organisation was established in 1952 by the Third International Conference on Family Planning to provide an international family planning movement. It is linked with about sixty autonomous national family planning associations in countries all over the world. Its work is based on the belief that people have a right to knowledge about the size and the spacing of families and that the achievement of a correct balance between the population of the world and its natural resources is a necessary condition of human happiness, prosperity and peace. The main purpose of the I.P.P.F. is to establish family planning associations in countries throughout the world, and through the activities of these local national associations to gain acceptance of the ideal of responsible parenthood. It also assists in the training of medical and other personnel in the techniques of family planning and motivation and organises international meetings for the discussion of new advances in the field of family planning.

The I.P.P.F. can claim that national family planning associations have played a decisive role in many countries where governments have accepted responsibility for providing family planning measures. It has also stimulated awareness, at national and international levels, of the population problem. It has attained this through directing its influence at intellectuals, to whom it points out the humanitarian, demographic and economic consequences of unrestrained fertility, and at parents, to whom it points out the problems of families which are too large and suggests ways of avoiding excessive family size.

(b) PLANNED PARENTHOOD – WORLD POPULATION (P.P – W.P.)

This organisation was formed about fifty years ago and has, as its basic objective, making available to all the peoples of the world 'the most effective and acceptable scientific means of voluntary conception control, and to encourage them to use them so that responsible parenthood will become a universal reality'. It tries to get government and business support for stronger public action in the field of fertility control at national and local levels, through an extensive public information programme and the use of press, magazines, radio, television and publications.

(c) INTERNATIONAL UNION FOR SCIENTIFIC STUDY OF POPULATION (I.U.S.S.P.)

The Union is a professional association of demographers from about sixty countries and its main function is to facilitate the exchange of information among its members. It co-operates with other organisations in sponsoring conferences on population matters. It has recently compiled an international multilingual dictionary of demography and has conducted demographic surveys in various countries of the world on behalf of UNESCO.

(d) THE POPULATION COUNCIL, NEW YORK

The Council was established in 1952, to 'stimulate, encourage, promote, conduct and support significant activities in the broad field of population'. The Council is a private foundation and is essentially knowledge-oriented, i.e. it fosters activities in research, training and technical assistance in the social and bio-medical sciences. Its Board of Trustees has laid down the following objectives: to study the problems presented by the increasing population of the world, and the relation of that population to material and cultural resources; to encourage and support research and to disseminate, as appropriate, the knowledge resulting from such research, to serve generally as a centre for the collection and exchange of facts and information on the significant ideas and developments relating to population questions; and to co-operate with individuals and institutions in the development of programmes, and to take initiative in the broad fields which, in the aggregate, constitute the population problem.

In recent years the Council has concentrated on the development of highly trained people to guide policy-making in the population field by getting the necessary scientific information, interpreting it and presenting technical plans. It is financed by the Ford and Rockefeller Foundations. Its work is carried out by three technical divisions: the Demographic Division, the Technical Assistance Division and the Bio-Medical Division, which has its own laboratories. It also has resident advisers in fourteen different countries, who include specialists from the whole range of academic disciplines and professional fields involved in population, for example, demographers, social scientists, health educators and public health administrators.

The Council has recently begun a new phase in its activities, which includes various new focuses of interest, such as population policy, the moral and ethical issues as well as the political implications of fertility control – the long-run issues of the relation of population growth to biological and physical aspects of the environment, water, air and land – and a study has been commissioned 'on population geography and what might be called the ecosystems of advanced populations'.

(e) FOUNDATIONS
The Ford Foundation
Over the past sixty years the Ford Foundation has probably spent more on world population problems than any other agency, public or private, i.e. over $100,000,000. The Foundation believes that the quality of life is 'threatened by excessive rates of population growth – that the problem of balancing the human population against an environment capable of supporting it with a rising standard of life, is one of the greatest challenges of mankind' and 'that high priority should be given to helping nations reduce their fertility'. The Foundation has been active especially in establishing and financing research and training programmes in reproductive biology, university population study centres in the United States and assistance to population programmes in developing countries.

The Rockefeller Foundation
The Foundation has concentrated especially on the overall goal of population stability in the world and on financing projects which are complementary to rather than competitive with the programmes of other organisations. It has, for example, given assistance in the establishment within medical schools, of full-time family planning units for the training of specialists in the field of fertility control and has made grants to research in reproductive biology.

Among other groups which have taken an interest in the population problem are the following: the Brush Foundation, the Conservation Foundation, the Pathfinder Fund, the Milbank Memorial Fund and the Rockefeller Brothers Fund.

11. EVALUATION

After this brief survey of the world population problem in its global
setting, and international as well as national action to solve it, some
evaluation of the situation may be attempted. On the positive side
the following achievements may be mentioned:

(*a*) There is a general and growing desire among most overpopulated countries of the world to limit their families; this has been
borne out by a number of attitude studies carried out by United
Nations and private experts.

(*b*) There is a general understanding that a limitation of the
population increase can add impetus to economic development,
which in turn would create a better level of living, higher educational
levels, etc.

(*c*) The technology of contraception has vastly advanced and is
still improving, and it may be expected that before long a really
cheap and effective method will be found.

(*d*) The campaigns run by many governments on fertility control
have improved greatly, they are today focused more on information
and motivation than on pure propaganda.

(*e*) There is today a world-wide interest and support for the idea of
limiting families, a situation probably largely due to the unique
contribution by the United Nations in legitimating the idea of
family planning and making it acceptable on a world-wide scale.

(*f*) The existence of a vast number of institutions devoted specifically to population and its related problems, on the international,
national and local levels as well as in official and private spheres of
action, which have evolved over the last twenty years, with their
activities reasonably well integrated as well as differentiated; however, some observers feel that international action has now reached
its maximum level of effectiveness and that further action can only
be taken at the national level.

(*g*) There has been some drop in the population growth-rate in
some countries, but how far this has been due specifically to international action has not been established.

On the other hand, however, some unfavourable aspects should
also be noted:

(*a*) There is still relatively inadequate knowledge (i.e. inadequate
in terms of knowledge needed for concrete policy-decisions) of such
matters as the reproduction cycle, the relation between population
and socio-economic development, factors affecting family planning
and finally, the effects of family planning on the total society.

(*b*) Even if a major breakthrough does occur in motivating large numbers of people to limit their families and adequate methods become available to them, the actual decline of the population growth-rate would at best begin only in twenty to twenty-five years' time, but at that time the situation might be much more serious than it is today. Many observers have emphasised that the 1970s to 1980s should be considered the critical period during which a serious modification in the population growth-rate must be attained.

All this means that in the short run international action will have to be directed to an intensification of the present programmes of the United Nations and the Specialised Agencies, i.e. on family planning, economic development and food programmes, especially for emergency situations. At the same time, an intensified research programme is called for to provide new knowledge on such matters as the reproduction cycle, socio-economic causes and effects of population and between population and quality of living, which would include nutritional and educational aspects. Such research might perhaps indicate the dimensions of an *optimum population policy* for a country: which would for example provide enough for people to maintain present levels of gradual growth or for a small surplus to populate and develop its empty spaces, but would prevent a too fast growth which might cause an intolerable lowering in the standard of living.

In the long run, to which present research and thinking should be mainly devoted, the indications are that attention should be paid to what might be called our *global ecosystem*. This is probably the most serious and difficult task for the future. At present man is still continuing to exploit the earth and its resources at an uncontrolled rate and without regard to the necessities of future generations; his continued industrialisation and increased demands for higher levels of material wellbeing are affecting the environment to such an extent that it may be difficult to absorb and neutralise his wastes and pollution. But man is a part and a link in the natural cycle and to the extent that he destroys part of that cycle he destroys part of his heritage, part of his very existence. The tragedy is compounded by the fact, reported by various biologists, that some of the damage done today may from the ecological point of view be irrevocable and irremediable.

In the future therefore international action on the two inter-related and interacting factors of population and environment will have to be much more decisive and inclusive; no nation can opt out. In the absence of a true world legislative body, the existing machinery of multilateral diplomacy and action, through the United Nations and its associated institutions, will have to fulfil this function. They

K

will probably be able to do so provided that a distinction can be made between national or particularistic interests on the one hand and international or general interests on the other hand, and a reconcilation between these two sets of interests can be found. This would be a challenge not only to the scientists and technologists but also to the diplomats who handle our present embryonic legislative international systems, viz. to find bases for agreement rather than to find reasons for disagreement.

In concrete terms, such international action would involve two things: first, more research in order to know more about population and environment in order to inform the peoples of the world of the implications of population in relation to its ecosystem and, through diffusion and education, to build up a basis for constructive future support and action towards population control and conservation of resources. Second, through existing international organisations, a beginning can be made to building up global legislative measures or guide-lines and establishing minimum standards regarding the exploitation of natural resources and minimum standards regarding pollution of the atmosphere, space, the ocean and inland waters. This could be done, for example, through the establishment of model codes on conservation, on the exploitation of non-renewable natural resources and of the biosphere. Such model codes, internationally formulated and sanctioned, would have a strong persuasive effect on the governments of individual states, and make them guardians rather than exploiters of their national heritage of a territory which each calls a fatherland. In this way, perhaps, we can reintroduce an element of value into man's relationship with his environment, because it can provide him not only with sustenance, but also with values and with the fellowship of other human beings and in an ultimate sense with meaning for his own existence. Population may then change in meaning from overcrowding to brotherhood.

Notes

1. P. M. Hauser, 'Demographic Dimensions of World Politics', in Larry K. Y. Ng, and Stuart Mudd (eds.), *The Population Crisis, Implications and Plans for Action* (Indiana University Press, Bloomington, Ind., 1965) p. 63.
2. Hauser, op. cit., p. 64.
3. United Nations, *Science and Technology for Development*, vol. V, People and Living (United Nations, New York, 1963) p. 9.
4. O.E.C.D., Development Centre of the O.E.C.D., *Population, International Assistance and Research*, Proceedings of the first population conference of the Development Decade (3–5 December 1968), Paris, 1969, p. 208.
5. Hauser in Ng and Mudd (eds.), op. cit., p. 65.
6. United Nations Monthly Chronicle, vol. V/I, January p. 105.
7. P.E.P., *World Population and Resources*, P.E.P. and George Allen and Unwin, London, 1955–64, pp. 189–273.

8. ECOSOC, Official records: 27th Session, 1959, Supplement No. 3 (E3207/Rev. 1; E/CN9/156/Rev. 1), paragraph 14.
9. International Conciliation, Issues before the 24th General Assembly, September 1969/No. 574, Carnegie Endowment for International Peace, New York, 1969, p. 53.
10. For the general report, see U.N. Document E4667, 26 May 1969.
11. Ibid., p. 29.
12. General Assembly Res. 2467 (XXIII), 21 December 1968; 2413 (XXIII), 17 December 1968; and 2414 (XXIII), 17 December 1968.
13. General Assembly Res. 1838 (XVII), official records of the General Assembly, 17th Session, Annexes, Agenda Item 38, Document A/C.2/L.657/Rev.1/ADD.1.
14. Res. 1084 (XXXIX), official records of the Economic and Social Council, 39th Session, Supplement No. 9 (E/4109).
15. Quoted in United Nations, Report on *Science and Technology for Development*, vol. V, People and Living (United Nations, New York, 1963) p. 30.
16. Partners in Development, Report of the *Commission on International Development* (Praeger, New York, 1969) p. 55. (Pearson Report).
17. United Nations, Report on *Science and Technology for Development*, vol. V, People and Living (United Nations, New York, 1963) p. 12.
18. *Everyman's United Nations*, 8th ed. (United Nations, New York, 1968) p. 501.
19. David R. Wightman, Food Aid and Economic Development, International Conciliation, March 1968/No. 567, New York, p. 7.
20. United Nations, ECOSOC, Population Commission, 15th Session, Five-year and Two-year Programmes of Work, Report of the Secretary General, E/CN.9/234, paragraph 18.

Bibliography
1. Berelson *et al.* (eds.), *Family Planning and Population Programmes* (The University of Chicago Press, Chicago, 1966).
2. Donald J. Bogue, *Principles of Demography* (John Wiley and Sons, Inc., New York, 1969).
3. Jean Bourgeois-Pichat, *Population Growth and Development*, International Conciliation, January 1966, No. 556, Carnegie Endowment for International Peace, N.Y.
4. Colin Clark, *Starvation or Plenty?* (Secker and Warburg Limited, London, 1970).
5. Philip M. Hauser, (ed.), *The Population Dilemma* (Prentice-Hall, Inc., Englewood Cliffs, N.J., 1963).
6. Sir Joseph Hutchinson, (ed.), *Population and Food Supply* (Cambridge University Press, 1969).
7. International Conciliation, *Issues before the 24th General Assembly* (Carnegie Endowment for International Peace, September 1969).
8. Larry K. Y. Ng and Stuart Mudd (eds.), *The Population Crisis* (Indiana University Press, Bloomington, 1965).
9. Stuart Mudd (ed.), *The Population Crisis and the Use of World Resources* (Dr. W. Junk, Publishers, The Hague, 1964).
10. O.E.C.D., *Population, International Assistance and Research* (Development Centre of the Organisation for Economic Co-operation and Development, Paris, 1969).
11. Göran Ohlin, *Population Control and Economic Development* (Development Centre of the Organisation for Economic Co-operation and Development, Paris, 1967).
12. C. W. Park, *The Population Explosion* (Heinemann Educational Books Limited, London, 1965).

13. Political and Economic Planning (P.E.P.), *World Population and Resources* (George Allen and Unwin Limited, London, 1955, 1964).
14. Thorsten Sellin and Richard D. Lambert (eds.), *The Annals*; American Academy of Political and Social Science, January 1967, vol. 369, Special Issue on World Population, Philadelphia, 1967.
15. United Nations, *Everyman's United Nations*, 8th ed. (United Nations, New York, 1968).
16. United Nations, *Proceedings of the World Population Conference, Belgrade, 30 Aug.- 10 Sept. 1965*, vols. 1–4 (United Nations, New York, 1967).
17. United Nations, *Science and Technology for Development*, People and Living, vol. V (New York, 1963).
18. United Nations, *Yearbook of the United Nations* (New York, 1966).
19. David R. Wightman, *Food Aid and Economic Development*, International Conciliation No. 567, March 1968, Carnegie Endowment for International Peace, New York.
20. Louise B. Young (ed.), *Population in Perspective* (Oxford University Press, New York, 1968).

DISCUSSION

Panel Members: Professor A. F. K. Organski and Dr. Denis Worrall

Professor Organski agreed with Professor Louw that the United Nations had achieved much in the way of the legitimation of the control of population. In these efforts it had received important assistance from private foundations which carried on research into demographic problems. Research was a priority; perhaps more important than the present type of action.

Dr. Worrall contended that Professor Louw had accepted too traditional an approach to international action. Attitudes to Article 2(7) of the United Nations Charter had evolved considerably, particularly in the field of human rights. Population control was a matter of international concern, which should not be restricted by Article 2(7).

Dr. Worrall also stressed the importance of involving regional organisations such as the O.A.U. and O.A.S. in population control.

Professor C. J. R. Dugard agreed with Dr. Worrall and asked whether the existing world order, which insisted on state sovereignty, was capable of coping with the problems presented by overpopulation and threats to the ecosystem.

Dr. N. J. van Rensburg agreed that the United Nations was doing excellent work in the field of population control, but expressed doubts as to whether South Africa should participate in its programmes. Perhaps it would be better for South Africa to 'go it alone' in this field. *Professor Dugard* disagreed with Dr. van Rensburg, and suggested that this was an area in which South Africa could co-operate fully with the United Nations.

Professor Louw, in reply to Dr. Worrall and Professor Dugard, commented that in time population and particularly environmental problems might be taken out of the *domaine réservé* of Article 2(7) of the United Nations Charter.

APPENDIX TO CHAPTER 15

Population growth and economic development
General Assembly Resolution 1838 (XVII) of 18 December 1962
The General Assembly,

Considering that rapid economic and social progress in the developing countries is dependent not least upon the ability of these countries to provide their peoples with education, a fair standard of living and the possibility of productive work,

Considering further that economic development and population growth are closely interrelated,

Recognising that the health and welfare of the family is of paramount importance not only for obvious humanitarian reasons, but also with regard to economic development and social progress, and that the health and welfare of the family require special attention in areas with a relatively high rate of population growth,

Recognising further that it is the responsibility of each Government to decide its own policies and devise its own programmes of action for dealing with the problems of population and economic and social progress,

Reminding States Members of the United Nations and of the specialised agencies that according to recent census results the effective population increase during the last decade has been particularly high in many low-income less developed countries,

Reminding Member States that in formulating their economic and social policies it is useful to take into account the latest relevant facts on the interrelationship of population growth and economic and social development and that the forthcoming World Population Conference and the Asian Population Conference might throw new light on the importance of this problem, especially for the developing countries,

Recalling its resolution 1217 (XII) of 14 December 1957, in which the General Assembly, *inter alia*, invites Member States, particularly the developing countries, to follow as closely as possible the interrelationships existing between economic and population changes, and requests the Secretary General to ensure the co-ordination of the activities of the United Nations in the demographic and economic fields,

Recalling Economic and Social Council Resolution 820 (XXXI), which contains provisions aiming at intensified efforts to ensure international co-operation in the evaluation, analysis and utilisation of population census results and related data, particularly in the less developed countries, and which requests the Secretary General to explore the possibilities of increasing the amount of technical assistance funds for assistance to Governments requesting it in preparing permanent programmes of demographic research,

Recognising that further studies and research are necessary to fill the gaps in our knowledge about the causes and consequences of demographic trends, particularly in the less developed countries,

Recognising that removals of large national groups to other countries may give rise to ethnical, political, emotional and economic difficulties,

1. *Notes* with appreciation the report of the Secretary General, entitled 'The United Nations Development Decade proposals for action' which, *inter alia*, refers to the interrelationship between population growth and economic and social development;

2. *Expresses* its appreciation of the work on population problems which has up to now been carried out under the guidance of the Population Commission of the Economic and Social Council;

3. *Requests* the Secretary General to conduct an inquiry among the Governments of States Members of the United Nations and of the specialised agencies concerning the particular problems confronting them as a result of the reciprocal action of economic development and population changes;

4. *Recommends* that the Economic and Social Council in co-operation with the specialised agencies, the regional economic commissions and the Population Commission, and taking into account the results of the inquiry referred to in paragraph 3 above, intensify its studies and research on the interrelationship of population growth and economic and social development with particular reference to the needs of the developing countries for investment in health and educational facilities within the framework of their general development programmes;

5. *Further recommends* that the Economic and Social Council report on its findings to the General Assembly not later than at its nineteenth session;

6. *Endorses* the view of the Population Commission that the United Nations should encourage and assist Governments, especially those of the less developed countries, in obtaining basic data and carrying out essential studies of the demographic aspects, as well as other aspects, of their economic and social development problems;

7. *Recommends* that the second World Population Conference pay special attention to the interrelationships of population growth with economic and social development, particularly in countries that are less developed, and that efforts be made to obtain the fullest possible participation in the Conference by experts from such countries.

16 Conference conclusions

(Approved at Closing Session on 1 July 1970)

A conference was held in Johannesburg between 23 June and 1 July 1970 by the South African Institute of International Affairs on 'The Impact on International Relations of the Population Explosion', in which scientists from five continents participated. This Conference was impressed with the magnitude of the problems to which the rapid increase of population is giving rise, and recognised the urgency of dealing with these problems before they become more serious. While the primary obligation must rest with national governments, the co-operation of all countries is needed, and international organisations, official and private, have vital roles as initiators, organisers, co-ordinators and communicators.

The more developed countries should realise their strong moral responsibility in this regard.

While the direct effects of the population explosion on international relations require further study, there is already abundant evidence that its indirect effects in many fields require urgent and sustained action on the part of international and national organisations and authorities.

The Conference reached tentative conclusions in the hope that these might stimulate studies and actions by those organisations or institutions especially interested:

1. The key to the prosperity and power of a country lies in the quality and productivity rather than in the size of its population.

2. The widening economic gap between more and less developed nations, as evidenced by income per head, is partly due to continuing disparities in their fertility rates and is a source of increasing international stress.

3. It is the moral responsibility of each nation, shared by its government and people, to achieve an improving balance between its population size, food production and ability to purchase necessary imports.

4. Instability and strife may result from too rapid a population

growth, mainly because of mass urban in-migration and because capital formation to provide extra employment cannot keep pace.

5. The economic costs of high fertility rates and rapid population growth are not sufficiently understood by national leaders and public opinion makers. To remedy this dangerous situation international agencies should complement existing programmes by direct discussions with decision-makers to increase their awareness and understanding of these vital problems.

6. Government medical programmes should link policy with respect to fertility to action with regard to the reduction of mortality.

7. Governments should *inter alia* consider that the health of mothers and infants may be severely impaired by too frequent pregnancies and excessive number of births, and should take this fact into account in formulating their population policies.

8. While governments in high fertility countries should encourage family planning through education, through the emancipation of women, through economic measures and easy access to birth control methods and by instilling in parents a greater sense of responsibility for their children, the decision to have or not to have children is the responsibility of the individual.

9. Family planning and related policies in heterogeneous societies should be on a basis of non-discrimination.

10. The United Nations and its associated agencies have a constructive role to play in world attempts to resolve the population problem, especially in establishing legitimation and support for family planning programmes.

11. Inquiries by inter-disciplinary research teams into the varied reasons why fertility rates are not declining appreciably in less developed countries, and into ways by which motivations and practices might be changed, are urgently needed, and should be undertaken on a more extensive scale.

12. Assistance to less developed countries should primarily aim at the widest possible modernisation in order to increase their productive capacities and to attain a better balance between population and resources; such aid should be given in the spirit of helping less developed countries to help themselves, and it is becoming increasingly clear that developed countries have a special moral responsibility in this regard.

13. Priority financing should be extended to research to develop new strains and agricultural techniques to be used especially under tropical and semi-arid conditions, coupled with extensive field forces to give advice and assistance.

14. Because countries with rapidly growing populations find it especially costly to educate their young it is extremely important

that research be undertaken on the kinds of education and training required in such countries.

15. Even if all limitations on international migration were removed, emigration is not a feasible means of solving the problem of population pressures in most high-fertility low-income countries.

16. Given differential growth-rates of population and of employment opportunities among neighbouring countries, non-permanent labour migration can provide sufficient economic advantages to the countries concerned to enable them to promote the welfare of the migrants and to accept the social and political problems involved.

17. Developed countries restricting immigration should accord greater freedom of entry to imports from countries with population problems.

18. Because some population problems have regional implications, countries in the same region should work more closely together to understand and solve them.

19. The interaction between multiplying mankind and its environment should be thoroughly explored and the findings made available, so that national, regional and global measures can be taken to ensure that man and the environment will, in future, be in harmony.

The population explosion and international relations

Background Paper Prepared for the Conference

PROFESSOR B. COCKRAM

Lord Snow wrote in 1959 of the 'three menaces which stand in our way: H-bomb war, overpopulation and the gap between the rich and the poor'. Each of these three is sufficiently devastating in itself, but none of them can be separated entirely from the other two, and it is on their interaction that the future depends. In the words of Robert Louis Stevenson, written a hundred years ago, 'we theorise with a pistol to our head; we are confronted with a new set of conditions on which we have not only to pass judgement, but to take action, before the hour is at an end'. For the purpose of a conference on the population explosion and international relations, it would seem logical to consider Lord Snow's three menaces in a different order, firstly overpopulation, then the gap between the rich and the poor, and finally H-bomb war.

OVERPOPULATION

There are only four ways in which the number of people in any area can change:

(i) someone may be born;
(ii) an inhabitant may die;
(iii) an outsider may move in; or
(iv) a resident may move out.

For the world as a whole, however, while some may be born or some die, it is not necessary yet to consider the entry of outsiders from, or the departure of residents into outer space. There remain births and deaths.

I. EXTENT OF POPULATION INCREASE

The most striking fact which emerges is the comparative modernity of population increase. In the year 8000 B.C., the world's population may have been as little as 100,000, in *anno domini* possibly 200 million; by 1650 it had risen to perhaps 500 million and by 1850 to 1200 million. By 1950 it had doubled to 2400 million. It is already about 3500 million, and by the year 2000, if the 1950–70 growth-rate continues, there will be 7000 million, and in 2050, over 17,000 million. Professor Ehrlich, in his book *The Population Bomb*, expressed it neatly: 'A cancer is an uncontrolled multiplication of cells – a population explosion is an uncontrolled multiplication of people.' From 1957–67 Gunnar Myrdal investigated the extent of the population problem and its results in south and south-east Asia. He found that the population of Taiwan had doubled between 1905 and 1945 and increased from 8 million in 1953 to 13·5 million in 1968. In 1970 the population of India, he estimated, is likely to be between 523 million and 558 million, and in 1981 between 682 and 730 million; of Pakistan, in 1971 between 117 and 126 million, and in 1981 between 152 and 170 million; of Indonesia in, 1970 between 111 and 120 million, and in 1980 between 139 and 160 million; of the Philippines, this year between 36 and 39 million and in 1980 between 51 and 57 million. Other geographical regions where similar explosions of the population are taking place are Central and South America, North Africa and Nigeria, although the increase in the population of the latter since 1967 will have been reduced by the deaths from war and starvation during the Biafran civil war. Mrs Irene Green* has calculated that in the 60 years between 1915 and 1975 the population of the small island of Jamaica, in the West Indies, will have increased from 864,000 to approximately 2,343,600. The increase in the population of the even smaller island of Puerto Rico would have been even more fantastic but for the emigration of over 1 million Puerto Ricans to the United States, mainly to New York. In North Africa the increase in the population of Egypt between 1897, when the population was 9,715,000, and 1967, when it was 30,907,000, was over 21,000,000. In Algeria in 1881, the Moslem population was 2,860,000, in 1963, 10,670,000, and it is expected to exceed 14 million this year. In Nigeria the 1963 census showed an increase of 23·6 million over the 1952 census, from 32 million to 55·6 million, and the present population is believed to be at least double that of Egypt. Myrdal was unfortunately unable to estimate the present or forecast the future population of China (as his team were unable to work there), for China is the country with the largest population in the world. In 1965 Chairman Mao Tse-tung noted that estimates were as high as 690 million but doubted their accuracy: more recent estimates range

* In the first population study of the Department of International Relations at the University of the Witwatersrand, published 1966 by the S.A.I.I.A.

from 750–800 million, a difference of between 60 and 100 millions in 5 years.

By way of contrast the populations of the various countries of Europe and North America are not only known, but by and large are increasing at rates which constitute no threat either to their own economies or to their capacity to support the increases. The increase in the 6 countries of the European Economic Community is only 0·7 per cent annually; in the United States and Canada it has been 1·8 per cent and in the Soviet Union about 1·5 per cent: the projections for the period 1960–2000 are: for Europe (other than the Soviet Union) 5 per cent, for the Soviet Union 1·3 per cent and for the United States and Canada 1·4 per cent. It is also possible that the large increases in the populations of some African countries after independence may at least reflect the association of the taking of earlier censuses with the subsequent assessment of hut-taxes, when to be omitted from the returns was to practise 'tax avoidance', possibly even 'tax evasion' by the only means know to the tax-payers. In Swaziland, for example, while the estimate of the population by the British Administration in 1962 was 225,000, the post-independence census of 1968 recorded 390,000, and the near doubling of the population of Nigeria has already been mentioned.

It is therefore of the utmost importance that 91 countries, including the United States and the Soviet Union, and ranging from Greenland to South Africa, will this year (1970) be taking a census of their populations. More than 30 of them, from Somalia to New Guinea, have never held a census. Projections which have been made include 250 million for the United States, 241 million for the Soviet Union, 54 million for the United Kingdom and 20 million for South Africa. It is doubly unfortunate that China will again not be included.

Within individual countries important changes can be brought about by emigration from one country to another or by migration within a country from one region to another. Immigration from without was the major factor in the development of the United States. Between 1901 and 1910, 8,795,386 immigrants entered the country, or about 1 million a year: by contrast only 271,344 entered in 1961. Conversely, in Ireland, in the years after the Potato Famine of 1846, the population was halved from 8 million to 4 million by emigration to England, Scotland and the United States. At the end of the Second World War Poland ejected 7 million Germans into East Germany and 4 million Germans crossed from East into West Germany. 1 million Vietnamese similarly left North for South Vietnam in 1954–5, and 5 million Hindus and Pakistanis crossed their mutual borders in 1947. Algeria in 1962 returned

900,000 Frenchmen to France and Ceylon is now seeking to send 500,000 Tamils 'back' to India. Canada, Australia and Brazil are building their populations annually with approximately 150,000 immigrants each. The number of Jews in Israel has increased, in three-quarters of a century, from 150,000 to 2·25 million, mainly by immigration. The coloured population of the United Kingdom has increased from a negligible number before the Second World War to some 2·25 million, mainly as the result of immigration of West Indians, West Africans, Indians and Pakistanis.

The speed and relative cheapness of movement in the past decade has also led to temporary migration of millions of workers. There are now 6 million foreigners working in northern Europe, drawn mainly from Italy, Yugoslavia, Greece, Turkey, Spain and North Africa. In Switzerland at any time they number one-sixth of the population, and from West Germany they send home $740 million to their families annually. To what extent they will tend to bring in their families and become permanent settlers remains to be seen.

The internal distribution of population also fluctuates as a result of movements from one area to another, particularly in countries of continental size. Within the United States, 58 per cent of the population of the state of Florida, in the period 1950–60, had come from other states, 54 per cent of that of Nevada, 44 per cent of that of Arizona and 30 per cent of that of California, which now has over 20 million inhabitants. It has been suggested that Florida and Arizona are filled with 'oldsters' in search of the sun, Nevada with gamblers and would-be divorcees, and California with Mexicans, 'Okies' and would-be film stars, but the migration has in fact been widespread and general from many parts of the United States. It was the disturbed condition of China, after the overthrow of the Manchu Empire, which led to the emigration, between 1910 and 1930, of about 30 million Chinese into the bleak northern province of Manchuria, incidentally destroying the myth that Chinese would only move to countries with warm climates. During the period of Japanese expansion in south-east Asia between 1935 and 1945, about 600,000 Japanese moved overseas, but many of these were administrators and other personnel still based in Japan itself.

An even more important aspect of international migration has been the migration from the countryside to the cities, which has almost always been accompanied by a rapid increase of the population as a whole. In 1790 only 5 per cent of the world's population lived in towns whereas in 1960 70 per cent lived in them. In 1820 there were only 45 cities in the world with over 100,000 inhabitants out of a world population of 906 million; in 1950 there were 875 such cities out of a world population of 2400 million and we are

approaching megalopolis. In North America New York has already
over 14 million citizens, and Chicago and Los Angeles over 6: in
Asia Tokyo has nearly 12 million and Osaka, Calcutta and Shanghai
each over 6: in Europe London has about 11 million, Moscow 7·5
million, Paris 7 and Essen 5·5: in Latin America Buenos Aires
has nearly 6 million and Mexico City 4 million. Four-fifths of the
population of the United States are now living in 3 per cent of its
total area. The whole Atlantic coast from Norfolk in Virginia
northwards to Portland in Maine, a distance of 600 miles, has been
described as a 'linear city', in which one urban aggregation slides
into the next. Los Angeles has already covered the 65 × 50 miles
of level country between the mountains and the sea, and even
50 years ago a sprawl of automobile and steel cities linked Toledo to
Chicago. London now threatens to engulf the whole Thames basin.
Tokyo-Nagoya-Osaka is a vast urban bridge across Japan with
60 million people on it. Even in South Africa the urban sprawl of the
Witwatersrand extends over an area of 80 miles from west to east,
and will soon join the still separated communities from Pretoria to
Vereeniging over a similar distance from north to south.

The new censuses will, in many countries, also indicate the ethnic
and religious composition of the population, the distribution of
wealth among different groups and in different regions, and the
numbers in each age group. It is expected that for the first time,
the Russian people will prove to be a minority in the Soviet Union,
outnumbered by the total of the other 109 nationalities. In Northern
Ireland the number of Protestants and Roman Catholics will be of
vital importance for the future organisation of the country. In the
United States, the total of the Negroes is expected to be about 22·5
million and their geographical distribution will be vital to the approach to be adopted, in the next 10 years, towards their own
particular problems, and to the political future of the southern
States and the reconstruction of the northern cities. In South Africa
the Europeans are not expected to exceed 4 million, and their rate
of increase is likely to be shown to be continuing at a considerably
lower rate than those of the African, Coloured and Indian communities.

The comparison of the distribution of wealth between countries
and within individual countries will help to confirm or correct forecasts that the rich are getting richer and the poor poorer. Most of
the Negroes of the United States will almost certainly be shown to be
continuing to possess the least individual wealth and resources, and
to constitute, therefore, the major burden on the social services.
Similarly, the rates of increase of the average income of the inhabitants of the less developed countries may be shown to have failed to

exceed, possibly to have failed even to keep up with the recent increases in the cost of living, with the prospect of increasing pressure on the more developed countries for additional aid.

From the point of view of international relations, the most important result of the censuses may be the more accurate deductions as to the total population of the world, and the comparisons between the rates of increase of the races, and of the population in different areas, which will be able to be made when all the 1970 returns, however inconsistent they may be for the world as a whole, and however varying their accuracy, are available. Will India's population growth-rate, for example, be found to have increased from 2·5 per cent, or Ghana's from between 2·7 per cent and 3 per cent: conversely will the Japanese be found to have achieved as effective a degree of control of the birth-rate as they are believed to have done?

2. CAUSES

It is only to the city-dweller, and in recent decades, that children have ceased to be 'production durables', no longer producing income for their parents as they did in the agrarian period of the history of developed countries, or as they still do in underdeveloped countries. They have become instead 'consumer durables', costing money to bring into the world, to rear and to educate. The United States Department of Agriculture has estimated that it now costs $15,000 to rear an American child to his or her sixteenth birthday. Inevitably this is reflected in a decrease in the average number of children in each family, but earlier censuses have shown that the population explosion has been due mainly to a rapid decline in the number of deaths. This is so, even where the birth-rate has remained high. In India the birth-rate remained at about 45 per 1000 between 1880 and 1960, but the death-rate dropped from over 40 to under 20: the rate of natural population growth in the same period therefore increased from 5 to 25 per 1000. In Ceylon, where the birth-rate remained constant, at about 36 per 1000, and the death-rate dropped from 27 to 8, the rate of growth increased from 9 to 28. In Mauritius the birth-rate also remained constant, at about 36, while the death-rate dropped from 33 to 11. In Egypt the birth-rate remained over 40 while between 1900 and 1965 the death-rate dropped from 42 to 15. In Taiwan the birth-rate fell, during the same period, from 41·7 to 32·5, but the death-rate decreased from 33·4 to a fantastically low 5·5. In Japan the birth-rate dropped from 32·1 in 1900 to 19·3 in 1967 but the death-rate from 20·46 to 6·7. Conversely, in north-western Europe, where the birth-rate dropped from about 23 to 13, the death-rate declined only from about 13 to about 8, and the rate of natural growth decreased from 10 to 5.

In some underdeveloped countries both processes, an increase in the birth-rate and a decline in the death-rate, may have been proceeding simultaneously in recent years. In Algeria the birth-rate of the Moslem population was estimated in 1963 to have risen to 48·3 per 1000 while the death-rate fell to 11·0, a natural increase of 37·3 per 1000. The only countries which registered a higher birth-rate than Algeria during the period 1960–5 were the Cape Verde Islands, Dahomey, Ghana, the Ivory Coast, Mali (with an incredible 61·0 per cent), Soa Thomé, South West Africa, Zambia, Costa Rica, El Salvador, Greenland, the Dominican Republic, Guatemala, Haiti, Ecuador, Brunei and Jordan, and in all of them the Algerian variation from the general course is likely to have existed. Not one European country, on the other hand, registered birth-rates in equal range: the United Kingdom rate was 18·4 in 1965, the Germans 16·5 and the French 17·8, while the United States registered 19·4. The Algerian death-rate of 11·0, on the other hand, compared favourably with the French 11·7 and the British 12·2, Japan with 6·7, Canada with 7·8 (in 1963), Yugoslavia with 8·9 and Denmark with 9·8 all improved on the Algerian figure. The net effect of the decrease in the death-rate, whether or not accompanied by a decrease in the birth-rate, has been that in the past 200 years life-expectation in the western and industrialised countries has increased from 35 to 70 years, and from 30 to more than 50 in underdeveloped countries. Regionally the effect has been to increase the population of Asia from 650 million to over 1800 million; of Europe from 150 to 870 million, of North America from 10 million to 230 million, of Latin America from 50 to 220 million, and of Africa from an unknown but decidedly small figure to 300 million.

Nine factors have been listed as contributing to this decline in mortality:

(i) The first is the increase in the quantity of food produced. In the United States the maximum use of agricultural machinery on large farms has increased production to an extent which has made American surpluses of grain the standby of the world for relieving famines wherever they have occurred, yet only 5 per cent of Americans now work on farms. A similar process has occurred in Canada, Australia and to a lesser extent in western Europe. The massive use of artificial fertiliser has at the same time greatly increased crop-yield and the use of pesticides has greatly decreased wastage during growth. The development of refrigeration has permitted perishable food to be transported from one part of the world to another and canneries and canning machinery have made it possible to preserve and store almost indefinitely. The twentieth century has also seen an assault on the sea which has nearly exterminated the whale and threatens the fish shoals of every ocean.

(ii) The second factor has been the change to a machine-factory system, which by permitting specialisation, combination and automation has increased the amount and variety of the goods available to man.

(iii) The third factor has been the improvement in all means of communication which have become the conveyor belt of the world's larder. Ships of over 300,000 tons have replaced those of 300 tons common in the eighteenth century, railways criss-cross continents and even larger trucks and articulated container-vans have made the roads more than competitive with them. Intricate canals carry heavy freight, where cheapness rather than speed is the main consideration, and ship canals bring inland cities within reach of ocean-going ships. Where value and not volume is the criterion, air-freight has the advantage, since no part of the world is distant from any other by more than a day.

(iv) The fourth factor has been the effect of such social reforms as maximum working hours, minimum working ages, minimum wages, safety regulations, industrial feeding systems and essential medical services. Working a twelve-hour day did not conduce to the longevity of a three-year-old child, nor the haulage of pit trolleys by pregnant women to the lives of mothers and children.

(v) The fifth factor has been the improvement in public sanitation, especially in urban areas. The provision of piped water has fulfilled the double purposes of flushing toilets, providing bath-water and reminding the inhabitants of cities that water could be a safe, if unpalatable, alternative to beer.

(vi) The sixth factor has been personal hygiene. From the time of the Roman Empire until the twentieth century bathing had ceased to be practised.

(vii) The seventh factor has been the development of asepsis and antisepsis which, particularly in the First and Second World Wars, greatly reduced the death-rate from wounds and in hospital wards.

(viii) The eighth was the development of immunology, protection against the onslaught of disease, which drastically cut the number of cases of smallpox, diphtheria and yellow fever; and the corollary of immunology, the counter-attack on disease by such measures as destroying its vectors, for example, the anopheles mosquito for malaria, and the tsetse fly for sleeping sickness, or by weakening its onslaught by the use of antibiotics which also reduce its duration.

(ix) The ninth has been improvements in surgery from anaesthesia to the repair and transplantation of organs. Of the 13,000 amputations performed during the Franco-Prussian War of 1870–1, 10,000 proved fatal.

All these factors have so far been operative mainly in the more developed countries.

THE GAP BETWEEN THE RICH AND THE POOR

It is the interrelation of the problem of population increase with food production in the underdeveloped countries, and with those of industrialisation and urbanisation in the developed countries, which is contributing to the gap between the rich and the poor. Both underdeveloped and developed compete for the world's declining stock of materials and for the capital available for development.

(a) FOOD PRODUCTION

If the problem of overpopulation is sufficiently general to be called world-wide, it is most serious in those countries where it is accompanied by low incomes and marginal living standards. At present the percentage of the population living in countries with average calorie in takes for each individual below the minimum recommended by the World Health Organisation of 2400 calories a day is 39 per cent in Asia, 38 per cent in Africa and 29 per cent in Latin America, a total of 78 per cent of the population of the underdeveloped countries and 56 per cent of the population of the entire world. René Dumont, using F.A.O. statistics, concluded that 300–500 million people, or about 1 in 8, normally suffer from undernourishment or hunger, and 1600 million, or 1 in 2 of mankind, from malnutrition. A chronic state of food deficiency erodes the physical and mental capacities of its victims, ultimately causing premature death. Of the total of 60 million deaths each year, hunger and malnutrition account for between 10 and 20 million.

From the economic viewpoint, starvation reduces human aptitude and capacity for work and contributes to underdevelopment. It is only necessary to mention that the population of the underdeveloped countries includes 50 million sufferers from yaws, 150 million from bilharziasis, 250 million from filariasis and 400 million from trachoma, to realise the extent to which disease reduces output. That such diseases are difficult to cure in the countries where they are widespread is obvious when there is only 1 doctor to 50,000 people in up-country Burma, 1 to 15,000 in up-country Pakistan, and seriously inadequate medical facilities everywhere. Even if enough food and enough doctors were available, the rural worker could not pay for them. In 1954–6, the estimated income per head of a Pakistani was one fiftieth that of an American, of an Indian one fortieth. 'For the Indian villager, the Latin-American peon and the African tribesman, life is getting better at a rate which economists may put at 0·5 per cent a year, but which in terms of human experience may as well be put at zero.' If the rise in population is continued the poorer countries of the world could cease to have any growth-rate by 1975, and a minus quantity thereafter. To the poor of the underdeveloped world there is a bitter irony in talk of the 'revolution of rising expectations'. Is it possible for the food production to be increased in an attempt to meet the need? The F.A.O. has suggested that many countries could increase their production by 50 per cent or even 100 per cent if they made more use of organic and chemical fertilisers, and introduced a rational crop rotation system. But while only 10 per cent of the earth's land area is cultivated and it would be economically feasible to exploit about 20 per cent of what is now pasture-land or forests, the remainder is too cold, too arid or too mountainous, and there is therefore an ultimate ceiling to production.

Much might be done before this ceiling is reached, but the underdeveloped countries, in spite of the assistance they have so far received, have not yet achieved much in the way of increasing production. In the interior of Africa, chemical fertilisers, when they are available, cost 70 per cent more than in Europe, and are only economical when the yield can be expected to be good. Farm machinery is too expensive and the rate of deterioration too rapid. Major irrigation schemes have not only proved expensive, but require a higher standard of efficiency than the agricultural workers possess. Since 1958 the gap between population increase (2·7 per cent) and increase in food production (1·7 per cent) has in consequence continued or increased. In Morocco, the gap between population increase (3·5 per cent) and increase of food production (1 per cent) is now one of the highest in the world. Dumont's conclusion is that 'with a virtually neolithic agricultural system and a population expansion unmatched by adequate economic progress, the food situation in Africa is deteriorating rapidly'. And Egypt, in spite of the expenditure on irrigation, has now to import half of the cereals consumed instead of the quarter imported in 1960. South Africa and Rhodesia are among the very few countries in Africa which have been able to increase food production to overtake population growth. Elsewhere, 'population is increasing faster than food production, the terms of trade are deteriorating and the price of raw materials is still settled by large monopolies'.

In Latin America there has been only deterioration in food production. In the 1930s, Latin-American countries exported more grain than the United States and Canada combined, but in 1949 they became grain importers. The Paddocks have calculated that there is now 14 per cent to 15 per cent less food from local sources available to each person. In Latin America as a whole, cultivated land constitutes only 2 per cent of the total, and even in this 2 per cent the fall in acre yields, owing to inefficient methods of agriculture, lack of fertiliser and so on, is likely to become more and more evident because in some places land has already been put into production which lacks the qualities to maintain it.

In south-east Asia the total increase of population is greater, and the prospects of increased production to match it even less than in Africa or Latin America. Their numbers have driven the peasants in India to encroach on pastures and forests until 40 per cent of the whole is ploughed, compared with 10 per cent in China. In some areas the soil has so deteriorated that millet must be grown instead of wheat, and the deccan has been ravaged by erosion. The average size of the holdings has grown smaller and share-cropping leaves the farmer with only half his crop. With rice yields only 20 per cent of Japan's, many farmers are totally destitute. In Pakistan, Indonesia and the Philippines the increase in production during the decade 1955–65 similarly lagged well behind the population growth. In the Indus Valley of West Pakistan expensive drainage systems were required to remove the salt brought to the surface by irrigation followed by evaporation. In East Pakistan, where the Ganges-Brahmaputra delta is under water during the monsoon, and cyclones flatten everything in their path every year, and where cholera and plague are endemic, the problems of feeding the present population of 55 million, let alone any increase of it, are probably as great as anywhere else on earth. In Indonesia, famine is spreading insidiously in the south and centre of the small island of Java with its 70 million inhabitants. Africa and South America could, if vast development plans were launched, wait for one or two generations for the results, but south-east Asia cannot wait at all so far as food production is concerned.

In 1965 B. R. Sen, then Director of the F.A.O., stated that 'the F.A.O. had calculated that a sustained increase of 4 per cent per year in food production, against a population growth-rate of 2·5 per cent, would be needed over the next 15 years so as to avoid any serious breakdown of the precarious balance between population and food supplies'. 10–15 per cent of the world's population, he went on, was permanently hungry and sometimes starved and 30 per cent was undernourished. In 1966 his Annual Report went further: 'if the rate of food production cannot be significantly increased, we must be prepared for the Four Horsemen of the Apocalypse'. In 1968 the F.A.O. proposed that a world food reserve should be created, amounting to 8·5 million tons of cereals and $330 million of stocks of other foods in order to provide for disasters alone. Instead the rate of increase of food production in the neediest areas is now down to 1 per cent and the food surpluses, still limited to those in private or national hands, are but a fraction of what they were in 1966.

Two other sources of food are capable of being developed extensively, fish and synthetics, but neither at present seems able to meet the prospective deficit. Since the Second World War there has been rapid development of existing fisheries and their extension to new waters, but with declining yields. The shortage of fats and proteins after the Second World War led to deliberate and ruthless exploitation of the Antarctic whale fishery: the whale-catcher, the harpoon-gun and explosive charge, and the factory ship were made infinitely more deadly by sonar, until today the Antarctic whale fishery threatens to follow those of the Arctic and the Pacific to extinction. Local shallow-water fisheries have steadily declined: over-fishing of the North Sea has drastically reduced the catch of herring and flat-fish, and the breeding and migration cycle of the herring has begun to vary from year to year. Fast New England fishing-boats, with city markets at their posts, have drastically cut into the older trans-atlantic cod-fisheries of the Newfoundland banks, and there, as everywhere, sonar has reduced greatly the number of fish to escape the nets. Salmon fishing in the Pacific, from the Columbia river to Alaska, is threatened by river barriers to spawning and by over-catching of the returning fish. The Atlantic salmon is threatened by a development of new fishery off the west coast of Greenland, to which salmon migrate twice in their lifetimes. The tuna, off the Californian and Mexican coasts and off west Africa, are threatened by the mile-long multi-hook lines of the catchers, with regard to the much larger proportion of fish lost to sharks before the lines are hauled in. But nothing has compared to the massive catches of anchovies, pilchards and other small fish for processing either at shore factories or, more recently, at sea, for fishmeal for use as fertiliser and as one of the more inexpensive foods for animals. Millions of tons leave each major fishery each year. The competition for fishing has led to the extension of territorial waters, by the countries possessing the coastlines, from 3 nautical miles, to which 29 countries still adhere, to 6 (14 countries, including South Africa), 12 (40 countries), 100 or even 200 (Panama, the Argentine, Chile, Uruguay, Peru, Ecuador, el Salvador and Nicaragua). In a desperate attempt to preserve the local fishing industries and the livelihood of the local fishermen, the United States, Canada, the United Kingdom and France are among those claiming exclusive fishing rights up to $12\frac{1}{2}$ miles from their coasts, but sticking to the three-mile limit of territorial waters for other purposes. Until there are alternative sources of proteins and fertilisers, the exploitation of the fisheries is none the less likely to continue by moving into still untapped waters until none such remain. The underdeveloped countries suffer a double handicap. The cost of factory ships and catchers – the latter nearing the one million dollar mark – puts them outside their purchasing capacity, and the catch finds its markets in the developed countries, markets which are likely to expand beyond any increase in production.

Suggestions have been made for increasing the production of fish by 'farming' bays and inlets, as Japan is increasingly doing, but relatively few bays and inlets are suitable topographically, and only a few of these have the limited range of currents or tidal surge and the relatively high temperatures required. Edible algae also provide Japan with 400,000 tons of protein a year and some of these are also cultivated. There has been a successful experiment with algae in Chile – cars returning from the beaches at the week-ends are festooned with the favourite seaweeds – but while both fish and algae farming will be extended in the future, their contributions will for some time continue to be small.

Of the non-agricultural, non-marine foodstuffs, yeasts are the best known. By aerobic reproduction on sugar solutions, they ferment and convert the sugars into alcohol. They can also reproduce fast on the by-products of pulp and paper factories, have a very high protein content and are particularly rich in Vitamin B. Yeasts will also grow on such by-products of oil refineries as heavy oils and waxes: all the oil-refining countries could produce between them about 40 million tons of yeast concentrate or 20 tons of pure protein from them, but it will be years before they do so. Dried, the yeasts can be made into soups, cakes, bread and biscuits, but so far they have been used almost exclusively for feeding livestock in the developed countries. Of the synthetics, methionine is already used to feed pigs and poultry and to enrich soya bean cake, and, if production were doubled to 12,000 tons, 1 million tons less fishmeal would be needed, which in turn could be used to improve the protein intake of 150 million people.

Theoretically, the greatest increase of agricultural production would result from supplying water to the soils of the arid regions of the world, or warming the climates of the frozen ones. Efforts have so far been limited to making maximum use of the water which can be brought to the former areas and to experimenting with hydrophonics under glass in the latter. While, by the latter, fresh vegetables can be grown in the Arctic and their dietary importance make the cost worth while, only the former affords the prospect of real increase in production. Some of the great rivers of the world cross deserts to reach their deltas – the Nile, the Niger, the Orange, the Colorado, the Mekong, the Hwang Ho and the Indus. If they can be dammed and their waters utilised for irrigating fertile desert soils, these could produce one, two or more crops a year. Egypt has staked its future on the Aswan High Dam, which is not only to regulate better the flow of the delta, but to increase the irrigated area of the Nile Valley to the south, and to divert water to a former course of the river in the Fayyum.

For such immense undertakings international co-operation and external finances are essential: the World Bank project for the Indus is estimated to cost $350 million, which was approximately that of the Aswan High Dam. Even so the effect on the already irrigated lower courses and deltas of some of these rivers can be adverse and it has been suggested that each will lose as much in production from the older as it will gain from the newer irrigated areas. There are also the overriding power interests in the use of the water for industrial development, as from the Snowy and the Aswan High Dams, and the need of increased supplies of water simply for human urban consumption, as in the diversion of the waters of the Colorado over a distance of 300 miles to the city of Los Angeles. Competing national interests add further hazards to the major irrigation projects – the Sudan blackmails Egypt, and Ethiopia is threatening both with its plans to divert the upper waters of the Blue Nile. Fortunately, Mexico and the United States have reached an agreement over the waters of the Colorado, and South Africa and Lesotho will probably do so over the Orange, but within the United States the States of Colorado, Utah, Arizona, Nevada and California all dispute the allocation or use of the Colorado waters as between themselves.

Desalination of sea water is at present sufficiently costly to make its use uneconomical, except in special circumstances, as at Kuwait, where there is no water at all, but untold oil to pay for it, as in Israel, where deserts must be occupied for strategic reasons, and, possibly as in Los Angeles, where industrial development is already so extensive that water must be provided whatever the cost. In a few other places exploitation of minerals might make abnormally high costs economical.

Much more than balancing the more productive use of these rivers is the steady increase in the pollution of the waters of many of the larger rivers in the industrialised countries, which has already decreased their yield of fish, their potential use for irrigation and even their human consumability, so throwing additional burdens on the unpolluted small tributaries which now have to be tapped above the levels of existing use.

Country after country has had to realise that the local supply of water is no longer unlimited, can no longer be let run to waste, must be conserved, and must, if necessary, be used not once, but twice, thrice or more often for different purposes, even during the remaining 30 years of this century.

(b) URBAN RENEWAL

If the immediate need of the underdeveloped countries is for food to feed their increasing population, the immediate need in the industrial countries is to prevent the human environment deteriorating, and in particular the centres of the great cities.

The problem of urban renewal has already become the principal internal preoccupation of the United States, and one which as yet appears insoluble, because of the fantastic cost. In the dead hearts of the great American cities, run-down apartment houses turn into Negro ghettos, business and factories flee to the white suburbs, the value of property steadily deteriorates and the unemployed and unemployable are bringing the welfare services to a standstill: violence, arson and looting have become endemic. The city budgets show mounting deficits, and their administrators are unable to re-house, educate or look after the health of the inhabitants. Even burial of the dead is becoming a major problem. School buildings deteriorate side by side with the apartment blocks, and juvenile delinquency increases in both. Health services deteriorate as doctors and nurses leave and the cities already depend, to keep the services going at all, on the 20 per cent of foreign doctors licensed each year in the United States, just as Indian and Pakistani doctors and West Indian nurses supply the needs of the deteriorating centres of English cities.

One of the most serious aspects of the growth of the cities is proving to be the disposal of waste, solid, liquid or gaseous. Although burnt, buried, ground up or flushed, the material survives and technology adds to its longevity. An aluminium can will outlast the pyramids, and 49 billion are produced each year in the United States and the number increases each year. There are also 28 billion long-lived bottles and jars. New York city produces 375,000 lb. of solid waste per square mile of its area per day, and 1600 lb. of similar waste have to be removed each year for each American man, woman and child across the States. Each year Americans junk 7 million cars, 100 million tyres and 20 million tons of paper.

United States factories discard 165 million tons of solid waste. The disposal of this solid waste costs $3000 million a year. And, of course, the problem is not confined to the United States. The power-generating stations of the Trent Valley in England have already produced an accumulation of 30 million tons of ash. At present 10 trains a day, each carrying 100,000 tons, carry the ash to the holes left by disused brick-works near Peterborough. The pits and spoil-tips of the china clay workings in Cornwall have sterilised a 30 square mile area, possibly beyond all hope of reclamation. Scrapers can now move more than 300 yards of earth a minute, graders lift a ton of soil a second, excavators strip 1500 tons of hard ground or soft rock in 12 hours and draglines with buckets can move 1400 tons in an hour. The cities, the industries and their waste products are destroying agricultural land as fast as or faster than production can be increased on that remaining.

Sewage is polluting rivers and lakes all over the world. The river Rhine has been described as the world's biggest open sewer, and Holland, in consequence, as the rubbish bin of the world. The estuary of the river Elbe in the North Sea used to be a major fishing area: there are no longer fish to be caught. Nothing lives in the river Seine below Paris, and Lakes Zurich and Geneva in Switzerland are already biologically dead. The Norwegian fjords are awash with stinking cakes of solid waste. Lake Erie, between Canada and the United States, is not only biologically dead, but its water is a menace to man as well as fish: to deal with the detergents would alone cost $230 million. In the paintings of Tom Thomson, G. Y. Jackson and Arthur Lismer, the colour of the water of Lake Huron is a heavenly blue: had they lived a generation later they would have had to paint them a murky brown or grey. New York disposes of 200 million gallons of raw sewage into the Hudson river each day, and Philadelphia has similarly polluted the lower Delaware. The effluents of industrial plants add their gaseous poisons. At the same time, industry is syphoning water from the rivers and lakes at a rate which is rapidly reducing the quantities which have been available through the centuries for agriculture, and is threatening the supply available for human consumption. Johannesburg is going to have to take water from the Orange to supplement that of the Vaal. All the water available in South Africa will be distributed before the year 2000, and thereafter more can only be made available by rationing the existing supplies. Beaches suffer not only from oil pollution from wrecked tankers, but from steady pollution by every town or factory along the coast. 10 years ago the resorts of the English Channel coast were all polluted, and on the Riviera the sea at Cannes, Monaco and Monte

Carlo has been declared to be dangerous to health. The category of highest pollution includes 63 other west European resorts. In Australia Prince Charles found that 60 miles from Melbourne, 'it was like swimming in diluted sewage'. The people of Windhoek, in south-west Africa, are already drinking treated sewage water, and it has been forecast that by 1975 every other South African city will be doing the same. The pollution of water is destroying the human environment of the cities just as rapidly as the accumulation of solid waste and is perhaps the more urgent problem. Because so many rivers and seas are shared among several countries it is usually also a national or international one.

Only in the late 1960s has the danger of pollution of the air begun to be appreciated. In Los Angeles, the city whose clear light made Hollywood the centre of the film industry, it is now impossible, on most days of the year, to see the 7000 foot mountains which ring it. Air pollution can result in 39 tons of solids being deposited annually per square mile over London, 34 over Manchester, 32 over Birmingham, 30 over New York, 26 over Chicago and 22 over Johannesburg: a similar quantity has made the buildings in Newcastle a permanent black. Rotterdam has had to develop a fully automatic air pollution warning system, which is soon to be extended to cover the whole of Holland. California already has 50 per cent more nitrogen oxide in the atmosphere than the normal count: the effect is to reduce the rate of oxygen regeneration, and the amount of oxygen in the air could suddenly start to decline dangerously. The increasing number of cars has similarly increased the average American's lead content 125-fold since 1900 and it is now near the maximum of tolerance.

The first task of the developed countries will inevitably be to tackle their own urban problems, equally inevitably the poor in the underdeveloped countries will get only the crumbs from the rich man's table.

(c) DEPLETION OF MINERALS

The mineral resources of the world have been exploited most ruthlessly for man has been a miner much longer than he has been a farmer, and minerals do not replace themselves. The demands of modern industry for iron ore, chrome, tungsten, manganese, asbestos, antimony, lead, zinc, copper, bauxite, etc., have led to exploitation on an unprecedented scale. Australia exports 6·5 million tons of iron ore a year to Japan from the desolate north-west coast, as well as large quantities of antimony and bauxite. Swaziland has signed a ten-year contract for about 12 million tons of iron ore to be exported to Japan. Libya has accused the oil companies of running down its reserves, and demanded a higher price for smaller quantities in order to help its economy move beyond the next decade or two. The United Kingdom is having to spend £740 million in the next 5 years in order to develop a source of natural gas in the North Sea, and £1450 million for consequential changes. Even larger sums may have to be spent to tap the frozen Alaskan oilfields. With demand on this scale from the industrialised countries, and the investment costs of production so enormous, the underdeveloped countries are, except where they enjoy natural monopolies, unable to compete for supplies or to utilise their own for the development of local industries. Only in Iran, Venezuela and Nigeria are the oil revenues likely to raise the standard of living of any considerable numbers. Even so, whether there will be any oil left to meet the demands of the developed countries by the twenty-first century remains to be seen. The temptation will be to use economic and political power to exploit the mineral resources of the underdeveloped countries before those of the developed are exhausted. For their part the underdeveloped will, for the most part, lack the mineral and other resources needed for industrialisation, or the capital to finance it.

(d) CAPITAL

If more and more food must be produced and transported; if more and more minerals must be extracted; if water must be brought from ever greater distances or conserved and re-used at higher cost; if more and more care must be taken to prevent the pollution of land, sea and air by waste products; if housing, urban renewal, education, health and social services are to be expanded and improved; and if transportation is to be provided rapidly for increasing urban populations, the enormous sums of capital now needed for investment will become astronomically greater. The demand in the developed countries will be infinitely larger than in the underdeveloped, and priority will be given to them, because of their vast populations, their ability to use raw materials effectively and the returns which they can yield on both private and corporate investment. The first preoccupation of the developed countries will be to keep their own industries going, their own people employed, and to ensure their own supplies of food. Companies will develop their own sources of raw materials rather than take the risk that shortages will interrupt production, and will in this way tie the materials to the industries. The United States steel industry used to obtain its iron ore from the Messabi Range in Minnesota, and when the reserves there were exhausted, the Labrador iron ores were developed. Similarly, when Iran nationalised the Anglo-Iranian Oil Company's refineries at Abadan in the early 1950s, British oil companies developed the Kuwait oilfields to similar capacity. When Japan ceased to be able to import iron ore from Manchuria, contracts for large quantities over considerable periods of years were signed by Japanese steel companies with other countries.

The developed countries will also try to safeguard themselves against possible aggression, or possible threats to their sources of materials. Military expenditure in 1969 was the highest ever – R142,000 million – although there has been a recent tendency for the annual rate of increase of such expenditure to decline from 13 per cent to 5 per cent between 1965 and 1967. Of this total, the United States spent R58,000 million, the Soviet Union R54,000 million and the NATO countries, other than the United States, R19,000 million. By way of contrast the 93 developing countries spent only a small fraction of the remaining R11,000 million, even though their military expenditure increased during these years by 25 per cent. By 1980, military expenditures can be expected to reach R200,000 million. This military expenditure will be the second charge on the capital resources of the developed countries.

The third preoccupation of the developed countries must continue to be improvement in the standard of living of their peoples. Recent planned improvements in the United States are expected to cost between $8000 million and $10,000 million a year. And the costs continually increase. In Britain, £1000 million a year is being spent from public funds on housing, yet the number of units completed last year reached only 300,000 as compared with over 400,000 a few years previously, and examples can be multiplied indefinitely.*

Already the growing preoccupation with the problems of poverty, housing, health, education and employment in the developed countries has led to failure in practice even to keep up the level of aid given to the underdeveloped, expressed as a percentage of national income, let alone to increase it. The United Kingdom has restricted aid, at first to £200 million, latterly to £150 million, and has in practice tied an increasing proportion to purchases of United Kingdom exports and services. The United States foreign-aid programme has been cut each year by Congress until it is now but a fraction of

---

* The developed countries not only follow the principle of meeting their own needs of capital first, they also draw on the human capital of the underdeveloped by acting as focuses of immigration from them, and they draw a high proportion of those who have been specially trained. So much is this so that the recent United States Immigration Act, while opening the door slightly to immigrants from a number of countries from which immigrants were previously excluded, has at the same time made the choice selective, and reduced the total numbers. In the United Kingdom the operation of the Commonwealth Immigration Act has drastically reduced the inflow from coloured Commonwealth countries from over 100,000 a year to under 10,000, and those admitted must have special qualifications.

what successive presidents have recommended. Much of the remainder has taken the form of surplus United States food sales, with the further condition that these have to be carried in United States ships, whose freight charges are usually higher. The United Kingdom, the United States and France have increasingly offered the services of their own skilled but surplus citizens as aid, services paid for in part from the reduced resources they have made available. The effect has been that aid has been provided at the rate of about 1 per cent of the gross national product of the developed countries, or $7600 million in 1965, while to meet the needs of the developing countries would, the Lester Pearson Commission calculated in 1969, require a minimum of 4 per cent. With recession in the economies of many of the developed countries in 1970, it is doubtful if even the 1 per cent level will be maintained.

From the point of view of the developing countries, the situation is made even more difficult by the division of what is available into tied aid, project aid and aid-with-strings, and by the right which the providing countries retain to allocate aid between the would-be recipients. Some developing countries have received, for a variety of political or economic reasons, much more than their fair share, while others, equally deserving, have received much less. The Pearson Commission found that there was a sort of psychological barrier to any country receiving a total of much more than $1000 million per annum, whatever its population or its needs. India, for example, with a population of 530 million, has usually received about the limit, i.e. about 2 dollars per head. Pakistan, which receives about $750 million annually, with a population of 100 million, receives proportionately considerably more than India, with 5 times the population. At the other end of the scale, Jordan, with a population of about 1·5 million, plus half a million refugees, who are provided for under special arrangements, has received about $31 a head.

Much of the aid provided has been given in the form of loans, usually at very low rates of interest and with provision for long-term amortisation, but the total annual interest and repayment charges have increased over the years, until they now constitute a formidable drain on the new aid provided each year. In India, for example, the amortisation charges amounted to only $9 million in 1953, but are now over $450 million or nearly half the total of annual aid. Similarly, the total foreign indebtedness of Ghana has been reported, in May of this year, to have increased to approximately $500 million, the annual charges involved being approximately equal to the amount of new aid. United States aid to South Korea, Nationalist China and South Vietnam has been exceptionally large, for strategic reasons, but equally, an exceptionally large proportion of it has been in the form of military aid. Frequently, a revolution in a developing country has either cut off a source of foreign aid, or, conversely, stimulated aid as a form of *pourboire* to the revolutionary government to keep it loyal to previous commitments. Much project assistance has inevitably been motivated by the interests of the providing countries, whatever these interests may have been, and such projects may have subsequently imposed direct and even unwanted burdens on the local inhabitants.

The main complaint of the underdeveloped countries has however been that as producers of raw materials, which form the bulk of their exports, they are dependent upon the prices fixed in world markets, which they have been unable to influence to the extent of ensuring a reasonable degree of stability. Indeed they have suffered from generally declining prices since 1950. Importing countries have been able to play off rival producers, or to substitute alternative raw materials (aluminium for copper, tea for coffee, or vice versa) or synthetic materials, which they themselves manufacture (for example nylon for jute or other vegetable fibres). The only developing countries which have greatly increased their exports and have been able to make even better terms have been those exporting minerals in limited supply, and essential to the industrialised countries, for example, Venezuela, Libya, Saudi Arabia, Kuwait, Iran, Iraq and Abu Dhabi, exporting oil, Zambia and Chile, copper, and Malaya, tin, and all these with the exception of Iran have a total population of only 50 million. The developing countries with the large populations therefore have some reason for believing that the lower prices for their exports have in effect more than cancelled the total sums received by them as aid.

It was for this reason that these countries stressed at the U.N.C.T.A.D. Conference in Delhi in 1968 the importance of steps being taken by the developed countries to prevent fluctuations in the prices of those raw materials which constitute the bulk of their exports. Such a step could be the signature of agreements for bulk purchases, at agreed prices over a period of years, which would also provide guaranteed markets, and the purchase of buffer stocks, when supplies are in surplus, which would help to avoid competitive sales which might breach the purchase agreements. The response of the developed countries has been negligible.

In an attempt to counter the tendency of the developed countries to decrease aid, or at best to keep it at a strategic level, Mr. McNamara, on his appointment to the chairmanship of the International Bank for Development, proclaimed the duty of the Bank to provide greatly extended aid, a duty which could be met by increased contributions by the international banks. None of the international banks has come forward to make such a contribution. The Pearson Commission, assessing the situation realistically, has therefore felt able only to recommend that aid should be increased to provide the 1 per cent of G.N.P. already approved in principle, that it should be pledged for at least three years to permit of longer-term spending in the recipient countries, that it should be untied, and that the international agencies should be brought into its allocation, as between recipient countries, and should supervise its use where allocated. To top the multilateral pyramid, the Commission recommended that the United Nations should appoint a High Commissioner for Aid and that there should be a cadre of both national and international technical assistance personnel, to make more efficient use of the aid than do the present 200,000 who are temporarily employed for specific purposes in this connection.

It is obvious that with the precarious balance in the underdeveloped countries between development, standing still or actually or comparatively retreating, one factor is of supreme importance, the extent to which the increase of population is countering progress. India increased the number of jobs available by 5 million only for the population to increase by 13 million. Production in India increased from 1 per cent to 1·5 per cent a year, but the population increase was 2·5 per cent. It is the increase in the dense population of East Pakistan which has counterbalanced the development of West Pakistan. And in India and Indonesia the average food intake has actually declined since 1939.

THE H-BOMB

The implications for international relationships are as ominous as the facts themselves.

(a) Since the main cause of population increase all over the world has been the decrease in mortality, the obvious way to produce an immediate improvement in the overpopulated countries would be to make sure that there should be a speedy increase in mortality, either by removing the causes of the improvement or by removing the aged before they would otherwise die. The former course might be achieved by ceasing to supply antibiotics, sera, etc., and refusing to train any additional doctors and nurses for service in the countries of rapidly increasing population, but it would take time, and in the name of humanity would be rejected by all countries and the great majority of individuals. Euthanasia for the aged would probably be preferred if a choice had to be made: the death of children is always much more shocking than that of grandparents, towards whom the attitude is more likely to be that they have at least had a run for their money. Governments might even welcome this since they would save pensions and gain in death duties. The decisive objection, however, to this course, is that it would have no affect on the birth-rate, the age of removal would therefore have to be lowered with each generation, and, for various reasons, it would be most likely to be effective in those countries in which reduction of the population was least necessary.

(b) A much more humane solution would be to reduce the number of births and much could be done if all major countries were in agreement. As it is, the achievement is pitiful where it is most needed. In India, where the government has made a major effort, 7 million have been reached by sterilisation or in other ways. However, with the population nearing 540 million, and the monthly increase running at over 1 million, the outlook remains grim indeed. Nor is there agreement that reduction of births is necessary. In China, Chairman Mao regards 750 million Chinese as an insurance against the possible casualties of a nuclear war and as the guarantee of the ultimate domination of the world by the Chinese. And Indians and Chinese between them constitute already nearly half of mankind. Add a further 300 million people in southern Asia, 200 million in Latin America, where religion has reinforced the traditional trend to large families, and 200 million in Africa, and the prospect of successful limitation of the world's population by persuasion, before the increase has outstripped the available resources, is highly unlikely.

(c) If a solution to the problem is unlikely, can the day of reckoning be postponed? More might be done to improve food production even if the extra quantities are produced uneconomically, and such increases might tide over the next generation. India uses only 3 lb. of fertilisers to the acre, against Japan's 300 lb., but the price at which fertiliser can be made available from the national factories is at present far beyond the pockets of the peasants. Only 10 per cent of the world's output of fertiliser is indeed used in the under-developed countries. It has been suggested that if ammonia were produced at the oil-wells of the Middle East it could be sold to east Africa at half the present price (due to freight costs) of the ammonia produced in Europe or the United States, and east Africa might then in turn grow surplus food for India. Hundreds of similar co-operative arrangements are possible – and the Pearson Commission has stressed the advantage of regional co-operation – but the speed at which they can be organised may be too slow to meet the needs. Something might be done – as it has been in India and Pakistan – by planting short-stemmed Mexican wheat, which bears

L

twice the productive content of the taller varieties: the so-called 'green revolution'. The use of varieties of sugar or corn, with double or treble the normal chromosome counts, might help similarly, but their development to breed true is slow and costly, and in underdeveloped countries only one-five-hundredth is spent on agricultural research of the amount spent in the developed countries, and the research is needed on the spot. Irrigation can also increase the land available, but, as already indicated, it is for various reasons subject to diminishing returns. So is the harvest of the sea, as it is at present caught, and the production of synthetic food is so far too limited and too costly to hold out hope of doing more than up the diets of a relatively small number of the diet-deficient.

(*d*) The prospects of a more equal allocation of food and other resources, including minerals and capital, are similarly bleak. The combination of political instability and, in places, of civil or guerrilla warfare, severely reduces the ability of a number of developing countries to make better use of what is available to them. The financial instability of and economic pressures in the developed countries reduce the psychological readiness of the governments of the latter to give them even as much as they could. The probability that the next few years will see only limited increases in aid might however be utilised not only to reorganise the machinery for its distribution, as proposed by the Pearson Commission, but also to employ all the media of mass communication to bring home to as many people as possible all over the world the urgency of limiting the increase of the existing population and of making sacrifices to assist the underdeveloped countries.

(*e*) The efforts of the developed to help the underdeveloped countries are likely to continue to be on an ineffective scale until they have shown themselves to be capable of dealing with their own sociological problems, those created by industrialisation and urbanisation, which are bound to loom largest in their own eyes. The major one at the present time is preservation and reconstruction of the human environment. If these countries are unable to restore the increasingly dead centres of their cities, to provide in them, for all the citizens, the health, educational, communication and recreational facilities which they have come to expect, and to offer them the prospect of employment with the opportunity of improvement, they will themselves become less able to help, and the developing countries will see no reason to look to them for advice. If the developed countries similarly fail to satisfy the reasonable expectations of their own minority groups they will prejudice the success of all their efforts. So far there is scant reason to believe that they are within sight of finding solutions to these problems of their own or, therefore, of giving such efforts as they may make to assist the underdeveloped any real impetus.

(*f*) If the efforts of industrial countries, however great their resources, are unlikely to succeed in solving problems which are worldwide, the approach must be as global as it is possible to make it. This is the objective of the recommendations of the Pearson Commission. A prior requisite is, therefore, the constitution of an organisation with the maximum resources and authority. But, with the United Nations unable to keep the peace, dominated to an increasing degree by the votes of mini-states, and, for one reason or another, incapable of amending its own constitution, to seek to transform it into a world government would be to court defeat. There is greater likelihood that a group of major countries might agree upon a common policy in relation to so major a problem as population. If they seek to persuade they may have some success in particular areas but the limits of persuasion will soon be apparent: if they reach agreement that more is essential, they will have to coerce. The limits of co-operation against, for example, their own satellites or countries genuinely independent but within their own spheres of influence, would become obvious very quickly.

(*g*) Failure to deal with the problem, probably before the end of the twentieth century, could entail the breakdown of national and therefore international order. India has already over 14 million unemployed, the United States 5 million: in the United States there are over 30 million poor, in India over 500 million. By the end of the century, Calcutta could have 5 million unemployed, among a population of 35 million at the present rates of increase. The existence of destitution or even of continued poverty among such numbers, cooped in decaying cities, whose urban sprawl cuts the poorer citizens off from any change year in, year out, could only lead to rioting on an ever larger scale. Riots could be put down – no city can resist the ruthless use of modern weapons – but the casualties would be enormous, the government would lose support, and most governments, in such conditions, would seek to divert the subversive forces into external aggression.

(*h*) It is necessary, therefore, to face the strategic implications. If an increasingly small minority of the human race continues to get richer, and an increasingly large majority continues to get poorer, in relation to each other, then the temptation to the poor to take a larger share must become irresistible. They might rely upon useful fifth columns in the richer countries and they could afford much greater losses. The richer would be in a similar position to Israel among the Arab states: they could not afford to lose a battle, and a series of victories might bring them no nearer to security. From their point of view, the earliest and most drastic action would hold out the best prospect of success.

(i) Any such action would, by the geographical concentration of the population explosion, be bound to take on the character of racial war, with the 'haves' mainly to be found among the white races, and the 'have-nots' among the yellows, browns and blacks. This division in itself could reduce the possibility of voluntary limitation at an early stage, or acceptance of an imposed solution at a later. It has been characteristic of recent analysis of the population problem in an international context for the analysis to be clear and devastating, but for suggestions as to action to deal with it to be so limited as to be unconvincing, or so hesitant as to be disregarded. Time no longer permits this. If international action, and drastic action, is not taken soon, some country or countries will act to safeguard what they consider to be their vital interests. It is even possible that they might, like Dr. Strangelove, grow to love the bomb.

Opening address

DR. ANTON RUPERT
(*President of the Conference*)

May I welcome to our shores our distinguished guests from so many different countries. It is a pleasure to welcome you to the Land of Good Hope – a country which is a microcosm of the world tomorrow – often without the sympathies of the peoples of today. We are particularly pleased to have you here since your presence is eloquent proof of the world-wide recognition which this Conference enjoys.

Such an array of distinguished and leading authorities in so many respective fields is fitting tribute to the Institute's Chairman, Leif Egeland. He was father of the thought of having this important Conference in South Africa. It is a 'world first', since no conference has previously been organised to discuss the impact on international relations of the world population explosion. Allow me to congratulate you and your Committee on your foresight and initiative.

Moreover, you decided to hold this Conference in the Jan Smuts Centenary Year – fitting tribute indeed to a man who gave such deep thought to global problems. Some even might contend that he did so to the exclusion of thinking about the country of his birth. And yet he was in many respects ahead of his time. He was the spiritual father of the League of Nations and wrote the preamble to the Charter of the United Nations Organisation in San Francisco, only to have to leave the discussions in dismay at the turn of the tide in the affairs of Man. He wrote a philosophical treatise on holism before the birth of instant communication by means of television, before the era in which Marshall McLuhan could speak about 'the world becoming a village'; yes, even before the atom bomb and Hiroshima, after which one could declare in dismay:

> We all live on borrowed time like
> scorpions in a bottle.

Those of you from abroad and my fellow countrymen, and particularly the experts from universities, are here to discuss the impact of the population explosion on the relations between people.

The population explosion is a fact. One cannot have an infinite increase in population in a finite space. The most important by-products of the population explosion have thus far been:

1. LESS SPACE

Firstly, there is less space, less room for the individual.

2. THE GROWING EFFLUENT OF THE AFFLUENT

Secondly, there has been a sharp increase in pollution by effluent, pesticides, herbicides and other chemicals. And this is particularly true of the rich, industrialised countries where one could well speak of the growing *effluent of the affluent*. The people in these countries are the very ones who dispose of non-biodigestive materials such as plastic cups and bags by simply dumping them in Nature.

- Thus modern man is altering the systems of Nature without being able to predetermine the consequences.
- Modern man introduced D.D.T., a persistent poison, to lands from the Arctic to the Antarctic. This persistent poison has circled the globe and has now finally found its way into all our bodies.
- Modern man has used fertiliser so freely that Lake Erie has practically died.
- Vast areas of the world have been salted into wastelands by improvident irrigation. So, for instance, apart from the great benefits derived, the Aswan Dam has had two surprising negative effects:

The sea near the Nile estuary has become saltier, with the result that certain kinds of fish are disappearing. Furthermore, some authorities predict that the flow of Nile water to new farmlands, by means of irrigation canals, will result in a calamitous spread of bilharziasis, produced by parasites which spend part of their life cycles in the bodies of snails.

Thus every action has a reaction. Everything is related to everything else.

3. EXTINCTION OF CERTAIN SPECIES

Thirdly, the population explosion is leading to the extinction of certain forms of animal life. We all know about the demise of the Dodo, a large bird formerly found in Mauritius, unable to fly and thus an easy prey to man. But do we realise that the World Wildlife Fund now has to buy a few square miles of land as landing spots for the Crane, so that it can migrate from Sweden to Spain in winter and back again in summer?

On the first of this month I had the privilege of being present at the inauguration of the Marchauen-Marchegg Wildlife Sanctuary in Austria, on the border of Czechoslovakia.

4. IMPACT ON INTERNATIONAL RELATIONS

Fourthly, we have the impact of the population explosion on international relations – the theme of your Conference.

We already have the problem of rich and poor countries, of one-quarter producing three-quarters of the world's wealth, and the other three-quarters producing only one-quarter.

We have the problem of the rich becoming richer and the poor relatively poorer, because the population explosion makes an increased standard of living well-nigh impossible for the poor countries. There are just too many new mouths to feed, too many new bodies to clothe, too many new young to educate.

Resulting from these circumstances, we then have to deal with their feeling of hopelessness and their envy of those who prosper. This creates a playground for the unscrupulous politician.

Yet we dare not lose heart, for 'he who does not believe in miracles is not a realist'.

CONVINCE ... INFLUENCE ... ADVISE

May I suggest a few helpful aids in your probing of the problems of the poorer nations.

Firstly, *convince* the well-to-do that they will not be able to sleep if their neighbours do not eat.

Secondly, *influence* the knowledgeable to share their knowledge with their needy neighbours, thus helping them to help themselves.

Thirdly, *advise* the industrialised nations to risk the building of labour-intensive industry in the developing countries on a basis of industrial partnership.

There are the first hopeful steps now being taken to help our poverty-stricken neighbour, Lesotho. And the little that has been achieved has been from the grass-roots up. Yet the small factories are paying their way.

May I tell you how inspiring it has been during the past two years to have the help of South Africa's leading medical specialists, who sacrifice their week-ends in order to do major surgery and consulting work in Maseru. They have performed more than one thousand operations without a single loss of life in the operating theatre.

Senior medical students from our universities are at this very moment once again spending their vacation working in hospitals in our neighbouring countries of Lesotho, Botswana, Swaziland and Malawi.

'A very strange society', as indeed you might say (the title Allen Drury used for his book on South Africa). Yet you will find us no different – the good, the bad and the indifferent. But we are finding that we have wonderful opportunities of venturing out in order to serve our needy neighbours. This climate of opportunity may yet be instrumental in saving our youth from the 'crisis of purpose'.

When you have analysed the problems and come up with some answers, please

> *advise* us what to do,
> *influence* us to do it and
> *convince* us all to act.

There are no easy answers. Why, for instance, welcome medical aid when the problem is in fact one of overpopulation? Conclusive answers to and reasons why are not simple to find but I submit some thoughts for your consideration:

Firstly, only a healthy, well-to-do population will care enough to care for the future and thus be motivated to limit their offspring.

Secondly, life is always a matter of balance. We are now troubled by the possible danger of overpopulation. Were we to be eventually left with standing-room only, so to speak, someone is sure to use the atom bomb.

Worse still, since the artificial creation of the first gene this month by a team of scientists in the United States, the possibility exists that scientists anywhere could create a new kind of virus to which there would be no counter. This could be the beginning of the end.

There are easy ways to create smaller populations. The mere contemplation thereof calls for balance.

Meeting you, the balanced seekers of solutions, has been an inspiration to me. May I wish you well, and hereby declare this Conference formally open.

Dr Anton Rupert is Chairman of the Rembrandt Tobacco Corporation. Among his many public activities, he is honorary Industrial Adviser to the Prime Minister of Lesotho.

Closing address

DOUGLAS ROBERTS

May I commence by congratulating you on the choice of your speakers and on the efficient arrangements which have been made throughout the Conference. I would like to add my thanks to all the speakers for the contributions which they have made, and to our foreign visitors for having given of their time to visit us in South Africa. Its venue is an indication, if indeed we require one, of the very many scientists in the world who are appreciative of the technical and other developments which are taking place in South Africa.

Having had personal experience of a few international conferences held in South Africa over the last few years, I made some inquiries concerning the popularity of South Africa as a venue for scientific discussion, and I am amazed at the number of such conferences which are held in our country. In particular I am impressed at the number of conferences which are held by the medical fraternity and with the great contribution that our doctors are making in the development of medical science. It is not only Professor Chris Barnard who is known world-wide for his achievements, but many others of our medical scientists have made unique contributions to medical science. In particular I would mention the original research resulting in the production of a polio vaccine produced by Dr. J. H. S. Gear.

Last year the International Union of Pure and Applied Chemistry organised a conference in our country to discuss Chemical Control of the Human Environment. There is another international symposium on Gondwana Stratigraphy being held at this moment under the auspices of the International Union of Sciences, and at this there are some hundred participants from abroad. Our Department of Agricultural Technical Services holds regular conferences in South Africa, and there are many more.

It is very satisfying for South African scientists to know that they are acceptable and welcomed by all nations of the world. It seems to me that when men of thought and vision come together, politics are excluded. I am very happy to know, for example, that our scientists in a large number of fields exchange views very freely with their counterparts in all other countries of the world. Apart from formal international conferences, dozens of scientists visit us in their personal capacities each year to discuss problems with their opposite numbers in South Africa.

I have unfortunately been unable, because of absence from Johannesburg, to attend many of your Conference sessions, but in any case I do not propose to talk much about population explosion, for I obviously can contribute very little to all the vast amount of knowledge and the views which have been expressed during this last week. However, a few remarks from a layman in the subject may not be out of place.

Some years ago I began to hear the phrase 'population explosion', but it was some time before I appreciated the significance of it. During the last five or six years, however, I have constantly tried to make my friends and particularly those in my own industry, which is construction, aware of the problems resulting from this fact of life. I was about to say 'phenomenon' but of course there is nothing phenomenal about it all. It is a perfectly natural development, but one which I am sure is not appreciated by many people in our South African community. I became aware of it when I sat round the table with my co-directors to discuss forward planning of our company for the next five or more years, and since then I have constantly drawn attention to the implications of population explosion for our industry.

I have pointed out that we shall have to build in the next 25 years what has been built in our country during the last 300, for our population will at least double during this period. This means metaphorically speaking that we shall have to build another Johannesburg, another Pretoria, Durban, Cape Town, Port Elizabeth, East London, and in fact all our cities, together with all the necessary services to enable them to function. When I visited Richards Bay last month a friend of mine remarked that Durban Bay may have looked very much like Richards Bay when the first settlers arrived. Since that time the city of Durban has been built – in approximately 150 years. My guess is that a city the size of Durban will be built at Richards Bay in the next 25 years. In addition to all this new building, living standards will improve, so that the actual amount of work to be done will be more than doubled, and in addition we must replace or renovate existing buildings.

There was an inclination among the general public to dismiss all this as a flight of fancy, but the seriousness of our housing position in this country, which has become progressively more grave, is making them realise that we shall experience serious trouble in this field unless some quite revolutionary steps are taken by our Government. With the population increasing as it is, we are still subject to rent control and interest rates are extremely high, so that there is a progressively and rapidly decreasing interest in the provision of accommodation by private enterprise, and this naturally is very serious for the country. Until quite recently, in spite of rent control, property development for living accommodation was profitable, but with the marked increase in the interest rates an investor can show greater returns in other fields.

I often quote an example of population which can be easily appreciated, by reference to a little country almost on our doorstep – Mauritius. When I first visited this island in 1938, its population was approximately 240,000. Today, little more than 30 years later, it is over 800,000. This large increase of over 300 per cent in 32 years is due to many factors, most of them mentioned in papers which have been read at this Conference, but in this instance the most important of them has been the improvement in health services and the consequent appreciable decrease in the death-rate among children. Malaria was brought under control. Here we have an instance of the problem mentioned by our President in his opening address, i.e. the advance of medical science stimulating our very problem. I must agree with the President's plea that we should take a balance view in the solving of our problem.

The population explosion has a great influence on the construction industry. In the field of transport alone there is so much to be done – roads and railways to be built, harbours to be expanded, airport facilities to be increased, runways to be lengthened and strengthened to take the larger and heavier aircraft of the future. All this quite apart from the construction of new airports with all their necessary ancillaries. In South Africa I believe we have a further fact which will accentuate the South African population explosion in the not too distant future. The standard of living of our non-Europeans will improve quite rapidly, if they are to be used more in the labour market – and I cannot see otherwise – and then this large proportion of our population will also have to be provided with services which they do not require at present. Already the increase in their motor cars is significant. It will not be long before more sophisticated travel facilities, including air, will have to be provided for them and when this position arises the overall increase in population to be serviced will be accelerated. The need for increased supplies of commodities will necessitate the building of factories for production, storage space and shopping centres.

I do not need to expand further on the implications to our industry and the great challenge which lies ahead of it. This challenge would be serious enough in a normal community, but in ours, where

we must select from a quarter of our population all types of management and even artisan labour, our problem is even more difficult.
It is unfortunate that there is such a slow realisation that rigid
applications of policy simply cannot apply in our modern age if our
economy is to flourish. But matters are changing. I would have
hoped that we would have been brave enough to face up to the use of
non-European labour fairly and squarely, so that a phased and
properly controlled change could be made in our labour policy.

I am not here, however, to talk politics, but population explosion
has its impact on all our ways of life – economic, political and in
every other way – whether we like it or not. I am confident that our
industry will meet this challenge and many steps are being taken to
assure its doing so. As examples I quote the mechanisation of our
industry and the use of industrialised systems of building.

While I am not so involved in the humanities, I have been given
the opportunity of an insight into some of the developments in the
scientific work of South Africa and for this I feel not only honoured,
but extremely grateful. Perhaps you may like to hear a little of the
scientific developments which are taking place in South Africa and
in particular of those developments which have a bearing on the
problem you have been discussing.

We have many centres of research but the one with which I am
most familiar is the Council for Scientific and Industrial Research.
This Council controls some twelve research institutes, in many of
which there have been significant developments recognised internationally. I would like to quote a few examples of developments
which will help us in our population explosion problem. My
particular baby, as a member of the Council, is the National
Institute for Building Research, where not only basic research but
applied research is being conducted. This institute is a member of
the International Building Research Association and our Director
has been recently appointed to its executive committee. In the context of our Conference I am sure you will be interested to know
that this Institute has done a great deal of work on low-cost housing
for our non-European population, and, partly as a result of the
work, building costs in this field were halved. When it is stated that
over 400,000 of these low-cost houses have been built, the saving to
our country may be measured in millions of Rands. Many problems
of house-building and particularly of schools and hospitals have been
the subject of research by this Institute and in particular the effect
of the cost of services, i.e. roads, water, power and lighting, on housing
schemes, has also been meticulously studied. When one realises that
such services can cost as much as the dwellings themselves, one
realises the significance of such research.

Water is a scarce commodity in South Africa and in many other places of the world, and our Institute of Water Research has played a leading part in the use of water and its conservation. Recently a very significant achievement of this Institute was a demonstration that sewage and other waste waters could be reclaimed and made potable. I believe that the reclamation of water from the Windhoek sewage plant and its recirculation into domestic supply is the first example of this technique anywhere in the world. We are very proud of the fact that the Director of this Institute has recently been appointed President of the International Association for Water Pollution Research.

Our National Chemical Research Laboratory, among many other projects, tackled that of brewing Bantu beer, the consumption of which rose from 20 million to 160 million gallons per annum between 1954 and 1969, and the improvements in the brewing techniques have enabled processing costs to be kept low and the quality of beer to be improved.

The National Nutrition Research Institute has made its biggest contribution in the supplementing of deficient foods. A scheme for enriching bread, introduced in the fifties and costing R1½ million per annum, was conclusively proved to be yielding very little benefit, if any, and was abandoned. Subsequently a food mixture was developed to combat all forms of malnutrition, and this offers great possibilities for the future.

As you can imagine, the Institute of Personnel Research has been of great assistance in the development of aptitude tests for the selection of workers in the gold-mines and in industry, and this will help us increasingly to a better use of our population.

The Physical Research Laboratory has collaborated with other foreign countries in investigations of marine life, currents and other properties of the Indian Ocean. This may well lead in the future to the ability of man to recover food from the sea.

As a matter of interest you may like to hear of other notable achievements of the C.S.I.R., which perhaps are not so closely related to the population explosion problem:

Our Road Research Institute developed a hydro-densimeter, an instrument for measuring rapidly the moisture content of road material, which will optimise road construction procedures and limit premature failure.

The most spectacular achievement of our Institute of Telecommunications Research was the development of an instrument for the accurate measurement of distance by means of microwaves, known as the tellurometer.

This instrument has won world-wide acclaim and is being used by a number of military forces of the countries of the world, including the United States.

The activities of the Physical Research Laboratory extend over a wide field – optics, accoustics, geophysics, geochronology, nuclear physics, spectro-chemistry. Research in the field of cathode lamps enabled a new South African industry to be launched. Of particular interest to me in this Laboratory has been the development of an electrical anti-shark barrier, which has been developed to protect bathers against shark attack. This will be a 'first' in the world, I believe.

The Chemical Research Institute has assisted our mining industry, particularly, in the knowledge of rock stresses. South Africa has suffered a number of disasters due to rock-bursts in our gold-mines, but research is now teaching us how such rock-bursts may be foretold so that requisite action may be taken before an accident occurs.

All this knowledge is available to private enterprise and many inquiries have been received from overseas for assistance in these matters. This knowledge is also available particularly to all countries in Africa, but some years ago doors were closed to us. However, I am pleased to say that our Government is endeavouring to open some of them again, which will be to the greater benefit of the countries involved rather than to South Africa. It is a great pity and to my mind a very short-sighted policy of some of the African countries that they do not take advantage of all the knowledge which South Africa is prepared to share with them, and I can only hope that in future the trend will be reversed.

I hope our visitors may have seen some of our universities, which for the size of our country are very impressive. As a member of the Council of the University of the Witwatersrand, I am naturally not satisfied that either the Government or the private sector is giving sufficient funds for the development of our universities. But I believe our community is becoming more and more aware of the necessity to do so. There have been opinions expressed in the past that higher education should be solely the responsibility of the Government, but with this I do not agree. I believe industry should play its part, and play its part far more than it has done to date, and I am hopeful that we will be able to persuade it to do so, because we must pay particular attention to planning and must accordingly step up higher education.

I have obviously no time to speak of the many other scientific developments which have taken place in our Republic, but I hope our visitors will go away feeling that they have learned more of our sub-continent and particularly are now closer to our scientists.

In conclusion I would once again thank the Institute's Chairman, Mr. Leif Egeland, for his kind invitation, and congratualte him and his Committee on this most successful Conference. I am very pleased to hear that firm recommendations have been made and that your discussions have not been merely an interchange of views and ideas.

To our visitors I say thank you once again for visiting us. Farewell – *totsiens*.

Mr. Douglas Roberts is Chairman of Murray and Roberts Holdings Ltd, Johannesburg.

Authors
of main papers

Professor Jan L. Sadie	Demography and Economics
	University of Stellenbosch
	South Africa
Professor Willem Brand	Economics
	University of Leyden
	The Netherlands
Professor G. Ugo Papi	Economics
	Formerly Principal, University of Rome, and Italian Representative to the Food and Agriculture Organisation
	Italy
Professor J. J. Spengler	Economics
	Duke University
	North Carolina
	United States of America
Professor H. V. Muhsam	Demography
	Hebrew University of Jerusalem
	Israel
M. Jean Bourgeois-Pichat	Demography
	Director, Institut National d'Études Démographiques
	France
Professor C. A. Price	Demography
	Australian National University
Dr. Stephen Enke	Economics
	Tempo, Center for Advanced Studies
	General Electric Company
	United States of America
Professor W. B. Vosloo	Political Science
	University of Stellenbosch
	South Africa

Professor A. F. K. Organski	Political Science
	University of Michigan
	United States of America
Professor A. Sauvy	Social Demography
	Institut National d'Études
	Démographiques
	France
Professor Kei Wakaizumi	International Relations
	Kyoto Sangyo University
	Japan
Professor G. M. E. Leistner	Economics
	University of South Africa
Professor M. H. H. Louw	International Relations
	University of the Witwatersrand
	South Africa
Professor B. Cockram	International Relations
	University of the Witwatersrand
	South Africa

Panel members and other participants

referred to in Discussion Summaries*

Professor Marcus Arkin, Economics, Rhodes University.

Professor S. S. Brand, Economics, Rand Afrikaans University.

Mr. W. J. P. Carr, Johannesburg Municipality.

Professor S. P. Cilliers, Sociology, University of Stellenbosch.

Professor R. J. Davies, Geography, University of Natal.

Professor C. de Coning, Business Economics, Rand Afrikaans University.

Professor C. J. R. Dugard, International Law, University of the Witwatersrand.

Mr. S. O. Eklund, South African Road Federation.

Mr. D. F. S. Fourie, Political Science, University of South Africa.

Mr. M. J. Fransman, Economics, University of the Witwatersrand.

Dr. J. H. S. Gear, Director, South African Institute of Medical Research.

Miss S. Hall, Industrial Ethnology, National Institute for Personnel Research.

Professor D. G. Haylett, Agronomy, University of Pretoria.

Dr. Ellen Hellmann, Social Anthropology, South African Institute of Race Relations.

Dr. E. Higgins, Sociology, Rhodes University.

Professor J. D. J. Hofmeyr, Genetics, University of Pretoria.

Dr. C. J. Jooste, Director, South African Bureau of Racial Affairs.

Mr. Radford Jordan, Political Science, University of the Witwatersrand.

Mr. A. J. Karstaedt, Industrialist, Chairman of Eastern Province Branch, S.A.I.I.A.

Mr. Oliver Kerfoot, Ecology, University of the Witwatersrand.

Mr. Otto Krause, Editor, Johannesburg.

Mr. I. Knowles-Williams, Attorney, Potchefstroom.

Professor F. X. Laubscher, Genetics, ex University of Stellenbosch.

Mr. G. E. Lavin, Industrialist, Johannesburg.

* The names of those Panel Members who were also Main Speakers will be found in Annexure 4.

Mr. Gordon Lawrie, Political Science, University of the Witwatersrand.

Dr. J. M. Lotter, Director, Human Sciences Research Council.

Mr. H. M. Marsh, Johannesburg Municipality.

Mrs. Fatima Meer, Social Science, University of Natal and South African Institute of Race Relations.

Professor E. S. Munger, Political Geography, California Institute of Technology, U.S.A.

Mr. M. Nupen, Political Science, University of Natal.

Professor John Phillips, Ecology, University of Natal.

Dr. B. J. Piek, Demography, Rand Afrikaans University.

Professor H. P. Pollak, Sociology, ex University of Natal.

Mr. M. W. Richards, Chairman of Council, University of the Witwatersrand.

Professor H. M. Robertson, Economics, University of Cape Town.

Mr. T. C. Robertson, formerly Director of the Veld Trust of South Africa.

Professor L. H. Samuels, Commerce, University of the Witwatersrand.

Professor E. S. W. Simpson, Geology, University of Cape Town.

Dr. P. Smit, Africa Institute of South Africa.

Rev. L. J. Smith, O. P., St. Peter's Seminary, Hammanskraal.

Mr. A. W. Stadler, Political Science, University of the Witswatersrand.

Dr. C. Strauss, Economics, Standard Bank of South Africa Ltd.

Professor F. R. Tomlinson, Agricultural Economics, Department of Agricultural Technical Services.

Professor G. J. Trotter, Economics, University of Natal.

Professor P. D. Tyson, Geography and Environmental Studies, University of the Witwatersrand.

Dr. B. Unterhalter, Sociology, University of the Witwatersrand.

Professor Sheila van der Horst, Economics, University of Cape Town.

Dr. N. J. van Rensburg, Deputy Superintendent, Hendrik Verwoerd Hospital, Pretoria.

Professor H. L. Watts, Director, Institute for Social Research, University of Natal.

Dr. Denis Worrall, Political Science, University of South Africa.

Rapporteurs

Chairman:

PROFESSOR D. J. J. BOTHA

Economics
University of Port Elizabeth

Mr. D. Archibald
Sociology
University of the Witwatersrand

Dr. M. T. Bell
Economics
Rhodes University

Professor C. J. R. Dugard
International Law
University of the Witwatersrand

Mr. D. F. S. Fourie
Political Science
University of South Africa

Mr. O. Kerfoot
Ecology
University of the Witwatersrand

Miss J. Knox
Economics
University of the Witwatersrand

Mr. G. G. Lawrie
Political Science
University of the Witwatersrand

Miss A. M. Muller
Political Science
Rand Afrikaans University

Dr. B. J. Piek
Demography
Rand Afrikaans University

Mr. A. W. Stadler
Political Science
University of the Witwatersrand

Dr. B. Unterhalter
Sociology
University of the Witwatersrand

Dr. Denis Worrall
Political Science
University of South Africa

Sponsors

The following organisations assisted the Institute in the sponsoring of the Conference:

African Cables Limited
African Wire Ropes Limited
Alex Aiken & Carter
Anglo Transvaal Consolidated Investment Company Limited
Anglo American Corporation of South Africa Limited
Argus Printing & Publishing Co. Limited
Babcock and Wilcox of Africa (Pty) Limited
Barclays Bank D.C.O.
Barlow, Thos. & Sons Limited
B.P. Southern Africa (Pty) Limited
Cape & Transvaal Printers Limited
Cementation Company (Africa) Limited, The
Central News Agency Limited
Corner House Group, The
Cooper Brothers & Company
De Beers Consolidated Mines Limited
Delswa Limited
Douglas Low & Company
Dunlop South Africa Limited
Edgar Stores Limited
Engelhard Hanovia of Southern Africa (Pty) Limited

Fibreglass (South Africa) (Pty) Limited
Ford Motor Company of S.A. (Pty) Limited
Garlick Limited
General Mining and Finance Corporation Limited
General Motors S.A. (Pty) Limited
Gold Fields of S.A. Limited
Goodyear Tyre & Rubber Company (S.A.) (Pty) Limited
Greatermans Stores Limited
Hill Samuel (S.A.) Limited
Hippo Holding Company Limited
Holiday Inns (Amalgamated Hotels Limited)
I.C.I. (South Africa) Limited
Imperial Cold Storage & Supply Company Limited
International Computers (South Africa) (Pty) Limited
Johannesburg City Council
Johannesburg Consolidated Investment Company Limited
Legal and General Assurance Society Limited
Letaba Citrus Processers (Pty) Limited

Lion Match Company Limited

Marine Products Limited

Massey-Ferguson (South Africa) Limited

Mobil Oil Southern Africa (Pty) Limited

Natal Tanning and Extract Company Limited, The

Netherlands Bank of South Africa Limited

Oceana Group of Fishing Companies

Percy Fitzpatrick Memorial Trust

Price Waterhouse & Company

Rembrandt Tobacco Corporation (S.A.) Limited

Royal Insurance Company of S.A. Limited

S.A. Associated Newspapers Limited

S.A. Breweries Limited

Safed Services (Pty) Limited

Sagit Trust Company Limited

Schlesinger Organisation

Schwartz, Fine, Kane & Company

Senbank (Central Merchant Bank Limited)

Sentrachem Limited

Shell S.A. (Pty) Limited

South African Marine Corporation Limited

South African Philips (Pty) Limited

South African Sugar Association

Standard Bank of South Africa Limited, The

Stellenbosch Farmers' Winery Limited

Stewarts & Lloyds of South Africa Limited

Stuttaford & Company Limited

Total South Africa (Pty) Limited

Toyota South Africa Limited

Truworths Limited

Unilever South Africa Limited

Union Acceptances Limited

Union Corporation Limited

Volkskas Limited

Volkswagen of South Africa Limited

White's South African Portland Cement Company Limited

Woolworths (Pty) Limited

The following individual members of the Institute made financial contributions towards the Conference costs:

Adams, A. D.

Asbury, J. R.

Ash, Lt.-Col. S. H.

Bader, Brig. E.

Barratt, Mrs. J. K.

Baumann, L. G.

Bean, Miss L.

Blore, W. B.

Bostock, A. L.

Bramwell-Jones, Dr. T.

Brothers, M.

Buchanan, W. F.

Dickson, Miss S.

Douglas, Mrs. J.

Egeland, Leif

Emery, Mrs. M. A.

Falconer, Mrs. P. H.

Ferguson, W. T.

Fleming, K. G.

Garritsen, Mrs. E. H.

Gonlag, Mrs. A. E.
Haggie, I. S.
Harvey, G. E.
Hellmann, Dr. E.
Horwood, Miss C.
Jones, L. D.
Jordan, Mrs. E. C. L.
Kark, Dr. W. C.
Karnovsky, S. R.
Katz, J. N.
Katzenellenbogen, J.
Knight, A. P.
Knowles Williams, I.
Kowen, J.
Lavin, G. E.
Loveband, Capt. J. G. Y.
Macdonald, Mrs. D. J. M.
McGregor, H. H.
Martinovic, Dr. M.
Mullins, Mrs. D. M.
Murnane, Miss S.

Murray-Johnson, A. F.
Murray, R.
Myers, Mrs. S.
Ogilvie, Mrs. D. M.
Peer, Dr. S.
Peterson, Mrs. M. C.
Pollit, F. J.
Robertson, Prof. H. M.
Roos, Gideon
Selby Taylor, The Most Rev. R.
Shaul, F. D.
Sorour, J. de L.
Strachan, D.
Struben, Comd. R. F. C.
Sutton, Prof. W. G.
Travis, L. A.
van der Byl, Maj. P. V. G.
van Heerden, W.
Walton, Mrs. M.
Webber, Miss V. K.

Index

Latin-American Free Trade Association
180
Laubscher, F. X. 56
Lavin, G. E. 37
Law of diminishing returns 26, 36,
68
Lawrie, Gordon 159
Lebensraum wars 155
Leistner, G. M. E. 212
Lesotho 309
Less developed countries 56, 130–8,
140
Life, quality of xiv
Livestock 20, 34
Living-standards xiv, 26, 28, 40, 46,
131, 239, 299
Los Angeles 297
Lotter, J. M. 83
Louw, Michael H. H. xi, 17, 112, 159,
179, 184, 237, 275

McNamara, R. S. 203
Malnutrition 16, 44
Malthus, T. R. 26, 37–9, 68, 79, 80
Manpower 152
Marriage 85, 86, 96–9
Marsh, H. M. 84
Marxist doctrine 189
Mauritius 313
Medical aid 310, 313
Medical services 87
Meer, Fatima 56
Mexico 10
Migration 61, 77, 90–2, 96–101, 113–
28, 154, 172, 173, 188, 194, 220–2,
284. *See also* Emigration; Immigra-
tion
Military aid 301
Military expenditure 299
Military power 151, 157, 167
Military technology xii
Milk production 21
Mineral resources 70, 297–8
Mining 35
Monogamy 86
Moral formulas xv
Moral revolution 56
Morocco 290
Mortality and mortality-rates 86, 88,
92, 96, 101, 104, 172, 173, 187,
189, 193, 237, 287, 302. *See also*
Death-rate
Muhsam, H. V. 15, 16, 17, 84, 85, 92,
93, 94, 160, 177, 194, 235
Munger, E. S. 17, 94, 159, 160, 179,
181, 183, 234, 236
Myrdal, Gunnar 282

National Chemical Research Laboratory 315

National Institute for Building Re-
search 314
National Nutrition Research Institute
315
National power 151, 157, 161–2
National product and national product
per head 18
Nationalisation 78
Natural gas 298
New Delhi Conference 48
New Zealand 63, 116, 118, 120
Nigeria 10, 217
Nile estuary 308
Non-Proliferation Treaty xii
North America 101, 239, 283
Nuclear technology xii
Nuclear weapons 177, 178, 199, 251
Nupen, M. 160, 179, 181, 183, 236
Nutrition 22

Oceania 10
Oil 298
Opening address 307–10
Organisation for Economic Co-operation and Development 50, 258
Organski, A. F. K. 128, 161, 175, 176,
177, 275
Overpopulation 196, 281–9
causes 286–9
dimensions of problem xv
implications and effects of xvi
international issues xiv
long- and short-term solutions xvi
perception of problem xvi
problems of 241
See also Population, etc.

Pakistan 82, 199, 250, 289, 300, 302
Papi, G. Ugo 39, 57, 77, 83
Parents, rights of xiv
Pearson Commission 203, 260, 300,
302–5
Petroleum 24, 28
Philippines 115
Phillips, John 32
Physical Research Laboratory 315,
316
Piek, B. J. 16, 17, 94, 110
Planned Parenthood – World Popula-
tion 268
Planning for Better Family Living
Programme 256
Poland 191
Policy of structure 50–2
Political efficiency 169, 171
Political implications 143–60, 181, 264
Africa 226
and domestic implications 146–51
and international implications 151–
7